DIY
For All Seasons

DIY
For All Seasons

Gareth Parry

Illustrations by
Ros Asquith

FOURTH ESTATE • *London*

First published in Great Britain in 1991 by
Fourth Estate Limited
289 Westbourne Grove
London W11 2QA

Copyright © 1991 by Guardian Newspapers Ltd and Gareth Parry

The right of Gareth Parry to be identified as the author of this work has been
asserted by him in accordance with the Copyright, Designs and Patents Act 1988.

A catalogue record for this book is available from the British Library.

ISBN 1–872180–33–7

Typeset in Bodoni by Discript, London

Printed in Great Britain by Biddles Ltd., Guildford

Contents

Introduction

You might recall a Python sketch in which a mouse was interviewed, his profile anonymously blanked out behind a screen, about how he first got hooked on cheese. It all started, he said, with that first little nibble at an all-night party. Then he was doing more, stronger stuff too; soon he was taking it in secret behind the skirting boards. It was only then that he realised he'd never be able to kick the habit. Do It Yourself seems to have turned on a lot of people like that.

It is estimated people spend £3 billion annually on projects as diverse as putting up a shelf to building a house. They've had frustrating and expensive years being swindled by real Loadsamoney cowboys whose traditional tools of trade are an Old

Holborn roll-your-own kit, a radio with a volume control stuck on loud and a special sucking and whistling sound, as 'a quote' is expertly assessed on the social timbre of the punter's voice or the number of books on his shelves.

That's why the growth of DIY has been phenomenal; B&Q, founded by Messrs Block and Quayle, and one of the market leaders, opened its first supercentre in 1969. By 1987 there were 80 million people shopping at its 220 stores. By 1990 the company, which is part of the Woolworths group, had 350 supercentres. The big companies have established nearly 1000 such stores nationwide, and reckon the saturation point is close to 1200. They're invaluable places, as long as you know what bits and pieces to look for.

Given that the average person cannot saw a straight line, or drive a nail into a piece of wood without splitting it or his thumb, it is something of a miracle that DIY has caught on at all, let alone transmogrified into a semi-respectable set of craft skills which are regularly practised in thousands of homes thoughout the land by personalities as diverse as (of my acquaintance) a High Court Judge, an SAS booby-trap expert, a prize-winning fashion photographer and a (frocked) priest.

I know a millionaire beautician whose passion over the past few decades has been the face-lifting of old houses, buying dumps and selling 'palaces'. He got into the business when there was an abundance of houses waiting to be done up. Now he lives in a fashionable part of London in a Queen Anne home. He had bought it as a burnt-out shell and its front wall had sunk nine inches below the level of the back. This slight blemish was corrected very early one Sunday morning when a mammoth yellow machine lumbered up out of the autumn mist and, with a deep groan and unearthly cracking of old mortar, jacked the building up to its proper stance. The driver and his crew got what is known as 'big drinks' for their help, and the rig was back at its proper job on a nearby building site in time for the local pub to open. This beautician is of course quite an extraordinary person, but his basic knowledge on these matters came initially from the original *Reader's Digest* DIY Manual.

People like that make you slightly uneasy; but who doesn't want to live in some sort of comfort, and it really is achievable.

What this compilation of *Weekend Guardian* DIY pieces sets out to do is to advise you, as accurately as possible, what is achievable, without either breaking your neck or creating such domestic mayhem that even the dog leaves home. It has been set out in seasons; there's a time and a place for everything, including DIY jobs.

While the days of real house bargains may never return, as even the most unpromising building stock has been grabbed by the big-money developers, there remains considerable scope for home improvements of a real and valuable nature. Black and Deckerman, who used to be something of a joke, a closet masochist who spent his evenings and weekends blinded by dust and deafened by the whine of his ubiquitous drill, is now a respected person.

The near-evangelistic conversion to part-time building by otherwise quite lethargic people has a lot to do with the dinner party horror stories. I myself got home unexpectedly early one evening to find 'The Builders' preoccupied thus: one was headphoned on to my Beatles *White Album*, the Guv'nor was sprawled, shoes and socks off, on the bed making a phone call, and two others were in the kitchen Chasing the Dragon (that's sniffing heroin, folks) from a tea-leaf strainer they'd balanced on the gas stove burner. The real joke was that the team had been engaged by a firm of 'supervising architects', who eventually tried to sue me for their fees.

The Cowboys have a phrase for this behaviour: 'Taking the Piss'. So, most people eventually try to do things for themselves out of the sheer frustration of finding it impossible to get a real tradesman around, for any price. DIY, home improvements, call it what you like, is in my view saving money you really haven't got to spend anyway, and cutting down on 'aggravation', which is what the heroin sniffers told me they could 'well do without' when I threw them out. 'Aggravation' can also be your observation that there's a smell of burning because they've taped an electrical lead onto the central heating boiler, or put their foot through your favourite old rattan-caned chair because *you* didn't have a ladder.

Whether you do-it-yourself from choice or from necessity, the key to success is to recognise your limits, and then do it anyway. However, do not tear things apart without very carefully considering what is involved in terms of tools, expense and, perhaps more importantly, time. It can be demoralising, exhausting and domestically ruinous to pull about your ears a project which seems to have no end, despite many dedicated evenings battling alone under a naked swinging bulb while the rest of the faily, sensibly, spends the time with friends. Generally, do not attempt any job you do not fully understand from start to finish.

Professional electrical work, such as rewiring a house, is very expensive, but so, too, is electrocution. However, it really can be simple to install and reposition sockets, or introduce new lighting which, for perhaps some primordial reason, can have a profoundly cheering effect on your enthusiasm. But always use a good-quality current tester; in some electric wiring schemes, switching off at the mains does not render the entire circuit safe.

Plumbing, that other mysterious craft, is a more visible skill, as long as you carefully practise how to drain off the system, and know how to turn off the mains tap – very quickly – if needs be. Most plumbing jobs can now be done with plastic piping, which is light to handle and easy to bend, cut and join, although only time will tell whether its expensiveness over copper makes it a really viable alternative.

Do remember from the start that house renovation and a lot of DIY jobs are not the neat and tidy experiences which sometimes TV programmes compress into a few minutes' comfortable viewing. Inevitably you will have to begin from the very beginning. Whatever the job you confront, there'll be a book about it on the shelves of your local library. Browse through the collection, then buy the book; many home improvement jobs somehow seem to last a lot longer than two weeks.

There is a house I pass each morning and evening which I suspect has suffered GBH in the hands of a DIY madman. Its face to the outside world was once a respectable, even classic, example of what Victorian property developers probably considered to be appropriately modest dwelling places for the lesser artisans. Yet this mid-terraced house stands out from its neighbours because it has been redone in 'Cotswold Stone'.

I'm not suggesting for a moment that a *Guardian* reader would be so callous, but it may be important to bear in mind that one person's home improvements can be another's entrenched and very-expensive-to-move eyesore. Of couse, it's your castle and you're entitled to do what you want with it, but remember that while the midnight-black bathroom suite with contrasting tiles may be just the thing the Sunday colour mags have got the hots about this advertising season, the general conception in public tastes could have swung rapidly in another direction by the time you come to sell said black bathroom.

With the housing market in a generally downward spiral, estate agents, surveyors and building societies all seem to agree that certain types of property improvement on which a great deal of effort and money has been invested could now, more than ever before, leave you with a depreciating pup.

With a cautious vote of thanks to the bureaucracy of planning permissions and building regulations (which nevertheless missed out on the five-storey Cotswold Stone number) there are a number of things which do not necessarily involve the feared Inspectors. The big sell remains directed onto 'improvements' such as double glazing. But ripping out those draughty sash windows and replacing them with hermetically-sealed white plastic framed models could provide your house with a difficult sales point. Far better to keep out draughts with secondary glazing that is invisible from the road.

Similarly, those old window shutters may look as though they are dropping to pieces, but, stripped of their layers of paint and polished up again, they could sell the house by themselves. The original front door, with its beaten-up mouldings and scars of many lock changes over the years, can be rejuvenated with loving care.

Fitted kitchens very quickly get 'out of date' and tatty. This is, if you need it, an excellent argument in favour of spending £500 on a DIY range, rather than £5000 (at least) on a German job.

If you saw prospective buyers turning up their noses at your version of the most important room in the house, then you could rip it out and replace it with something more fashionable. What they do with the blue rag-rubbed hardboard cupboards isn't your problem.

But whatever the fads, the basic attractions of a warm, light, dry house will always prove a valuable investment. An efficient central heating system in a terraced house could add up to 20 per cent on its value. Cotswold Stone could mean that it's your retirement home.

Refurbishing: is it Worth it?

Refurbishing your house can make it more valuable and more pleasant to live in. The money you invest in improvements seldom yields a pound-for-pound return, but when you do eventually sell-up, some revamping projects will return much more than others.

Estate agents are convinced that face-lifting a bathroom with a basic but good-quality suite is probably one of the most financially rewarding jobs. You could expect to get about 75 per cent of your money back on this, and a second bathroom will return only slightly less. If you choose fancy fittings, such as an all-round shower spa or whirlpool bath, you might sell the house, but you're unlikely even to get your money back.

Spending money on improving one bathroom to an excellent state, perhaps putting in two washbasins, makes more financial sense than cutting corners to stretch out the budget to afford a second, guest bathroom. Plain colours always represent best resale appeal. Remember, white permanent fittings are acceptable to just about everyone, and you or a new owner can ring the changes with accessories that are vastly less expensive than having to hack off a wall of expensive, unsuitable tiles.

Kitchen improvements offer similar high-rate returns, although the smaller your investment in a face-lift, the higher the potential for recovering costs. Avoid budget-smashing extras such as state-of-the-art hobs and coloured sinks. Some buyers might be frightened off by complicated digital oven-timers, gory red sinks and central heating programmers which would challenge Mensa.

An added room could be a valuable asset, as long as you take care not to over-develop the house in terms of its neighbourhood. Every district has its maximum price, and you're highly unlikely to breach this, no matter what improvements you carry out.

A ground-floor family room that can be used as a third bedroom is a wiser investment than a dedicated fourth bedroom. Extensions that sympathetically replicate the style of the building will indeed prove an immediate benefit to you and also the eventual selling price, and that's a fact endorsed by building society research. An extension providing an extra bathroom or shower room and a bedroom is usually a winning attraction. But do not sacrifice a bedroom by irrevocably converting it into a second bathroom.

It really ain't what you do, but the way that you do it that brings results. You could spend thousands for what, in your view, is the best possible taste and still reduce the value of your home.

Sometimes you can't win, but there's no need to take another person's views too personally. I once returned to my former home to discover its new owners had smashed the roof off my quite stunning Victorian summer house because they wanted to use it as a 'barbie'.

Of course you can have your ranch-fenced Ponderosa in Pinner or Cotswold stone-clad Rose Cottage in Rotherham, but such bestial assaults on property are not only obviously and aesthetically wrong, they're also more than likely to mean that you'll continue to stay put when the housing markets start moving again. Surveyors sometimes suspect, with justification, that exterior cladding has been used in order to hide much more sinful things like serious structural cracks.

Well-installed double glazing will, undoubtedly, improve comfort, cut fuel bills and improve window security, but you generally won't get half its cost back in the selling value of your house, even if you fit an elaborate and expensive system yourself. And that doesn't take into account the devastating effect a gleaming white set of hermetically sealed windows will make to say, a granite cottage. Instal a modern, efficient central heating system – many buyers won't consider a house without one anyway – and you'll get the money back, and more, as the cost of installation, as with all building labour costs, will continue to rise, whatever the state of the house market. A new central heating boiler, alone, is a good investment.

Garages are one of the most sought-after adddition. Apart from keeping a car safer from vandals, they provide attractive storage space, workshop facility and a safe place in which children can play.

However, it's straightforward and simple things like good lighting, conveniently sited power points, thorough and, again, neutral-coloured, exterior painting, clear effective drains, toilets that flush properly and a waterproof roof which are most important.

Taps that don't drip and washing machine connections that don't leak; windows that bar icy draughts, shelves that don't collapse, stairs that don't squeak, safe and sound bannister rails and an absence of trailing electrical leads – all these are of paramount importance, right now and in the future.

Tools for the Home

In the beginning there was 'the electric drill'. And the multitude heard the words, Go forth and bore not only holes in the wall but all your friends, with tales of new shelves and neat fountains of water which spring eternally from hidden, punctured pipes. And there were flashes of fire, acrid smoke, the whimpering of panic and the total darkness of a house with electric wiring of such wonderously melted contortions that people travelled far to gaze in wonderment at it. And lo, the skips of the land were bountiful with half-born 'projects', pine spice racks, quietly aborted before Christmas-time arrived.

It was of course Black and Decker who brought real power to the people – and, it must be said, made it easier than ever before for the careless amongst them to zip off the entire finger-count of one hand with a quickness that not only deceived the eye but also the nerve-endings, so graphically illustrated by legends of people strolling to hospital with their pinkies in their pockets.

It is really to firms like Black and Decker that the aspiring DIYer must still turn for reasonable quality in power tools, reasonably-priced and backed up by the most obliging and consoling repair service in the country. Enthusastic beginners sometimes want not so much to drill a hole, but rather a new exit for the Channel Tunnel.

But (very) carefully handled, power tools save time, and although they cost money, they save it too by enabling the novice to accomplish a job he or she would not otherwise be able even to contemplate, even if it is ostensibly as simple as cutting a straight line in a piece of wood (which could be your first ever shelf). You'll always need something to hold things on, safely and securely. The B&D Workmate has its own vice, and it's a useful 'step-up' platform for standing on.

Power tools fall into two distinctive groups. First there are the one-job purpose-built saws or sanders, for example, and then there is The Drill, with its long list of accessories and

attachments which take so long to attach and, in cutting applications, are usually so unwieldy and innacurate as to make the
whole excercise pointlessly frustrating. This is particularly so
if you have to stop in the middle of a job to change your drill
from one use to something entirely different. For the first
project which will really test your nascent skills as a tyro
carpenter it is therefore well worth hiring a particular 'dedicated' tool from one of the many hire shops found in the *Yellow
Pages* (see next chapter).

However, a good, general purpose drill will have the following – minimum – specifications: two speeds (high speed for wood,
and a low gearing for denser materials), a half-inch chuck which
will easily cope with half-inch steel and concrete. Typical price
target: around £50, but for another £10 you could get a vari-
able-speed drill which has a reversing facility enabling it to be
used as a power screw-driver. It will also have a hammer action
for which you will be eternally grateful should you ever try to
drill a hole in a solid concrete wall or engage in work in what is
sanguinely described as 'a demanding environment'. Note that
the power tool business is notorious for its discounting. Some
firms regularly sell 'reconditioned' drills which are often, in
fact, slightly out-dated, but brand-new tools being cleared out
of stock. They all have a one year guarantee. There are similar
bargains in *Exchange and Mart*.

The power tools I consider next in value for home-based jobs
are the jig saw and the circular saw. A single-speed jig saw is
quite adequate for most tasks; you'll use it a lot for cutting
curves, round and square holes (for example the aperture for
a kitchen sink or hob unit) and profiles in just about any flat
surface. It's also good for just general hacking, although it is
unsuitable for long, precise cuts in boards, such as kitchen work
surfaces, large sheets of block board or the increasingly used
MDF (medium density fibre) boards from which a lot of contemporary furniture is manufactured.

A circular saw will have a rip-fence, which will facilitate long
accurate cutting, although ideally this will be done with the sole
plate of the saw bearing against a batten that is fixed adjacent
to to the cutting line. A circular saw's most important asset,
both in terms of safety and performance, is its power, which

must be adquate enough to cope with the heavy cutting jobs and therefore no smaller than seven and a quarter inches in diameter. The electric motor for such a saw will be in the 1100 watts range. Anything less is not really worth buying because saws of this size can also be fitted with metal and masonry cutting discs. Incidentally, a hard-tipped TCT blade is expensive, but will last up to 20 times longer than a conventional HSS steel blade.

It is worth considering the convenience of cordless electric drills, jig saws, sanders and screwdrivers; (the latter are in my view rather a novelty unless you can forsee a job where literally hundreds of screws are going to be screwed). Cordless means of course being free of the tedious and dangerous likelihood of tripping over long lengths of extension lead trailing from some distant power plug. Unfortunately cordless can also mean that you may find the power tool dead and useless because you have forgotten to charge its batteries. But cordless tools are infinitely more mobile than the conventional versions. Even with the big discounts available, buying the above basic implements may well ruin your budget, particularly when your first projects will probably come soon after the considerable expense of buying and moving into a new home. In that case hand tools must be the answer.

While they do need a lot more practice, the cost of hand tools will be very much smaller, and they can be a pleasure to use. But they must, really must, be British-made. This is not my own peculiar chauvinism. It's simply that Britain continues to make the best tools in the world. Stanley, of Sheffield, say theirs are the best you can lay your hands on. Consider the humble hammer; surprisingly perhaps, many accidents involving cheap, market-stall hammers happen not when people hit their fingers instead of the nail, but when fine chips of steel fly off the hammer head with injurious speed. Stanley's electrically-smelted steel heads are drop forged so that the grain structure of the steel flows with the shape of the head, making chipping improbable. And that's a simple example of the craftsmanship involved in a very simple tool which is, nevertheless, in frequent use – and abuse.

Stanley also offer one of the latest versions of another vital piece of DIY equipment, the pocket measuring tape on which most jobs rely. The Autolock has an innovative locking device which prevents the spring from withdrawing the tape (blade) in mid-measurement and is only released when the power return lever is operated – the usual locking mechanism for tapes is applied by the thumb. Also, the blade itself is 16 mm wide, wider than most, which means it is kept more rigid when measuring long distances. Consider the advantages of this when there is no-one around to hold the end taut against a wall. Prices range from £4.25 for the 2 m to £8.45 for the 5 m, which I would consider the best size, particularly when you may have to size up large areas such as floors.

The purchase of a handsaw is slightly more problematic: there are so many versions, cross-cut, rip, back and panel saws, all of which can be rendered useless in the second it takes to hit a hidden nail in a floorboard. So you can waste a considerable amount of time and money seeking out the services of the quaintly-named 'saw doctors' for the re-sharpening or re-cutting of saw teeth. The best general-purpose saw has got to be the 'universal' panel saw with a 22-in blade and 'hardpoint' teeth, which are extremely sharp and long lasting (about five times longer than conventional teeth). However, they usually cannot be re-sharpened, so they are in that respect disposable. Brand leaders in hardpoint, Sandvik, sell a saw like this for around £12. The other essential saw is ridiculously cheap by comparison. The Eclipse Junior – the type is universally known as a junior – hacksaw cuts metal and plastic and costs around £1.60. Packets of spare blades are equally inexpensive.

You will need several versions of screwdrivers: two single-slots for screw sizes 6 to 8, and 10 to 12 gauge, a Phillips or Pozidrive No. 2, which will fit most 6, 8 and 10 gauge screws, and an indispensable neon mains tester-cum-electrical screwdriver with a fully insulated blade. The handle contains a neon bulb and a one megaohm resistor. By touching a mains terminal with the blade and holding the metal stud on the top of the handle with your finger, you complete a circuit with the earth and the bulb lights, indicating live power. The resistor guards you against shock, but buy the best, and check it regularly against a socket you know is live.

The ubiquitous Stanley knife, with a safely-retractable blade, is another essential tool; it can also be fitted with wood and metal cutting blades. The 99E with five spare blades costs under £5. Also terrific value are a good-quality wire stripper, pliers, a G-cramp (or two) for holding down work, holding glued pieces together, and even as third or fourth hands.

Apart from high-speed drill bits for wood and metal you will also need masonry bits, but don't buy expensive packs, which will include sizes you may never use. Instead, buy them one bit at a time, as required. A bolster chisel, for cutting cavities into bricks and channels for wiring, a 1 in wood chisel, a torch and a pencil will complete your starter kit. And don't forget a piece of string. I know someone who spent all day in the loft of his house until his wife returned home. He was holding up a broken ball float valve which would otherwise have deluged the building with water. If he'd had a piece of string in his pocket, he could have gone for a pint instead.

Hiring Tools

I've already discussed putting together a fairly basic set of tools, but sometimes you will want to tackle jobs that need specialist implements. These are invariably far too costly to buy unless, perish the thought, you face years of evenings and weekends doing up a succession of houses instead of settling down with a good book and an apple. The fast-growing popularity of the gladiatorial sport of DIY has, in its turn, spawned hire shops where you can, for a price, get hands-on experience of a huge variety of tools from a vibrating plate to a miniature excavator and digger.

You should insist on specific instruction and a demonstration on how to use a tool. Also, fastidiously observe all the safety rules involving dress and protective gear like goggles, gloves, footwear, masks and ear defenders even if, at the time, they seem inconvenient or irrelevant. Hiring some tools can be pretty costly, particularly if you might not use them for more than an hour or so. But you'll be saving yourself a great deal of hassle and, in many cases, a good tool will make up for your lack of expertise.

Many people rely on a chair and a rickety old step ladder to do their own interior decorating but a continuous working platform of trestles and staging is both safer and more comfortable, particularly if you have to put up lining or woodchip paper to hide a cracked ceiling.

Heavy-quality cotton dustsheets are far better than their polythene equivalant which can also prove dangerously slippery on some floors.

Wallpaper strippers are perhaps one of the most blessed inventions. The heavy duty models will help you strip the most stubborn paper effortlessly, but beware, the steam generated within about 10 minutes can scald you if you're not reasonably careful. Really difficult-to-remove wall coverings are best first attacked with a wallpaper perforator, a spiky-headed device which allows the steam to penetrate more easily.

A hot air gun is the quickest and most effective way of

stripping paint and varnish. It's also safer and more pleasant to use than the gas blow-lamp or liquid stripper alternatives, and the guns available on hire are much more powerful than those on the DIY market. But again, take care, they can burn both you and the wood, unless you play them back and forth over the material being stripped. They can also damage light switches and melt things like room thermostat covers, surface cables and plastic fittings.

Pasting tables are cheap enough to buy, but don't get 'bargain' stripping knives: the handles fall off and the blades can blunt quickly, or even shatter. Good ones last years, and are useful for other jobs like filling holes.

Ever thought of hiring a portable paint spraying unit? Then stop it at once. It's difficult not to over-spray; paint-mist is hazardous and even if you like the mono-colour look, the cat won't.

Tiling is one of the most pleasant jobs because the cosmetic result is immediate. A good tile cutter with a carbide wheel will make easy work of quarry and ceramic wall and floor tiles, but if you've chosen a particularly thick tile, first take a sample along to the hire shop for a demonstration.

If you really *have* to hack off wall tiles, rather than take the sane, cowardly but completely satisfactory course of tiling over tiles that may be ugly but sound, get a light electric hammer. Eye protection is imperative and cover up as much of your face as possible. Tile splinters are as sharp as glass shards.

Redecorating a room will also give you the opportunity of cutting chases for new lights and sockets, and an electrically operated chasing machine will do this neatly and quickly in solid plaster (but not lathe and plaster walls) as well as in brickwork and blockwork, but it cannot cope with concrete or the hard (usually blue) engineering brick. These materials require an angle grinder with a cutting disc – a ferociously noisy and, in tired hands, potentially lethal machine.

If you're not sure where existing cables run in a wall, you can hire the most impressive CAT – Cable Avoiding Tool – which electronically detects buried cables much more effectively than DIY models. (A CAT signal generator traces runs of cables and pipes in spaghetti-built systems).

I'm hesitant about recommending you try exterior decorating. Even if you've a good head for heights, it's still the most dangerous of projects, and putting up a large ladder is a skill in itself. Even carrying one is tricky. But if you must, then hire scaffolders to come and erect a safe structure for you. Three potential snags: they'll want cash in hand; scaffolding is a burglar's gift; and the scaffolders may come and take it away before you're finished with it.

Consider hiring light-weight alloy access towers which are avaiable in three basic sizes from 2 ft 8 in by 5 ft to 4 ft 3 in by 5 ft. Towers come with decking boards, safety toe boards and adjustable base plates or wheels. They're not too difficult to erect, but they must stand firm and be tied to a part of the house, such as a window frame. Always climb up the inside, otherwise the tower can unbalance and topple over.

Heavy duty rope-operated ladders are best: a double 16 ft for two storeys, a double 20 ft for modern three-storey houses or a treble 16 ft for older three-storey buildings. A modern four storey will need a treble 20 footer. Hire a ladder stay which clips to the top and stably holds the ladder away from the wall to prevent damage to guttering and provide a more comfortable working position. The foot of the ladder must be on even, solid ground, and it must be tied to a couple of stakes, and/or supported by a bag of sand. The ladder must rest at the correct angle, which is 1 ft out for every 4 ft in height. Don't work alone if you can help it, and never look down.

Following a piece on hiring tools, I've had many requests from readers for information on hiring tools for tasks I haven't yet mentioned. Be patient, I'll continue on the tool hiring theme, but remember that some of the tools available for hire are intended for skilled and experienced tradesmen, and as such require extreme care, practice and advice, which the hirer is obliged to give you. I won't repeat this warning. Just heed it, and don't write to me with a pen clenched in your teeth.

Somewhere, out there, a reader has attempted to sand the planked wooden floor of his living room using an electric drill fitted with an abrasive disc. Not surprisingly, it has, he said, so far taken three weeks, and scored circular marks all over the surface. Solution: he can either cover the uneven floor with

hardboard and carpet it or hire a disc floor sander (about which
more later). It's Sod's Law that you'll too often read how to do
something when you've already done it.

Many people who've written in want to know about floor
sanding machines, and while it's true that some old houses do
have potentially beautiful wooden floors, most have been
ravaged in one way or another and you'll waste a lot of time and
money trying to restore them, unless you're prepared to begin
by replacing all the damaged planks, which will always, no
matter how carefully you stain them, look odd.

There's a variety of floor sanders available, from lightweight
to industrial. Most look, and handle, a bit like lawn mowers; all
have dust collection bags which pick up about half the dust. The
rest spreads to almost every corner of the house unless you
carefully seal the doors of the room you're working in, and keep
them closed until you reckon you can safely take your face-mask
off.

It's vital to prepare the floor before sanding, naturally checking that all the floorboards are secure, removing tacks and
remnants of old covering, and punching nail heads – which
would otherwise rip the sanding equipment – well below the
surface. A floor sander should effectively remove old and thin
coats of paint, stains and varnish. If the floor is thickly painted
you're in trouble, and you might reconsider the whole project,
for you must first remove the paint with a proprietary liquid
stripper and scraper, by hand. If you don't, the paint will not
only quickly clog the machine's sanding discs, but will also be
irrevocably friction-rubbed back into the wood.

Buy more than you think you'll use of coarse, medium and
fine abrasive sheets; the hire shop should buy back unused ones,
but check. Hire a drum floor sander for most of the floor area,
working diagonally across the boards first in one direction and
then the other, going down through the grades from coarse to
fine sandpaper.

Clear the floor of dust between each operation – a hired
industrial vacuum cleaner will save your own vacuum from
certain death.

The drum machine generally won't sand right up to the
skirting board. For this you'll need a lightweight disc floor

sander sometimes called an edging sander. Both sanders can be hired as a package for about £30 a day or, to give you more time, £55 for a week. Work carefully, as every mark will be instantly highlighted when you finally stain and seal the wood.

For a really perfect finish, you'll need yet a third, floor-finishing, sander to use between coats of sealer, and which can also be used to clean cork or terrazzo floors.

Some hire shops will also try to sell you floor varnish. Samples I've seen were an all-purpose 'one pack' polyurethane. After all that effort, you'd benefit more from advice from a paint merchant who will take into account the described state and colour of the new floor surface.

You can also hire a floor polisher for the final shine, and a lightweight back-pack vaccuum cleaner for clearing the dust which might, despite your best endeavours, have gathered on the walls of stair wells and on picture rails. Also recommended for nascent Flash Gordons, but tie long hair well back.

Removing an old floor covering like vinyl, carpet tiles or linoleum which has been firmly stuck down is best done with a floor tile stripper which has a wide blade which vibrates at high frequency. The blade angle is adjusted to meet the required severity of attack. Grubby solid concrete floors can be cleaned with a scarifier which uses wire brushes that are avaiable on a sale or return arrangment. Vacuum floor scrubbers that scrub, dry and polish are, however, cumbersome to handle because they've got usually got a large, six-gallon water tank. All the carpets in a three-bedroomed house can be cleaned in a day with an industrial carpet cleaning machine which simultaneously heats its own water, mixes it with special cleaning fluids and sucks up most of the dirt and moisture. If this seems almost too good to be true, you're half-right because you can give the carpet a soaking which could take many days to dry out. Attachments for deep-cleaning furniture are also available.

You can hire a set of rods and a chimney-sweeping brush if your house is already really filthy, otherwise call Sooty. Grimy exterior brickwork can be rehabilitated with an electrically powered turbo-washer operating at about 2000 psi, with a chemical injection gadget for stubborn stains. A wet sandblasting attachment is also available. But this can make more of a

mess than you've already got, and can destroy pointing (the
gaps between bricks) which might otherwise have lasted years.

'Easy to handle and gives good penetration from a fast
compaction rate of 600 strokes per minute'. Told you DIY can
be fun. Especially if you're powered by a two-stroke petrol
engine. But always make sure you're wearing sturdy boots with
steel toe caps. The Vibratory Rammer so described in my tool
hire catalogue is used to ram down hard core rubble and earth
when you're preparing foundations for anything from a brick
wall to a driveway, or even a house. In the latter case its
portability and smallness, compared to its bigger brothers you
see jumping about mending roads, make it ideal for working in
the confined space of a foundation trench. Together with a
portable electric concrete mixer, it's just about the best hire-
tool bargain you can get, even if, like Winston Churchill at
Chartwell, all you want to do is to build a modestly relaxing
brick wall around your country estate. The human effort such
instruments save is more than gargantuan – you just cannot do
without them. If you try, you'll end up in bed with a very bad
back.

The Vibrating Plate isn't part of the paraphernalia of a bogus
seance, either. Although it delivers almost the same message as
the rammer, in that it is used for quickly compacting rubble and
foundations for paths, its lightweight lawn-mower-like appearance belies the strength of the vibrating action which exerts a
compacting force of well over a ton. With a protective rubber
mat attached to its base plate, it is ideal for levelling paving
bricks without damaging them.

A friend, a man of the cloth, once told me he became so
attached to the faithful concrete mixer he hired during a pro-
tracted bout of vicarage extending he ended up buying it. But
that too is what you'll have to do if you absent-mindedly leave
the mixer half full of quick-setting mixture.

Hire shops take a very unsporting view of equipment returned in a bad condition, which is why they demand quite a
substantial deposit, which is normally returnable.

No matter how modest your building work, if it takes more
than a half a dozen cement, sand and aggregate (ballast) mixes,
a portable electric mixer, which comes on a stand, enabling you

to tip the mixture straight into a barrow, is a blessing. It turns out 85 litres of perfect, pliable concrete every time. You'll need a transformer to step down 240 volt supplies to 110 volt equipment and a heavy-duty power extension (usually about 50 ft), which is best all wound off its drum to prevent overheating.

Don't use a a common-or-garden wheelbarrrow: heavy, wet concrete mixes will destroy it. Hire a builder's barrow and a shovel. It's best to buy your own builder's spirit level, which will always be invaluable for other tasks. Hired ones do get bashed about, and even the most minimal inaccuracies in levels can have disastrous effects the higher, or wider, your wall, drive or concrete floor is. A Cowley level is a precision automatic surveying instrument, which comes with a tripod, staff and target, and can be used for setting concrete forms, foundations and gradient levels.

Hirable concrete forms provide the edge formwork needed for the construction of largish slabs like foundations and garage drives. If you want to lay concrete slabs, a portoscreed vibrates, compacts and levels simultaneously. If you have to work at a height over a large area, say building or repairing a wall, it's vital you use a continuous platform provided by steel trestles, sometimes called hurdles, or bandstands supporting scaffolding (or builder's) boards. These are far stronger than the trestles used for interior decorating, for they have to support not only yourself but also the considerable extra weight of materials. You'll also use the boards to form a path for your barrow over uneven ground, up slopes and on soft earth.

All this sort of work involves lifting heavy things – a bag of cement will seem rooted to the ground. Quantities of sand and aggregate come in half-bags, otherwise you'd never move them. Keep your back straight and use your knees to power the lifting. Unfit and overweight? Don't do it.

If you have a huge amount of digging to do, say foundations (footings) for drives and walls or digging or excavating for a garden pond or even a swimming pool, hire a mini-excavator, which is powerful, manoeuverable, and has an amazing capacity for work. It can work in very confined spaces, digging over six foot deep, but also has stabilisers giving a wide, firm base. It moves under its own power once you've got it on site, but it does require some practice to enable you to use it efficiently.

Take extreme care with demolition work – do not touch things like chimney breasts and load-bearing walls. As a general rule you can identify a non-load-bearing wall if the joists in the floor above run parallel to the wall. The joists of a load-bearing wall run at right-angles, and rest on it. If you're in doubt, get a builder in, just for a quote.

Hire a demolition hammer for breaking brickwork and concrete up to 4 in thick. A heavy breaker will demolish concrete up to 1 ft deep.

Domestic electric drills with 600 watts can burn out if used for a lot of tough masonry and wall drilling. A heavy- or medium-duty rotary hammer drill is best. They can be fitted with a core bit for making holes for pipes up to 4 in in diameter.

Hired tools are invaluable for coping with one-off plumbing problems and disasters. A blocked sink, bath or shower tray can be cleared with a manually-operated Sanisnake. A powered drain cleaner can be used for more serious blockages. Blockages in straight drain runs between outside inspection chambers can be quite easily cleared with drain rod sets, but always hire a scraper head which will de-gunge the drain, and lessen the chances of recurring problems.

If you do have a flood, particularly in a basement or cellar, clear it with an electric submersible pump. 'Wet' vacuums will help dry out soaking carpets and a dehumidifier can be hired to dry out a room as big as 5000 cu ft. These are of course also invaluable for removing heavy condensation, and speeding up the curing of plaster before decorating, but be careful not to do this too enthusiastically as it could cause severe cracking.

These are the often much-loved beasts of DIY tools and, once tamed, your only true friends as the thin Saturday morning drizzle works into your shoulders, the time you wish you could join your neighbours in Sainsburys instead of building the damn fool-idea patio which they'll all come and enjoy on halcyon summer evenings which seem a hundred years away.

Winter

Winter concentrates the mind on tasks so easily put aside in more pleasant seasons. It's when most people feel the draught, both financially and physically, and they suffer the cruel and punitive power of Sod's Law as central heating systems collapse, pipes burst and the damp patch appears on the bedroom ceiling, usually on the morning after a particularly late night.

Repairing Central Heating Systems

As Richard Nixon would tell you, some plumbers can be ruin-ously expensive. Their 'minimum call out' charges for de-bugging your system should be sufficient incentive for you at least to try and cure a problem yourself. You might enjoy plumbing, but I doubt it. It's dirty and messy. But you'll certainly save a lot of money and heartache, pleading with the 'no job too small' merchants you ring on frosty January mornings. Let's face it, if they were any good they'd be at work by 9 am.

The heart of any central heating system is its pump, and this over-worked and neglected component is the one to examine when your radiators suddenly go cold. But check simple things first: is the thermostat on the boiler or the roomstat on the wall set too low; are the timer and programmer working satisfactorily?

The likeliest sign that the pump isn't feeling too well is banging or hissing sounds in the central heating system or boiler. The pump, which is quite easily identifiable on the bottom face of the boiler, may also be overheating; it will be extremely hot to touch, but the pipes on either side will be lukewarm. If the pump is still running, and you can tell this by 'listening' stethoscope-wise through a screwdriver touching the casing, then there's probably air trapped inside. The bleed screw valve on the pump is usually marked as such; if not, look for a countersunk screw on the top or side of the casing. Open the screw *very* gently, and if you hear a hiss of air followed by a dribble of water, you can re-tighten it and go and spend the £40 or so you'd have had to pay an emergency plumbing service for doing precisely that.

Pumps also suffer from sludge accumulating in the filthy black fluid that runs inside your nice white radiators. The sludge might have jammed the pump's rotor – although this usually happens when the central heating system is first switched on after an inactive summer. (Make a note in your new diary now to run the central heating system for an hour on alternate weeks throughout the summer.)

Make sure the heating is on 'continuous' and turn up the wall thermostat. Try and free the pump's rotor with a screwdriver inserted in the slot in the middle of device (there might be a hexagonal nut there instead) and move the rotor backwards and forwards from the 11.45 to 12.15 position. You'll need to do this fairly vigorously. If all that fails, then you probably need to replace the pump itself, but you might first try removing it and cleaning it out.

Replacement is best, however, if the system is elderly, and it is easy, as long as you can buy a pump which is exactly the same make and model as the old one. Get new sealing washers at the same time. Turn off the gate valves either side of the pump, thereby isolating it from its water supply. If there are no valves, I'm afraid you'll have to drain the system from the stopcock at the bottom of the boiler. Switch off the electrical power to the pump, and remove the fuse for that circuit from the fuse box. Put the fuse in your pocket, and so prevent any well-intentioned 'helper' from electrocuting you. Remove the cover plate off the pump and disconnect the wiring, carefully noting which coloured connections go where.

Cover the floor around the boiler with old rags and newspapers, and have a bucket handy, as a certain amount of black water will come out of the pump when you remove it. Undo the two compression nuts on either side of the pump and fit the new unit, tightening the compression joints, opening up the gate valves and reconnecting the electric power. When you replace the fuse and switch on you'll probably find that the pump needs bleeding again.

Control valves, sometimes called motorised valves, can stick or break down completely. They're a nusiance because if they need replacing the whole system will have to drained down, as it's highly unlikely that the installers will have spent an extra ten minutes and £10 on installing gate valves on either side. The method for renewing a valve is similar to fitting a new pump, but these box-type valves are usually in an awkward position, and you probably won't be be able to take the old valve out of the pipe run simply by unscrewing the nuts on either side, so it's best to pay a plumber to do it.

If the pump is operating normally but all the radiators

remain cold, check the thermostat and timer. Still nothing? Switch the power off and check the electrical connections in the controls. A single cold radiator could simply mean that its inlet valve is closed, or a thermostatic radiator valve is not properly set. If the bottom of the radiator is hot and the top cool, there's an airlock. Use a radiator key to turn the bleed valve found at one of the top corners of the radiator until you hear the air escaping, followed by a dribble of water. Have a rag handy to catch this, and put some newspaper underneath.

Radiators that need constant venting in this way can be a sign of drastic corrosion within the system. If you hold a lighted match to the quarter-open vent valve and it burns with a blue flame, this means hydrogen in the system. The other product of corrosion is the black iron-oxide sludge which is drawn through the system by the magnetic field of the boiler pump. This is the corrosive sludge which siezes up the rotor. To lessen the chance of this happening you will have to introduce a corrosion inhibitor.

Turn off the boiler and drain the central heating system via the stopcock on the bottom, connecting with a hosepipe to outside the house. Do not stop the water supply into the small feed and expansion tank in the loft because this of course will allow the system to flush out. Allow at least 30 minutes for this to happen; in fact let the water flush through until it looks fairly clean. As the system is flushing out, tap the surfaces of all the radiators with a heavy piece of padded wood to free any clinging sludge. Start at the radiator furthest away from the boiler. Close the boiler drain cock and put the chemical corrosion inhibitor into the feed and expansion tank.

Repairing Central Heating Boilers

*'Sorry it's a trifle warm — we always test
the boiler at this time of year . . . '*

It's part of the boiler-manufacturer's sales philosophy to persuade people that replacing an old central heating boiler will save fuel bills. It's true, of course. If your boiler is more than ten years old, it may be getting a little doddery; a new model will be so much more efficient and it will offer at least a 10 per cent saving in running costs. Better control over combustion and enhanced heat transfer through the boiler means that much less heat goes wastefully up the chimney. The new generation of boilers are also smaller, which may give you a little more floor space, and the wall-mounted versions are far more efficient than the old floor-standing models.

But a new boiler will also cost an awful lot of money; it's going to take you a long time to recover that extra expense. It therefore could be far more cost-effective to repair rather than replace; spares for most popular makes and models made as long as 20 years ago are still readily available. You may have to ring around a little, or maybe even send off to one of the heating-by-mail-order companies you'll find in Thursday's *Exchange and Mart*.

It doesn't really make a material difference to the checks whether you have gas, oil or solid fuelled heating. Although the components will look and work differently, the maintenance is elementary and similar. Before you start, write and ask the manufacturer whether they still have stocks of the original servicing book appropriate to your old boiler.

The boiler simply has to be clean and nicely adjusted. A well-tuned gas boiler will have a clear blue flame, with very little traces of yellow in it. At the same time, check that the thermo-coupler trips out after ten seconds or so. They're not expensive, so buy a new one if it doesn't. It is essential that major overhauls on gas boilers should be carried out by a CORGI registered fitter, but you can make your own checks to establish whether servicing is necessary. Switch off the gas and remove the fuse to the electrical power supplies, and cover the surrounding floor with a stout old dust-sheet. The following can be a messy business.

With the front cover removed, you'll see the heat exchangers, which get gunged up with sooty deposits. If you're not confident about their removal and safe replacement, they can be carefully wire brushed and vacuum cleaned. The same applies to the burners. They may have metallic gauze inside their elements so take care not to damage these by too vigorous brushing. If the elements can be removed, they're best cleaned by soaking them for a few hours in a caustic soda solution.

It cannot be overemphasised that it is illegal, as well as potentially dangerous, for an unqualified person to do any work in connection with the gas supply itself.

Central heating pumps are a potential problem, not because

of their design, nor even the enormous workload – some are working winter-long. They often break down because of the severe pressure put on them by some uncaring or incompetent builders who have taken time-saving short cuts, not only in the routing of central heating pipes, but in doing things like using cheaper – to him but not to you – 15 mm pipes and fittings when the design called for 22 mm. Such modifications can make an enormous difference to the frictional resistance and operational loading on the pump. Remember, when you employ them, that builders build, and that central heating installation is a specific and sometimes very complicated craft of pressures, heat values and balanced, bespoke design.

Another way to give a pump heart failure is by installing too many thermostatic valves on radiators after installation, without making a simple circuit operation to ease the stress on the pump which is being 'called' and shut off that many extra times. So if you have got thermostatic valves, a controlled by-pass would not only give the pump a longer life, but also boost fuel savings by increasing the response to the settings of the boiler thermostat.

The rotors of pumps that have done nothing all summer may have seized, resulting in the radiators remaining cold. This can usually be cured quite simply by rotating the nut in the centre of the casing, clockwise and then anti-clockwise, half a dozen times. Remember, you can hear whether a pump is working all right by using a long screwdriver, placed on the casing, as a sort of stethoscope. This is not as unamusing as paying a plumber a minimum call out fee to do exactly what I've just described.

Many older heating systems have matching inadequate controls like a simple time switch and a single room thermostat – usually in the hall. They do little to control the various space heating demands of different parts of the house, and nothing to monitor hot water temperatures. At today's fuel prices, they're squandering money. You might consider fitting at least a separate room- and hot-water-cylinder thermostat, activated individually by motorised valves, and a good programmer. Although the digital micro-chip controls look very impressive, and are selective enough to switch on various days, when you're away in the winter for example, I prefer the simple reliability, and fixability, of mechanical controls.

Have a look at the radiator valves which may have been permanently closed for the summer season: they may have seized too. Squirt some penetrating oil on the spindles, and leave it to soak in overnight. You may find that some radiators won't heat up at all because of sediment, or rather sludge that has accumulated in them. A good chemical cleaner like Fernox (full instructions on the container) will probably solve the problem, although you may have to close off the valves on each side of the radiator, remove it from the wall and take it outside before flushing it with water from a hosepipe.

I don't want to bang on about heating problems any more than some of your boilers, pipes and radiators seem to have been doing recently, but I guess that at this time of year the subject is likely to be a lot more pertinent than how to level the legs on a kitchen table. The reader who asked about this will, I'm afraid, have to wait until more desperate dilemmas are resolved.

A coupling means different things to different people, but for the purposes of this piece, it's the sort of remedy you could implement if you suffer a burst pipe. It is a purpose-made fitment which will replace the part of the pipe that has burst. You will of course have already closed down the boiler, turned off the mains stopcock and drained the central heating system. You will also have confronted the agonising decision of what to do with the bulging ceiling, given it a good poke with the end of a broom and watched in fascinated horror at the result collapses onto the carpet, entirely missing the plastic dustbin you've rather pathetically put there 'to catch the worse of it'.

It's important to remember that closing the mains stopcock might have no effect whatsoever on a burst pipe that is coming down from the cold water cistern in the roof space. If this is the case, open all the hot and cold water taps on the way upstairs and close the gate valves on the cold water supply and the pipe leading into the hot water cylinder.

Now for the coupling. Replacing the damaged bit will be a lot easier if you've bought a length of hand-bendable copper with compression fittings. Fitting a replacement piece of rigid copper in the gap won't be particularly easy unless you can quite easily move the two cut ends apart in order to get the replacement in.

Cutting into a fixed pipe is best accomplished by lifting it from its fixing bracket and wedging wood between the pipe and wall or whatever it's on. This will give a comparatively stable base on which to cut with a Junior hacksaw. You'll then have to file the cut ends to make sure they are perfectly square, otherwise you're wasting your time. Carefully remove all the filings.

Companies like Kontite, Delta and Conex make 'slip' couplings which are like ordinary compression fittings in appearance, but are much longer and, more crucially, have no internal shoulders where the cut ends of the old pipe buts into the new fitting. Consequently these 'slips' are the ones to use for a DIY repair as there's no soldering involved. The only imperative is that the piece of burst pipe cut out is shorter than the length of the coupling, which is then slid down one pipe and back into the other. Forming the connection is then simply a matter of tightening two nuts on either end.

If you do get an initial weep from a slip coupling, tightening the compression nut using a spanner, with another spanner on the fitting will cure it. Be very gentle though, as too much force will make the joint leak even more, and you'll have to go through the whole procedure of turning off the water, draining, and so on. Incidentally, Kontite make a slip fitting which will repair a burst lead pipe.

Plumbers will tell you that such a remedy isn't as good as a soldered joint; that being, in effect, compression joints, they are susceptable to weakening as pipes expand and contract under normal working conditions. All this is true, but they cost only a couple of pounds to buy, and you can do the job yourself. You can practise soldering a capillary joint some time next summer.

When you refill a repaired central heating system you will of course be introducing fresh water and fresh air, which could create air locks and require the bleeding of radiators and possibly the pump. More worryingly, you'll also be creating ideal conditions for corrosion, so make sure you add a dose of Fernox (MB-1) corrosion inhibitor to the feed and expansion (header) cistern. The same firm also produces an internal leak sealant (FP-FH) which might cure leaking radiators that have corroded and are on their last legs, depending on the severity of the damage.

There's no particular mystery to making a joint with a capillary fitting either. They are a lot less expensive than compression fittings. You might understandably consider it imprudent to try it out for the first time in a confined space or a loft, for you'll have to use a blow lamp. Make sure you don't set any of the surrounding area alight, by placing an asbestos mat behind the work. A butane-gas blow lamp is easy to use and very effective, as long as you turn the flame down to a medium-blue colour.

The soldered capillary fitting is so called because inside each socket end there is a reservoir groove holding enough solder to ensure a good joint. Preparation is all-important; the pipe must be completely dry, for even the slightest glimmer of water will prevent the solder from reaching the right temperature. The pipe needs to be cut square making allowance for the depth of its fit into the socket. Clean off any burr and, using fine wire wool, also clean about two inches of the end of the pipe and the inside of the socket. The copper should be shiny bright; try not to touch the clean bits with your hands again. Now do a dry run making sure the pipe buts neatly up to the shoulder within the socket.

Remove the fitting and smear plumber's flux on the mating surfaces, that is the inside of the fitting and the outside of the pipe end (flux prevents oxidisation, which could prevent the solder from bonding). Refit the pieces, wiping off any excess flux. Heat the joint with the blow lamp, playing the flame evenly over the fitting. The joint is complete when a ring of solder appears around the edge of the fitting. Heat for a few seconds more and allow to cool. And don't in your enthusiastic concentration hold any part of the pipe with a bare hand; copper is an excellent heat conductor.

It's best to prepare and fit all the pipes entering the fitting at the same time so that they are all heated together, ensuring that the joint is correctly aligned and that solder in an unused socket doesn't just melt and run away out of the end. If for some reason you have to leave a socket empty while heating the other, put a short piece of uncleaned, unfluxed tube into the empty end and wrap a damp cloth around it.

Emergency Plumbing

One in seven homes has suffered the chaotic effects of a burst pipe during the last two years. Apart from opening the front door to a waterfall coming downstairs and a curtain of ice encasing your favourite Whistler prints, the most apalling sight must be the uncovered top quarter of the rear end of a plumber on hands and knees as he gropes under the kitchen sink for the recalcitrant mains stopcock which hasn't been turned for many years. So, a simple knowledge of how it all works and an ability to effect an emergency repair is essential. But don't wait for the worst to happen; locate and clearly label the various stopcocks in your domestic water system so you can turn off the mains supply, and buy some tools and a couple of the various pipe-mending kits. Do it today.

You'll find the mains stopcock on the rising main, and gate valves leading from the cold water cistern to the cold taps in the bathroom and upstairs WC, and another gate valve on the cold supply to the hot water cylinder. There should also be one at the lowest point of the central heating system.

Pipes burst, of course, when the water inside them drops below freezing and expands, splitting the casing. You won't know about it until the pipe thaws and the flow is re-established. Then you'll really know. An occupied and heated house stands little chance of suffering a burst, as long as the pipes in vulnerable places such as under the ground floor floorboards and in the loft are well insulated.

So if you go away for a weekend, or even a night, this winter it will prove an absurdly false economy to turn off the central heating. Most systems have a clock or some form of timer which will enable you to blast some hot water through the system at least a couple of times during the night and during the deadly cold hours before dawn. Turn down the thermostat to a minimum of 50°F and prop open the trap door to the roof void. Some recently-installed heating systems can be left in charge of a 'frost-thermostat' but as these have been known to stick, or malfunction, I'd always prefer to rely on heating the water by clock or timer.

There are pipe-heating systems, usually in the form of low-wattage electrical cable wrapped around the pipes and connected to a 13 amp electrical outlet. Some are linked to a thermostat which will switch them on as the temperature drops to freezing, others have a control which progressively increases the cable's heat output as the ambient air gets colder. They are inexpensive to run, not much more costly than leaving a light on, but quite pricey to buy. Typically, 10 ft of pipe-heating cable and a thermostat will cost around £40. But such a system would, I reckon, only be a viable proposition in a home which was unoccupied for long periods at a time. On the other hand, if you've got an isolated holiday cottage in Wales, it's highly unlikely its water supply will ever get a chance to freeze up.

If you intend leaving a house empty for a long period in winter, the only safe measure is to drain down both the hot and cold systems. Drain the cold supply by first shutting the mains stopcock, often found under the sink. This is usually solidly seized through disuse, so squirt some penetrating oil in the direction of the spindle before you try using any force which could itself spring a leak. Then turn on all the cold taps. There might be a few cupfuls of water in the pipe above the stopcock, and this can be dealt with by attaching a short length of hosepipe to the draincock found in the immediate vicinity, opening the draincock and collecting the water in a bucket.

Draining the hot water pipe runs is slightly more complicated. First, be absolutely sure to switch off the central heating boiler and any immersion heater. Put a large label near both noting that this has been done. Then open the draincock near the bottom of the hot water cylinder, connecting it to a hosepipe pointing outside. Open all the hot taps to drain the pipe runs to them, but remember that opening the taps alone will not drain the hot water cylinder.

Do not drain the central heating system, for a number of reasons. Reason One: it should already contain an anti-freeze and corrosion inhibitor in the water; these will of course be lost. Two: when you refill it, the combination of fresh air and fresh water will create perfect corrosive conditions. Three: the filthy black water found in a central heating system will stain anything it touches, and if you drain it into the garden it will not do much for your roses. You can add a specially formulated anti-freeze (and anti-corrosion fluid) to your system by first taking a few litres out of the small feed and expansion cistern (you can do this by holding the ball-float down so that it leaves the house through the overflow). The feed and expansion cistern is the markedly smaller of the two cisterns usually to be found in your loft. Do not use anti-freeze anywhere else in the house.

So what to do if you ignore all these precautionary suggestions, and a pipe bursts or, just as likely, a compression joint (which is the one with nuts on either side) springs apart. Turn off the water at the mains stopcock and turn on all the taps, both hot and cold, in the house. Close the gate valves supplying the cold water cistern and the hot water system. Turn off the hot water boiler. Once you've mopped up the flood as best you can, set about repairing the damage. It is not difficult, and a semi-permanent repair can be made quite easily by using one of the many emergency kits. There are three types: sealants for small leaks and clamps and couplings for bursts.

Some sealants are two-part: you mix the contents of two tubes and apply to a clean and dry pipe. They set very hard in a day, but you can shorten this time by playing a hot-air paint stripper on it, set at its lowest heat. Some kits recommend you reinforce the repair with special glass fibre or self-adhesive PVC tapes. Clamps wrap around the pipe. They are usually made of rubber-cushioned gaskets enclosed in stainless steel and they are tightened onto the burst section with a wing or hexagon nut. The coupling repair method is by far the most permanent. They're also a bit more complicated. Cut out the burst section and replace it with a 'slip' coupling which can be slid onto one pipe and back up onto the other. Polycell make a repair kit using polybutylene pipe, in 15 mm and 22 mm sizes with push-in fittings.

The minimum things you'll need in an emergency are a selection of the burst pipe repair kits, including a slip coupling and leak sealant, a pair of plumber's grips or mole wrench, a large adjustable spanner, a sink plunger, penetrating oil, a radiator key, a junior hacksaw, a length of hosepipe with a jubilee-clip fastener (for draining), a shallow container such as an old litre ice cream carton to catch leaks in otherwise inaccessible places and a torch with leak-proof alkaline batteries.

Insulation

The chances are you're living in a house built much longer than 20 years ago, when the first real moves towards energy conservation were made by architects and builders. Any form of insulation is worth having, and it will pay for itself in a period of time but the amount of money spent does not necessarily correlate with the the amount of heat energy conserved. Some of the more expensive systems of double glazing, for instance, will take many years to repay their initial costs.

By far the biggest proportion of heat is lost through walls; typically a terraced house will lose £90 worth of heat a year, a semi-detached £160 and a detached £250. Older houses have solid walls which, if they are dry, can be excellent insulators in themselves, but most houses since 1920 have cavity walls made up of two 'skins' of brick or blockwork with a 2 in (51 mm) gap which should prevent damp penetration and improve insulation – particularly if the inner skin has been made of blocks which are themselves insulated. Heat loss through these conditions – and there are specialist firms which will provide infra-red 'thermo-grams' showing exactly where heat is escaping from a building – are dealt with by the following methods.

The cavity can be filled with urea-formaldehyde (UF) foam, rock- or glass-fibre particles or expanded polystyrene beads. All these are meant for professional installation (and if this isn't done properly, it can actually bring damp into the house) and such treatments are expensive. However, the particularly cold walls of a house can be greatly improved by 'dry lining' – fitting so-called thermal boards which are simply plasterboard with up to 60 mm of polystyrene insulation on one side. There are two types of thermal boards, one with a white paper interior facing which you can paint, wallpaper or add some form of textured wall covering, and a grey interior face which is intended for a plaster skim finish.

It's a good idea to damp-proof the wall first with one of the many brush-on compounds available, and then fix the thermal boards onto a framework of timber, although the board can, rather less effectively, be fixed directly onto the solid wall. This is an obvious stage to reinforce the insulation by fixing a mineral- or glass-fibre blanket in the framework, keeping it in place by stapling heavy grade polythene sheeting to the wood. You might also want to run new wiring for power points within the framework before the thermal boards are fixed. Of course this method will marginally reduce the floor space, and means that the treated wall will have to be redecorated, but the room will, immediately, be noticeably warmer.

Cladding with interlocking tongue-and-groove wood panelling is another excellent way of warming a room with a 'cold' wall, particularly if you place half-inch (12 mm) insulation material between the panelling and the wall – except in kitchens and bathrooms, because air needs to circulate behind the panels in these rooms. Wood panelling will also hide a poor or ugly surface, and this seems to work particularly well when you also want to cut down condensation in a bathroom or a kitchen. There's an interesting-looking variety of tongue-and-groove boards: plain, linen-fold and ornamental but the easiest to work with, and probably the most available, is known as a 'false-vee' tongue and groove, which gives the impression of the boards being much narrower than they in fact are. Such panelling is usually about three-eighths of an inch (9 mm) thick and 4 in wide, although a couple of nominally 4 in-wide boards will cover only 7 in when interlocked, so a wall 12 ft long and 8 ft wide will need just under 42 8 ft-long boards. It's best to buy half a dozen or so more to allow for wastage, splits and dead knots in inferior quality 'knotty pine' (which invariably fall out) and buy them all from one batch as the tongues and grooves can vary considerably, even from the same supplier.

You'll need a roof or ladder rack on your car to get it home, although most wood suppliers will deliver. While you're buying the panelling, get new matching architraves for window and door surrounds, and skirting board. It's also important to bring all the bought wood into the house a week or so before you fix them so that any damp they've gathered in the timber yard will have an opportunity to dry out. Fixed vertically, tongue-and-groove boards make a room look higher, fixed horizontally they will give an impression of length.

Nail or, preferably, screw 2 by 1 in wood battens to the wall in the opposite direction to the run of the panelling, about 20 in apart, replacing existing skirting boards, and architraves around window and door openings with battening. Ensure the battening presents a level, flat surface by packing out hollows with scrap plywood. The quickest and simplest way of fixing the panelling on to the battens is to face-fix them with inch and a half panel pins, punching in the heads to avoid hammer marks, and filling the holes with plastic wood.

You could also use a technique called 'secret nailing' which means driving the pins into the tongue at an angle so that the next groove covers it. However, until you master this method you'll bend a lot of pins and split many tongues.

Most importantly, use a spirit level to ensure *every* board is absolutely level (or vertical). If it isn't, take it off and realign it. If you don't, the fault is exacerbated along the wall, the last panel you try and fit won't fit, and the wall will look ridiculous. Finish the boards by staining and sealing them, rubbing down with medium-grade wire wool rather than glasspaper, between two or three coats of the sealer. Existing ceilings can be clad in the same way by screwing battens through the plaster into the joists. Re-route the wiring to electrical sockets and switches into the new metal boxes, which are fixed to the wall surface and framed by battening. In this way the socket and switch plates will cover the sawn ends of the panelling.

People are usually more comfortable when their feet are warmer than their heads, so floors insulated with a good underlay and carpet covering are excellent value.

Roughly a quarter of the heat from a house escapes through the roof. Insulating your roof space by simply laying insulation quilts of mineral or glass wool across the joists will make another instant difference – there are still council grants available in some areas to help pay for this sort of material. It is not difficult work, just messy and dusty, so wear some sort of eye protection and rubber gloves for the unpleasant duration of the Saturday morning it takes to complete. Once it is insulated, your roof space will probably be one of the coldest places in your house, so wrap and tie insulation blanket around the cold water tank, make a cover for it out of a piece of plywood, and insulate that too. It hasn't got to look pretty, just warm. But of course do not insulate under the tank; rising heat will help prevent the water from freezing in the coldest of weather.

All pipes in the loft can be easily lagged using lengths of the foam-moulded liners available to fit the 15 mm and 22 mm pipework normally found in lofts. One of the economical so-called black light heaters can be put into the loft while you're doing this. The heater, which can be run from a junction box into a socket, can be safely left on throughout the winter months. It simply takes the chill out of the air; its heat is otherwise imperceptible.

If you anticipate using your loft for storage you should of course lay the insulation between the joists, and board over them. If you can see the underside of your roof tiles, staple heavy-duty polythene sheet to the underside of the rafters. But if you don't do another thing, ensure that the domestic hot water cylinder has a smart new jacket which conforms to British Standard Kite Mark BS 5615. Measure the height and circumference to ascertain the right size. This measure alone could pay for itself in only a couple of weeks.

Double Glazing and Draught-proofing

'We were going to draught-proof, but this way it keeps the kids from under our feet.'

The fundamental economics of keeping a house warm can be daunting: you will get a maximum of only about 25p worth of heat for every £1 spent. Between 10 and 20 per cent of heat goes straight out through the windows, a fact that is graphically illustrated by thermal 'photographs' which show uninsulated buildings outlined in blue with only the windows and doors picked out in pink, indicating the parts where the warmth is leeking into space.

It is a myth perpetuated by some double glazing companies (the reputable ones don't even try it on) that double glazing will cut your fuel costs by 50 per cent; yet simple arithmetic shows that it is not a cost-effective way of cutting heating bills. It could cost anything between £500 and £5000 to have double glazing professionally installed, taking between 10 and 60 years to repay the capital outlay.

So unless all your windows are so rotten they need replacing anyway, a complete set of replacement windows is nowhere near being a financially viable project. Unless of course you do it yourself, in which case you will also miss having to listen to the salesman's account of the fortnight in Acapulco he won by topping his firm's sales target, and the theatrical opening of an entire family of Samsonite suitcases to reveal working doll's house models of sliding windows. And of course you'll miss out on the substantial 'discount' (I was once was offered £1000 off if I'd sign up on the night).

Double glazing can indeed cut heat loss (but not your bills) by up to half, reduce condensation and noise from the outside and eliminate draughts, and it can be an attractive asset when you eventually sell your house. There are so many different versions to choose from, but unlike many other home improvement schemes, the cost of double glazing is not necessarily relative to its effectiveness. You can for example 'double glaze' an entire house for around £50 using the simplest of all methods: stretching a plastic film, similar to kitchen cling wrap, across the window, holding it in place with double-sided adhesive tape and shrinking it into a taught, near-invisible covering with a hair-dryer. It's marketed by Sellotape, who call it Seasonal Double Glazing, and Scotch, who call theirs Thermal Seal.

These coverings can be removed in the spring; so too, I'm afraid, will strips of unsound paint on your window frames as the double-backed tape is peeled off. Left in place in, say, a bedroom, they will last a year or so. Make sure the insides of the windows are clean before you put the film on or you'll be looking at the smudges for a long time. Versions involving heavier-duty PVC film and polyester sheeting are available and these can be carefully removed and stored for next winter. Frail as they are, they work splendidly well.

So too did the Victorian pine night shutters, which also provided a solid security barrier. If you're lucky enough to have a set which escaped the ravages of post-war 'modernisation' or 'the new look' in which beautifully-panelled doors were also replaced, with ones of patterned glass, and graceful mahogany bannister rails were hidden under hardboard, then do all you can to repair them. They are not, for that matter, too difficult to make, provided you have a set to act as a pattern, and reasonable room to work in, because they do become unwieldy once you start putting the parts together.

The wooden shutter's modern equivalent is the highly efficient thermal shutter which has a plastic core, about one and a half inches thick, and folds back on itself during the day. Consider, too, detachable thermal interlinings for your curtains; they are weighty enough to need a track of their own, such as the ones offered by Harrison Drape.

Hermetically-sealed double glazing replaces the existing glass with two panes which have a built-in air gap usually of between 6 mm and 12 mm, although the optimum thickness for reducing heat loss is in fact 20 mm. Sealed units can be bought, made to measure, from double glazing manufacturers or from glass merchants. Secondary double glazing is perhaps the best buy because it too is permanent, openable and comes in kits versatile enough to fit almost any sort of window.

Firms like Polycell market a variety of specially designed systems, both in the original white rigid plastic UPVC, which is a good insulation material and resistant to ultra-violet discolouration, and aluminium-framed kits which are finished in white. A horizontal sliding system is recommended for casement windows, and there is a vertical sash system for sash windows as well as a fixed pane kit for non-opening panes. They are all easy to fit and come with clear instructions. A kit would cost between £30 and £40 for the average 2 sq m window; the prices of fixed-seal replacement windows seem infinitely variable. But be careful when using glass with DIY kits. Even the lightest permissible grade, 4 mm, can be heavy to use in any significant size, and it can cause serious injury if your first attempts are not too secure.

It could be best to start by using plastic sheet materials. They are considerably safer to handle and are usually cheaper, although most materials, like clear polystyrene, which does not have the clarity of glass, will last no longer than three to five years before degrading. Plastics can be cut, sawn, drilled and planed, but they do scratch very easily, and should be carefully cleaned with soapy water. Acrylic costs around the same as glass, and will last as long as ten years; polycarbonate is about the best plastic presently available. It is virtually unbreakable.

But, for all the double glazing schemes on offer, it's the rather more prosaic systems of simple insulation and draught-proofing which will produce the most signficiant value-for-money results. You would be hard pressed to spend a total of £30 on draught-proofing a four-bedroomed house, although you would save as much as that in the first year after installation. It's estimated that more than half the country's homes have little or no draught-proofing whatsoever, and consequently lose another 15 per cent of heat through ill-fitting doors, window frames and floors. Total draught-proofing would of course result in condensation; but don't worry, you're unlikely to be that successful.

Simple and inexpensive things like foam-backed radiator foil reflects 90 per cent of the heat back to you, rather than being soaked into the fabric of the wall. Radiator shelves which simply drop-fit onto the top of the panel will throw heat back into the room instead of letting it drift up the wall.

Discover where draughts are coming from by holding a lighted candle at window frames (taking care not to touch the curtains) and other suspect places. Gaps and crevices in floor boards, and particularly at the bottom of badly fitted skirting boards can be filled in with shredded newspaper boiled into a pulp in a little water with a couple of large spoonfuls of plain flour – or with a proprietory filler like Polyfilla. Mix it in a stout plastic bag, cut a corner off and pipe the filler in, like icing a cake. If there are large gaps below a skirting board, then buy strips of one and a half inch 'quarter-round beading'. Nail it to the skirting, not the floor.

If the floorboards are generally bad and draughty, secure them as best as you can and cover the entire floor with sheets of hardboard, which should be laid smooth face downwards if you intend to carpet over them. You should also first condition them by brushing in about three-quarters of a pint of water into each 4 sq ft sheet, stacking the sheets, flat and back to back for 48

hours in the room where they will be fixed. In this way the
boards dry out once fixed, tightening up on the panel pins to
form a perfect surface. But beware of damaging under-floor
pipes and wiring; use only quarter-inch pins. A staple gun which
can also fire small nails is a big help.

Cracks in door and window frames, both inside and out are
best sealed by a flexible sealant applied with a caulking gun.
There are many types of foam, vinyl coated rubber and plastic
strips for fitting around door and window openings. The foam
versions are inexpensive but need regular replacement. Phos-
phor bronze strips pinned into the rebate of the door are fiddly
to fix, but will last longest.

The best excluder I've tried for under door draughts was
made by a WI lady: it is a snake with a lazy grin and dramatically
crossed eyes. But since it has to be moved every time the front
door opens, a PVC strip with a brush seal might be better. A
brush seal can be fitted over the inside of the letter box, and if
you have any doubts about the need for a cover on your key
hole, peer closely in through it on any winter night. You'll feel
the warmth oozing out. But don't get arrested.

Repairing Appliances

Most people spend a lot of money calling in repairmen when household appliances break down. It's an understandable panic reaction, but many faults can easily be cured, just by switching off the machine, disconnecting it from the electricity supply and undoing a handful of screws. The fault is invariably quite evident at first glance. A broken drive belt doesn't need any special diagnostic skills, and you don't have to endure the expensive sharp intake of breath which signals the imminent arrival of 'never seen anything like this before' as a thousand drachmas are removed out of the washing machine's drainpipe.

Never, ever, try and look into a broken machine before disconnecting it from its electricity supply. Switching off at the plug is not safe enough. And if you really can't figure out how to disconnect a fused switch unit on, say, a washing machine, then switch off at the mains. Ignore this warning at your own peril. But remember, the most usual cause of a stalled machine is a blown fuse in the plug. Check the fuse and connections within it as well as the ones to the appliance itself.

Now that many people can't cook, washing machines are probably the most overworked household machines. Most have at least a year's warranty and some have a five year optional extension to this. If this is your case, fiddling about with it may void the warranty. Sorry, but you'll just have to wait in all day for the service engineer to call. Service 'manuals' with new machines sometimes have helpful diagrams of various parts.

Like humans, older models can behave badly in a number of ways, one of the most common being a refusal to drain off the water once the final washing cycle is over. You may be able to get rid of the bulk of the water by turning the programmer straight around to the spin and draining section. If you can't, prepare for a flood with lots of newspapers on the floor and containers at hand. *Disconnect the power* and turn off the water supplies – usually red and blue hosed taps leading into the machine. Haul the machine out from under the worksurface.

Remove the back, and check the filter for drachmas, buttons, etc. Unfasten and remove the inlet and outlet hoses and look for bigger obstructions here. This could, by the way, solve The Mystery Of The Missing Odd Socks. But the trouble could be as simple as the hoses kinking as the machine is pushed back into a tight space below a worksurface.

If the pump doesn't spin freely, and its connections are sound, it has probably had it. Disconnect, remove it and take it around to the local dealers for an *exact* replacement. Front doors leak because the rubber seals around them have perished. Fit a replacement – it helps to warm it gently with a hair-dryer. Banshee screams and screeching during the spin cycle indicate worn or slack rubber drive belts. Don't try and adjust the tension; they've probably stretched too much. Simply replace them – the serial number is usually on the belt. However, even new belts can get greasy – wipe the grease off with a dry cloth.

If the water in the machine remains cold, there's probably a fault in the heating element. These can be tricky to remove and expensive to replace, so you might as well call in Repair Man. Machines that over-fill usually have a faulty air pressure switch which should automatically turn off the supply. It's usually a blockage in the pipe running into the switch. Detach and blow through it. Don't suck.

Your second best friend, the tumble drier, is also one of the simplest, but it also suffers from blockages. The main filter, which traps lint and fluff, needs cleaning out before every session, otherwise the contraption can overheat, burning out the quite expensive heating element. The filters should be easily accessible and removable; the ones slotted into the side of the drawer are obviously best, otherwise it's a mini-potholing expedition to reach it at the back of the drum, but it's worth the trouble. Replace broken or torn filters or risk a loadful of clean washing impregnated with a blowback of brownish fluff and cat hairs.

Squeaking machines probably have bearings that have been dried out by the same hot air that dries the clothes. As long as the tension on the drive and fan belts are all right, a few drops of (light) oil on the bearings will work wonders. But if the bearing on the edge of the drying drum seems to be the noise source, do *not* oil it. If it's made of nylon, lubricate it with a light coating of PTFE spray. Lubricate a fabric bearing with just a touch of silicone grease.

A dryer that constantly runs cold almost certainly has a thermostat failure. This is the little device protecting the heating element. It's usually fixed with just a couple of screws. Disconnect the spade-connectors and buy another one for about £3. The thermostat may have just stuck open, but if the new one similarly fails, call Repair Man.

If the motor is running, but nothing much else seems to be happening in the way of hot air blowing, suspect a broken fan belt. Replacement as per exact part number – don't try and make do with something similar as it may damage the machine.

If a tumble dryer vibrates so much it looks like taking a walk around the room, first check there is nothing you can do to adjust the stubby legs on some models; otherwise I'm afraid the bearings are likely to need replacing – at a cost.

Refrigerators are usually quite trouble free. Door seals do get damaged and are easily replaced by lifting up the edge and removing the securing screws. If power is reaching the fridge, but not cooling it sufficiently, the first check is to see if the condenser-evaporator at the back of the cabinet is warm. If it isn't, select a colder setting.

If it still doesn't get really cold inside have the heating element checked professionally. Alternatively, the compressor might have failed. Leave the door open for a few minutes with the temperature set to maximum. The condensor motor should start, if it doesn't call Repair Man and tell him you probably need a new one, so that he can bring it with him. If the little light inside fails to come on, I wouldn't insult your intelligence by describing its replacement. But I make no apologies for warning you, just one more time: always switch off and disconnect before doing anything.

Repairing Gadgets

*'Your irony does not escape me, but
I'm not fixing a thing tonight.'*

Every gadget in a home is a potential source of irritation. They break down from over-use and abuse. In the last section I discussed things you might consider doing to marshal things like washing machines and dryers back into action. These are expensive items and cannot lightly be replaced or thrown away. With other, less costly things, steam irons and kettles, for example, it might be best to cut your losses and replace them, but if you do think a repair is feasible, then do have an attempt, but not before running a few very simple checks.

A continuity tester is, I think, essential for these; it's an inexpensive tool which will instantly detect faults in the fuses and flexes on most household gadgets; in the latter case whether an electrical circuit exists between two points. Such a tester will also find fault in batteries, light bulbs, etc, but as with all things electric, take great care – switch off and disconnect an appliance before looking inside. And remember that although a continuity tester will perform simple tasks like those I've just mentioned, there is no better substitute for a proper inspection by a qualified electrician.

Flexes on electric irons get twisted, torn, burned and severed and if they show any signs of such torture they should be replaced as a matter of course with proper, braided flex, probably of a much longer length than that originally provided. Replacing a flex is not a case of trial and error; if you have any doubt at all about which terminals are live and neutral, don't do it.

If the temperature on a (non-steam) iron cannot be controlled, the thermostat is faulty and you might be able to buy a replacement. If the thing won't heat up at all, then it could still be a faulty thermostat, or a loose connection in the iron but probably, and more seriously, the element has gone. Fitting a new one is a fiddly job and if the iron has badly burnt out, it really isn't worth trying to do it. About the only other simple DIY remedy for a recalcitrant steam iron is to descale it. It's perhaps worth mentioning that although some manufacturers say that ordinary tap water is suitable, the use of distilled water will ensure a long and trouble-free life.

Scale also causes one of the few problems suffered by kettles. If a kettle element is badly gunged up, it's quite easy to replace. If a jug kettle won't heat up and the red light also remains out, (and the plug connections are sound) this too means the element must be replaced. If on the other hand an automatic kettle won't switch itself off, it's also possible to replace the thermostat or steam switch.

Vacuum cleaners take an awful battering, and the things that always seem to go first on upright models are the brush inserts on the roller. These are usually a slide-in fit, and no trouble to replace. The ominous smell of burning rubber usually means that the drive belt which turns the roller is loose. Examination of the underneath of the tool will reveal whether or not it can be tightened; but it's usually easier to fit a new belt. Cylinder cleaners have even less to go wrong, but they do rely on internal filters which must be regularly replaced. This type gets pulled about a lot by the flexible hose, and if this cracks or leaks, there's really no alternative other than to replace it.

Both type of vacuums use a brush-type motor. If this stops and starts, then the two brushes at opposite sides of the commutator are either worn or badly pitted. They are spring fitted, and can usually be quite easily unclipped or unscrewed. Note if there are any guide marks indicating their fixed position and take them to a dealer to buy matching replacements. Before refitting them, carefully clean the commutator with methylated spirits.

All heaters, whether they be fan, convector or radiant, have an electrical element, and this is the part that usually goes wrong. Radiant heater elements can usually be removed by undoing a couple of nuts, but it's best to take fan heaters to a dealer, as they are easily damaged by inexperienced hands. Fan heaters can suck in a lot of dust through the rear or side vents, and this is easily removed with a small, dry paintbrush. Apply a tiny drop of light oil to the bearings at the same time. The constant flow of air is meant to keep the heated elements 'black'. If parts of the elements glow, then not enough air is reaching them; suspect blocked vents, and remedy them as above. If, after cleaning and minimal oiling, the elements still glow, then the heater is potentially a bad fire hazard – particularly if it's left unattended for any length of time.

Ironically, it's usually the oldest electric cookers that are the easiest to fix. If nothing works, check the fuse at the consumer unit or fusebox – the cooker will usually have its own circuit – and if this fuse has blown then it's likely there is a fault which will blow it again. Switch off at the mains and check the connections in the cooker control unit and the cable outlet box. If you don't find anything wrong, call in an electrician. Ditto if the state of the cable itself is suspect.

Although separate elements heat the hot plates, grill and oven, only the hot plates can be replaced on a DIY basis. It's simple. Lift the hinged top cover and remove the screws holding the element-terminal cover. Removing this will reveal the terminals, and removing these will enable you to lift out the old ring element and take it to a dealer for a replacement of the exact size and rating. Replace them in reverse order. Solid plates are renewed in the same way.

Security

'But now I'm worried that if there's a fire, the men may think
we're at home and risk their lives trying to save us . . .'

Every few weeks, or so it seems, someone dies in a fire in their own home because their anti-burglar security is so invincible no-one, including firemen, can break in. The police and the fire services are at loggerheads; the former encourage people to do everything they can to help protect themselves and their property. The firemen say steel-plated front doors and windows caged in high tensile lattice work are a potential death trap. Both are right. This time, I believe it's the customer who too often gets it wrong. Too little security is as bad as too much.

Of course, burglary is a terrible experience, striking deep at a person's psychological inner-guard. On two evenings in the 30 years I've lived in London I've glanced up from a book or the television and seen a face at the window. On the last occasion I caught a glimpse of a distinctive green and white banded sports shirt. Within an hour I'd visited all the local pubs and told the police where to get him, which they did. He was arrested, charged and, later, freed. Insufficient evidence. He had a long record for housebreaking.

It took those experiences to make me do something about my house's security, and if you haven't been robbed yet then you might read the following with only mild interest. Indeed you might skip the whole thing. But if you do get 'done' – for one house in every 35 does get broken into – you'll be very sorry you turned the page.

Some of the facts about burglary are boringly obvious as long as you take the stereotype view of the robber as a scheming cat. But about 80 per cent of burglars have no particular target. They'll just be walking down your street at 3 pm and will find your open door or window irresistible, so you have in your hands the prime psychological advantage: ensure they feel you are not easy prey.

Fix an alarm bell box on the wall, even if you haven't an alarm system, similarly a Beware of the Dog plate on your front gate, as well as Neighbourhood Watch and property marking scheme stickers in your windows. Roses, holly or any prickly plant below the window sill level are also useful disincentives, but do not hide the front of the house with tall walls, fences or a hedge and don't plant bushes near the front door; they're excellent cover for the burglar. If you have a video recorder or any other electronic equipment, turn its winking lights away from the window and try and position the television set so that it's not in a direct line of sight. So far you will have spent about £20 and you're quite a bit safer.

If you live in a high risk crime area (London, Merseyside, Greater Manchester and Northumbria) and, not totally irrelevantly, you've got a job too, you could instal a DIY burglar alarm system from between £100 and £200 for a three-bedoomed house. A professional job would cost at least £500. (You may be able to claim tax relief on a loan to pay for it.)

Many thieves get into a house through the doors and windows, whether they're shut or not. Securing the most vulnerable windows, particularly at the back of the house, can be cheap and easy. Polycell make a wide range of locks covering sash, casement, pivot and sliding windows. They all prevent the window from being opened through a smashed pane of glass, but try and fit the same type throughout the house so that you do not have a confusing bundle of different keys. Shop around and make a note of the dimensions of your window frame before you buy. But don't lock yourself into a fire trap; hang a key close to each window and make sure everyone knows where it is and can find it at night, or in a smoke-filled room. And fit smoke detectors on the ceiling of each landing.

Most of the recent fatal incidents in which people have trapped themselves in a fire have happened because the victims have armour plated not only the doors, but also the frames. A solid hardwood door, or one made of hardwood chippings bonded together, can resist a powerful battering, and both are ideal for fitting strong security locks. Panelled doors may look prettier and stronger, but will collapse to a hefty kick. Some locksmiths will recommend fitting a steel sheet behind the door, but this is expensive; obviously the steel has to be cut to exact size, with gaps for locks and letter plates, and as this also adds considerably to the weight of the door, you will need new extra-strong hinges. Far better to buy a solid door.

Good-quality locks are of paramount importance. A front, or main entrance, door should have a five-lever mortice deadlock and a rim automatic deadlock. They should conform to BS 3621. Back doors should have at least a five-lever mortice sashlock.

A door is only as good as its frame, so make sure this is also hardwood, and securely fixed into the surrounding brickwork. Amazingly, some exterior door frames are simply wedged into the doorway, and 'secured' with a few nails driven into wooden plugs.

Wooden French windows are a problem because they are usually not too strong. Most open out into the garden, and consequently the exposed hinges can quite easily be knocked out. Combat this by fitting hinge bolts which lock the doors into the frame when they're closed. Although very few thieves will break glass and climb through its jagged edges,they will try and reach the locks, so fit a lockable ornamental grill on the inside which can be swung open for cleaning purposes.

A burglar will be stopped by noise and light in the house. You can buy a recording of a barking Alsatian which sounds just like a recording of a barking Alsatian. Of course a real dog is the best deterrent (next to a flock of geese, of course).

A plug-in time-switch, offering a 24-hour to seven-day control can operate the radio at different times of day or night; don't use it for the TV set – that could cause a fire.

By using lighting intelligently, you can make your house look permanently occupied when you are away. But don't buy cheap devices; they can fail or burn out. There are several on the market but the cheap ones have unreliable detectors which don't work half the time.

Racal-Guardall make Autolite, which combines a passive infra-red movement detector and daylight sensing device; this can replace your porch or front door light. It can also be powered via a flex to a socket connection. At dusk or at night, it will detect a moving person or car in the vicinity, and the light will switch on and stay on for a pre-determined period after movement ceases. A special sensing device ensures that the light does not come on in the daytime. Unlike many of its market rivals it incorporates a fluorescent tube which consumes a fraction of the power used by a special bulb and still a lot less than that of a standard bulb. It costs around £50.

Much less expensive but just as reliable are the Polycell security lighting devices. The Automatic Security Light is suitable for all internal bayonet fittings (ceiling, table or standard lamps), turning them on at dusk and off at dawn. There is an override switch which allows the security light to be used as a normal light fitting, so it will never have to be removed once fitted. It costs £10.49.

The programmed security light is also suitable for all internal fittings, and again turns on automatically at dusk. But then a built-in timer turns the light on and off at 30 minute intervals, throughout either a four or eight hour period, depending on the selected programme. That too has an over-ride switch.

Fire Alarms

Christmas should be a relaxing time and, bilious bad tempers and over-spending apart, it generally is. Unfortunately, it's a season where a lot of accidents happen in the home. In fact the average home is said to be a much more hazardous place than a factory, where strict safety laws apply. Fires are a particular hazard: a lot of people in the house, the annual Yule log crackling in the hearth, candles on the tree and, of course, all that relaxing spirit. There were nearly 56,000 house fires last year; now every home may soon have to be fitted with a smoke alarm by law. New legislation is being drawn up by the Government and is expected to come into force soon.

A three-year Home Office experiment in which 10,000 homes in Tameside, Greater Manchester, were given £10 smoke alarms free in 1988 indicated that the early warning system saved lives by giving householders vital minutes to escape. In Britain 38 per cent of homes now have smoke alarms compared to nine per cent three years ago and it is estimated that a change in the law would cut the annual toll from 750 to 450, as well as drastically reducing the 10,000 casualties.

In the United States, where legislation resulted in four out of five homes being fitted with smoke detectors, the death toll has been almost halved.

Remember that smoke detectors are intended to give early warning so that you can get out of the house before the fire gets too big; they are not a signal to fight the flames yourself. Get out and stay out; advise the firemen.

Fire alarms cost from around £10 and the smallest house will need two. There are two popular types; the majority are ionisation detectors, which have chambers enclosing two electrodes. When smoke enters them, the current flow is reduced and the alarm sounds. These types are good at sensing fast-flaming fires. Photo-electric units contain a light beam and a photoelectric cell. The alarm sounds when the beam encounters smoke. These units react quickly to deep-smouldering fires, such as those caused by carelessly discarded cigarettes.

There's a third type which combine both apparatus. Only two have so far passed *Which?* tests – First Alert SA3001 and BRK SA3001. They each cost £30.

Some detectors have extra features such as escape lights – invaluable if the electrics are damaged – a low battery indicator and a test button. The British Standard Kitemark to look for is 5446.

Fitting a smoke alarm is easy; they are battery powered. All they need is a firm fixing on the ceiling and, as most ceilings are plasterboard or lath and plaster, the simple way of doing this is to find a joist and screw directly into it. You can sometimes do this by looking for the nails securing the plasterboard, or by tediously tapping the ceiling until the more solid sound indicates the mass of a joist. Drill a small hole where you think the joist is; if you've missed it, push a piece of bent wire though the hole to 'feel' for it. Alternatively, use a special hollow wall fixing – but be careful not to penetrate electric wiring or pipes.

Install alarms where there is a risk of fire, but not in bathrooms or kitchens where steam or smoke from cooking may accidentally trigger the alarm. There should be an alarm on every level of the house and one outside each sleeping area – it's important that the alarm can wake sleeping people. Fix them on the ceiling near the centre of the room, at the centre of the hall ceiling and the top of a stairway, or the highest point on a sloping ceiling. Try and avoid mounting them on walls, but if you must, make sure the alarm's 4 to 12 in below the ceiling, and never in a corner or a 'dead air' space. Some detectors can be interlinked so that if one sounds, they all will. It's not a difficult job, but hiding the wires is.

Detectors shouldn't be difficult to reach, or you won't test them – weekly – to make sure they work. If the alarm hasn't got a test button, use the smoke from a candle or cigarette, but be careful not to start a fire. Never leave an alarm disconnected. If it becomes a nusiance from false alerts, eg, from cooking, check it or resite it. Change alarm batteries at least once a year, on a date that's easy to remember such as when the clocks go back. Clean detectors when you change the batteries and never paint them.

Some detectors may fail to work properly because they're too old. They'll give either false alarms or nothing at all. Like any other electronic device, they have a useful life. Unfortunately, there appears to be no consensus about how long that is, but some fire experts reckon on it being around 10 years. There's not been much research into this problem, but one Canadian study, completed in the eighties, found that smoke alarms failed at a rate of three per cent a year, irrespective of their age.

Once a smoke detector sounds, it's crucial for everyone in the house to know how and where to get out. Here are the key points: Draw a floor plan of the house which indicates two exits – a primary and a secondary in case the primary exit is blocked by smoke or fire. Designate a meeting place outside for everyone, once they've got out of the house; ensure everyone knows what the detector alarm sounds like, and never go back into a burning home.

Kitchen Planning

Judging by the proliferation of advertising in the colour supplements by the direct, (and very hard-sell) kitchen companies, most of our fantasies would seem to revolve around the models of either gleaming, streamlined galleries of gadgets or, to the other extreme, the so-called traditional country kitchen, the walls hung with shiny copper pans, and a huge, scrubbed, pine table, on which is carefully arranged perhaps a brace of pheasants, a sea trout, a handful of herbs and some russet apples.

The reality is, of course, very different; many kitchens are a chaotic after-thought of a room in the back of the house, and clearly came last in the family budgetary priorities. But with very careful, cunning planning there are ways of simultaneously economising on space and making the kitchen/eating room one of the most attractive parts of the home.

This is not difficult – which is why the kitchen-fitting industry has become one of the most profitable businesses around. First make a list of everything you want from you kitchen. For instance, are you happy eating in the kitchen and if so, when you entertain, do you mind being seen cooking? Does your family eat together in a well-ordered manner or do individual members help themselves at odd times, as and when they please? Be honest, are you that keen on cooking that you really need an electric double-oven and gas hob, or would a simpler single oven, or a small microwave oven cope with all the ready-made meals you eat?

Once you've targeted your ideal kitchen, that is, a kitchen that's going to work for you, and hopefully the house's next owners, take a look at the space available, and if you need more, consider the possibility of removing part of a wall, and stealing space from an adjoining pantry or hallway.

Kitchen units are likely to be your smallest problem. If the only thing wrong with your present ones is the colour, and they're otherwise quite sound, you can easily buy new doors to the standard-sized 500, 600 or 1000mm wall and base units.

New drawer fronts are also available. Central heating boilers are often an ugly, intrusive nusiance, particularly the floor-standing models. Consider hiding them in a so-called 'larder unit', which will also give a useful amount of shelf storage.

Similarly, you can get lengths of fresh-looking worksurfaces, often half-priced because they're 'damaged'. (I've never discovered why they're called worksurfaces because you can't cut or chop things or put anything reasonably hot on them without badly marking the plastic covering.)

I think the finest alternative for a practical, working, work-top is one fashioned out of strips of pine or hardwood laminated together. The more you mark it the better it seems to look; and you could tile a section of it next to the hob, especially for putting hot pans on, and even inset a slab of marble for pastry-making (available as inexpensive off-cuts from monumental masons). But all-marble worksurfaces are a dead loss: a piece of bloody meat, or even a slice of lemon can stain them forever.

Scheme your kitchen on graph paper, making an accurate floor plan and noting existing plumbing, electrical sockets, windows and doors. You'll find such kitchen planners together with cut-out models representing the three different sizes of units, in some brochures and the specialist magazines. The work-triangle, the well-beaten path between the fridge, cooker and sink should not be more than 6 m. If it is, then re-design.

The outside wall – the 'wet wall' containing all the plumbing is the best place to start, so that after the sink is positioned, the cooker and fridge-freezer, with worksurfaces on either side of them, should go within the 6 m triangle.

Make the most of your walls with the biggest units you can find, and bear in mind that you can save precious space by stacking a tumble-dryer over a fridge or washing machine, providing the dryer can be sasifactorily vented through an exterior wall.

Similarly, cooker hoods need venting out into the open air; extractor hoods that are said not to require this are a waste of time; they just don't work. A cooker in the middle of a wall can be quite satisfactorily vented through hidden ducting running along the top of a run of wall units. Smaller kitchens work better in a one-line or galley lay-out, or L-shape configuration.

The DIY super-stores are the best for DIY kitchen bargains, (the trade think MFI stands for 'made for idiots', but that firm usually has terrific 'special offers').

Unfortunately, because they're usually so busy you won't get much, or any, help or advice unless you go on a mid-week morning. Be sure that you buy all the units you need at the same time, for these places do suddenly cancel various colours and models and quickly run out of stock. If you do find yourself short of a particular unit and have to resort to telephoning around different super-stores, be wary of relying on their computer's assurance that what you want is in stock. I once travelled for hours up the MI to such a place to discover that although the computer said they had an item – 'the only one left in the firm' – in reality they did not. So persuade the assistant to actually go and see that they've got what you want.

Before leaving a super-store with flat-packed kitchen units, insist on examining them to ensure you've got the right model and colour and that, as sometimes happens, the units are not incomplete or damaged. They'll hate you for the hassle, but you could be saving youself a lot of future trouble.

Although most DIY store kitchen units are almost exactly the same – made out of cheap chipboard with a shiny plastic skin – you will pay extra for solid wood doors, glass-fronted wall-cupboards and new paint finishes. Be sure to examine the hinges of the units for strength and durability and try and discover whether you could, independently, fit tougher, better-made hinges which won't let the door fall off after a few days. Inexpensive kitchen units won't last long unless you make an effort to toughen up their carcasses by backing them with plywood, and varnishing all the cut chipboard edges, which otherwise can soak up water like a sponge.

Builders' merchants stock the much more expensive, but also more durable, rigid carcass units, but usually from one big-name manufacturer. Rigid units save a lot of the time you would otherwise spend putting the flat-pack units together. But this isn't difficult as long as you have a helper and throw away the usually inept construction instructions.

The direct-sell companies say they offer a complete kitchen package. But this doesn't usually include such essential components as tiles, a new floor covering and possibly a new ceiling and lighting. Tiling really is easy and pleasing, as long as you're fastidious in getting the first row square and horizontal. Don't hack off old tiles unless they're very unsound or you're putting in a new run of power points. Throughly clean off any grease with a strong solution of Flash, and tile on top of them.

A new floor can make a tremendous difference, and the new vinyl sheeting, which comes in 2, 3 and 4 m widths is simple to lay and comfortable to stand on. It is also easy to clean, which is fortunate if you choose a light-coloured covering which shows up every tiny spill and crumb. Carpet tiles, which can be loose-laid are a tougher proposition, particularly as individually dirty tiles can be picked up and washed under a tap. Cork is inexpensive and comfortable to walk on, but unsealed cork tiles need to have at least three coats of polyurethane varnish.

Patterned or glazed ceramic floor tiles or plain, unglazed quarry tiles last longest, but are very hard on your feet, and unforgiving should you drop anything on them. A kitchen depends on good lighting for safety and hygiene but, as in other rooms, a selection of different, dedicated lights is best. Overall illumination can be provided by an attractive central pendant fitting with a 100 or 75 watt reflector bulb, or a 30 or 40 watt fluorescent light fitted with a diffuser. 'Direct task' lighting can be easily achieved by small linear filament bulbs or mini-fluorescent tubes fitted beneath wall units.

The same effect can be had using downlighters or track-mounted spot-lights positioned directly above the front of the work surface so that the light shines on your hands and not in your eyes.

Renovating and Replacing Kitchens

When walls look dowdy they get a fresh coat of paint or paper. But when your kitchen yells out for revival do you rip it all out, buy new units and spend a couple of weeks patronising the local take-aways while you refit? Not necessarily. There's a couple of other options. If the cabinets are basically sound and functional you can resurface them and make them look new.

Resurfacing simply means replacing cabinet doors and drawer fronts and covering the exposed frames and end panels with a new material such as thin adhesive-backed veneers or plywood, fixed with contact adhesive. There are several advantages to resurfacing not least the saving of a lot of money. It's quick and not much harder work than, say wallpapering or tiling. The mess is minimal; of course there will be a bit of sawdust around, but the worksurfaces, sink and appliances can be used throughout the process which, with a bit of careful ordering and planning, shouldn't take more than a longish weekend.

If the only thing you can't live with is the colour of the cabinets, they can sometimes be given a new look by simply painting them. This is most successful if the cabinets are made of wood, hardboard, medium density fibre board (MDF) or covered in wood veneer. Although laminate finishes can be smartened up with a matt or thinned gloss paint, such a covering tends to chip off, but you may think it's worth the experiment. The laminate must be thoroughly washed down with sugar soap and be spotlessly clear of any grease, then lightly sanded with wet and dry abrasive paper to provide a key for the paint finish. Wipe it clean with white spirit before painting. It's best to use two coats of primer before the top coat.

You could have a go at stencilling. The Stencilling Advisory Bureau, PO Box 1609, London W8 7TN, offers free leaflets on the technique. If this doesn't work, then try a stick-on laminate which has a powerful pressure-sensitive adhesive on the back. These laminates are available at most DIY stores and come in a variety of colours and woodgrain effects.

Resurfacing is not necessarily a cheap and cheerful remedy, and can look terrible if you don't take care, but if your kitchen is poorly designed, lacks adequate storage space or is just too tiny, then it's going to be a waste of time. Of course a cabinet or two can be added, but resurfacing is not a space-enhancing project.

Almost any cabinet can be resurfaced, regardless of its age or style, just as long as the insides are square and sound. There's a huge range of door styles to choose from – they're usually advertised in publications such as *Exchange and Mart*, *Do It Yourself* and *Practical Householder*. But, for ease of work, you're limited really to doors that can be surface-mounted – that is to say, the hinges you use will be visible. Firms like Bordercraft of Peterchurch, Hereford HR2 0SD will make doors – and lovely solid wooden worksurfaces – to order.

I have used quarter-inch plywood to resurface cabinets with pleasing results. Plywood comes in a variety of facings and can be stained to any colour and then sealed with a clear varnish. The cheapest is often known as 'Far Eastern'. It has no grain pattern and I think it looks awful. Most wood yards have a pile of damaged plywoods – that is to say a corner has been broken off, or there's a scratch on the face. They're sold off cheaply, but of course you need to buy a quantity of the same veneered covering. The snag is that plywood comes in 8 ft by 4 ft sheets which are very unwieldly, and it's worth £1 to have it ripped (cut) down its length to a more manageable size that will fit on a car's roof rack.

The only tool you really need, apart from a drill, and a Stanley knife for cutting veneers, is a circular saw to cut the plywood to size, and if you've always wanted an electric screwdriver, this is your excuse – each door and handle has at least 12 screws.

Use a contact adhesive to fix the plywood in place. Dunlop Thixofix is excellent because it gives you to time to reposition work if you initially misalign it.

Cut veneers face side up, using a steel straight-edge and sharp Stanley knife. The backing paper peels off to expose the adhesive. Painstaking surface preparation is important if you want the veneer to look good and last. First wash the face frame with a mild solution of dishwashing liquid and rinse it. Smooth any uneven joints with a file or sandpaper and fill any gouges with something like Plastic Wood. It's best to use a veneer roller to fix the veneer in place. Use light pressure at first, because once you apply heavy pressure, contact veneers are almost impossible to remove without splintering, if you make a mistake.

Remember, when you are measuring for mail order doors and drawer fronts, that accuracy is imperative. Plan ahead – some suppliers take a long time to deliver.

The method of replacing drawer fronts depends on the drawer's construction. You're in luck if it's a four-sided box with the front screwed onto it. Simply unscrew the old front and replace it with a new one. If the drawer front is fixed to the sides of the drawer you'll have to trim it before adding the new front.

When two doors cover a single opening, add three quarters of an inch to the width of the opening, then divide by two to determine the individual door widths. Drawer-front width should be the same as that of the door below it. Drawer-front height is normally three-quarters of an inch taller than the drawer opening.

Elderly cabinets may be out-of-square and crooked. Overcome this by using slightly oversize doors. Although stick-on veneers will cover nails and screw holes, they won't level dents and cracks of more than about three-eighths of an inch. These will have to be levelled with filler.

The cabinet stiles (the upright pieces) may be too narrow to accept the new surface-mounted hinges – they need to be at least two-and-a-quarter inches wide where two new hinges meet back to back, and a quarter-inch wide at inside corners. Widen the stiles by screwing or glueing and nailing small strips of wood to them. Do this before you measure and buy new doors.

If there are gaps between wall cabinets, it's best to clamp them together with a G-cramp (this *is* the correct name), then drill and retighten them with quarter-inch bolts. Cabinets which have pulled away from the wall can be re-anchored with screws driven into plugs.

If you plan to replace the worktop, do this first. Many are fixed so firmly to the base framework, you're likely to cause damage as you prise them off.

Spring

Rot and Woodworm

Houses are incredibly resilient things. They can withstand a considerable amount of assault and battery from the most unskilled hands, yet will capitulate quite quickly in the face of a rot attack, especially if this gets into the structural timbers of the floor or roof. Don't think that you're safe because you've bought a brand new home. Bad practices in the building trade, when wood is left around sites getting soaked for months before being used, means that some houses actually have dry rot built into them.

If you do discover dry or wet rot in your house, be assured of a couple of things: the damage is likely to be far worse than it looks, and do not be panicked into calling in an expert for treatment. People spend thousands of pounds on such measures, and are still unable completely to eradicate the rot. However, some specialist firms will give you a free (doom-laden) survey which will help you assess the extent of the damage. It's vital to take some immediate, but elementary, measures towards a cure, but first identify what sort of decay it is.

Rot happens when the wood soaks up more than 20 per cent of its mass, and remains wet for a considerable time; months rather than weeks. The misleadingly-named dry rot, by far the worst because it spreads very quickly, particularly relies on damp to breed in places like roof voids, bathrooms and kitchens and especially where wood beams, for example, are tied into walls which are themselves damp.

Its effect on timber is to produce a rusty red spore dust on the surface, while the body of the wood will shrink, splitting into cubical patterns, and cracks will appear along the grain of the timber. Brittle grey strands by which the rot spreads can often be the first sign of attack, or there could be cotton-wool like patches on the timber. In the worst possible forms of attack, a soft pancake-like growth develops. Wet rot is found in extremely damp places like cellars and roofs and exterior doors and window frames. The wood is darkened, with severe cracking along the grain. But wet rot does not spread anywhere near as rapidly.

The treatment for dry rot amounts to quite drastic surgery; rotted wood must be cut out allowing a safety margin of at least 1 m each side of the damaged portion and replaced with sound wood which has been soaked in a dry-rot-killing liquid, which of course should also be liberally sprayed onto surrounding timber. A garden-type spray with a coarse spray head is ideal for this.

The best method of fixing the replacement timber is by bolting pairs of steel connector plates onto both it and the existing sound timber. It is of paramount importance to remove and, preferably, burn the infected timber as soon as possible. Infected plaster must also be removed and, allowing similar 1 m safety margins, the walls should then be scrubbed with a wire brush and sterilised with a masonry dry-rot killer. The treatment of wet rot is similarly messy and tedious, but remember that in both cases it is vital to discover the original source of the dampness which led to the rot, and cure that.

Woodworm is just another pest to consider, and the best time to attract the beasts is in the spring and summer when the adult insects are at their most active. Again, the sight of the typical minute flight holes can mean that the offending beetle has been – and gone. The furniture beetle, which despite its name will eat into any sort of wood, whether it's painted, polished or structural, is perhaps the most common, but the treatment is similar for all the beetles. The timber must be thoroughly cleaned, and sprayed with anti-woodworm fluid.

This is much easier said than done if woodworm is found in an inaccessbile place like a loft, in which case all the thermal insulation material will have to be removed before the joists and rafters are thoroughly sprayed. The popular expanded polystyrene pipe insulation and electrical cables must be protected as these can be damaged by the fluid. Water tanks must also be covered. Woodworm in floorboards are much more easily treated by lifting every, say, third board and spraying underneath the wood using a lance extension to the spraygun.

But take care with chemical treatments. Most smell quite evil and can irritate your skin and eyes, so wear plastic gloves and goggles. There have been reports linking them with serious illnesses. The chemicals mainly used in timber preservation treatments are lindane, pentachlorophenol (PCP) and tribu-tyltin oxide (TBTO). They are licensed under the Control of Pesticides Regulations, and the British Association of Wood Preservation says that the chemicals are safe provided they are used under approved conditions which should be stated on the container. Keep out of the treated areas, and keep them as well ventilated as possible for a couple of days. Do not use fires or heating appliances during this time, or store food there. Pets should also be kept away for 48 hours. If you'd rather not use lindane, PCP or TBTO, buy a treatment whose active ingredients are either permethrin or cypermethrin.

If you think that DIY rot-proofing is too much of a project, you'll be forced into paying for the treatment. Don't trust one firm, get several quotes, and you'll see that they vary widely. When *Which?* tested 10 firms, two didn't even bother to turn up, a third cancelled their appointment and four out of the remaining seven refused to give an estimate but instead wanted to do exploratory work costing from £80 to over £700 to reveal the full extent of the rot. Membership of the British Wood Preserving Association (BWPA) may also be a guide – members have to have been trading for at least three years, and have undergone a detailed assessment before they can be admitted. They are then eligible to register with the Guaranteed Treatments Protection Trust.

Timber treatment firms offer a 20- or 30-year guarantee for their work, and this could, eventually, be a useful selling point; on the other hand, it could raise unwelcome spectres which could stymie a sale.

Damp and Condensation

Rising damp is not a comedy. It can appear in your home at any time. If it is left unchecked it could in a couple of months lead to wet rot, which is bad enough, or dry rot, which is catastrophic. It will transform your desirable semi into something even the estate agents couldn't describe as being 'in need of some decoration' – their euphemism for 'demolition'. Still glad you got out of bed this morning? Maybe not. But even if you find *merulius lacrymans*, the thinking man's dry rot fungus, sprouting in the cellar, don't pack the pram yet, there's a reasonable chance you'll cure it.

Rising damp is particularly unfunny if your house was built before 1875, when the damp-proof course (DPC) was made obligatory. This layer of water resistant material does deter rising damp. It can range from the earliest model, which was made of a couple of courses of slate bedded in the mortar near the bottom of the house wall, to impervious blue 'engineering' bricks or layers of copper; bitumous felt or thick polythene. But these sometimes break down, inviting rising damp. Damp will introduce itself in a number of ways, but the one it likes best is by blistering paintwork, peeling off wallpaper and crumbling plaster.

There are several remedies, all rather tedious and time consuming, so first check that the damp isn't caused by broken down-pipes or gutters, damaged rendering, or porous or damaged flashing, plumbing leaks, faults in the drainage or broken window sills. All these can have the same effect as rising damp, and you'll feel very silly indeed if you go to the trouble I'm next going to recommend, only to find that RD came in via the most common fault of all, garden soil banking up over the years against the outside wall, effectively bridging the DPC. Some damp can be caused by poor ventilation underneath the floorboards. This can be cured simply by fitting a bigger air brick: an hour's work.

It's worth buying a battery-powered damp meter which has

two prongs for prodding gently into plaster, and lights that indicate damp, but remember that some of these meters have to be carefully calibrated according to the instrument's instructions. If not they can indicate damp on a dry wall because the concentration of salts is high. Some damp-proofing firms make thousands of pounds 'curing' such walls.

The most effective remedy is also the most difficult – (sorry, but the story doesn't change) and that is to cut out a row of bricks *only three feet at a time* and insert the engineering bricks in mortar to which you have added a waterproofing compound – the DPC should be about 6 in off the ground. It's tempting just to cure the spot where damp occurs, but far better to do the whole wall. Alternatively, hire a special masonry chain saw, or an angle grinder, this time cutting out a horizontal mortar course between the bricks, again 3 ft at a time. Don't do more. You could, as a surveyor might say, seriously interfere with the integrity of the wall; to you, Premature Burial. You then insert the new purpose-made membrane strip into the gap and seal it with mortar.

The easiest DIY solution is to inject a silicone water repellant – a chemical DPC – which will act as a barrier throughout the thickness of the wall. Hiring the complete outfit will cost around £130 for a week. It consists of an electric pump with half a dozen nozzles, a powerful rotary drill – do not use a hammer drill as this could crack elderly brickwork – and, of course, the fluid. The efficiency of this method depends on how well the fluid permeates the wall. It involves drilling 20 mm diameter holes 100 mm to 150 mm apart, preferably from the inside of the house, but it's easier and less disruptive to work outside. Angle the holes slightly downwards, about 15 degrees.

You will of course have to drill both inside and outside a cavity wall, and the depth of the holes will depend on the thickness of the wall. Aim at going half-way through the brickwork. The injection nozzles are inserted and the chemical DPC is forced in, saturating the wall at one level. Watch the pressure gauge on the pump; if it drops dramatically, the fluid (which costs about £60 for 100 litres) is wastefully running into a void or the wall cavity. Stop the pump, discover which nozzle is doing this, and re-drill a shallower injection hole. It will take a few days to take effect, but after about a week – depending on the ambient temperature – it's likely that the plaster on the inside of the wall will have soaked up the chemicals from the new DPC, or become saturated by salts brought up from the rising damp.

You will have to remove the skirting boards and hack off the plaster to a height of about 1 m. Plastering isn't easy, so pay to have the area re-plastered with a damp-retardant plaster, and 'remind' the plasterer that the new plaster should not drop below the line of the new DPC, otherwise all your efforts will have been in vain. There is likely to be some residual damp in the skirting board, so brush some timber preservative onto the back.

You will need neighbourly approval if the party wall of a terraced or semi-detached property needs damp-proofing, for the chemical might seep straight through the wall and affect their wall covering. Before deciding to do it yourself, remember that if you wish to borrow money on the house from a bank or building society, they will invariably require a guarantee from a specialist firm.

The floors and walls of basements and cellars are below the normal line of a DPC and are therefore particularly prone to damp if the damp-proof membrance protecting them has failed – unless there is an obvious fault like a broken drainpipe. The traditional method of 'tanking' the walls with a four-coat sand and cement render containing a damp-proof compound is still the most reliable, but difficult work for an amateur. Floors are more easily treated by a damp-proof compound covered with a sand and cement screed. But if a floor is really wet, the only solution is to dig it up and re-lay it over a thick damp-proof plastic sheet membrane. Only for the brave and very fit.

Preparing for Painting and Decorating

'Have you got any Hospital Corridor paint? You know,
nice pale green mixed with wood chips?'

I seriously hate painting and decorating. To me it's the DIY
equivalent of 'knit-your-own-royal-family'. But trying to get
someone to do it well for you is just as tedious, and of course
vastly more expensive. A famous cartoonist once showed me,
with a grim smile, the wallpapering work of a 'little man' he'd

captured in a pub. The windows, fireplace and doors had disappeared under rolls of mock William Morris. Little man, in fact an oafish but possibly genial brute, was going to cut them out later when the paste had dried. He said. He never returned.

This sort of thing is ridiculous. Decorating can be one of the most aesthetically and financially rewarding of all DIY as long as you persevere from the start at getting each stage throughly right. Preparation is ineffably boring, but it is everything. Spend as much, if not more, time on it as actually decorating, and the result will look and last beautifully. It's the professional's secret. So off with Question Time, and on with your old pyjamas and amusing baseball hat with built-in radio, tuned to Radio Three.

Remove as much furniture as possible, and pile the rest in the middle of the room. Remove the fittings; you'll find an electric screwdriver will remove 100 screws on a single charge, takes all the wrist-ache out of this. (Protect switches and immovable fitments, etc., with kitchen cling-film.)

Dust and vacuum everywhere. Cover everything with proper, hired, dustsheets and use masking tape to fix them carefully down on the edge of the carpet, (enabling you to work on the skirting board).

Remove radiators so that you can paper behind them – close the wheel valve at one end, the lock-shield valve on the other, counting the number of turns it takes (that way you won't unbalance the entire sytem). Undo the large nut connecting the valve at one end – *after* placing a washing-up bowl underneath. When it's full, push the coupling back on it, empty and repeat, unscrewing the bleed valve to increase the flow. Careful when you lift the radiator off the wall, there's always some dirty water left. This part is well worth the effort, particularly if you use lining paper on the rad wall alone. Otherwise the wallpaper will, eventually, definitely, lift.

No paint or wall covering will bond properly to dirty, crumbling or otherwise unsound surfaces. Woodwork in good condition doesn't need stripping. Lightly sand it with a fine 'wet and dry' paper, constantly dunked in water. W&D is best; it doesn't produce dust, (this is vital if you have old paint which might contain lead) but it's expensive; it will last longer if you first smear it with soap. Wash down with a strong sugar soap or Flash solution – if you regularly change this there's no need to rinse.

If you intend painting a wall, use a soft broom to wash it from the skirting board up – otherwise you'll have sugar soap stripes which are difficult to paint over. Rubber gloves won't stop the misery of water dripping down your sleeves, so fashion bracelets out of something like foam rubber.

If large areas of old paintwork are peeling, or bear so many coats that they are chipped and uneven, perhaps to the extent of losing the shape of decorative turnings and mouldings – a particular problem on stairs and some potentially beautiful doors and skirting boards – then you must strip off old paint.

If you want to return the wood to a replica natural finish, by staining and then sealing, the wood must be in really excellent shape. If stripping reveals decades of filled-up marks and gouges, immediately abandon ambitions of a natural finish for, despite a lot of time and effort, it will never look good. You must also strip varnish before painting, rubbing or sanding down since it just doesn't provide an efficient key for new paint.

Stripping paint and wallpaper is no one's idea of fun; most people make the fundamental mistake of using a filling knife, which is flexible, instead of a scraper with a thick and rigid blade. This may seem a pedantic point, until you consider the amount of energy wasted on each stroke in bending the former tool's blade before it is transmitted to the the scraping edge. Buy a scraper and a shave-hook, invaluable for cleaning moldings, in a specialist shop.

Oil-based paints and varnishes are best removed by the hot-air strippers or heat guns; these have supplanted paraffin blow-lamps which are heavy, potentially dangerous and can badly scorch the wood. The basic single- or double-heat gun can also burn wood, so you must not work too long on one area, nor use it near window glass without fitting a heat shield. Of course you can be restricted by the length of the power cord, (if you use an extension cable, wind it all off the reel) and you must take great care working near flammable materials since you can't see the very hot air stream.

However, these problems are a great deal assuaged by state-of-the-art guns like the Black and Decker BD1610E which electronically maintains five different temperature settings, from 100 to 560°C. This facility also enables you to solder plumbing, do roofing repairs, heat-shrink the film-type double-glazing, remove old floor coverings, and thaw and dry just about everything except your hair.

Chemical strippers are, I think, a lot messier and more hazardous. They usually contain methylene chloride (dichloromethan) as the main solvent and this is powerful, moderately toxic stuff, so cover skin and wear goggles. Be careful; don't use it near a naked flame, nor in confined places for prolonged periods; it can cause dizziness. Don't use it at all if you have any heart trouble.

Liquid chemical strippers are, however, the best solution to clogged-up and intricately detailed wood and metal surfaces. They're particularly appropriate if the wood is going to be left in its natural state or varnished. They're simply brushed on, worked well into mouldings, and left for 10 to 15 minutes, after which the paint or varnish is soft enough to remove both easily and cleanly. You will probably have to use wire wool or an old (natural bristle) toothbrush to scrape the stripper into awkward crannies. After stripping, it's imperative that you neutralise the chemical with water or white spirit, or whatever the manufacturer recommends. This will raise the grain on wood, necessitating a final light sanding.

Paste chemicals, generally based on caustic soda – so again, care – are best in removing a multitude of coats from a flat surface. They're applied in a thick layer and left for several hours, during which time the paste must be kept from drying out by covering it with polythene or at least newspaper. They may darken the wood – try a sample area first if possible – and never use them on veneer or on plywood, as the caustic soda will melt veneer glue and delaminate boards.

Textured paint, such as Artex, is an excellent way of covering cracked or uneven ceilings – so consider what's undeneath before you set about removing it. If you really must, the best specialised products, which resemble gel-type liquid strippers, are made by Nitromors and POB Salvent. They're brushed on and after about 30 minutes you start scraping off the softened mess. Surfaces must be washed down afterwards, of course. It can be a lengthy and messy affair.

It's almost inevitable that however much time and painstaking care you've spent on the sort of preparation for decorating, the walls of a room – particularly those in more elderly houses – will retain lots of little imperfections which won't manifest themselves until you're actually wallpapering; a slap-dash coat of white emulsion makes the remaining gaps and holes more visible.

Painting and Decorating

Photographs in some glossy magazines of all the decorating equipment you'll need, laid neatly out on a table like in a kit inspection, suggest some complex SAS-like assault afoot. It's quite possible, of course, that some simple tactical errors will be made in the white-heat of enthusiasm to get the job done. It is childishly easy to hang a piece of patterned wallpaper upside-down, or step gently into a roller-tray of emulsion. At times like these, the Raid on Entebbe seems positively straightforward.

Nevertheless, you will need a few good-quality tools, the best you can afford, which will last for countless years of fun. There are no such things as all-purpose tools, so for most woodwork painting you'll need three hog-bristle brushes, because they hold paint best – half inch, 1 in and 2 in. Walls and ceilings require a 4 in brush. Even brand new brushes have loose hairs, so break them in by using primers and undercoats, and don't later clean off gloss with turps as it hardens the bristles. Use a proprietory brush cleaner.

Rollers make things easier for the DIYer but use one with a mohair or short woolpile sleeve for covering plaster, lining paper and hardboard and sheepskin for covering brick, concrete or cement rendering, which of course has first been properly sealed. Fit a broom handle to the roller to decorate ceilings while standing on the floor; this method also means you don't get splashed so much, because the roller will be applied at an angle, and will not be directly above you.

Old ceilings that have badly-cracked textured surfaces can be returned to pristine condition with an all-in-one repair and decoration treatment like Polytex, which is easily applied with a roller and covers cracks up to 2 mm wide. It's durable – flexible enough to keep cracks covered for years – and the standard white finish, which won't yellow with time, can be overpainted when dry. A 2.5 litre bucket of Polytex will cover up to 60 sq ft.

Don't try to paper without a proper paste table, a soft pasting brush, paper-hanging brush, plumb-bob for dead vertical drops, long-bladed wallpapering scissors and a seam-roller. You'll already know about the ubiquitous Polyfilla, but if you confront patches of crumbling plaster you will have to hack them off to a sound surface. No need to try and call in irascible 'spreaders', use Polyplasta for a really smooth finish, obtained with a float on big areas, but a trowel or filling knife is adequate for smaller repairs.

It's easy to calculate the number of rolls – with a calculator. Ignore doors and windows and measure the distance around the room, then multiply by the height between the floor and ceiling and divide by 5.4 for metric or 57.63 for imperial. It's an estimate, of course, (based on the British standard 33 ft roll – continental and special papers will differ), but you'll be grateful for the extra roll or so you buy, particularly if you are matching a large-patterned covering, which could mean a lot of waste.

Estimating the amount of paint, primer and undercoat is problematic, as the guide given on each, usually referring to the amount of square metres covered by each litre, doesn't take into account the porosity and/or colour of different surfaces. As some sort of benchmark, a door will take about a tenth of a litre of gloss.

Colour can vary considerably in different batches of paint so if you're using several tins, as soon as the first can is half-empty, stir in the contents of a second container. Keep a note of all the materials (paints, rolls, paper adhesives, etc.) used for a particular room, so that next time there will be no waste. Even if you won't use it again, the next owner of the home could be grateful. Equally, if you're using a large quantity of a particular paint throughout the house, note that too, and buy in bulk at discount prices. Some of the best discount 'trade paints', particularly primers, still contain quantities of lead; there's no reason why you shouldn't use them as long as you're aware of what you're handling. You obviously wouldn't paint a nursery or any other child-accessible place with such stuff.

If you must store left-over paint, don't keep it in the house; it's a potential fire-hazard. If you need to re-use stored thixotropic 'non-drip' (and non-stir) paint, discard the liquid that's gathered on the top. An old pair of nylon tights is still the best for straining other paints through. Always try to work in good natural light – strong sun or electric lights cast shadows – and always finish a complete wall or other surface before taking a rest, otherwise the break between the two applications will be clear.

Many people are forced to decorate after a wall has been re-plastered; it's best to wait at least three months before wallpapering, especially if you're going to use vinyl. Even then, walls should be sealed (sized) with thinned wallpaper paste containing a fungicide. However, you can apply matt emulsion on a wall as soon as the plaster is touch dry. Similarly, a cured damp wall will take several months to dry out, as remaining moisture surfaces, bringing with it alkaline crystals from building materials causing efflorescence. Otherwise, you can use a waterproof sealer such as Aquaseal 77, which will allow redecorating within hours.

The best product I've used for covering and sealing stained but otherwise dry walls and ceilings, and preventing the stains from leaching through time after time, is the new Stain-Block from Polycell. This ozone-friendly aerosol is really superb; it not only blocks and seals water-based stains like the one on the bedroom ceiling from last winter's leaking roof, but also deals with the grease, rust and (perish the thought) your child's 'wonderful' crayon pictures on the bedroom wall. It dries white and you can paint over it within 10 minutes.

Stripping wallpaper has been voted *the* most hated DIY job among the 6.5 million households who each year buy 90 million rolls of wallpaper. But don't risk putting new paper on old as it's probable that both will bubble up. You can soak and then scrape off paper (tedium of Stygian depths) or you can, for under £30, make the job very easy with the new Black and Decker BD1200 wallpaper stripper which, with a touch of a button softens wallpaper adhesive with five high-powered steam jets. It will remove all kinds of wallpapers, although washables should be scored first with a perforator (B&D A9840). It also uses water straight from the tap and (unlike some hired machines) is well-balanced and lightweight.

Stripping Woodwork

It's tempting when painting woodwork simply to scrape off the loose bits, fill a few holes and gaps, maybe even dispense with an undercoat and get the job over with as quickly as possible. Don't do it; it's an entire waste of time, money and effort. Stripping paint is, next to watching paint dry, an ineffably boring occupation, but that, and thorough preparation, is the professionals' secret. There's no escape. The slightly better news is that with modern methods and materials, stripping isn't the mind-numbing chore it used to be – well, not quite. Modern paints and varnishes are intended to last years, and can be freshened by regular washing, but there eventually comes a time when there is no alternative other than to strip – and start all over again.

The development of chemical paint strippers, plus the invention of the hot air gun, makes a fresh start easier. You'll need to learn how to use paint strippers; they have to be powerful, but they won't differentiate between your fair skin and eyes and the dark-green thirties gloss on the hall dado. Read the instructions on the container: it's important to find out which surfaces the stripper can be used on.

Liquid chemical paint strippers are the only answer to clogged decorative wood. Typically they need to be brushed on and left for 10 to 15 minutes while the paint softens and blisters. It can then be removed with a scraper or a shavehook. If there are several coats of paint to be removed, and the chemical hasn't reached the wood in this time, don't scrape off the softened top layers, as the stripper will continue to act. Add a second coat, and when the paint blisters, break the blisters and press them back onto the surface again.

You'll find to your considerable financial cost however, that you can go through tins of the stuff and still find layers underneath, so try the old-fashioned method – caustic soda – before using the more expensive preparations. The soda must be added slowly to the water as it will boil up – and you will of course be wearing thick gloves, not washing up models – and goggles. The solution can be thickened by adding whiting or lime, so that it will gel and stay on vertical surfaces. The cleaned surfaces must be neutralised: well-washed with water, then with diluted vinegar, before a final scrub with water.

Most of the proprietary liquid paint strippers are non-caustic, and are made up of a solvent and thickener. Intricately moulded areas will inevitably need scrubbing with fine wire wool or an old toothbrush with natural bristles – strippers will simply melt plastic ones. It's again vital that the stripped wood is neutralised with water or white spirit, according to the makers' instructions. This procedure invariably raises the wood grain, and there'll be quite a few wooden whiskers around, so a light sanding and/or a rub with wire wool will also be necessary before painting.

Chemical paint strippers give off fumes, so work in a well-ventilated area, and don't smoke – the strippers aren't usually inflammable, but inhaling the fumes through a cigarette can obviously be very harmful indeed.

Liquid strippers are available in runny or gel versions; the latter are best for vertical surfaces but cost a little more. The gels are also better for dealing with wood which will eventually be given a clear finish, for moulded surfaces and for working on windows, where the heat from a gun could crack glass. The gel strippers don't act as quickly as the runny ones, and will not penetrate very thick accumulations of paint without several applications.

Paste strippers are simply a modern version of the old caustic soda solution. They usually need to be left in place for several hours, and stopped from drying out either by covering them with old newspapers or polythene, or lightly spraying them with water. The paste layer is then peeled off with, one hopes, all the paint. These strippers work well on both emulsion- and solvent-based coverings.

Paste strippers are also likely to darken the wood slightly, so only use them if you intend painting, rather than staining and varnishing. Paste strippers may also badly stain oak, iroko or hemlock – so try them out on a small area first.

Never use chemical paint strippers on veneered surfaces,

plywood or hardboards; they'll lift the wood covering as well as the paint. Veneered surfaces can best be cleaned by laborious hand sanding or by the very gentle use of an electric sander, using fine sandpaper. Textured emulsion paints and the tougher coverings such as Artex present different problems to other paints because of their special ingredients; however, brand leaders Nitromors produce a non-acidic, non-caustic gel-type liquid which is simply brushed on and left for 30 minutes. The softened paint can then be scraped off.

Heat stripping is quicker and cheaper than any chemical method. It won't, however, work on emulsion or water-based primers and undercoats. Use a blow lamp or hot air gun to strip solvent-based paints and varnishes; the heat simply causes the paint film to bubble up. Don't use a blow-lamp on anything that won't require repainting. No matter how careful you are in keeping the flame moving, it's difficult to prevent scorching the wood. Charring the wood is less of a problem with a hot air gun, but it can still happen and, frankly, once it does it's difficult to eradicate, so painting may be the only remedy. A blow lamp or hot air gun will crack window glass in seconds and the shields available for the latter are not terribly effective. Great caution is also needed when working close to inflammable materials because you can't see the hot air stream.

Mechanical stripping is fast and comparatively effortless, but use it as a last resort; it is only really suitable if you're dealing with flat areas with no intricate detailing. This method creates an awful lot of dust, and many old paint systems probably contain lead, so always wear a dust mask over your mouth and nose. Sanding discs fitted on electric drills tend to score the surface badly, so only use this method where the standard of finish is not too important.

Finishing Woodwork

After the messy business of stripping paint from interior wood-work – no one's idea of a good time – the next step is smoothing and preparing the surfaces for painting or another finish. This isn't too much fun either, but you might be encouraged to the effort once you've seen the promise and beauty of the newly-revealed woodgrain. Fine old woods may have suffered some knocks and scratches over the years, and indeed your own over-enthusiastic scraping could have done some damage too.

If you've used a chemical paint stripper, you will have had to neutralise it, usually by scrubbing the wood with water, then with diluted vinegar before a final scrub with water (some strippers are neutralised with white spirit). It's important that the wood is absolutely dry before you continue.

If you intend to repaint the stripped wood, then the surface can be restored with a cellulose filler such as Polyfilla. Fillers generally come in two grades – the general purpose kind for filling in deep holes and the fine filler for a perfect final finish.

Cracks and scratches on wood which will be varnished or clear-finished should be filled with a wood filler such as Plastic Wood or 'woodstopper'; these come in a variety of matching shades. Alternatively, melt coloured beeswax, which can be bought in small sticks. Leave the filler or stopping to harden, and shave off the surface excess with a razor blade. Although fillers are sold in wood shades, the repair work will be noticeable as it breaks the pattern of the grain. Some will take wood dyes, which are best mixed into the filler before application.

This is also the stage when you might confront surface stains and black or grey water marks, often found on windows. These can be removed with a proprietary wood bleach; you could also use a solution made up of one tablespoon of oxalic acid, available from a chemist, to one pint of water. This is cheaper, but also poisonous. Bleaching will of course lighten the colour of the surrounding wood, so you may have to treat the whole area, or use wood stains to restore the original colour.

Power tools will make the smoothing ('rubbing-down') of wood considerably easier as long as they're used with some restraint. They'll give off a lot of dust – wear goggles and a face mask – and this will have to be carefully removed from the workplace before any decoration takes place. The best way of doing this is with a lint-free cloth dampened with white spirit.

Belt sanders are far too powerful for finishing wood and disc sanders which are fitted into an electric drill will almost inevitably and perhaps irrevocably score the wood. So too will drum sanders, although these are ideal for inside curves. Orbital sanders are best – they vibrate rather than rotate in one direction. Always sand in the direction of the grain and work from coarse through medium to fine grade papers.

Silicone-coated 'wet and dry' paper – used dry of course – is probably the best – when the paper gets clogged up, the old paint can be simply be rinsed out. If you are sanding by hand, use a cork or wooden sanding block to ensure the paper remains flat on the surface.

Traditionally, wood finishing is a laborious and painstaking skill, but modern stains and varnishes have now made excellent results possible to the novice. First there are the oils, such as linseed and teak; they're only suitable for hard or oil woods; they quickly discolour and dirty soft wood. They're applied by rubbing, sparingly, along the grain with a lint-free cloth. Leave the oil to soak in for a couple of hours and wipe off the excess. Leave to dry for about two days and reapply the oil over the same time sequences, until the wood won't accept any more oil. Buff and wax. A lengthy process, but oils will not mask the grain, and will disguise a lot of superficial scratches. Some proprietary oils can be sealed with a polyurethane finish.

French polishing or shellac will produce a mirror-like finish, but I'm afraid its successful application is well beyond the scope of DIY. Wax is easy to use; it's applied in one heavy coat and worked in. It will beautifully highlight the grain, but needs frequent maintenance renewal.

The clear, usually polyurethane-based, varnishes and lacquers offer excellent, highly durable finishes in gloss, satin or matt finishes. They're easy to apply. Dilute the first coat of varnish with 10 per cent white spirit and let the mixture stand until clear of bubbles. Brush the varnish on very thinly along the grain, laying the tip of the bristles flat against the starting edge to prevent a build-up of varnish.

In between coats, lightly sand down with fine glass paper, and remove all traces of dust with a vaccum cleaner hose or slightly damp cloth. A minimum of three coats is usually recommended. You may have wondered how the professionals achieve that glass-like finish. They work in a clean dust-free environment – they'll even damp down the floor with water. Because dust travels down, suspend flat surfaces with the side to be treated facing downwards and work underneath. Fine-grade wet and dry paper (used wet) is used for sanding. Before the final coat of varnish, dust off after sanding and lightly rinse the surface with a damp, not wet, chamois leather. Allow to dry before applying the last coat.

Wood dyes or stains can be used to alter the wood quite dramatically, without masking the grain. These are best on light-coloured woods, and deep colours are easily obtained with successive applications. How well wood takes colour depends on its porosity. Softwoods will drink up stain, so apply it diluted for more economic use. A very thin coat of shellac first will help minimise absorption. Compatible dyes may be mixed to individual shades – always mix enough stain to finish the job. They can also be diluted to compensate for dark patches in wood.

Dyes and stains, however, don't offer surface protection and you'll need to provide this with a sealer. Never leave part of a job unfinished, watch for runs at edges and build-up of colour in corners, and check for missed spots before leaving to dry.

Ceilings

'Here's to thirty-five years of textured paint.'

Ceilings are supposed to be flat, level things, but too often they're in such a poor state of repair or decoration, they can spoil the effect of an otherwise quite reasonable room. They may not get a lot of wear and tear but they're neglected because of the obvious difficulty in working on them.

There's no really easy way to do this that doesn't involve a lot of neckache, but if you plan such an assault, and you don't want the project to become a Laurel and Hardy tragi-comedy, hire purpose-made decorators' trestles and a builders' board to provide a safe and comfortable working platform. Wear goggles.

Older houses are likely to have the original lath and plaster ceilings which, like ladies of a certain age, are sagging, bulging and in a generally bad state of preservation. It's not easy to tell lath and plaster from below, so the simplest way is to lift a floorboard in the room above. If only part of the plaster has come away from its laths, you have a reasonable chance of repairing it by lifting and supporting the bulging portion with wide boards held in place by lengths of timber or, better still, screw props, which can be hired. Then you drive countersunk plated screws fitted with galvanized or plated washers at intervals of up to 12 in through the plaster and into the ceiling joists. They will become embedded into the plaster, and are concealed with filler. Whenever you do this, try to leave the filler slightly proud of the surface, so that it can be rubbed down to a smooth finish with glass paper when it has dried.

A more elaborate method of rehabilitating a sagging ceiling would be to prop it up as before, then clean from between the joists above as much dust and debris as possible. Mix up a quantity of plaster of Paris and tip it over the damaged area. This will set quite quickly, and hold the ceiling in place. Again strengthen the repair with plated screws.

It would be a good idea to go over the rest of the ceiling, carefully nailing it back to the joints with large-headed galvanized clout nails, often simply called plasterboard nails, which won't rust when they are later dampened by wallpaper paste. Always 'cross-line' such ceilings (meaning the first lining paper is fixed at right angles to the window wall, and so in the opposite direction to that normally taken for the final ceiling paper.)

If a lath and plaster ceiling is webbed with fine, hairline cracks, they're nothing to worry about, but don't think that a good strong coat of emulsion will hide them. If you wish to use emulsion, the ceiling will have to be cross-lined first. Use inexpensive lining paper if you want a smooth finish or, alternatively, one of the embossed papers such as Crown Anaglypta.

Long, thin cracks need to be raked along their length with a pointed filling knife. This is to enlarge the crack sufficiently to take a filler, and also to get rid of any loose material. Fill the crack by loading the filling and first drawing it at right angles across the crack before drawing it along its length. Rusty stains, grim reminders of winter bursts, reappear on freshly-painted ceilings, and will continue to do so unless the stained area is treated with an aluminium primer-sealer which has a scale-like composition that effectively seals the stain and prevents further 'bleeding'. But it's worth checking in the loft that the leak which caused the trouble has been effectively dealt with.

Modern ceilings are usually made of large sheets of plasterboard. Perhaps you've suffered a leak or, just as likely, someone clambering about in the roof space has put a foot through the bedroom ceiling. Locate the joists either side of the damaged area and ensure there are no pipes or electrical cables in the vicinity. Make a start hole with a chisel so that you can get a general-purpose saw blade through to cut out a rectangle which includes the damaged area.

Wooden battens will now be needed to frame the aperture, to enable you to nail a new piece of plasterboard into it. You might be able to use the bit that's been cut out as a template for the new board, which should be fixed with the ivory-side down if you intend papering the ceiling. Try not to break the paper surface of the plasterboard and fill any gaps.

Bad ceilings often have received a covering of polystyrene tiles. There's no easy way of removing them. Slide a scraper underneath and remove as much as you can. This will almost certainly leave blobs of adhesive on the ceiling. Use a hot air gun to soften these and scrape them away.

Some older ceilings may also have been covered with a textured finish which can, with a lot of hard work, be removed with Nitromors textured paint remover, which is a non-acid, non-caustic, non-drip splash gel. Nevertheless, wear old clothes, goggles and gloves. Apply the remover with a brush or plastering float, but don't spread it thinly as this will reduce its penetrating power. It needs to soak into the covering for at least half an hour. Remember that some of the earlier textured paints contained asbestos, so never try to scrape or sand them off. After removing materials like Artex, you'll need to scrub the ceiling with hot water and detergent before you start redecorating.

You may be fortunate enough to have an original, rather pleasant decorative ceiling rose, but unlucky enough to find it's clogged with paint. Hours of nit-picking, shoulder-aching work lie ahead with copious amounts of paint remover dabbed into the nooks and crannies. It can be done, but you'll be bound to wonder whether it's worth it in the end.

You may even break bits off, but decorative ceiling roses and ornate mouldings can be repaired by using the sort of rubber

moulding compound sold by some craft shops to copy an un-
damaged section. You will need to form a female mould into
which plaster of Paris can be poured. When set you need to
make a gap in the damaged section, and stick the new piece in
with PVA adhesive.

Cornices

There are various ways of enhancing the ceilings; fitting a cornice is one of them. It will take away the box-like appearance of some rooms and, perhaps more beneficially, cover the unsightly cracks which often appear between the walls and the ceiling, particularly in modern houses.

Cornices are usually simply glued and/or nailed into the angle between the wall and ceiling; the only fiddly part is cutting the mitre joints for the corners, but most manufacturers supply a paper template which makes this easier. In any case, gaps in joints can be quite neatly filled in and covered completely once they're painted.

Expanded and high-density polystyrene, polyurethane and gypsum and fibrous plaster covings are available in a wide variety of patterns. The simple cove mouldings are most popular, and best for the low ceilings of modern homes. Older rooms with higher ceilings can take elaborate and heavier cornices, and these often include a frieze which is fitted flat against the wall below the cornice.

The least expensive cornices are made of expanded polystyrene; they're usually a simple cove moulding and, being super lightweight, are extremely easy to fix, although you may have to substitute ceramic tile adhesive for the recommended one where wall or ceiling surfaces are badly deformed.

Polystyrene covings are soft and quite susceptible to damage, so take care not to dent them when cutting or fitting. They're easily cut to length and mitre angle with a sharp craft (Stanley) knife. They can be effectively painted with emulsion, but not oil paint as its chemicals would destroy the material. High-density polystyrene is a bit costlier than the 'expanded' type but rather more robust. The same methods of cutting and fixing are used.

Polyurethane coving is used for both simple cove mouldings as well as large cornices which may also have a frieze that fits flat against the wall. The material is the most dense of all the plastics used for such mouldings, and it's more expensive.

However, it's a material which is as hard as wood, and therefore won't dent when you fix it, using either the special adhesive provided by the manufacturer, or ceramic tile adhesive. The difference is that it needs to be pinned to the wall until the adhesive has gained full strength.

Gypsum plaster is made like plasterboard – the cove consists of a gypsum plaster core encased in paper and is one of the most popular cornice materials. It is made in two sizes: 100 mm, which projects about 67 mm from the wall and comes in easy-to-handle 3 m lengths, and the 127 mm girth coving, which projects from the wall about 82 mm and comes in 3 m, 3.6 m and 4.2 m lengths. It is heavier to handle, and a helper is required in the fixing process, which is usually by means of the Gyproc cove adhesive. It can also be fixed to the wall with galavanised nails while the adhesive sets. Gaps in joints are made good with adhesive and cutting to length is easy with a fine-toothed saw, although you'll have to sand lightly the rough edges away to get a neat joint.

Gypsum plaster coving can be decorated with most types of treatment, although if you want to paint, it must be primed. Templates are usually included in the pack. These help make the cuttings of mitres for external angles a bit easier. The templates also enable you to make square cuts accurately, or to scribe internal angles.

The classical cornices, complete with friezes and elaborate patterns, are made of fibrous plaster. They are expensive and heavy, but nearest now available to the authentic original cornices which were made made of stick and rag, the plaster-soaked materials originally used as reinforcement. Fibrous plaster with the most fanciful patterns, such as egg-and-dart and egg-and-leaf, only really look good in the lofty rooms of older houses. This type of coving is invariably nailed and glued; it's likely to shatter if dropped, and therefore is not generally recommended for DIY work.

Wooden 'mouldings' are an ideal way of giving a room interest as well as visually altering its dimensions. They are the traditional method of providing (or restoring) an ornamental finish to most kinds of joinery, and are simply pinned on to doors, architraves and skirting boards. There's a wide range of off-the-shelf wooden mouldings available – most of the large sizes. Skirtings, architraves, weatherboards and hand rails are machined from softwood such as pine; the smaller, more intricate designs are cut from one of the cheaper hardwoods like ramin.

Dados and picture rails were popular from Victorian times to the 1930s, and they're now coming back into fashion. Dados were fixed on the wall at waist height to protect the plaster from damage from carelessly-moved furniture, and also provided a natural break in the wall's colour scheme. The area below the dado was usually panelled, while that above it would be papered or painted. The picture rail, usually fixed around 600 mm below ceiling height, allowed pictures to be hung and moved about, and also provided a visual break in rooms with lofty ceilings.

Exterior Decorating

Decorating the exterior of a house isn't difficult or dangerous as long as you organise safe, confident access to the heights, you plan carefully and you're lucky with the weather. If your home seems to need redoing every couple of years, it's not getting the treatment such a valuable investment deserves. A thorough job should last about five years depending, of course, on prevailing climatic conditions.

Exterior work, even on a bungalow, means working at heights, and you might be forgiven for salving your conscience about paying someone else to take the risks of balancing on ladders were it not for the easy availability nowadays of hired towers and platforms. These allow faster, safer and more thorough work because you can use both hands, and your fear of falling is substantially calmed, even at the maximum tower height of 30 ft. Towers must stand on firm ground and be securely tied to the house; the wheels you move them about on should always be locked. If you're not sure how to erect them – it's a pretty commonsense operation – then pay a scaffolding firm to do it. Only two other things, always climb a tower from the inside, and make sure that your windows are extra secure at night.

There are no excuses not to do exterior decoration yourself, for there's now plenty of time for the planning. Late summer or early autumn are usually the best time for the work, when the weather seems set into a longish, dry spell which dries out all the exposed timbers. You'll need the time to shop around for the best buys in paint, because you'll probably need quite a lot. Never go for cheap job lots; good paint is expensive, but it will last. The quality of such materials is conveniently demystified by a regular subscription to the Consumer Association's *Which?* magazine, a must for DIY – I reckon it has saved me thousands, and a good deal of trouble, over the years – in 'Best Buy' selection alone.

Don't decorate when the air is damp, or wind is blowing dust around. This is a waste of time. In general, you follow the sun – making an early start as soon as the dew has dried, and working on areas that the sun has already passed over. That way you're not working in direct sunlight when eye-strain is likely to lead to a lot of missed patches, or 'holidays' as they're known in the trade.

Start at the top and work down with each stage of cleaning, repair and painting (which will consist of under and top coats); complete one side of a house at a time, gutters and eaves first. Keep a bucket of water handy if you're burning off paint with a blow lamp as it's easy to set fire to an old dry bird's nest, and consequently your house. Many homes have been raised that way – by professionals, too. This is very embarrasing, so use a hot air gun instead.

It's better really to sand-clean metal gutters, eaves and downpipes, but wear a face mask as many exterior paints, particuarly primers, contain lead. You'll need a really tough sander for metal pipes and gutters, or they'll take for ever to clean.

You should take the opportunity to clean and rust-proof the gutters, after which you can best protect the inside of metal gutters with any left-over gloss paints of different colours, mixed together into an unearthly colour and strained through an old pair of tights. Incidentally, never employ the bright idea of flushing the debris from gutters with a hosepipe; you'll almost inevitably block the downpipes.

Use a drill-powered disc sander for flat surfaces, but be careful not to dig in and irrevocably mark wood. It is possible to paint faded plastic guttering and downpipes but it must all be rubbed down with a super-fine Garnet paper, *nothing* else will do. Even the finest sandpaper will destory the delicate surface, leaving fluffy marks which look terrible when painted. Dust off and apply a couple of coats of gloss paint – prime or undercoat is unnecessary – but ensure you go right round the backs of pipes, or rain will eventually lift the edge of the paint film.

Save yourself a lot of extra cleaning by spreading dust sheets over paths, the roofs of lower buildings and and plants before you start, as there are bound to be falling splashes of paint.

(Paths can be deep-cleaned quite easily with Polycell Patio Renovator.)

Newish masonry, whether brick, cement rendered or pebble-dashed, are all cleaned with a stiff brush which removes dust and loose material. At this stage, mark or note damp areas – usually signalled by white crystals – for extra further treatment before final painting. Moss and mould must be treated with a solution of one part bleach to four parts of water, and allowed to cure for two days before painting. Similarly, fill cracks and holes using quick-set cement; it's worth the extra money for the time saved.

Repointing portions of brickwork, conventionally, calls for the old mortar to be raked out to a depth of 20 mm, but with Polycell's repointing kit, which comes with a dual-purpose repointing tool and plastic builder's hawk – which you must have – only 6 mm needs to be raked out. The 18 mm difference saves an enormous amount of time and effort, when it really matters.

The whole surface must then be sealed with a proprietary stabiliser, which will not only kill any remaining alkali but will make it less absorbent, and the first coat go much further.

Masonry already covered in an oil-based paint is best washed down with household detergent and rinsed well. Easier still, hire a high-pressure jet water cleaner, which simply connects to an ordinary garden hosepipe. Be careful not to get too enthusiastic, as the powerful jet can knock out a lot of pointing too, making a lot of extra work.

Emulsioned walls can only be washed with water; anything stronger is likely to damage the paint. Cement-based paints just aren't washable at all; you'll just have to dry brush them until the surface is sound. Resin-based masonry paints, although waterproof when dry, tend to peel off once moisture gets behind a crevice, so scrape off, then prime, any loose bits.

After all this cleaning and preparation you'll be glad to know the actual decorating is comparatively simple and easy. Textured and pebble-dashed surfaces really require the deepest pile roller or, better and quicker still, spraying, for an effective cover.

Select the type of paint with great care – tell a paint merchant what it has to cover, and if you're using a roller you must also buy a deep, rectangular paint tray which hangs from a convenient tower pole or ladder rung. If you're dying for a cup of tea, or find you're running out of paint, stop at a natural break like a window or door frame, otherwise the colour variation will be glaringly obvious. Wear soft shoes with lots of grip if you're working on a tower platform, but hard-soled footwear on a ladder. And the moment you start feeling tired or dizzy, stop.

Co-ordinating Carpets, Curtains and Covers

'Elspeth . . . where are you, Elspeth?

Decorating is much more than the basic slave labour of stripping paintwork and wallpaper. The real skill and work is in the creating of a new and beautiful illusion. It always seems a holy irony to me that all the sweat, tears and toil will go into the basics of construction, wiring, plumbing and so on which are put in, forgotten and, hopefully, never seen again. Yet paper and paint complete the picture and turn a building site into a comfortable place to live. Comparatively speaking, decorating is all done in very little time.

While the proverbial lick of Brilliant White will always brighten things up, a new and carefully co-ordinated colour scheme – taking into account floors, walls, ceilings, lighting, curtains and furniture coverings can dramatically transform a pretty ordinary room into something quite special.

Just as Black and Decker, B&Q and Texas *et al* have de-mystified and made DIY available for even the most fumble-fingered, so firms like Laura Ashley and Sanderson have encouraged the nascent interior designer to achieve splendid results, even though this might be brought about by a little judicious cribbing from the catalogues' set-piece illustrations.

An overall colour scheme is the first thing to consider, and this is of course much easier if you start from scratch. Colours, like just about everything else are subject to a cyclical fashion-ability, and many people pay the price of going for voguish colours, only to see them not only drop out of favour, but frankly become something of an irritation.

The wooden kitchen in its various forms will stand the test of time, never looking sensationally new, but on the other hand never seeming old hat. Similarly, white bathrooms are a good idea; it's a lot easier to buy royal blue towels and curtains than hack off a wall full of tiles.

Carpets are massively expensive, so choose colour and quality well. It's not a bad scheme to carpet most of the rooms of a home in the same material and shade – you could probably get a better discounted deal too – possibly stepping out of line in a bedroom, to match or co-ordinate with that room's own scheme, and the bathroom and of course the kitchen.

Forget patterend carpets; they may not show up marks and wear so much, but you may quickly tire of them, and trying to co-ordinate things like curtains and other fabrics is very difficult indeed. Choosing a carpet colour depends a lot on whether you want to lighten a dark house or alternatively add some depth to an airy one. It's worth considering the outside surroundings. In a rural setting, you may want to extend the natural colours into the home, but in an inner-city location something bright and cheerful might compensate for the grey-ness outside.

Live in a new home for several months before deciding on the decor – even if you do have the money after the expense of moving.

Colour co-ordination is now the buzz-phrase, but take care; matching everything can be as hard on the eye as clashing colours. Sanderson were the first to introduce co-ordinated wall covering and curtains, and many of their ideas are still the most sensible. Although prices seem to have taken a collosal leap this year, few companies on a comparable price scale have got their co-ordinating act together better than have Laura Ashley.

They charge £3.00 for their catalogue – I think that's a bit of a cheek for an advertising brochure – but it can turn into a valuable investment in avoiding terribly expensive mistakes in that you can browse through it at leisure, mixing and matching their various designs in furniture fabrics and tiles, and costing them too. Have no doubt, an affair with Laura Ashley can be a very costly business, particularly if you choose to have curtains and covers made up at the LA factory.

Next shops and the bigger branches of Marks and Spencer also carry co-ordinated wallpapers and curtains, but don't go wild on the really fancy patterns; you'll only want to change them next season – which is precisely what the shops want you to do.

Curtains and furniture coverings say a lot about the family that has chosen them and instinctively set the style of any home. They are, like everything else, increasingly expensive, but for the most part curtains are decidedly more affordable than carpets and large furnishings, and go a long way towards an entirely new look.

If you are in a new house and have so much work to do on it you don't know where to begin, once you've decided on a colour scheme, new curtains help to give your home its character, and they can be made and hung DIY. If you are not ready to decide on colours, lace curtains, which are enjoying a new popularity, make many windows look much prettier. If you make them full enough, they will also provide some privacy. Lace panels are ideal for small bathroom windows, and for the long narrow windows often found on landings.

If no one in the family likes to sew, there's a wide range of blinds abundantly available, from the plain and elegant to the now somewhat dated festoon blinds. Plain roller blinds are quite easily made up from kits and represent excellent value if you need a quick and colourful window covering. Festoon blinds can also be made at home but are much more difficult to put together. However, festoon blinds for, say, a large sitting room window can cost anything between £500 and £1000 so, given that frills are going out of fashion, I'd stick to the rollers. Many of the colourful and sometimes surreal *trompe l'œil* versions are great fun, and can divert attention from the mess the rest of the room is in.

Incidentally, don't buy ready-made curtain poles; they cost an inordinate amount of money. Instead purchase the fittings, such as the supports and end caps, and buy a length of the appropriately-sized dowelling at a wood yard, and stain or paint it whatever colour you like.

If in doubt in a new home, and something just has to be done to the decor, paint it all white, and develop a colour cheme as you learn to live with the house.

The final, and one of the most important, touches are the light fittings. They need not cost a lot to look really good and if you are on a tight budget head for a British Home Stores lighting department. Some of the grandest lighting effects I've seen in older houses have been Victorian gas mantle holders converted to electrical fittings. Try to select light fittings that are reproductions, or better still originals of the same period as your home.

Carpets and Flooring

Although many carpet shops offer 'free' fitting when floor coverings over a certain value are bought, there's no such deal on the odd piece, often be sold at bargain price, which is just right for a small spare bedroom, for example. The trouble is that laying carpets isn't a task with which you're likely to have had much practice.

If you are buying new material and intend fitting it yourself, remember that foam-backed carpets are much easier to lay, not least because the more expensive hessians have to be stretched into position. Do this too enthusiastically and any pattern will appear deformed; if a carpet is laid too slackly there'll be unsightly wrinkles, and it will wear unevenly.

Estimating the amount of carpet can be difficult, so it's easier to take a detailed plan of the room with you to the store, and let them do it. You'll need to hire a 'knee kicker', which does the stretching, and have a sharp Stanley knife, a hammer, a bolster chisel, a stapler, a pair of pincers or pliers, adhesive carpet tape, a tape measure and a felt tipped pen.

The floor must be level, smooth and dry, because although a carpet will initially cosmetically cover dents and hollows, these will show through almost immediately you start walking on it. An uneven concrete floor can be remedied with a self-levelling compound, which is simply brushed on and allowed to dry. Nails on wooden floors must be punched below the surface and loose or unsound boards fixed. It usually better to screw a loose board down but be very careful putting new nails or screws in a floor which might contain electrical or plumbing supplies. The £10 or so you could pay for a cable/pipe detector could save an awful lot of trouble.

If a wooden floor is in quie a bad condition, it's a lot easier to cover it with hardboard sheets, laid smooth side down after you've given the other (rough) side a dampening dose of water.

You can tack hessian carpets down, but it's worth the extra cost of buying lengths of spiked wood, called gripper strips, which are nailed down along the perimeter of the room, with the angled edge to the wall, leaving a gap which is just slightly less than the thickness of the carpet. Break the strips up with pliers, and be careful: the spikes are very sharp.

Hessian carpet does need an underlay. It is comparatively cheap and will make a big difference to both the feel and wear of a cheaper covering. It's not necessary to fix an underlay down, but this will help prevent it moving during the laying work. Fix it inside the gripper strips, using a stapler on wooden floors and double-sided tape on a solid one. Unroll the carpet in the room so that it is approximately in the right position, with any pattern at right angles to the doorway and the pile leaning away from the window – this is so that uneven shading, a problem with some inexpensive carpets, won't be too noticeable in daylight.

Secure the first edge – the longest or straightest or otherwise least complicated – by sliding it up about 10 mm onto the skirting board, and then pressing it down with your hands on the gripper strip, ensuring the spikes grip the hessian backing.

The 'knee kicker' or stretcher has adjustable spikes which can be raised or lowered to suit the thickness of the carpet backing, just gripping the pile, without going into the underlay. Its use is fairly self-evident: place it on the carpet and push it with your knee. When all the edges are in place, trim them back so that a 10 mm overlap remains and, using the bolster chisel, ram the overlap into the gap between the wall and the gripper strip.

Floors can be a problem if you need to lift them to reach a light fitting in the room below or you need to put in new sockets. Even new houses don't seem to have enough, and overloaded adaptors are a major fire risk. Lifting floorboards is much easier in an older property, where they are likely to be square edged, rather than connected with each other by tongue and groove joints. Whatever, buy a pipe and cable detector.

It is obviously best, wherever possible, to begin with a shorter, cut length of board. Pick one near the centre of the room, to avoid damaging skirting boards as the floorboard is levered up. Use a bolster chisel (the thin-bladed 'electricians' bolster' to prise up square-edged boards enough to get a claw hammer underneath; place a piece of wood underneath the lifted board and work along to the next set of nails.

To lift a continuous board, start at the middle, where you can see it is nailed to a joist. Hold it clear with a piece of wood as before, and cut the board with a tenon saw, ensuring that the cut is directly over the centre of the joist, so that it is properly supported when it is nailed back again. Removing tongue-and-grooved boards is rather more tedious. The tongue has first to be cut away, working carefully along the joints with a floorboard saw, which has a curved leading edge, specially for starting cuts in flat surfaces.

Wood Flooring

'You're not going to like this . . . I just got the
carpet up and the floor's concrete.'

A beautiful warm wood floor, with its variations of colour and grain, can really transform a room into something quite stunning and special. It costs less than a good-quality carpet and underlay, and lasts much longer, actually improving with age and a minimum of maintenance, as long as stiletto heels don't come back into fashion. There are only a couple of places where you cannot install one – on solid floors which are prone to dampness, and over an underfloor heating system.

If you're not sure whether a solid floor is damp, lay a small piece of glass onto a circle of putty or acrylic sealer, press it firmly to the floor to make sure it is airtight and leave it for a couple of days, preferably in rainy weather. If you later find there is condensation on the underside of the glass, then the floor's damp-proof membrane is probably defective. Moisture on top of the glass indicates condensation from within the room. Similarly, central heating pipes running under the floor must be adequately lagged.

Although floorboards in older houses can often be successfully sanded, it's a hard, dusty and tedious job, and could really be a complete waste of time if the the boards have badly split and warped, usually after the installation of central heating.

If you still want a wooden floor then the old boards must be levelled with hardboard, which must be treated before being fixed with coppered diamond-headed, rust-proof hardboard pins. These are put in at 4 in intervals. In this case hardboard is laid rough side up. Treatment can mean simply stacking the boards separately and on edge for three days in the room where they are going to be used.

Before fixing boards in an old house, you might consider increasing the insulation of the floor. Products like Styrofoam, which comes in large sheets, will raise the floor level a little. Hardboard used in a new house, a kitchen or a bathroom should first be conditioned by brushing the rough side with about a litre of water to each standard (2440 mm by 1220 mm) sheet. There are bigger and smaller sizes though. All this is to lessen the possibility of buckling caused by a later change in the moisture content of the room.

Some makes of DIY wooden flooring can be laid directly onto vinyl or cork tiles as long as they are secure. Some can even be laid over carpet, as long as it is short-piled needle felt. However, I wouldn't risk laying a new wood floor on a carpet, which may well deteriorate long before the wood does.

Most manufacturers recommend cork lining paper or cork roll, which will also enhance the insulation of the floor. Solid floors are often quite uneven, and these need a self-smoothing levelling screed of around 3 mm. It is simply poured on, brushed out and left to dry. Before applying the screed, thoroughly clean the surface and remove any loose pieces with a scraper.

There's a great choice of wooden floor coverings. The cheapest is plywood, in which case you can screw the sheets down into the joists. A large sheet can be cut, very accurately, into four, and the pieces laid with the grain running in different directions to form a chequered pattern. It must then be lightly sanded, cleaned, stained and sealed. It's a budget option, and you might not like the effect, so try it in a small room first, and if you don't like it, carpet it.

Remember that all wood floors need about half an inch expansion gap around the side. This is normally covered with quadrant moulding or a cork buffer strip. But you could also raise the skirting board in order to hide the gap. Although some wood coverings are little thicker than a carpet and underlay, most will raise the floor quite a bit, and this might mean planing or cutting an appropriate amount from the bottom of doors.

Wood is so wonderfully varied in colour that you have a wide range of choice. Ask to see specific samples of the wood; pictures in colour brochures can be misleading. But make sure it is guaranteed kiln-dried to a moisture content of around 10 per cent, otherwise it will shrink, and leave ugly gaps between the boards. There's the reddish Merabu and the yellowish-brown Iroko; both are smooth, hard and stable Class One woods, which means they are unlikely to be affected by normal heat and humidity changes.

Popular mahoganies include Sapele and Meranti, which have subtle pink and red tones and a rather softer more grainy surface. Of the lighter woods, Ash and Beech are beautiful, but they're Class Two and Three and so are rather more unstable. Beech is also lovely, but soft. So to is Kampala. Use these in bedrooms. White Oak is one of the most popular choices for modern homes; the light, open grain blends in particuarly well with pastel shades. It's expensive compared with the rest.

Mosaic panel, parquet or wood block and wood strip are mostly offered for DIY application. They come with full fitting instructions, which vary too much to generalise on, except to say that some are glued onto the subfloor, others are fixed with panel pins, and some use special clips. The mosaics are the least expensive and the easiest to fit, and are widely available. (They're basically the offcuts from other types of floorings.) The panels, usually 300 mm square and containing fingers of wood, are laid at right angles to each other in groups of four to form a basket pattern.

Wood blocks are made from solid blocks of wood, and are much more of a substantial covering than the rest. They're therefore most hard-wearing, and costly unless they're laminated, rather like a plywood construction, and only the top layer is made of hardwood.

I think wood strip offers a good compromise in price, quality and looks. It comes in a variety of widths, some similar to traditional flooring, others much narrower. This too is either made of solid timber or laminated.

Laminated floor coverings are coated either with lacquer or PVC and are therefore easier to maintain, but some solid wood coverings come unfinished, that is to say they need sanding and sealing, and waxing or varnishing. So check before you buy. Once a floor is properly sealed and finished, maintainance amounts to an occasional wipe over with a damp cloth. (My wife wouldn't agree.)

When you come to order wooden floor covering, it is wise to allow around five per cent extra for wastage, from cutting around awkward shapes.

Summer

Garden Paths

'Doctor, I'm afraid she's gone crazy, paving.'

It's all very well talking, dreaming about making the garden 'another room', an extension of the house, and so on. Of course, this is all possible. But be realistic, for goodness sake. The pretty pictures you see in the hedonist mags aren't for people who have got to do it themselves because they can't hire a safari-suited 'garden consultant'.

Like many aspects of DIY, fancy paving, patios and pergolas are not all that difficult, as long as you really want them. But remember it's quite heavy work and the more you do in terms of garden building, the less space you'll have for the traditional uses like growing things (which for busy people may not, after all, be such a bad thing). Although it could be considered to be nothing more than tragic vandalism to pave a small urban back garden from wall to wall, most home owners would rather sit in the sun than work in it.

But before you drive off to your garden centre for an axle-breaking load of paving stones, do some rudimentary surveying. A plan sketch of your house and 'grounds' on the back of an envelope will solve a lot of problems before they manifest themselves.

If you plan a patio, check things like the where the sun shines most on the garden and where it rises and falls. A site facing south or west is usually best, but this could mean that your paved sitting-out area might not be in the conventional position outside the back door, but in the top left-hand corner instead. This would mean planning for a communicating path, and maybe a honeysuckle-clad pergola to give a modicum of privacy from next-door observers.

Consider too the prevailing wind; this could be an interesting consideration if you'd like to incorporate a built-in barbecue. And where are the dustbin and washing line going to go? Sort it all out on graph paper and produce a scaled drawing which will enable you to buy sufficient, but not too much, of the materials I'll now discuss.

Concrete is probably the most versatile and cheapest garden-building stuff. It's best used as a solid and durable base for other, more attractive things like ornamental flagstones, clay or brick pavers or crazy paving, which can indeed be maddeningly difficult to piece together.

Concreting also involves quite a lot of hard labour, in preparing the site and in mixing, laying and finishing the surface. Don't attempt to mix a large amount by hand; it will half-kill you. Hire an elecric mixer. And if there's a lot of work to do, ready-mixed concrete is the answer. Of course it is all delivered in one alarming gush, and you'll need more than two willing, and fit, helpers to lay it before it sets.

There are only two basic mixes to use for DIY work. Paths will need a mix of one part cement, two parts sand and three parts coarse aggregate, which gives bulk and strength to concrete. Aggegrate, sometimes called ballast, is stone crushed to a consistent size of particle; in this case three-eighths of an inch. The other mix, one part cement to three of sand, is perfect for paving that is less than 2 in thick, and for bedding down paving slabs.

Natural stone slabs, such as York, are undoubtedly the most attractive, heavy and expensive; better choose precast paving in something like a Cotswold blend, which may sound mock horrible, but in fact looks quite nice once it has weathered a little. Avoid self-coloured slabs, they soon fade quite appallingly.

Flagstones, pavers and crazy paving can all be laid in a mortar bed (that's concrete mix with a stoneless aggregate but if they're going to support heavy loads, like a car, they must be put on a concrete base.

Both types can be laid over an old concrete base that is in good condition, but beware of raising the level so much that it rises above the damp-proof course of the house. It goes without saying that all patios and other impervious flat areas next to the building must slope slightly away from it.

If there's a cracked concrete base already there, then I'm afraid it must be broken up, but use the bits as hardcore, well compacted, for a new sub-base. Hire a Kango hammer to do this. Don't try to prove anything to yourself with a pick-axe. A sub-base should be 50 mm deep for a path, and twice as deep for a car-carrying drive. You can also lay flagstones or interlocking pavers for a path or patio on a bed of sand.

Different types of pavers have varying laying instructions, but you'll certainly need to hire a plate vibrator with which to bed them down solidly. The flagstones then need to be pointed with a fairly dry mortar mix, which can be forced down the spaces without staining the stonework.

Gravel paths and drives are the easiest alternative for flat surfaces. Gravel also gives that country-house scrunchy noise (much despised by burglars) and is easy work. Spread rounded pea gravel 50 mm deep on hard-core base containing at least a 150 mm layer of hardcore which is covered with a thin layer of sand. You'll need to edge the path with some form of stone edging or preservative-treated timber.

Gravel is usually delivered when you're out shopping, and

dumped in a huge pile on the road outside. Barrow it in, tip it out and rake it level. Gravel needs regular weedkilling treatments and raking, and keep a few sacks of it in reserve for filling in patches caused by settlement.

Tarmacadam, black or red and perhaps made more interesting with coloured chippings laid into it, makes a reliable enduring flat surface, but it has to be supplied in two hot coats, each of which are rolled. This is really a specialist job. Find a member of the British Aggregate Construction Materials Industry in the *Yellow Pages* under asphalt contractors.

Garden Ponds

The sight and sound of moving water can make a rather dull, small garden, or even dingy backyard, into a pleasurable retreat on the long hot summer evenings. Frankly, I'm such a hopeless gardener, I consider green-fingeredness to be something akin to a conspiracy enjoined by millions of others each week through secret signals given out by Mr Clay Jones. Yet one of my 'gardens' once appeared in a very glossy magazine as an example of urban slum gentrification. The trickle of water on a few polished pebbles cost £20, but sold the house to the first viewer who was, incidentally, Chinese.

Don't be discouraged by the prospect of digging out huge heaps of soil, it just isn't necessary or desirable; this is a pond for people who want to enjoy its pleasures this month, not next year.

Ideally, the pond should be sited in a sunny position, away from trees and bushes, otherwise you'll spend a lot of time clearing it of fallen leaves.

As electrical fountain pumps are the the best, and probably most practical, way of moving water around, your hole in the ground has obviously got to be deep enough in one part at least to submerge the pump's casing, and in any case not shallower than 15 in.

So first buy your pump; the smallest submersible, something like an Otter, delivers about 200 gal an hour, which sounds an enormous amount, but of course it's the same water that's being continuously recirculated. A fountain cascade produced from an outside source will, apart from being horrendously (and illegally) wasteful of water, will continually disturb the biological balance of a pool, and water will remain forever cloudy.

The pump is simply placed in the pool and connected by waterproof cable to the mains electricity supply, about which more later. The pump, deftly hidden by a pile of rocks, or similar, can then be positioned either with its outlet spout just below the surface, or, only if you really, really must, be connected to the umbilicus of 'The Grecian Water Carrier'.

There are lots of smashing, cheap, non-naff alternatives. You could for example cast your own 'millstone' using an old shallow plastic washing-up bowl. Use a one-to-three mix of cement and sand and a layer of chippings atop the wet mixture will add an attractive surface, which will also will 'weather' more quickly. Place a wooden dowel, wrapped in a bit of polythene, through the middle. When the 'mill-stone' is set, this can be replaced with a piece of piping retrieved from a skip.

There are two simple ways of ensuring the water stays in the hole you've dug. Buy a moulded glass-fibre pool, which can look tremendous when set carefully among rocks, but otherwise these inevitably commit you to digging down to the necessary depth. The edges of a glass-fibre pond are simply hidden by an overhang of edging slabs or flat rocks – the water level is of course kept just below these. Glass-fibre ponds are the more expensive option, but they can be bought with 'shelves' for marginal water plants, and they're less likely to leak.

Alternatively you can quite simply line the hole in the ground with a tough liner made either of butyl synthetic rubber or terylene reinforced PVC. This way you can make a pond of any shape – experiment with shapes beforehand by moving a length of tope or garden hose around. Once you've settled on a shape, mark it out with pegs and string. Don't be tempted to use ordinary thick polythene sheeting such as that used for damp-proof membranes in concrete floors. They quickly deteriorate in sunlight.

Flexible liners can be repaired if they leak, but it's better to take precautions against punctures by laying them on a few inches of sand spread over the bottom of the hole in the ground. To find the size of liner you need, simply measure the maximum length and maximum width of the hole, adding double the maximum depth figure to each of these dimensions.

Pool pumps run on a low voltage, which gives you a choice. You can run a mains voltage supply to somewhere near the pool, and connect this to a transformer, which definitely must be securely mounted in a waterproof enclosure. Or you can fit the transformer inside the house, garage or shed, and then run the low-voltage cable from there to the pump.

The cable must either be buried in its entirety, at least 500 mm beneath the surface to guard against them being damaged by digging, or run along a (solid) wall before being put underground. The best type of cable to use is known as MICC or 'Pyro-safe', an orange-coloured, three-core, copper-clad, mineral-insulated armoured cable. Armoured cable needs special glands which enable it to be fitted into rocket outlet boxes. This is a job a competent electrician would take only minutes to do as he should have a special tool for stripping back the copper cladding. 'Pyro-safe comes in ready-made lengths which cannot be cut. You'll probably find it easier to use ordinary PVC cable, threaded into a tough, rigid PVC conduit.

Wiring for an outside outlet is simply taken from an existing socket inside the house. This is done by knocking out one of the blanks in the back of the existing outlet box and drilling a hole through to the outside. (When you drill a hole in an outside wall to take a cable, always dangle it slightly down, and cement the PVC conduit in place to protect the cable.)

The new outside cable can then be taken as a spur from the existing socket's terminals. If you're using ordinary PVC cable in a PVC conduit outside, ensure the edges of the knocked-out hole are protected with a rubber grommet, and the cable exit hole is sealed with a flexible, weatherproof mastic. However, you will be able to do this only if the socket outlet itself is not a spur or feeding a spur. The alternative is to take the power from the most convenient junction box, or fused connect unit wired into the ring.

As in all electrical work, safety is paramount. Switch off at the mains before starting, and if you have any doubts about how to do it, don't. Pay an electrician.

Specialists in aquatic plants have lengthy and detailed catalogues you can browse through, but basically if you want fish (frogs from tadpoles are more interesting and a good deal cheaper) you must have submerged oxygenators to absorb the carbon monoxide, keeping the fish healthy and the water clear.

There are several hardy varieties of pretty water lilies to give fish shade, but you must also put in some floating aquatics which, although not very decorative, provide fish dinners and keep algae in check. Avoid duckweed; it spreads sensationally in warm weather, and needs constant purges.

Electricity for Gardens and Sheds

'*I'm going out to read in the garden.*'

A power supply outside the home can make an enormous difference in terms of convenience, comfort, safety and security. No need for trailing extension leads for mowers and power tools, straining to read the last of *Guardian Weekend*, or fumbling for your simmering G&T on a humid evening. And when visitors or burglars come to call in the dark nights to come, they'll either be surprised or horrified as automatic lights click on.

It's quite easy to extend the house wiring to add power sockets and lights, but swot up on electrical work in one of the many detailed electrical DIY booklets available and *switch off* before you start. You might forgive me for stating what should be the obvious, but I'd rather be tedious than tried for conspiracy in person-slaughter.

Getting the electricity out of the house was described in the last section; basically, you run a spur extension from an existing power socket, or junction box, out through a hole in the wall to a weatherproof outdoor outlet which has a switch.

There are numerous types of outlet available, and the industrial ones you buy in electrical wholesalers are the best, because they have their own built-in RCD (residual current device), which is absolutely essential. RCDs provide additional protection to the fuse and earth and will immediately cut off the power if a cable is cut. They're much more expensive than plainer types, and you'll also have to buy plugs designed for their use. But I wouldn't consider anything else for outdoor use.

You can of course get an RCD adaptor which fits between the plug and socket; however, the best, but most expensive, safeguard of all would be an RCD incorporated in a new consumer unit, fitted by your electricity board.

There is now an interesting selection of sympathetic garden illuminations, light years away from the apalling colours which jaundiced faces and turned barbecued sausages green. For lighting *only* you can take a 1 mm twin and earth from the most convenient junction box or looped-in ceiling rose to the outside light via a new junction box concealed in a floor void above a ceiling, or in the loft.

You will recognise a looped-in ceiling rose (as opposed to one at the end of the circuit) by the three red and three black wires entering it. The last rose on a circuit has only two red and two black wires. Do not connect your new spur into the terminal which has only one black and one red wire – those are to the light switch.

The convenience of running outdoor lighting from a power socket is somewhat lessened because it's essential to incorporate into the circuit a fused connection, fitted with a 3 amp fuse. However, the fused connection can incorporate a light switch inside the house, which may be more convenient and will of course make a more expensive weatherproof switch unncessary.

The same wiring techniques, through a fused connection unit, apply to the excellent friend-welcoming/burglar-deterrent passive infra-red sensors which react to the body heat of a person approaching a house, and will flood the front or back (or both) with a very bright light.

You could, using this method of wiring, connect several lights around the exterior of your building. But two considerations: most of these halogen lights are intended to be dazzlingly bright, and some of the less expensive mail-order models, which incorporate both PIR censor and light, and which aren't that brilliantly illuminating, have poor-quality photo-electric cells which can quite quickly fail under normal use.

Power to a detached garage, greenhouse or shed instantly enhances their value, as long as you go for both light and power while you're at it. You will, though, have to have an extra circuit, protected by an RCD, wired right back to the consumer unit. You will make a considerable saving by using PVC cable inside the house and connecting it with an interior junction box to the exterior armoured carrier. This circuit will normally be a radial type, using 2.4 mm twin and earth cable protected by a 20 amp fuse at the consumer unit.

But why not provide for decent heating in a garage or workshop by spending (quite a bit) more on 4 mm twin and earth, guarded with a 30 amp fuse? If the outbuilding is more than around 15 m away, you will need even larger cable to prevent a drop in the voltage.

Power supplies to any outbuilding must never be run from a socket outlet on an outside wall. The armoured cable (MICC or Pyro-safe) coming outside the house and down into a trench must be buried at least 500 mm deep. If you consider using the trench for pipes to a new outside water supply for a garden tap, near the garage or greenhouse, you'll need to go down to at least 750 mm to avoid winter freezing. Plain PVC-sheathed cable can be run overhead if the outbuilding is close to the house. It must be at a minimum height of 3.5 m over a walk-way or 5.2 m over a drive, and if the overhead length or span is more than 3 m it must be hung from a supporting catenary wire, which itself is earthed.

The cable inside the garage or shed then goes into a small

two-way consumer unit with a 15 amp fuse or ideally an MCB, for power sockets, and a 5 amp fuse for the lights.

Ring circuit wiring inside the outbuilding provides power to the sockets, and a junction box makes easy work of the lighting circuit.

It might be suggested to you by 'know-alls', who invariably appear on the garden fence at the sound of anyone else's activity, that as an alternative to having different lighting and socket circuits, you could allow more loading for the sockets by using a 'one-way' switchfuse unit, and then running the lighting from fused connectors. Well, of course you can, but if a fuse blows, you'll be left totally in the dark.

Protect vulnerable cable runs with PVC or metal conduit, and afford the extra cost of metal sockets. The best light switches are, by far, the pull-cord ones you'd use in a bathroom. They're fixed at ceiling height, and out of the way – it's all too easy to absentmindedly come in out of the garden with wet hands and get a nasty shock from wall-switches.

The best lighting for outbuildings is the flourescent light fittings, usually available free, or for a few pounds' 'drink', from skips outside offices or commercial buildings that are being refurbished. Don't rely on fluorescents if you're using a lathe; their flickering is a bad combination with a fast-revolving work-piece. Skip-given fittings may need a new starter switch, which is an inexpensive plug-in gadget, but always buy new lighting tubes, as used ones are uneconomical to run. Anyway, you might not like pink lighting.

Pests

Uninvited guests are a pest, particularly when they seriously damage furniture, smell, and don't know when to go. You may have instantly thought of a name but I am in fact describing animal creepy-crawlies. What used to be a strictly warm season problem – from about May to September – has by virtue of domestic heating systems become a constant potential nuisance.

Of course there are a number of basic precautions to take to stop pests getting into the house. Seal gaps around pipes where they pass through a wall and put mastic sealant around window frames. Ensure all rooms are well-aired and there's no persistent damp. If you intend storing clothes for any length of time, have them cleaned first; moth larvae will thrive on the most minute traces of food.

And of course keep food covered when it's out of the fridge – flies leave their vomit and excreta behind in the form of black spots. Seal all domestic refuse in bin bags, and regularly clean out the drains, to ensure they are not blocked.

Remember that some household pests, cockroaches and rats, for example, can carry life-threatening diseases. But the proprietary 'killer' solutions or even their vapours can be equally dangerous to children, pets and the ozone. I recommend to you *C for Chemicals; Chemical Hazards and how to Avoid them* by Michael Birkin and Brian Price (published by Green Print, ISBN 1 85425 027 2). This £4.99 paperback lists most of the chemicals you may confront. But in any case read the manufacturer's information thoroughly before using pesticides.

There are about 30 species of ant in Britain, but only the black or garden ant (which is dark brown) is a regular house-caller in the spring and summer. The worker ants, which are around 5 mm long, will come looking for sweet or fatty things along a well-defined path from a nest often hidden beneath a large stone or path. At the height of visitation the path will resemble the M25 (anytime), so trace it back to, and pour boiling water over, the nest. If this doesn't work, block their point of entry with cotton wool soaked in paraffin. Some proprietary products will be taken back into the nests and will kill the whole colony.

Your house may be squeaky clean, but that old piece of furniture you've bought might harbour bedbugs or woodworm. Bedbugs can hide in cracks in the floor and wall, or underneath the loose edges of wallpaper. They're tiny (5 mm); so too are the marks they make on human skin after early breakfasting on blood. They can be killed by an insecticidal aerosol such as Rentokil Insectrol, although the local Environmental Health Department may help with serious cases of infestation.

Woodworm, the grub of the furniture beetle, is a much deadlier attacker because it can literally start eating your house. Don't panic, it takes its time (it is estimated that over half the houses in Britain have it somewhere). The grub appears accompanied by the familiar holes and tell-tale mounds of what looks like sawdust. The trouble is, woodworm often attacks the under-side of floorboards, and so will go un-noticed.

Small areas in furniture can be treated with proprietary fluid; softwoods can be liberally sprayed but hardwoods need an injection into the wormholes every 4 in or so; the fluids come with a thin nozzle specially designed for this. But if you find infestation in structural beams, call in professionals; choose a reputable company which will give you a free, but firm quote, and which is likely to be around when the guarantee runs out in, typically, 30 years' time.

Do not confuse the cockroach with the harmless black beetle. The former thrives in the right combination of food and warmth and can carry diseases such as typhoid and gastroenteritis. They have a distinctive scuttling motion and an equally ugly smell when they're disturbed under cookers, behind refrigerators and under heating pipes. They emerge after dark and can be very difficult to eradicate. Spray the roaches themselves and their routes, nooks and crannies with an insecticide. If there are no children or pets around to touch it, sprinkle boric acid powder to stop the cockroaches returning. This is a slow, inexpensive, but sure, deterrent.

Boric acid, mixed with a little sugar, will also catch the small, cigar-shaped silverfish which appear in damp areas of the house such as the bathroom. They love the taste of starch, glue and, consequently, books.

Flies can carry over 30 different diseases, and the methods of their prevention are pretty obvious – not leaving uncovered food around, and so on. But if they swarm around your dustbin, wash it down with hot water, allow it to dry and sprinkle soap powder inside, along with some mothballs. Put a few drops of oil of lavender on settling points like window sills – they hate it. Fly killer strips or papers are effective for an instant, non-atmospheric defensive, but some are unsuitable for rooms used by children or elderly people.

Common and German wasps come in the late summer. The odd one is little more than a nusiance, and can be dispatched with the help of a squirt of hair spray. They usually nest underground, and remain out of harm's way unless disturbed. A wasp nest discovered in the attic or in a cavity wall should not be tampered with under any circumstances. Call your local environmental people for advice.

House and field mice can carry salmonella, and their droppings will infect food. They'll chew through most things, including food packets, papers and electricty cables. They are also fast breeders, so deal with them as quickly as possible. A cat is best, and if you haven't got one, borrow one. There is also a wide variety of humane traps – but you'll probably need many more than you think and ideally set every 5 ft or so along a run. Bait traps with chocolate or nuts. Mice hate cheese.

Rats also carry an extremely serious health risk and they'll gather anywhere where rubbish has been allowed to pile up. They thrive in existing Victorian sewers. There are many poisonous rat baits available, but the local authority rat catcher is safest and best. Councils have a duty under the Prevention of Damage by Pests Act to keep their area free of vermin, and also have powers to deal with insects where they represent a health risk. Some urban services are free, but you are unlikely to get a guarantee that the pests won't return.

Warning: leave spiders alone; it's well-known they like flies, and they will also deal with a variety of unwelcome pests.

Renovating Bathrooms

The change in the householder's perception of the bathroom as a place of relaxation, or even sybaritic retreat, rather than the austere, pipe-ridden chamber of horrors confined in its use to the Puritan tradition of ablutions seems to have taken an inordinately long time.

A bathroom remains usually the most neglected room in the house, probably because of the belief that its fixtures are indeed very fixed and changing them would be a major and costly job. It ain't necessarily so. Big discount superstores like B&Q will sell you a bath, pedestal basin and toilet package, including all the taps, waste and fittings for around £300. Their Maturin suite, for example, is offered in five colours, if you count white.

So, even though the acrylic bath might scratch and mark quite easily and without great cleaning care won't keep its new look long, it is light and easy to handle on a DIY basis (a luxury cast-iron version takes at least three strong men to heave upstairs). And for that price you will have a complete bright and shiny new bathroom for a lot less than some firms would charge for a pair of taps.

Before you decide on any new bathroom, ask yourself exactly what fittings and what kind of plumbing you'll need. You may have to make provision for very young or old people (both classes need to turn taps easily, as well as accessible storage and sturdy safety handles). And you may even have enough room to build in a washing machine – after all you've got all the water and drainage services almost literally on tap, and it makes adequate sense to fling dirty washing directly in the machine rather than on the floor or in a basket.

Measure the room, transfer the dimensions onto graph paper and, using scaled templates of the various fittings, see if they can be re-arranged in a more convenient and comfortable pattern, bearing in mind what architects, and Department of the Environment guidelines (no, there is no escape from bureaucracy) call the 'activity area', the amount of space needed around each fitment.

Basins need a 1000 mm wide by 700 mm deep area behind the bowl, toilets 800 mm wide by 600 mm deep. Baths, with rather more elbow/drying room allowed, need 1100 mm by 700 mm, while shower trays enclosed on three sides need a 900 mm wide by 700mm deep drying space. The depth can be reduced to 400 mm if the tray is set into a corner. These are minimum dimensions for comfortable use, so be practical, don't get caried away by the glossy colour magazine adverts.

Do you really need a much bigger bath? There's no point in it if it impinges into the available space too much, and you'd probably be better off leaving space for a shower unit or bidet. Of all these considerations, drainage is the most important and problematical to alter – hot and cold supplies pipes are, or should be, in slim 15 mm copper which can run, hidden, practically anywhere, unless you're in a basement flat with a solid concrete floor. In this case you can box them in on the surface (usually an ugly solution), cover them with a special greasy protective tape and channel them into the walls or give in and retain them in their present positions. I've seen them quite effectively painted in a starkly contrasting colour in what some builders call 'making a feature' of them.

There's no problem with the bath waste, as it's hidden under the bath panels, but waste for a shower tray must have a 'fall', however slight, dropping, hidden, below the floor level, otherwise soap deposits and hair will soon block it. (This is an excellent case, of course, for installing a shower over a bath).

You really shouldn't hack a waste space into a solid floor – it could, amongst other things, breach its damp-course. The difficulty with timber floors is that if the joists run across, or at right angles to, the proposed new waste, you can't remove sufficient wood for it without seriously weakening the floor structure. If you can't, run the shower waste in the same direction as the joists, not forgetting that any waste needs to slope slightly downwards along its length. If you have a concrete or other solid floor, the only solution is to build a platform under which all the pipes, both service and waste, can be hidden.

There are also restrictions on the maximum length of waste pipes to the house soil stack, known universally to plumbers as the stink pipe. The biggest problem involves the 100 mm diameter toilet waste, and you'd be advised to keep the WC in its original position. There are solutions involving devices like macerators, which break down solid waste but these add considerably both to cost and breakdown potential.

Ideally, bathroom fittings should all be bought at once – easy in a super-store, but a little fraught if the local bathroom shop hasn't got the complete set, and can only 'guarantee' (hope) they'll get it in the 'next few days'. It's obviously best to choose all the fittings from the same manufacturer, but if you are tempted by special offers on single pieces of sanitaryware, don't risk trying to match what looks like a similar shade, for even whites differ considerably. Mixing co-ordinating colours is only really successful with the pastel shades and this can produce a novel designer-look at a bargain price.

Another possible economy would be to choose a cheaper suite, but spend the extra on a good thermostatic shower or a bidet. Alternatively, you could buy an expensive suite, but the cheapest possible taps or mixers (sometimes called bath-fillers), replacing them as soon as affordable with the latest ceramic disk type which last a long time and operate at the flick of a wrist, which is marvellous for young weak, or old rheumy, wrists. Good taps are very expensive; as an example, top-of-the-range ceramic discs could cost over £100 for the washbasin alone. On the other hand, smart new taps may be all you need to brighten up a dull, but perfectly serviceable, bathroom suite.

Bathroom Fittings

There's an enormous and bewildering choice of bathroom fittings, and just choosing a suite could be one of the biggest problems. It might be tempting to pick one of the latest fashionable colours, but remember you may never revamp your bathroom again. Select a colour which is easy on the eye, even erring on the side of being unremarkable. Dramatic deep purples, blacks and vivid primary colours may at first thrill you with their novelty, but could offend a depressingly long line of prospective buyers.

The now rather tired perennials, avocado, sand and so on have been supplemented by softer pastel shades. If you really longed for something more dramatic, be consoled with the thought that pastels show hard-water scum marks much less than the novelty colours. Alternatively, choose anything as long as it's white, which is invariably less expensive and more available. You will always be able to pick up dominant colours comparatively inexpensively with tiles, towels, floor coverings or accessories like roller blinds.

There's a still only a rather limited number of basic materials to choose from. Washbasins, toilets and bidets come in vitreous china, which is hard, strong and simple to keep clean, but ceramics are also easy to crack or chip, so check for defects if they are delivered and take extra care in their fitting. Cast iron makes the strongest, most rigid and durable baths but these are extremely heavy, and therefore not the best for DIY. Vitreous enamelled pressed steel, also strong but not as rigid, is also used for vanity basins and shower trays. It is lighter, but also quite easy to chip or damage. Stainless steel bathroom suites are still occasionally available. But again they are such an unusual option that they could be abhorrent to a potential buyer.

There has been some exciting progress in the use of plastics, both in bath colours and shapes. The newer plastics also have the bonus that the colour goes right through the material, making scratches less of a problem, though cleaners recommended by the manufacturer must be used. Plastics are warm to the touch and the easiest to handle, particularly if you're fitting a suite yourself. But they're also pretty flexible and need fixing in a solid timber frame and/or substantial chipboard bases with metal supports to stop them moving in use.

If space saving is a vital priority, consider replacing the standard 1700 mm (5 ft 7 in) bath with one of the much smaller 'sitz' or continental soak-tub versions. This could give you room for a separate shower, bidet or a substantial storage cupboard. Armitage Shanks' Moritz is, at 1394 mm by 797 mm (4 ft 7 in by 2 ft 7 in) about the smallest, and costs around £240, although there are other makes, which are only inches bigger but less expensive.

Corner baths may seem to take up a lot of space, but in fact the smallest models offer more bathing space per wall area than conventional baths, and may be ideal for fitting at the end of a long, narrow room. They're more difficult to screen off if you want to install an over-bath shower, and it's also awkward having to reach across into the corner for cleaning purposes.

Washbasins are most often wall or pedestal mounted – the latter have the advantage of concealing all the pipe-work, but the former can be hung at any height – good news for the long and the short of them all. There are also corner basins, and ones that can be semi-recessed into a wall, but these are often too small for anything but occasional cloakroom use. Buy the biggest you have space for – water slops out of the modishly shallow saucer basins, making even hair shampooing a messy business.

Vanity basin cabinets obviously take up more floor space, but the storage they provide is a big compensation. They're angular and pretty unattractive and the price of manufactured units seems ridiculous when you can inexpensively devise your own out of a 500 mm kitchen base unit. Use a jig-saw to form the hole for the basin in an off-cut of (kitchen) worksurface usually available, free, from most neighbouring skips where builders are fitting a new kitchen.

Enamelled cast-iron baths which are badly stained are none-theless well worth rehabilitation, because they're super hard-wearing, the best at water heat retention and also very expensive to replace. The classic roll-tops are much in demand by skip-scavengers who sell them on to dealers in 'nostalgia' bathrooms. But bear in mind that their sometimes tapered shape makes them difficult to side-panel. You'll have to buy similar 'period-style' basins, and so on, to match, and these reproductions are usually more expensive than the modern lines.

Cast-iron tubs are almost always white, and chips can be repaired by bath enamel paint. To refurbish the entire bath you'll need about 10 fl oz (285 ml) of enamel. Remove the chain from the waste cover and wash the bath down with hot water and washing up liquid. Rub the surface down with wet-and-dry paper, frequently dipped in water until the surface is really smooth, clear up all the dust, rinse and dry off. Rinse again with white spirit and dry again. Apply the enamel paint as thinly as possible with a medium, flat varnish brush, using long cross-strokes to avoid runs.

Paint the bottom first, then the sides and rim. Leave over-night. Apply a second coat and leave for another 48 hours. Replace the chain and fill the bath with cold water for another 48 hours. During the first week back in use run some cold water in before the hot. This process is, in fact, repainting, and not re-enamelling, and the new surface won't last years. But it only costs a few pounds. Professional re-enamelling companies will do it for you, at a price, and they'll also give you a guarantee, usually a year. It's worth trying to renovate a grand old bath, for the horrendous alternative involves breaking it up into manageable pieces with a sledge hammer, just to get it out of the house. If you are faced with this sad task, be sure to wear proper eye- and face-protection, heavy gloves and clothing – and ear defenders. It's a very noisy business.

Bathroom floor covering is, of course, governed entirely by the room's users. Purpose-made shaggy waterproof-backed carpets are a luxurious option for an adults-only home, but kids would quickly convert it into a bedraggled soaking mess. Far better to choose one of the sheet vinyl or cushion-floor coverings which come in a range of super patterns and colours and are easy to fit. Ceramic floor tiles look good as long as long as they're laid on a perfectly flat sub-floor, made of a suitably water-proofed boarding which, incidentally, is also a suitable remedy for uneven floors of any sort, particularly when you want to lay a quite expensive covering.

You'll save yourself a lot of tedious tours of bathroom shops if you narrow your targets by sending for information on manufacturers of cast iron and steel baths from the British Bath Manufacturers' Association, Fleming House, Renfrew Street, Glasgow G3 6TG. Tel: 041 332 0826. The Council of British Ceramic Sanitaryware Manufacturers, Federation House, Stoke on Trent, Staffs ST4 2RT, also offer a postal-only information service.

Heating, Extractors and Lighting for Bathrooms

Completely remodelling a bathroom offers you the opportunity to refine the various important elements which will make the final difference to the new room. Skimp on improved heating, ventilation, insulation and lighting, and you might as well not have bothered buying that streamlined new suite in the first place. Few places are as cheerless as a cold, dank bathroom on a winter's morning, and good heating – a minimum of 72°F – will also combat condensation.

If the bathroom is on the same central heating run as the house, then consider replacing the usual single-panel radiator with a double-panel finned or convector radiator with a towel rail over it. This is great heater in the winter but leaves you a problem with drying towels in the summer when the central heating system is resting. You can solve this by having the bathroom radiator fed off the hot water supply to the bathroom. But this only works satisfactorily if the hot-water cylinder is in or very close to the bathroom.

Perhaps the best all-year-round solution would be a radiator *and* an electrically-heated towel rail. (Alone, the latter would lend some ambient heat to a very small bathroom). Manufacturers like Myson make several radiator/towel rail combination models; there are of course the latest 'designer' towel radiators which incorporate a detachable telescopic drying rack that prevents wet towels from mopping up all the heat. Unfortunately, the prices also tend to be 'designer', but for about a fiver you can buy a clip-on towel rail.

Wall-mounted fan heaters are much more efficient than infra-red heaters which take ages to have any effect. Fan heaters generally come in heater/light combinations. Mounted above a mirror, they will keep it free from condensation. But remember, as with all things electric in a bathroom, they *must* be connected to a fused connection, and not to a socket outlet (which is in any case illegal in a bathroom), and they must not be in the reach of someone using the bath or shower. They also *must* be operated by a pull-cord switch. You could fit a gas heater, but it would have to have a balanced flue fixed to an outside wall. Frankly, not worth the hassle of rerouting a gas supply, unless you really have no alternative.

Baths and showers produce huge quantities of moisture vapour, which calls for lots of ventilation – a minimum of six complete air changes an hour. You could always open the window – in the summer of course. An extractor fan is therefore essential. Building regulations make one mandatory if there is no window. A good fan will not only remove moisture-laden air, but replace it by drawing in air from adjoining rooms, rather than cold draughts from outside.

It is vital to buy a fan giving the correct performance for the room size and so prevent excessive air extraction and consequent heat loss. Discover the volume of the room in cubic metres or feet (length by width by height), and multiply by the number of air changes per hour needed, to find the correct capacity of the fan required, as shown in makers' catalogues.

It is also important to position an extractor fan correctly in order to create the best possible airflow between it and the door – the point where fresh air is drawn into the room. Avoid, if you can, putting the fan directly opposite the door as this will give only fairly effective ventilation. A diagonal airflow across the room is best and the position of windows should not inhibit you doing this as most models can be wall- or window-mounted.

Personally, I prefer the wall-mounted fans; they look neater and I think it's a lot easier to take out a couple of bricks than cut a hole in the middle of a window. If you agree, choose a fan with a centrifugal impeller, (the inside looks a bit like a water-wheel). This is more expensive than the alternative axial impeller – rather noiser too – but extracts air at much greater pressure, works better against back-draughts and has the power to suck air through the ducting you'll have to put through the wall to the outside.

Extractor fans can also be fixed to the ceiling (of a top-floor bathroom), and vented into a ventilated space which must, in turn, have good access to the outside. This usually means using quite long lengths of ducting to channel the steam out of the house in order to overcome the building's atmospheric resistance, which would otherwise affect the output of the fan.

Extractor fans are no more costly than a light-bulb to run, but don't buy the cheapest, which are single-speed, manually-switched by pull-cord and designed for extraction only. Pay a little more for one which is wired into the light switch and stays on for 15 minutes or so after the light has been turned off. More expensive versions have a humidity control – a humidistat – which switches the fan on and off automatically, adjusting its speed according to the bathroom's humidity. The electrical wiring for fans, heaters, lights and possibly an electric shaver point, can very easily be hidden behind wooden tongue-and-groove softwood panelling on a wall and/or the ceiling.

T&G is simply fixed on a network of 2 in by 1 in battens running the opoosite way to the panelling. It will hide problem walls and there'll be no need to replaster surfaces which you've damaged by installing the fan or replumbing. Its great benefit will be in providing 'warm' surfaces to compensate for tiled walls, and it will very effectively reduce condensation. I like wood, but if you don't, or think it clashes with the colour of the bathroom suite or whatever, there are UPVC versions of T&G in a wide range of colours.

You can also get laminate-faced cladding boards which are also waterproof but these are not quite as good as wood in lessening condensation and, because of their size, are rather more difficult to fix. They too are tongued and grooved at the edges, and can replace tiling in bath and shower areas. There are also translucent 'illuminated ceilings', as used in chip shops.

If the bathroom is particularly cold, maybe an extension with three outside walls or a northerly aspect, 'warm' the walls by dry-lining them with insulating plasterboard before the fittings are installed, and think about double-glazing the window. A T&G cladding on a ceiling will enable you to incorporate sleek new light fittings, instead of the usual centre light. Remember, they must all be 'splashproof' – suitable for bathroom use – and have competely enclosed lampholders. Down-lighters look best. Either flush into the ceiling above various fitments or install the 'eyeball' kind, which can be directed to throw a soft wash of light on chosen areas. You could also fit a strip light incorporating a shaver point, over the basin mirror.

Preparation for Showers

Why is the British shower generally such a piddling disappointment? Some of the rubber tap attachments seen in otherwise well-ordered households are truly pathetic. Could it be that for too long, a shower-bath (as it was rather quaintly known into the fifties) has been aligned in our subconscious as something unpleasant, at best cathartic, and cold.

Wallowing in a warm bathful of millions of pieces of your own skin's detritus – among other unattractive additives – can't be be that healthy. Pig's don't do it. Besides, a long soak plays havoc with your waterproofing keratin and oily secretions, increases measurable skin flora, allowing microbial guests to gather into populations of over three million per square centimetre in your most hospitable zones.

Still not sold on a shower? Then consider the speed (a few minutes) and the economies (a quarter of the amount of energy needed for heating a bath). Think it an uneconomic addition? Thirty per cent more showers were sold than baths last year. One of those punters may fancy your house one day. Showers are galloping in popularity, the fastest-growing portion of the £500 million bathroom equipment market.

The smallest home will have room for one; fitting it over the bath is an obvious space-saving option, with the benefits of *in situ* drainage, but installing one in a separate enclosure or, better still, in another room, brings its obvious morning crush-hour advantages.

You don't need a lot of space in the corner of a room, or even under the stairs – the average shower tray is between 700 mm and 900 mm square. Discount anything smaller; it's impractical. But don't get too carried away with using nooks and crannies. The plumbing has to be taken into consideration. Although it's easy to run water to a shower, long pipe-runs will seriously affect efficiency through heat and pressure loss, and will also make drainage problematic. You might as well get free advice from your local authority building control officer before you start. Building Regulations say you'll need his approval anyway.

In a two-pipe drainage system, with separate runs for WC
waste and water from baths and basins, the shower waste can
run directly into an existing hopper head (the box-like thing
atop drainpipes), or simply be directed into a gulley. A system
which combines all existing drainage in one pipe requires the
waste to be connected directly into the soil stack. Plastic stacks
usually have spare blanked-off connectors, making this an easy
job, but if a new connection is required, regulations again,
forbid its position within 200 mm of the WC inlet.

The circumference of the shower waste gets bigger as it gets
longer. Use 40 mm (one and a half inch) pipes up to 3 m, and 50
mm (2 in) thereafter. Long drainage runs are not recommended,
because they may need additional venting.

Theoretically, all shower trays connected into a one-pipe
system should have a deep-seal 75 mm trap, but as there's
usually not enough room for this, a shallower trap will do. A
shower trap will eventually get clogged up with strands of hair
and bits of soap, so mount the tray on a plinth with a removable
panel so that you can easily clear it. Some trays enable you to
reach the trap from above.

You must have good ventilation like a powered extractor
venting to the outside air, either directly through an adjacent
wall or through ducting. All internal walls must be thoroughly
waterproofed by tiles or special waterproof (not water-resistant) laminate fixed and grouted with specially-made adhesives,
sealants and so on. And of course a good fixed enclosure is
infinitely preferable to shower curtains, which invariably are
vacuumed around the bather by the downdraught of water-displaced air.

Showering can be dangerous (see also *Psycho*), so if you're
installing a shower over the bath and if there aren't already
non-slip mouldings on its base, make sure you always use a
rubber foot mat, and fix a handrail to the wall. (I once slipped
using a smooth-bottomed French-Vietnamese version, recovering consciousness some time later very headachy, and dried
soapy-stiff by the Saigon heat.) Safety glass screens are four
times more expensive than plastic, which eventually scratch and

can crack. Glass is also much easier to clean (insist on BS 6262).

The trays upon which independent shower screens are fixed come in several shapes, colours and materials, but a shower based on a simple square version fitted into a tiled corner is much easier to DIY waterproof simply because there are less screen joints to leak.

You'll be saving hundreds of pounds by doing all this yourself, so it might be worth affording one of the ready-made cubicles which come as an integrated unit incorporating a tray, screen and backing wall and with the shower mixer and handset already fixed. They're expensive, but easiest to install in a bedroom, because you don't have to do any tiling whatsoever.

The efficiency of a shower relies almost entirely on a good head of water – that is, the height between the base of the cold water cistern and the shower spray or rose. A target flow rate of around 5 l per min requires a head of 4 ft (1.2 m).

Most British domestic plumbing systems are 'indirect' – the cold water storage cistern in the loft gravity-feeds and pressurises water into the copper hot cylinder down below. But beware, showers run off such systems can suddenly run scaldingly hot if cold water is drawn off elsewhere in the home, perhaps by a washing machine or flushing a WC. You really must fit a thermostatic shower which will automatically stabilise the temperature of the water. If the head of water isn't that good, then there are alternatives, but you will, as builders say through clenched teeth, 'get involved'.

If the cistern is, as usual, in the loft, it can be raised on blocks or, better still, on a – very – stout wooden platform (you're dealing with a massive weight of water) which will lift it into the apex of the roof. Obviously this means a good deal of carpentry and plumbing work as the feed connecting pipes are also extended.

In flat roofed homes or ones with shallow-pitched roofs, or even if the cistern is slightly below the water spray, you've little alternative other than to fit an electric pump between the mixer and the shower head. Pumps are expensive, and can seize in hard water areas, so fit gate valves, which are basically in-line taps, on both the hot and cold pipes supplying the pump so that you can isolate and remove it for cleaning or maintenance, without having to drain the domestic water supply throughout the home. The Mira showers have an excellent and sympathtic technical advice service, which I've used quite a lot.

So far, I've presumed that the shower would be run off existing hot and cold water supplies on an indirect system, but some homes have a 'direct' cold water system where every cold tap is fed from the rising main. Sometimes there will also be a small storage cistern for feeding the hot water runs, or you may have a multipoint gas water heater linked to the rising main. Unless you are prepared to install a new storage cistern in the loft, you are, in these cases, rather limited to an instantaneous electric shower unit.

Installing Showers

Many people give up the idea of installing a shower, beaten hollow by the most common bug, that of insufficient water pressure. This is usually the result of a poor 'head' of water above a shower or bath and shower mixer. The solutions, including lifting the cold water storage tank into the apex of the loft space are, I admit, pretty daunting, but the latest instantaneous electric-powered showers solve a problem which obviously frustrates quite a lot of people. Two out of every three showers now sold are 'instant'.

They're not too expensive (from about £50 to £150), safe, cheap to use, and simple to operate. Current models bear little resemblance to the early versions which were both inefficiently low-powered – frequently burning-out under even moderate use, ugly, and sometimes hair-raisingly perilous, particularly in a DIY application. Water and electricity still don't mix too well, so if you are not absolutely sure of the electrical work involved, don't touch it, call in a professional, and settle for a big saving in doing the rest of the work, which is basic plumbing, yourself.

Instant showers work off the rising mains supply, rather than the cold water tank, heating the water within the unit as it passes through it. Again, unlike mixer showers, which rely on heating up a fairly full copper storage cylinder of hot water, you only pay for and heat the water you use in three or four minutes. But of course, in the normal swings and roundabouts manner of home economies, during the short time they're in use, they consume a hefty amount of electricity.

However, a caution before you rush out and buy one. If you have an old, leaden rising mains system – and thousands of houses still do – make sure the water pressure is high enough for the shower you fancy. You could otherwise be wasting a lot of time and money, unless of course you fit a new copper rising mains, lug the old lead around to a scrap merchant and make a too-frequent trivial sale. There are a lot of doctored scales around.

The minimum pressure needed is about 0.8 bar (about 12 lb per sq in), but it must not be more than 6.8 bar (100 lb psi). Water mains are usually at around 3 bar. (Incidentally, a lead mains connected to a modern system is still considered legally acceptable, although it must now be near the end of its useful life, patched so many times and looking rather like a garter snake which swallowed a rugby ball. Drinking water which lies in lead for some time will absorb toxins from it, so if you have that situation always run off a quantity of water before using it.)

The general principles of instant showers are simple. The slower the water flow, the hotter the water. This is the reason why you will probably get a disappointing performance if you choose a model of less than 7 kw or 8 kw power rating. It will just not be strong enough to give a showerhead flow which is both hot and reasonably forceful. It's also the reason why the spray is weaker in winter, for the mains water is likely to be very cold. Only the models of 8 kw and more really succeed in the considerable task of almost instantly converting icy water coming in from the road into a comfortable heat.

But even if you're cost-confined to a lesser-powered 'instant', make sure it has at least two important features. The most important is temperature stabilisation, which automatically maintains the selected water heat, even when a kitchen tap, which should also be on the rising main, is turned, starving the shower of water and surprising you with a near-scalding spray.

The other vital item is a choice of power settings, enabling you to select three-quarter-, or half-power in the summer, when the water coming into the house is relatively warm. Instant showers really come into their own in warm months, when you can abandon central heating and heat water for other domestic usage in much more economical ways.

Although the electric unit must always be fixed out of the direct line of spray, remote control models make it possible for a control panel alone to be installed in the bathing area, allowing the actual heater to be positioned somewhere else.

Instant electric shower units must have their own radial circuit, directly from the consumer unit. A shower with a current demand of up to 7.2 kw, needs a spare 30 amp fuseway, usually the one with red dots, in the consumer unit. It is prudent also to fix a miniature circuit breaker (MCB) at the meter end. Showers up to 9.6 kw need protection from a 40 amp fuse. If there is no spare way into the consumer unit, then you must get the electricity board to install a separate switched fuse unit connected to the meter by 16 mm single-core cables.

The size of cables, and the distance they will have to travel from consumer unit to shower, could be an important consideration in your decision to install this kind of shower. Wiring regulations are subject to change, and local electricity boards are constantly being updated on new technical requirements, so check with them. Currently the minimum cable size is 6 mm twin core and earth, but for a unit of 8 kw or more, you'd be safer with a 10 mm twin and earth. There's quite a difference in prices between these two cables and a long run will be expensive (a good argument for having an independent shower somewhere like under the stairs). The Electricity Council specifies that when 6 mm cable is used in conjuction with the now rather outdated rewirable fuses, it must not exceed 18 m.

When used with a modern MCB consumer unit, or cartridge fuses, a cable up to 25 m long is permitted. These hefty, flat, white PVC-sheathed cables are quite difficult to manipulate as they travel up from the meter point to the bathroom; they're certainly too unsightly to run bare on a surface. You can hide them in cable conduits and trunking, but this is awful-looking. So, this means quite a lot of floorboard and carpet-lifting. This is not too difficult, but is tedious.

If you have a new house with the dreaded (in this case) tongue and groove chipboard floors it's best to hire an electrician's chaser that forms neat slots in walls for the cable. Fit protective trunking over it before replastering. Chasing into an already tiled wall isn't a great deal of fun. Take extreme care not to crack surrounding tiles, or you'll spend a lot of time searching for matching replacement tiles. Sod's Law says they are likely to have just been discontinued.

A fitted ceiling pull-cord switch with a pilot light is, for safety reasons, also essential. It must be a double pole, 45 amp isolator. So too is 'bonding' – a protective conductor must be connected to the earth terminals throughout the circuit, beginning at the earth terminal in the consumer unit and from there to the earth terminal in the shower heater.

Indoor Tiling

Tiling seems to be one of those jobs that confound otherwise confident tyro builders. I can understand why; it's expensive and rather permanent. Make a mistake in the bathroom and you, anyway, will be hypnotised by it every tub-night for a very long time.

Yet ceramic and mosaic tiles have always been popular as a splendid way of providing a waterproof, decorative and almost everlasting finish. The difference that new tiles can make to a dull kitchen or bathroom is often quite spectacular. The job isn't that difficult, just pretty tedious. The hardest and most painstaking part is setting out the wall surface, or wherever, and deciding on the starting point. Then once the first tile, then the first row, has been set accurately in place, the rest will, given a few escape clauses of Murphy's Law, follow with pleasing speed.

You will rarely have a wall that is mathematically vertical with a true horizontal floor and ceiling line, so you need to organise the task so that the main area of wall is covered with whole tiles and the irregular edges can be filled with tiles which have been, usually, individually trimmed and cut to size.

It's a great help in planning to have a measuring staff – a reasonably long (relevant to the room size) but absolutely straight piece of wooden battening marked out in tile increments. By holding the staff horzontally and vertically you will be able to see how tiles will finish up in relation to windows, baths, sinks, shower trays and corners. If you can, centralise the tiling so that you have reasonably equal bits to be used as 'fillers' on each side of the wall.

The all-important starting point for tiling is determined by fixing a horizontal batten to the wall, at the height of one tile from the lowest point on the floor line. The batten is best fixed with masonry nails, but use a spirit level to ensure it is horizontal.

Tiles can be fixed on practically any sound, dry surface as

long as it's perfectly even. If it isn't, and you proceed anyway, even the smallest dip or bump will be amplified by the tiles. Check the surface of the wall with a long, straight-edged piece of timber. Small defects can be levelled off using plaster filler; larger hollows can be filled with Polycell's Polyplasta, which is a ready-mixed material made especially for small patches of DIY plastering.

If there are only a very few slight defects over a pretty wide area, then you may be able to lose these by using a thicker bed of tiling adhesive. But if the wall is very bad, then one course is to have it entirely replastered – *not* a DIY job, I'm afraid. This will add considerably to costs and hold up the whole project while the plaster dries out to a pinky-white colour. This could take over a month. However, as with most building problems, there is an alternative (Fanfare of Trumpets).

First plug and screw 25 mm by 20 mm wood battens to the wall – it's worth the little extra cost to buy vacuum-impregnated timber which is moisture resistant. These battens will probably have to be packed out with scraps of timber so that they present a firm foundation at 90 degrees to the floor in order to counteract the deformity of the wall.

Then you can fix exterior grades of plywood or chipboard sheets onto the battens and tile the sheets. If for some reason you can't get exterior grade boarding then both ply and chipboard will have to be coated with diluted PVA adhesive to seal them from damp. It's also possible to use blockboard and of course plasterboard, but I'd rather you didn't use the latter as it's important to get a plastering grade board, which is coloured grey on both sides, and which is not as widely available as the alternative materials, and if you're not sure what you're looking for it's easy to get the wrong sort of plasterboard.

Wallpapered surfaces will have to be stripped bare before tiling – do buy or hire a steam-stripper for this mind-boggling and awful task.

Flaking paint must also be removed, but sound paint, whether it's emulsion or gloss, will take tiles as long as the surface is sound and clean. Check for soundness by firmly sticking some Sellotape on the wall and ripping it off. A gloss-painted surface should be throughly rubbed with coarse sandpaper to provide a key for the tiling adhesive.

I've known people who were scandalously ripped off by being persuaded that old tiles had to be hacked off before new ceramics could be fixed. This used to be the case but nowadays such drastic measures are often quite unnecessary, as long as the old ceramic tiles are clean, dry and firmly stuck to the wall.

Ensure kitchen tiles are absoluely free of grease. You don't even any longer have to roughen the old tiles to provide a key for the adhesive. Most of the adhesives now available make it perfectly acceptable to stick new tiles on top of old. Scrape out dirty or loose grout with an old screwdriver or chisel. It's important to lay the new tiles so that the vertical joints do not coincide with those of the old tiles.

Any loose tiles should be refixed with adhesive. If this is not possible, because maybe the tile has cracked, then the space can be refilled with plaster or a sand and cement filler.

If, however, you do have to hack off tiles using a hammer and chisel, be very aware of the danger of flying fragments of tiles. Heavy gloves and eye protection are absolutely vital – and of course the wall will eventually have to be replastered.

If you have to retile a whole wall which has previously only been half-tiled, there will of course be a step in the middle where the old tiling finishes. If you want an entirely smooth finish, then you have no alternative other than to build out the top half of the wall to leave it level with the tiled surface. It's quite a fiddly performance to get this right – you can use suitable thicknesses of plaster or the other building boards I've already mentioned. You could also line the entire wall with the building sheets, packing out the battens to allow for the thickness of the old tiles.

Alternatively, 'make a feature' of the step between the old tiling levels and the new. This acutally doesn't turn out to be as much of a bodge as it sounds, for you could pin and glue wooden beading in either scotia or glazing bead profile to bridge the gap. Use wall panel adhesive, (Dunlop Thisofix is excellent for this). The wood must be stained and sealed beforehand. Use hardened galvanised or masonry pins through holes already predrilled in the beading.

I've just discussed the elements of a tiling project in fairly general terms; the following is intended to guide you through the details, starting with the tools you'll need. A spirit level is probably the most indispensable; it's used for setting vertical and horizontal levels and, as it is invaluable in just about every DIY task you can think of, it's worth paying extra for a shock-proof quality model.

There are various gadgets for cutting tiles and spreading the tile adhesive; they all work well and make trimming around awkward shapes quite easy. They're inexpensive enough to be discarded, for the cutting points on most of these do wear out quite quickly. Then you'll need a filling knife, a rubber-bladed grouting spreader, a steel rule, a sponge and patience.

As tiles are often placed in places where there will be a good deal of water splashing, it's not worth using any adhesive other than the specially waterproof compounds, which are buttered onto the wall and then marked with a serrated comb in order to achieve a smooth coating. Don't cover more than a square yard of wall at a time.

It is usually sufficient to base the tiling on a horizontal batten, but it's also helpful to have a vertical batten, similarly marked in the increments of the tiles, nailed to the wall. The first tile is fixed in the angle where the two battens meet. This tile, like all the ones that follow, should be pressed firmly into the adhesive with a firm, but slightly twisting, motion.

The tiles are then built up in horizontal courses, but make sure that each tile butts closely onto its predecessor. If the tiles you are using have no spacers, place two scraps of cardboard in each joint to maintain even joint lines. Success is almost guaranteed – but do make frequent checks on the horizontal and vertical planes of each course. Fix all the whole tiles you can, and leave them to set for six or seven hours before removing the battens and dealing with the tiles that have to be cut and placed around the perimeter of the wall.

If you have to tile around a window, remember it's likely to be the focal point of the room, so pay extra attention to details such as having equal-sized tiles on each side of the window. On sills and reveals – the sides of the windows – use whole tiles at the front and cut tiles nearest the window.

The edges of baths, washbasins and other fitments should be dealt with in the same way as tiling from floor level, that is, fixing a horizontal batten above the fitments while the remainder of the wall is completed.

Cutting a tile into awkward shapes is always a problem. It's best to make a template of the required shape out of cardboard and transfer this to the face of the tile. Use the template to score along the cutting line and nibble the waste away with pincers.

Accessories such as moulded soap dishes and towel rings are much too heavy to tile in with the rest, so temporarily dry-place a tile in the space where the fitment will go, fixing it with tape. It's merely acting as a spacer. When the surrounding tiles have been in place for a day, remove the spacer, butter the back of the accessory with adhesive and press it firmly into place, holding it there for 24 hours with strong tape.

Grouting, getting the neat lines between the tiles, finishes the job. It usually comes in powder form, and is mixed with water into a creamy consistency, although some adhesives also have a grouting function. Grouting is carried out some 24 hours after the tiles have been fixed. Use a squeegee to press the grout into place and remove surplus with a wet rag or sponge. Again, deal with about a square yard at a time. Draw the end of a a piece of dowel along the joints to compact the grout. After about 24 hours, polish the tiles with a damp cloth.

All gaps between the bathroom fittings or the kitchen work surface must be sealed with a silicone rubber sealant, which is applied using a sealant gun. The sealant tubes have plastic nozzles which can be cut to adjust the amount of sealant required.

Ceramic floor tiles are fixed in much the same way. Find the centre of the room by stretching intersecting strings across, and work from the centre of the room. It's really best to hire a floor tile cutter for the job. These tiles can be laid directly onto a sound, dry and flat concrete floor. Any surface cracks on a solid floor can be filled with a mortar mix of one part cement to three parts sharp sand, but uneven floors need to be treated with a self-levelling compound which is simply poured on the floor, spread with a soft floor brush and left to dry. If the floor is only slighly uneven, you can solve the problem with a thick bed adhesive.

Suspended timber floors really aren't ideal for tiling; the

weight over a large area could also be considerable. However, it can be done. Floorboards must be covered with 12 mm water-resistant resin-bonded plywood or chipboard, screwed down at 220 mm intervals across the middle and 150 mm intervals around the edges. You may have to prime the boards before applying adhesive – ask about this where you buy the boards. If there are pipe runs under the floorboards, lay the panels in strips which can be lifted for access purposes.

Generally use a 3 mm bed of cement-based adhesive on solid floors; a thick bed adhesive means something about 12 mm thick. If you intend using it on boarded floors, the boarding will almost certainly have to be primed. A cement rubber adhesive is probably best for timber-constructed floors. Try not to walk on a newly-laid floor for at least 24 hours. If you really have to, protect the floor with a sheet of board. Floor tiles are grouted in a similar fashion to ceramic wall tiles.

Use the same sort of adhesive for quarry tiles; lay it 3 mm thick for smooth tiles and twice that for textured tiles. However, if you are laying quarry tiles on a new solid floor, fix them in a sand and cement mortar bed.

Creating more Space

Lack of space can drive you crazy. It is probably the most pressing and obvious reason for wanting to move out, but of course buying and selling houses has never been so fraught as it is now, so consider first what you can do in terms of conversions and improvements inside your house. But consider any such changes thoughtfully, and very conservatively. A stud partition can turn one seemingly large room into two large cupboards which won't be particularly useful to you and may seem abhorrent to a prospective future buyer.

Be convinced; the best results in converting or altering a place come from acknowledging and respecting the characteristics of a property and working in sympathy with them. An elevated sleeping platform will only really work in something like a warehouse conversion with acres of space. Slam it in the corner of a large Victorian drawing room and you'll lose a lot of sleep over the mistake.

Professional planners and interior designers put an enormous premium, and price tag, on meticulous attention to detail, and even a £30 DIY plasterboard partition can grow into its surroundings when furnished with skirting board and door architraves which match or complement the rest of the room.

But smooth aesthetics aren't the only important consideration. Whatever you are doing, it must be carried out in accordance with building regulations. Of course your home is your castle, but try and sell a house with a windowless room, or one with a ceiling that isn't high enough, or an alteration with awkwardly-placed access and the follies of your independent designs will be brought tumbling about your ears by even the most lackadaisical surveyor.

That's the bad news, but the good is that, in my experience at least, I've found local planning officers and building inspectors quite helpful – even enthusiastic – as long as you're prepared to do a certain amount of appallingly sycophantic creeping to their superior knowledge. Never be assertive or in the least argumentative with them; play ball, but remember the ball's theirs. On the other hand, don't go round to the planning department with vague notions. Draw your plans as clearly as possible and to scale, on graph paper.

The basic requirments of conversion are pretty straightforward and commonsense. For example, a wc must not open into a habitable room, and every new room must have its own window or a mechanical means of ventilation, and so on. But you can get bogged down in technicalities such as the requirement that the opening part of a window must have a total area equal to one-twentieth of the new floor area. This is where your neatly-drawn plans on graph paper will be invaluable in order to get building consent which might also have to satisfy fire (escape) regulations.

The most common problem in old houses is that the main rooms are too big. A division can be made by using stud partitions which are essentially lightweight, non-loadbearing frames faced with plasterboard. They are extemely easy to erect.

Ingenious colleagues in a Northern Ireland newspaper office once built their own, providing an airless, but comfortably womb-like, retreat in which to rest away the rigours of Guiness and oyster 'snack-lunches', as they were called in the days before madness prevailed. The snug, as it was called, had no visible doorway, just a hatchway hidden behind a desk. Its only accoutrements were a Lilo inside and a framed picture of The Laughing Cavalier with bored-out peephole eyes on the outside wall; this was used to keep watch for unwelcome visitors surveying the 'bureau'. The snug was only discovered and quickly demolished when a head office bureaucrat paying a surprise visit was alarmed by stentorian snoring which seemed to be coming from the classic painting.

But back to the basic stud partition. Its principal components are the vertical pieces of 3 in by 2 in timber – the studs – and two horizontal members, one called the head, which is fixed to the ceiling and the other the plate, which is screwed to the floor. Short horizontal pieces of timber called noggings stiffen up the whole structure by being nailed between the studs. This framework need not be a thing of beauty; roughly-sawn timbers are adequate.

First cut notches in the head in which to fit the vertical studs, which should be about 2 ft apart; this step will make fixing the building boards easy. (You will of course at this stage have to decide where the door is going to be fixed, and allow an appropriate space for it within the framework of horizontal studs.)

Do the same with the floor plate. Now screw the head to the ceiling (prod the plaster with a bradawl until you find the centre of a joist). The next joist should normally be about 18 in away. If the line of the new partition runs across the joists you can fix it anywhere. If it runs parallel to the joists, then you're confined to moving the postion of the partition until it comes under one.

Alternatively, you can fit bridging pieces of timber between the joists on either side of the partition. This is rather more bothersome as you will have to take up the floorboards of the room above; if on a top floor, you will need to go into the roof space.

Once you've fixed the head, the rest is easy. Drop a plumbline along the wall and fix the floor plate which you will have notched in an identical way to the head. Both head and floor plates are best fixed with sturdy No. 12 screws at around 2 ft intervals. Don't try and hammer nails into the ceiling joists as you'll almost certainly damage the plaster. If you're fixing the plate into a wooden floor, use nothing bigger than two and a half inch screws to avoid damage to hidden pipes or wiring. Fixing a plate onto a concrete floor requires three and a half inch screws, driven into plugs. Finish the framework by skew-nailing the noggings into the studs.

It's easiest to buy a door kit with a ready-made frame and door. Nail the plaster or insulating board onto the framework using plasterboard nails, making sure all the boards are fixed tight up against the ceiling, but allow a half to quarter inch gap at the bottom; this will evenutally be covered by the skirting. You'll need help to manoeuvre the boards into position.

Finally, cover the joins in the boards with special plasterboard tape. You can now skim plaster or paper the boards.

Sound-proofing

*'It's not so much the noise that bothers me,
but the constant feeling of inadequacy.'*

Noisy neighbours playing their favourite tapes, vacuuming,
DIYing, quarrelling or on the other hand regularly indulging in
athletic night activities, sometimes diagnosed as the Headboard
Banging Syndrome, can be more than irritating. Some houses,
particularly those built in the fifties, were thrown up with little
regard to acoustic insulation, and you'll know only too well if
yours is one of them. The sounds of constant partying coming

through party walls is usually tedious and sometimes extremely unpleasant.

Of course there are legal remedies you may seek, but the local council's environmental expert, whose personal audience of your Little Night Music noise might be necessary, is hardly going to stay around all night waiting for evidence. Therefore a person who brings a complaint must prove the annoyance was 'substantial', and that is often difficult to do.

Anyway, who wants to fall out with the neighbours, however noisy, by taking them to court when you could do a great deal yourself in terms of sound-proofing adjoining or party walls?

Sound comes in waves, of course. The lower the pitch or frequency, the louder and more difficult it is to stop or block, which explains why the insistent low-frequency thrum of a base guitar rhythm is the only thing you clearly hear of next-door's Pink Floyd album.

Noise nusiance problems can be considered by two approaches: absorption or insulation. The first refers to the attenuation of noise within the same room or area as the noise source itself. This normally would involve lining the walls, floor, roof or ceiling of a building or room. You'd use this method to keep noise confined to an area; I've seen it used to great effect in a children's noisy play room which had been converted out of an integral garage. I'll return to this later.

The second approach is all about silencing the noise from next door by insulation. Employing a rule of thumb, known to specialists in acoustics as the 'mass law', it can be seen that doubling the mass of a partition wall will normally reduce the sound transmission through it by one quarter.

The Pilkington company insulation division are among the world leaders in creating golden silences. Pilkington told me there are many popular misconceptions about acoustic insulation; principally that it is necessary to use heavy sound-absorbing materials to gain any real effect. It need not be an expensive remedy either.

Basically, what you need to do is form another leaf, or stud partition, next to but not directly on, the 'noisy' wall. This is done by attaching a timber framework of battens to it leaving a minimum 25 mm gap from the existing wall (I dealt with stud partitions in the last section).

Use less expensive rough-sawn timber (75 mm by 50 mm is ideal) to form the studs, the uprights, which are placed at intervals to suit the insulating material. Fit Pilkington's Supa-mat, which comes in 370 mm-wide rolls, into the framework, and face it with plasterboard, if you want a skimmed plaster finish, or a dry-lining board such as Gyproc; this has an ivory-coloured surface which can be painted, wallpapered or covered with a textured wall coating.

If you want to do this, buy taper-edged boards which, when butted together, form a shallow groove which has to be filled by bedding-in strengthening tape with a joint filler, and smoothed over with joint finish to provide a flush surface ready for decorating. The strengthening tape also hides the galvanised plasterboard nails (30 mm or 40 mm depending on the thickness of the board).

Take care with electrical fittings which will of course have to be extended to the new wall surface. And don't forget to buy sufficient length of new, matching, skirting board to protect the bottom of the new acoustic partition. When handling insulation which, by the way, is easily cut to size with a bread knife, it is best to use a disposable face mask and and rubber gloves to lessen skin irritation. You'll almost certainly get some bits of fibre down the cuffs of a glove, so rinse your hands under running water before washing.

You may, on the other hand, consider wall-to-ceiling book shelves or modular blocks of cupboards and display cabinets. Lines of books in themselves would enhance the sound-proofing qualities of the new wall.

Insulation also works well on ceilings and, in conjunction with double glazing, on exterior walls. But in the latter case you'd use a vapour-check plasterboard which has a metallised polyester backing that will resist moisture penetration. The timber framework would also best be made of preservative-treated wood.

Timber floors can be insulated from rising noise from a flat below by removing the floorboards and suspending Pilkington Supamat on plastic garden netting fixed across the joists.

Many householders have, by the skilful use of insulation

materials, been able to convert garages into comfortable multi-use rooms or even sound-proofed play areas. You will of course need change-of-use planning permission.

Garages with outward-opening hinged wooden doors are most suited for easy conversion. One door can remain bolted shut, while the other operates normally to provide access. I would always line the wooden door that's fixed shut with something like 25 kg roofing felt, nailed on batttens, to provide a vapour barrier, and the same applies to exterior walls. You can then apply the Supamat insulation as described earlier.

However, by far the best alternative with regard to access is to brick up with lightweight concrete blocks behind the door that is permanently closed. Because they are not load-bearing, these blocks will not need a footing foundation, neither will they have to be tied into the walls each side. A building-block wall built in this way can later be easily demolished if you want the garage returned to its original function.

The conversion of integral garages with up-and-over doors isn't such a good proposition, because unless you remove them and brick up the entrance to provide a door in that, you've little option other than to erect a stud partition at sufficient distance into the garage to allow the doors to open. You then put your door in the partition and, although you lose a lot of valuable living room space, you'll have a storage area for bikes, tools and things.

Planning permission will almost certainly require adequate ventilation, and probably the only way to do this would be with an extractor fan, ducted to the outside through an external grill. A sound attenuator, which is a metal tube similar in effect and construction to a car silencer, can be connected into the ducting, just before the exterior grill.

Conservatories

Continuing the theme on the possibilities, and practicalities, of creating extra habitable space, it's worth considering the merits of an extension, sometimes more grandeloquently called 'the conservatory'.

It really doesn't have to be the sort of greenhouse-like addition train travellers can see stuck down in surburban back gardens. Built with care and some sympathy towards the style of the house itself, it can be of considerable practical and aesthetic value.

This may be the only way of finding extra space, maybe providing an all-year round dining room, or perhaps just a sunny garden room which could bring light and vitality to an otherwise dark house. Frankly, if you just want a space to store things, it would be consideraly less disruptive and expensive to buy a bespoke cedar shed, site it at the bottom of the garden and clothe its boxy shape with climbing plants.

So first decide where you're going to put your extension and then ask the planning department whether you may. Plannning rules restrict the maximum volume of extensions. Basically, they must not be more than 15 per cent of the original volume of a semi or detached house and 10 per cent of a terraced home. Remember this original volume will include the roof space.

It is really easiest to buy a packaged kit. Its plans and written specifications will, for a start, make it much easier to get planning permission. Expect to pay around £2000 a room measuring about 17 ft by 19 ft. Most kits will not immediately provide you with a year-round room, you'll have to double-glaze walls and celings and pay particular attention to insulating and damp-proofing the floor. You'll also need back-up heating for winter months.

There may already be a structure of some sort where you want to site a conservatory; you may be in luck because if this is structurally linked to the back or side of the house, and built of the same material, its foundations could be substantial enough to provide two rooms, one on top of the other. If this is the case, extend the roof of the house over the new structure – it will add to the cost of course, but a pitched roof will not only be far more efficient than a cheaper flat one, it will also make the extension look much more like part of the original building.

One-storey extensions may, however, be prohibited by covenants in the title deeds, so check with your solicitor. If you want to finance the extension by topping up your mortgage, you will have to seek building society approval.

The floor of a conservatory-extension should be dealt with in the same way as that of the foundations of the house itself. Common sense – and building regulations – mean that you cannot just lay it on paving stones as you would a greenhouse.

Before you start, check where the drains are. You can have drains rerouted, and man-hole inspection covers moved, if you are determined to build on a particular site. Depending on the stability of the soil, you'll need a trench foundation filled with a minimum of 18 in-deep concrete, and at least 12 in wide, extending in front of the conservatory wall by at least 9 in.

The new solid floor should be laid over compacted hard-core, over which is spread about 2 in of sand to cushion the damp-proof membrane. A damp-proof membrane should be linked directly into the damp-proof course of the house. Then comes the concrete floor which, when set, is laid with a sand and cement screed. If you're already on Economy Seven night heating, you might consider laying cables for under-floor heating before the screed is put down.

If there are air-bricks in the house wall, it's esential to incorporate similar ventilation in the base of the conservatory. These can be linked quite satisfactorily with ducting made of one and a half inch plastic waste pipes. Assuming that the conservatory will lead directly from the house, if there is a substantial difference between interior and exterior levels, it is much easier to lay floorboards, or tongue-and-groove chip-boarding over rot-proof joists, rather than build up the solid concrete floor.

A suspended floor like this will not, however, be strong enough to take stone slabs or the heavier ceramic and quarry tiles. Sealed cork tiles, or insulation-backed lino or vinyl sheeting are ideal coverings, but if you want to lay carpet directly onto the concrete floor, make sure it has a thick foam or rubber underlay.

It is generally safer to keep the floor of the conservatory at the same level as the floor of the house. If there are steps down into the conservatory it is best to cover them with covering of a different colour than that of the conservatory floor: it's quite easy to be dazzled and fall coming out of the shade of the house into bright sunlight.

Conservatory roofs can be problematic. They often leak, because the house walls upon which they are placed are not vertical and smooth. Rough-cast and pebble-dashed house walls must be chopped back to the bare brickwork for a perfect seal. Most conservatory kits offer an option of a solid roof with a 'light'; clearly these are the best for insulation and, consequently, all-year-round use.

Most kits come with toughened glass walls; don't use anything else, particularly if there are young children around. It's well worthwhile fitting laminated glass for doors and fixing safety film over windows, to the height of the eaves.

Do not try and save money by using anything else, although some kits which come without glass suggest you can cut costs on the roof at least by overlapping small panes of 3 mm horticultural glass. Don't. These can collapse under a heavy loading of snow and in the summer the overlaps trap green algae, which are very difficult to clean out.

Other options include wired glass and polycarbonate sheeting. There's a version of this which is said to have excellent insulating properties. But plastics do tend to discolour over a period of time.

Kit conservatories require no special skills or tools other than an electric drill, spanner, screwdriver and, most important of all, a spirit level and plumb-line to get all the angles correct at every stage in construction.

Autumn

Safety in the Home

Safety precautions in the home seem fairly commonsense, until one considers that each year about a million people sustain injuries which need attention, and a further 6000 are killed in accidents in the house. It's a depressing and ludicrous situation, compounded by far too many advertisements for DIY activities which show the operators attractively dressed in tight jeans, open-necked shirts and trainers.

Even the simplest jobs require basic safety measures which minimise the risk of hurting yourself, but how many people bother to wear safety glasses to protect their eyes from flying materials when mowing a lawn?

Specialist gloves are widely available in a variety of materials. Common-or-garden gloves won't do if you're using a chemical paint stripper, and stout rubber gauntlets you'd use for that would give little protection compared with the industrial leather gloves you should wear if you're using potentially dangerous machinery.

There is, at last, a growing awareness of the danger of dust and, thanks to so-called scare-stories in the press, not many people would start demolishing anything with asbestos in it. If you suspect there is asbestos around the house, just don't touch it, and call in the council's health and safety people.

Make sure you wear the right sort of mask for the job; many only protect against non-toxic dust and powders. So if you're, say, sanding a floor you'd require a mask meeting meeting BS 6016 standards, particularly if you're sanding hardwood; this gives up a much finer dust, which is also likely to be toxic.

Paint-spraying equipment is increasingly being offered to the DIY market, and there's little doubt about the fine finish it produces, as long as it's not your own. Only a special paint-spray respirator will do (BS 2091) and this should have the appropriate filter for the substance you're working with. Two-part paints, where you have two components to stir together, need similar protection against poisonous fumes.

Safety goggles are inexpensive enough to buy; they can be a nuisance if you're laying blanket insulation in a loft, because they keep on misting up, but these, as well as gloves and a mask, are absolutely basic protection against airborne particles of mineral wool or glass fibre. But only impact-resistant polycarbonate goggles will safely protect your eyes when you're using an electric saw or router. These activities are also extremely noisy, so look for something like Vitrex's foam ear plugs which will be effective at levels up to around 80 dBA.

Protect your knees when you're kneeling a lot by buying a pair of inexpensive knee pads. The lightweight polyurethane foam versions are enough for most jobs. Old clothes are fine for messy jobs as long as they don't have sleeves and trouser legs that flap about. You'll soon deplete the stock, and feel more comfortable in proper overalls. I've found the rather lurid lightweight coversuits are fine for one session, but they do tear, and you'll probably find something much better, and cheaper, in an army surplus shop.

It may feel a bit cissy to wear a safety helmet until a falling piece of masonry drops on your head. The best, and there's no point in getting anything else, are expensive, but can be hired from hire-tool stores such as the HSS chain.

Demolishing things like heavy masonry is obviously a potentially dangerous activity. Industrial steel-capped boots can save your toes from amputation.

So many accidents are caused by people trying to over-reach while at the same time balancing on a stool. Lightweight aluminium steps, with a grab rail, a platform for paint pots and trays and just eight treads, are essential. But if you're reaching higher, don't be a ladder lout. Shop around and buy or hire a Class Two ladder which is often yellow-tagged, and appropriate for 'light trade'. How long it needs to be really depends on the height of the house; add up the ceiling heights of each room and add a metre to allow for the angle. One with three sections is much more portable and easier to use and store.

Go to a lot of trouble to ensure that a ladder rests on solid, even and, if it's soil, compacted ground, and that its foot is tied to a stake or supported by a sandbag. If you haven't got a bag of sand, don't be stupid; go out and buy one for a couple of pounds, and use it afterwards for castles.

Government safety facts and figures include horror stories of people falling off ladders because they were tired or had been drinking. The appropriate ladder standard is BS 2037, which does not include a breathalyser.

Big exerior repair or decoration work should be done from a platform tower. Domestic types built from aluminium or steel H-frames can be safely built up to only 12 ft, although this can be extended by additional supports fitted around the base to 18 ft. The basic price would be around £200. Unless you anticipate using one quite frequently, or you need to reach higher, it would be best to have a scaffolding tower put up for you. (Note that scaffolding left up overnight or while you're out is an invitation to burglars.)

Every slipped disc has a story; it's not funny because the injury will probably stay with you for life. The lifting rule is to keep your back straight and use your knees, but if you have difficulty in lifting anything – to the initiated a bag of sand is only half full, otherwise it will seem rooted to the ground – don't do it until you can get help. Some things are very deceptively heavy – a door is feather-light until the last screw comes out of the hinge, and then it can flatten you. A modestly-sized mirror or sheet of glass can be extremely heavy, unwieldy and danger-ous, as can a severed tree branch. Never work on a tree from a ladder, you can be swept off it by a falling branch, so get in among the branches, after securing the ladder-top, of course.

Other outside cutting jobs involve the use of a chain-saw, which is a very effective tool but it can be a lethal one too. A recent *Gardening from Which?* reported that, astonishingly, there are are sometimes fewer safety features on the growing number of chain-saws available to untrained amateurs than on larger professional models. Serious, often fatal, injuries to the head, face and neck are caused by kick-back, when the tip of a running chain-saw touches another object and is thrown viol-ently back. A chain-saw must have a chainbrake which stops the tool automatically, and in less than a second, if it starts to kick-back.

Gardening from Which? has also called for lawnmower blades which stop quickly once the on/off switch is released, and with a lock-off switch which would require two separate actions to activate the motor, and reduce the risk of someone, perhaps a child, operating it accidentally.

Always, always, plug an electrical power tool into a residual-current circuit breaker (RCCB), which would immediately cut off the supply if the cable is severed.

Children and Safety

Most parents have horror stories of near-tragedies involving children in the home; according to ROSPA, at least 160 youngsters die from their injuries each year. But how do you child-proof a home? It's not easy to second-guess a two year old who, given just a moment, can crawl or clamber into the most dangerous places and with devilish dexterity open an upstairs window (which has resisted adult attempts for years) and climb out onto the ledge. It happens.

Some of the danger zones are pretty obvious – the stairs for instance – and bedroom windows seem to share a fatal attraction with medicine cupboards and the under-sink place where you store the bleach.

Think about how many pieces of glass you have at child-height; not just things like French windows, but articles like glass-fronted bookcases. Shattered glass can, and does, kill and glass window and door panes need either to be replaced with safety glass or covered with the special film you get at shops like Mothercare. The film must conform to BS 6206.

There's some confusion about types of 'safety' glass, so remember that laminated glass crazes on impact, but is held together by the strong transparent interlayer, while toughened glass shatters into tiny pieces in the same way in which a car windscreen smashes. The BS glass number is 6206. Never put anything a child can climb onto near a window and decorate large and low panes with stickers, to re-emphasise their existence.

It's possible to provide a comfortable and safe environment in which children can sleep and play only if you adapt and reconsider your ideas and furnishings right from the start. (On a cosmetic note, it may be all too tempting to decorate a child's bedroom with frills and nursery wallpaper, but be practical and go for primary colours which can easily be repainted to cover the stupendously good first attempts at art. There are lead-free washable paints made especially for nurseries. If you must have bunnies or Jemima Puddleduck running around the walls, restrict them to a frieze and remember they'll quite quickly be replaced with poster portraits of the cast of *Neighbours* anyway.)

If you're going to use painted, possibly second-hand, furniture in a nursery or child's bedroom it's safest to strip it completely, just in case the covering contains lead, and repaint it.

If you do buy second-hand things like cots, make sure they conform to current safety standards in details such as the spacing of the bars. Write to the Child Accident Prevention Trust, 28 Portland Place, London w1 for the latest relevant BS numbers.

When your child moves into a 'grown up' bed, fit a safety rail onto the side; the better versions form a tubular framework and have a soft mesh infill. You'll certainly need one of these if you intend later to put children in bunk beds.

Before decorating a child's room consider whether there are enough suitably-placed electric sockets for the music centres, TVs and computers yet to come. In the meantime, make sure that every socket has a cover, and there's absolutely no need for trailing flexes. Mothercare also sell a self-adhesive video shield to protect your recordings from infantile erasure. You might consider replacing the wall switch with a dimmer switch or buy a plug night light to comfort any child scared of the dark. The candle night lights that could be stood in a saucer of water are, these days, a black joke.

You'll of course always use a fireguard on open fires, but fit guards that totally enclose the radiator(s) in a child's room, or have a thermostatically-controlled valve fitted, so that you can modify the radiator's temperature to a safe level.

A three year old has enough strength to pull a packed bookcase over onto itself, so firmly secure free-standing furniture like this onto the wall – you could use one and a half inch mirror plates for this, or if the bookcase has a solid back, screw through this into wall plugs.

It's easy enough to buy safety gates for the stairs, but shop around for the type that can be opened with one hand and make sure the floor support is not too high to step over. They're a nusiance for adults, but they must be kept in place day and night. Some children are nocturnal wanderers, and I know of a parent who glanced out of the window as she woke, early one summer's morning, to see her daughter playing in a pile of bricks some builders had left on the side of the road.

Fit proper safety catches to all windows – the Yale P117 Safety Lock allows the window to open slightly for ventilation. But do make sure they can be quickly unlocked in the event of a fire.

The kitchen is potentially the most dangerous room in the home – even half a cupful of hot water left in a kettle can cause scalds, so fit something like Mothercare's Kettle Guard which is secured to the wall at the back of the work surface. You can lessen some of the risk of pans being overturned by habitually cooking on the back rings or burner. Kitchen cupboards and drawers and fridge/freezers can be locked with a number of simple and inexpensive devices, and it is worth spending £6 on a Boots Door Slam Protector to prevent tiny fingers being crushed.

Living in Small Spaces

*'This is probably the best vantage point
from which to view my etchings . . . '*

Living in one room is a necessity for some, an enthusiastic choice
for others. Once I lived in a hotel room for two years – it was
one of those foreign assignments meant to last a month. By the
time I returned to normality, I was one of the many adherents
of bedsit living, who found that the obvious limitations of space
were well out-weighed by a compact home in an interesting part
of town which I would not otherwise be able to afford. Rates in
the Royal Borough were half those in the then nascently-trendy

Islington, even before the first khaki-painted front door appeared there. Moreover, a bedsit was cheaper to heat and light, and easier to keep clean, and secure.

Life in one room can solve a lot of problems, like how to give teenagers their own space and, with obvious modifications, what to do if a granny who comes to stay is of an age and mood to entitle her to her own privacy. But living in a boxy shape can become both claustrophobic and extemely tedious if you have to move the bed out of the way in order to cook an omelette, and the concept calls for clear-sighted and meticulous planning and an abundance of ideas. Here are some.

You've got to decide whether you're going to live in a bedroom or sleep in a living room. The latter is the better option, I think, and this means you have to draw up a – short – list of the various activities: sleeping, eating, washing, cooking, relaxing, etc, and apportion parts of the room to them in the order of your own priorities. Then, and only then, can you think about things like having people around for a meal or to look at your etchings. You won't often even open a can of beans if you have to remove the 'kitchenette table' to get at the stove.

The paramount problem of course is one of space, and this won't often be solved by Heath Robinson-like dual-purpose inventiveness. In any case, constantly having to re-engineer most such pieces is a bore.

But you really do want to hide, or at least disguise, The Bed, and steer away from the tawdry bedsit look. Convertible sofa-beds of a price you or I can afford are not the answer, uncomfortably failing in both roles. There are, now, comfortable beds which can be tilted on end and hidden in a cupboard. They're expensive, so consider building a bed-cum-day-lounger into an existing or specially-made alcove. This can be as simple as cutting up two or three 1200 by 2400 mm (4 ft by 8 ft) pieces of 18 mm chipboard to form the sides and rear of the alcove. Make pull-out storage units, fitted with wire baskets and mounted on castors; these will provide an enormous amount of storage under the bed or lounging area, whatever you want to call it. The mattress is supported laterally on 19 mm by 75 mm planed softwood slats, which rest on 25 mm by 25 mm battens.

The bed would, and should, be too high to climb onto so you

must make a two-step unit, rather on the lines of a horse-mounting block, which can also contain valuable storage space and double as a seat.

Obviously, one end of this sleeping alcove should be on a sound wall of the house (not a stud partition). But the construction of a stout but hollow wooden pier at the other end (bolted to the wall, floor and ceiling joists) could provide even more storage space, dividing this sleeping area from, say, the living-room part. The pier could also be a place to build-in a television set, and hi-fi system.

If you have an old and high-ceilinged room the sleeping area could be raised considerably higher, providing room for a desk and storage area underneath, virtually doubling the activity area. Of course you'd need a wall bar ladder, a miniature version of what you see on gym walls, bolted to the wall and, if you're a restless sleeper, a guard rail. However, I'd only recommend this to a pretty efficient DIY person who could ensure very secure fixings in walls floor and ceilings.

This sleeping area could be completely hidden by concertina-like folding doors. You mightn't have the space or possibly even the tools (principaly an electric saw) to move around and cut 4 ft by 8 ft boards, but you could explain what you want to a carpenter and have him make it up for you in kit form. It would save an awful lot of hassle and paint smell if all the parts were stained or painted, or at least primed and undercoated, before delivery.

Bought tables aren't so much of a problem; there isn't a huge choice of models which, quite essentially, convert from dining to coffee modes. I've seen some remarkably good value and well-designed models at both Habitat and IKEA stores, (if you live anywhere near IKEAs at Brent Park in north west London, or Warrington, you're in luck, but avoid the horrendous weekend queues.

You could, at less than half the price, buy a flush hardboard door, seal, undercoat and gloss it, and put it on a couple of trestles bought at IKEA, which are specially made for their more expensive table tops. Better still, have trestles made for you which will fold flat and hang on the wall with folding dining chairs when not in use. Trestle tables can also usefully double as wallpaper pasting boards, providing you protect them from adhesive marks.

Site a kitchen next to a house wall wherever possible. It may have to double as a washing area, although ideally, and if you're starting more or less from scratch, a separate ceramic bowl can be plumbed in to the space adjoining the sleeping area. But good ventilation is absolutely vital and is best achieved by an electric extractor fan.

There are several ready-made mini-kitchens available, designed to fit into a largish cupboard. These incorporate sink, fridge, two-ring stove, oven and electric water heater and are pretty expensive. You'll probably find a better buy at a caravan dealers or advertised in one of the caravan magazines.

If you're really short of space, a fold-away shower unit, which packs into a cupboard, could be the only solution. You'd probably find an 'instant' electric shower heater, run from the mains cold water supply, best, but in view of the usually small distance involved there should be no problem with running its own electric circuit from the consumer unit.

The shape of some rooms, particularly those which are L-shaped, lends them quite naturally to an open plan bed and bathroom providing there is adequate heating and ventilation to prevent condensation problems. The division between the two could best be marked by a change of flooring, say from carpet tiles, or it could simply be a floor-to-ceiling bookcase-like room-divider, backed on the bathroom side with a mirror.

But a wc will almost invariably require its own ventilated room; you must consult your local planning department.

Storage

'I've just ordered an eight-part series on shelving.'

Many people have, at one time or another, had the distinct impression that their home was shrinking around them. A lack of storage space, whether for clothes, books, pots and pans or even tools, can lead to frustrating searches and delays in getting things done. It's common to underestimate your storage needs, although most items filed under 'may be useful – one day' are best consigned to a skip.

The builders of many older houses, even up to about 50 years ago, had little inkling about the battery of domestic appliances in today's kitchen, for example. So even if you've got a basic washing machine and tumble dryer combination, where do they all go?

Most kitchens in older houses are too small, but considerable extra space can be gained by converting a pantry or outside loo into somewhere for appliances. Garages make marvellous utility rooms as long as they're not too far from the house, and so don't need expensive new water and electricity supplies.

I've seen under-pavement coal-holes so used – but with poor result; they're invariably damp beyond any reasonable remedy.

Shelves are an obvious first resort, and probably one of the few options in a small house or flat where the walls must be made to work for their keep. Fine for books of course, but do you like to keep all your other posessions permanently on display? Also bear in mind that the width of shelves is important. It is a much neater and space saving solution to have such ledges made just deep enough to take a lot of items which are roughly the same size, whether they be paperbacks or plates. Deep shelves where things tend to be stored in two rows are of little help.

There are generally three arrangements for shelving. They are most popularly mounted directly on the wall, and so must have strong fixings. There can be problems, not so much in ensuring a secure anchorage point, for there are many purpose-made screw plugs – but because of the possibility of drilling a hole into a hidden pipe or electrical wiring. Inexpensive battery-powered detectors can show you where these lie in a wall, stud detectors will also enable you to fix a shelf on one of the vertical timbers supporting the plasterboard or other material covering a hollow wall.

If there are alcoves, for example those either side of a fire-place, shelving can be built into place, supported by wooden battens of planed all round (PAR) 2 in by 1 in timber battens. There is a large selection available of bracket and track systems to support the shelves.

Wood is the strongest material for shelving. It's easy to cut, attractive and can be painted or stained to suit the existing decorations. Large quantities of wood can however be costly and blockboard, which is basically pieces of softwood strips compressed between sheets of veneer, is better if your budget is stretched. The only snag is that it is generally sold in 8 ft by 4 ft boards, which must be cut down to size. If you haven't the equipment and space to do this, some small DIY shops and

Sainsbury's Homebase will cut to specification. The sawn edges of blockboard also need to be covered with beading or lipping to hide its core.

Bathrooms notoriously suffer from storage problems. You could fix shelves high around the perimeter for bottles and cosmetics, and use any available wall-space to fit shallow cupboards. When you are choosing shelving materials, take into account the steam generated in a bathroom which could warp wood and rust steel.

Boxing-in the bath in tongue-and-groove panelling, fixed onto a rudimentary framework of 2 in by 1 in battens, could provide storage space as long as you include a door in the panelling. There is often a space between the end of the bath and the wall, which will provide another cubby hole.

If you have a pedestal washbasin, you might replace it with a vanity unit where the basin is set into a floor-standing cupboard. Corner washbasins and baths could be a solution if the size and shape of the room allows it, but never replace a bath with a shower if you plan to sell the place one day.

Some built-in wardrobes make no use of the space between their top and the ceiling. It's quite simple to replace the fixed panel with doors, which will provide space for suitcases and spare bedding or unseasonal clothes.

Drawers fixed on castors can be slid under some beds, or part of the floor could be raised into a platform to provide storage space underneath and a mattress or futon on top. Similarly, window seats with storage underneath could be fitted into the small bays found in older houses. Alcoves each side of a bedroom chimney breast are usually too shallow to be boxed in to form wardrobes, but they would take shelves.

Larger bedrooms, usually found in the older houses, can be divided into two, using a fitted wardrobe as a room divider. Some of the cupboards would open into one room and the others onto the other side. Sliding mirror doors save space and give a visual feeling of roominess.

Another scheme for dividing a large room which has a window on each of the two outside walls is to have a zig-zag stud partition constructed, faced with plasterboard which has fitted wardrobes built on each side.

Attics are in most cases used pretty inefficiently but cleared of junk they can provide invaluable storage. Good accesss via a sturdy retractable loft ladder is the first requirement and a storage platform is another – don't just balance things across the joists or you may eventually damage the ceiling. Lay panels of hardboard screwed on battens placed at 12 in intervals. There are also purpose-made loft-boarding panels, cut to a size which will pass easily through the loft opening. Use can be made of the void towards the eaves but make sure you do not block the ventilation gap between the insulation and the roof.

The space under the stairs is usually a cluttered mess, but it can be organised into a mini-room in its own right as long as you box in the gas or electric meters and provide a light source. Or with some shelving and hooks, simply make use of it as a cloakroom.

Flat Roofs

Heat waves and their attendant droughts may play havoc with your roof, tortuously and continually expanding and contracting its timbers and tiles and cracking cement flashings around the chimney. On flat roofs they shift a felt covering around like Rubik Cube moves, before blistering its surface, nice and ready for the rains to come.

Don't wait until it's too late. The first sign of trouble is likely to be a damp patch appearing on the bedroom ceiling, maybe accompanied by the chilling drip-drop of water. This almost invariably happens on a wet and bleary Sunday morning when you plan a lazy lie-in, a very late lunch followed by a delicious umpteenth viewing of Casablanca.

In this, the first of two parts on roofs and roofing, I'll concentrate on felted flat roofs, generally loved by few but their mothers – and the builders who hoisted them with profitable speed – because they're far more prone to trouble than pitched, tiled roofs.

However, their great attribute is that flat roofs are, by comparison, easy to inspect, maintain and repair on a DIY basis during their normal 10 to 15 year life-span.

Flat roofs are also found on many extensions and garages and above dormer windows; as such, they are usually safely accessible.

It's important to understand something of the structure of 'flat' roofs which, for a start, are rarely so, having a small degree of slope or 'fall' – a minimum of 1 in 15 – in order to speed the shedding of an average of 750,000 gallons of rainwater each year.

Most are built-up from a three-layer felt construction laid on a sub-base or decking of concrete, or timber boarding such as tough exterior-grade plywood or chipboard and, depending on their built-in insulation, called 'hot' or 'cold'.

The layers of felt are bonded to each other using a bitumen-based adhesive. Unlike tiled or slated roofs which are built of several separate parts that are designed to move independently of each other, roofing felt relies on its elasticity alone to move – expanding and contracting in response to changes in the surrounding atmosphere. It is a hostile challenge. When there is excessive movement caused by extreme temperatures like those recently experienced, felt roofs become extremely prone to tearing, cracking and delaminating as one piece of felt expands or contracts at a different rate from the others.

A very hot summer's day can soften the felt layers, dragging them against each other and blistering them. In the other extreme, a cold winter's day could make the felts brittle while the deck beneath expands from the humidity inside the house.

Flat roofs should be inspected at least once a year. Their maintenance is the common-sense removal of wind-blown debris, the careful inspection of the points where the felt covering reaches the side of a chimney stack, surrounds on upstands such as central heating flues or soil pipes or the edge of a dormer window. One should also clear the gutters of chippings blown into them, before they block down-pipes and impede the all-important matter of shedding water.

Take particular notice where fixings, like TV aerials, have been made through the roof covering. Satellite TV companies love flat roofs for their dishes, but any such fixing will make a leak inevitable.

Invariably, flat roofs are surfaced with some means of reducing solar damage. Although some manufacturers offer reflective coverings including special paint, in general domestic reference this is done by a covering of white stone chippings.

The most likely faults may all be inter-related to these chippings, and you will give yourself a flying start in damage prevention by never going onto a flat roof on a hot day, when the chippings can be pressed into the softened felt, with potentially disastrous effect. Look for patches where chippings are missing, for it is in these areas that you are likely to find cracks, blisters and bubbles in the felt.

Deal with a crack by first scraping away any embedded chippings from and around the damaged area. Use a hot-air stripper gun to dry out the area and soften the felt; don't use a gas blow-torch – unless you're extremely careful with these,

your problem could, dramatically, be one of major house re-
building.

When the area is dry, brush it clean, reapply the hot air gun
to further melt the felt and press it down with a wooden wallpaper seam roller. Let the area cool, paint it with flashing strip
primer, and then stick and roll down a strip of self-adhesive
primer along the crack.

Blisters and bubbles are caused by rainwater finding a way
between the layers of felt, and then being 'boiled' by the sun.
Repair them in the same way as you would a crack, except that
an x-shaped cut should first be cut in the blister, enabling the
edges to be folded back while you hot-air dry the underneath.

After heating, the cut flaps should be raised and coated
underneath with cold bitumen compound before being pressed
and rolled flat back into place. The repair is finished again by
sticking a patch of self-adhesive flashing over it. Needless to say,
you should cover all repairs with a good layer of chippings.

All the above procedures are at best aimed at prevention or
damage limitation. If leaking has already occured, then it's very
difficult to find the precise point of failure in the felt covering.
It could only be little more than a pin hole and, once inside the
roof decking, water can track along amazingly long and illogical
routes before deciding to drip drop onto the bedroom ceiling.
If you've had a bad leak, which appears to have been happening
for a long time, it may have rotted the wooden decking and/or
the supporting timbers. Beware of dry-rot having set in. If you
suspect it might have, call in a specialist firm who'll bring along
a 'damp-meter' and a hefty estimate for replacing and treating
timbers.

However, when a damp patch does appear, take an internal
measurement to provide some sort of clue to the area you will
be examining at roof level, where you will have to make a
painstaking and systematic search. Mark suspect spots with
brightly-coloured tape, or you'll certainly forget some of them.
The hunt for a leak should take into consideration possible
faults in walls, window openings and flashings.

Gingerly treading over suspect areas may pump water or air
bubbles up through a fault. Patch repairs are fine for small
areas of damage but if the felt has become mottled it's a sign it

is degrading and is likely to be nearing the end of its useful life. There are a number of paint-on compounds which will give it another few years. Their value is debatable. You have to clear off all the old chippings, moss, dust and other debris, and first apply a special primer before the final paint-on compound which solidifies into a rubberised sheet. The only snag is that this method can cause problems by sealing in any dampness, creating perfect conditions for condensation snags in the roof structure below.

If your bank balance allows you to decide on a professionally-laid new roof covering, probably the best felts available are the very high-strength polyester based ones. These are made with either standard bitumen or polymer-modified bitumen. The addition of polymers greatly improves the suppleness of the felt, enabling it to cope excellently with temperature-caused expansion and contraction.

Pitched Roofs

Professionally-erected scaffolding will give you justified confidence to complete most repairs on conventional pitched roofs. It's the biggest, but most necessary, expense – don't try and effect repairs balancing on top of a ladder. You'll need only a few basic tools, soft shoes, and a still, preferably overcast, day.

There are a number of temporary repair systems for the treatment of entire slate roofs which are in poor condition. These include coating the roof with bitumastic liquid and while this is still wet, unrolling reinforcing fabric onto it. This is then covered with another couple of coats of bitumen. It's too messy to be recommended as a DIY treatment, and can lead to condensation problems within the loft. The companies specialising in these treatments also won't tell you that such remedies are much despised by surveyors when you come to sell the house.

Most roofs suffer from cracked tiles or slates at one time or another. If you have, or think you have, a leaking roof, the site of the damage probably won't be obvious from inside the house unless you climb into the loft when it's actually raining. As this usually seems to happen at night, it is not recommended.

But in the morning, use a pair of binoculars to make a visual inspection of the roof. Once you think you've found the damaged area, wait for the scaffolding to be put up. To reach the damaged area you'll need to hire a roof ladder with a ridge hook which you run up the roof on its wheels, then flip over to secure it over the apex of the house.

Leaks often happen at abutments, typically the head of a lean-to extension or around a chimney stack where weak fillets of mortar crack or break away. These can be inexpensively cured, in the short term at least, by bitumen-backed aluminium foil. Lead flashings last much longer but inevitably are much more costly and difficult to fix.

The most common fault is cracked slates or tiles. Don't try to repair either; it's much easier and effective to replace them, although in an emergency, when you cannot find a matching tile, wire brush the damaged one, paint it with flashing strip primer and when dry cover the crack with flashing strip, tucking it in underneath the tile above.

Replacing a plain tile, the type most commonly used in recent buildings, is easy, as they're usually piggy-backed on top of each other, secured by two nibs which hook over roof battens or laths. Make a couple of wooden wedges to lift the tiles in the row above the damaged one, and slide a brick layer's trowel underneath it. You'll see how simply it is fixed when you remove the broken one, and replacement is similarily obvious. Support the new tile on the trowel, and slide it into place until the nibs hook on.

Concrete tiles are slightly more difficult to replace, because they usually have interlocking grooves on the sides. You may also discover wire clips holding some types of tiles, or they may even be individually nailed, but a fair bit of wiggling about will free any sort of defective tile.

Ridge tiles on the apex of the roof, and hip tiles on the external corners of pitched roofs where two roofs join, often work loose after high winds. This is because the mortar they're fixed with is, because of the juxtaposition of tile and roof, merely a fill-in material and has no real strength. Affected tiles should be carefully prised up and away – they are not difficult to crack – given a thorough soaking in a bucket of water and then bedded down again on a cement mortar (one part cement to four of sharp sand). You should first clean off the old mortar and seal all the ends and edges of the replacement tile, but try to keep the underside of it clean and open to enable air to circulate.

Alternatively, builders' merchants sell clips which will give ridge and hip tiles a much stronger hold on the roof. End hips, at the bottom of a run, are kept in place with curly ended irons which are screwed directly into the rafter.

If the mortar between hip or ridge tiles has only hairline cracks, and is otherwise quite sound, you can save yourself a lot of effort carrying buckets up and down by using a caulking gun to inject the cracks with a non-setting mastic.

A slate has to be replaced differently. Elderly slate roofs suffer from 'nail sickness' – the original copper nails fixing them rot, allowing the slate to slide down and away.

If the slate is damaged and loose, but still in place, it will simply pull out. If it's still firmly fixed you'll need to hire a barbed, sword-like weapon called a ripper, which is slid underneath the damaged slate, moved sideways over the nail and pulled down, severing it.

If you do have occasion to renail tiles, copper or, at a push, aluminium nails should be used. Never use galvanised, or anything else.

Tiles are replaced by 'tingles' – lead strips about 8 in long by 1 in wide, the top part of which is nailed to a fixing batten. The new slate is then pushed into place and the tingle's bottom is folded up on it to hold it in place. It's a simple job, but can come undone when a heavy load of melting snow moves.

Roof and Fence Repairs

Not surprisingly, many people are concerned about their gale-battered roofs, leaks, missing slates and recalling horrendous tales of cowboy roofers in the aftermath of the hurricanes in 1987; they naturally don't want to ripped off again, even if the insurance company *is* paying.

Many roofing jobs don't require a high level of skill or elaborate tools, most of which can, in any case, be hired. Safe access to the roof is of paramount importance; trying to work from the top of a ladder is not only futile but extremely dangerous. If you cannot arrange a safe way of getting on – and off – the roof, don't even think about trying. Ask the National Federation of Roofing Contractors, 15 Soho Square, London W1V 5FP (Tel: 071 734 9164) for the name of a recommended local roofer.

If you still want to do it yourself, then look in the *Yellow Pages* for scaffolding contractors and phone around for often amazingly varied quotes on hiring and erecting a very sound and safe tower.

You'll certainly need to hire a roof ladder with a ridge hook. This is slid up the roof on its wheels and flipped over so that the hook secures onto the apex of the roof.

Remember, you probably won't have much idea about the size and type of slate, clay or concrete covering, or how many you need until you get up onto the roof, so make sure you know where to get replacements, and that they definitely have what you want in stock, and not simply listed on their computer list.

Manufactured tiles usually have a groove each side to create a lateral overlap. It will be clear once you get on the roof how the tile is replaced, but basically it is simply a matter of creating an overlap at the top of each tile.

Some tiles are made with nibs which hook over the roof battens. This type is often laid with little or no nails or clips. You can quite easily lift individual tiles surrounding the one that needs replacing with a trowel, hold them up with wooden wedges, ease out the damaged one and insert the replacement.

However, nails or clips are used on some rows of tiles, particularly if the house is in an exposed position, and these have to be removed with a (hired) roofer's rip, which is slid up underneath the unit.

Broken slates are removed in a similar fashion; these are always nailed. The majority of slates are nailed just above the centre. Always try and use copper nails, or alternatively aluminium, but never ordinary or even galvanised nails – they simply don't last.

The gales will have dislodged many ridge and verge tiles, along the top and edge of the roof. They are particularly vulnerable because the mortar used with them merely serves as filler, and provides no fixing strength. However, ridge clips are now obtainable.

If the entire row of ridge tiles look dubious, consider replacing it with a dry-fix system like Redland's Dry Vent. If a contractor offers to put a covering material over the roof, usually a chemical compound, remember that this can only be a temporary treatment.

Similarly, there are spray-on treatments for the underside of roof surfaces. These bond slates or tiles by a chemical foam which sets or cures into a rigid layer. Such treatments are, again, only a stopgap and have, I think, considerable disadvantages to weigh against fulsome cure-all claims, including heat saving, made by some firms. If the roof is structurally weak, or the slates or tiles are old and unsound, they are a total waste of money.

They are no remedy for deteriorating roof timbers; some contractors will spray everything in sight, simply hiding rot and other faults. Undersealing a roof will certainly cure a draughty roof, but can make it vulnerable to condensation unless proper ventilation is provided in the eaves and ridge.

All foam burns, so such treatments can be a fire risk, although I have to say that bitumen sarking, the lining present inside most pitched roofs, is itself highly combustible. Most, if not all, such systems use a chloro-fluorocarbon gas to form the cells for the foam.

Household insurance policies do not usually cover garden fences blown down by high winds. Fortunately, replacing the posts is quite simple. They can either be fixed into concrete or supported by special spikes. The former method is cheaper but messy, involving boring or digging new holes. As a guide, about a quarter of the post should be below ground, and of course treated with a preservative.

Throw some hardcore into the bottom of the hole, to create a means of drainage, place the new posts into the holes and ram hardcore around them, using a spirit level to ensure they are upright. Then the concrete goes in: three parts aggregate, two of sand and one of cement. The fence posts will of course have to be braced and held in place while the concrete sets. To do this, nail two wooden battens either side and fix them in the ground. Rather than go to the trouble of mixing concrete, you might consider using a purpose-made product such as Super-mix's Post-set. This is a pre-mixed concrete powder which is simply poured into the hole, two litres of water is added, and the concrete sets in around five minutes.

What a performance to mend a fence! It's much easier to go to a Texas superstore and buy the required number of Larch Lap Erectrapost spikes and matching larch lap fence posts at very reasonable prices.

The spiked sockets are simply hammered into the ground, but when you're doing this, be careful to protect the tops with a piece of wood. The fence panels can then be refixed by driving something like 2 in or 3 in nails slightly downwards into the posts through pre-drilled holes in the the panel frame. Galvanized fence brackets do the same job more easily.

Unfortunately, these spikes are unlikely to work well in very soft or sandy soil, and they can be difficult to hammer into stony soil.

Televisions and Telephones

If your television aerial suffered in the gales, then it could be a good time to install a new one, or at least improve previously mediocre reception. It's surpising how many people put up with 'snow', blips and two people sitting in the Mastermind chair.

Aerials are, necessarily, neglected things, up there and out of reach. If you really do need a new one, then get your local TV dealer to arrange it, but try and supervise the work so that you see if any slates or tiles come tobogganing to earth; you don't want the addditional grief of a leaking roof.

A visit to your TV dealer, together with a survey of other aerials in your street, should give an indication of the best type of aerial for your area, as well as a rough idea of the direction in which it should point, but both the BBC and IBA have engineering departments which will provide useful information about the transmitters from which you receive signals.

Don't be persuaded that a super new state-of-the-art aerial plonked in your loft will be just as good once fixed to the roof; the signals have got to be very strong for the former to perform satisfactorily. In weak, or fringe, reception areas you'll need an extra high-gain aerial with maybe up to 20 elements.

So you have the best aerial fitted, and the reception still isn't excellent. You will of course know, won't you, that the TV set is properly tuned, and that the aerial plug, as well as the mains lead and its plug are in sound condition. Check that the cable, which should be 75 mm 'low loss' coaxial is connected outside the home by soldered joints in waterproof connector boxes. Often the higher the aerial is the better its performance, but check you don't need planning permission, and be nice to your neighbours. Nobody wants to live next door to what looks like a KGB listening post.

Signals can be boosted quite dramatically by fitting amplifiers. The best, and most expensive, are fixed onto the masthead and need their own electricity supply which is fitted next to the TV set and uses the coaxial cable. These are especially valuable if more than one TV set is being run off the same aerial. Some amplifiers can be fitted inside the house, and simply plugged into a socket by the set.

If you experience problems with only one channel, it's possible that the signal strength is too strong. An attenuator is an inexpensive little device which is fitted between the end of the coaxial lead and the socket on the TV.

A reader who lives on the boundary area of two ITV transmitters and who wants to receive both will need an extra aerial, with its coaxial cable taken down into the house, and joined with the first cable with a 'combiner'. Alternatively, she could have a change-over switch fitted next to the set.

It's worth knowing that interference from electrical equipment inside the home gives a variety of screen symptoms. Interference from appliances with brush-type motors such as vacuum cleaners show up as dots, while refrigerators, indeed most things with thermostats, will give a white band. Old light-dimmer switches will also interfere with radio recpetion. It's the law now that all new equipment which might cause interference must be fitted with suppressors, but if you're experiencing problems from older equipment, an electrical dealer should be able to fit a suppressor.

Electrical interference can also cause voltage 'spikes' which can damage a television set and wipe out the memory on a computer. Anti-spike plugs protect against this; they'll also guard a TV set against lightning damage. Most don't have to be attached to the set or computer, but simply inserted into an adjacent power socket.

Sometimes CB or police radio transmissions can break into TV and radio reception. This is usually caused by a fault within the system, and is invariably cured by having a 'high pass filter' fitted between the end of the aerial cable, and the TV or radio. If this doesn't work, then the equipment should be taken to a dealer who should be able to help.

Interference to hi-fi radio-tuner reception could also be caused by leads to loudspeakers that are too widely separated. The remedy is obvious, but if you don't want to cut into the expensive speaker cable and remake soldered connections, try simply looping it; if that doesn't work, then the tuner will have to be fitted with filters.

The BBC Engineering Information Department is at Broadcasting House, Portland Place, London W1A 1AA. The IBA Engineering Information Service is at Crawley Court, Winchester, Hampshire SO2 2QA.

From TVs to telephones; a reader wants to know how to fit an extension. British Telecom, no doubt facing the fact that some people have been doing it illegally for years, have brought out kits which make it easy to fit another phone point in just about any part of the house – but they're not recommended for bathrooms. There's a range of kits available at BT shops; the instructions provided are excellent, but you must have a modern plug-in master socket to start from. BT will have to provide one; you're not allowed to do it yourself because the new socket contains extra wires needed for testing circuits.

The only tools you'll need are a small screwdriver and a Stanley knife. A disposable thing for pushing the fragile six different colour-coded wires into their respective connector clips within a new socket comes with the kit, but as it won't last longer than two or three fittings, it's worth buying an extra one. It's also worth buying an extra pack of cleats with which to fix the extension cable.

A ready-wired convertor plug is simply pushed into the master socket where it locks in. There are only a few restrictions, apart from avoiding steamy conditions; the total distance from the main socket to the last extension must not exceed 50 m (150 ft), and the phone wire must be kept at least 2 in away from electrical wiring and sockets. More extensions can be run off a junction box, but they must be installed in series, one after the other, so that a socket never has more than two sets of wires. You can have as many extension sockets as you want, but the RENS (Ring Equivelance Number) found underneath the phone tells you how many will acutally ring, if there's a phone attached to every new point. Add the RENS numbers together from all the phones, and if the total exceeds four, the phones probably won't ring.

Fireplaces

'So we ripped out the old marble fireplace and there was this super orange and purple Formica cocktail cabinet . . .'

Open fireplaces are increasingly back in fashion. The Clean Air Act of 1956 that banished the acrid yellow city smogs of the early fifties created smoke-controlled areas that made fireplaces defunct unless smokeless fuel was burnt. Central heating quickly came into its own, but then experts discovered that without efficient insulation, it was pretty expensive. However, if a home was too closely sealed to conserve heat, excessive condensation could ruin decorations and, even worse, encourage rot. Of course adequate ventilation combats that; houses need to breathe and the real fire with its working chimney is, apart from its aesthetic attractions, a natural way to good ventilation and can, these days, add significantly to its market attraction.

Bear in mind that although it is generally not difficult to re-open a fireplace, making it work efficiently again could be a problem. A room sealed against central heating losses would work against efficient burning; prevailing winds, ambient house temperatures, through draughts, ventilation, suspended floors and chimney heights in relation to newer neighbouring buildings are all-important factors.

Domestic fires may look similar in design, but each one has its small differences. So you would be wise first to get expert advice from the Coal and Energy Service, still found in *Yellow Pages* under its old name, the Solid Fuel Advisory Service. The fee charged for an inspection will reflect the amount of work done, but they are the people who can ensure you have all the right safety and legal specifications, and put you in touch with the appropriate tradesmen if you don't fancy doing the job yourself – give them a call anyway, for the free leaflets they offer. It would also be a prudent to talk to the local building control officer if substantial structural work looks necessary.

The first thing to find out is how much is left behind the bricked- or boarded-up fireplace. At worst you'll discover the entire hearth, fireback and surround have been removed leaving the unmistakable 'builder's hole' in which the fire was originally installed. But if you're lucky, the whole thing will be there. If the fireplace was properly sealed with a ventilator near the floor, then the flue lining should not have deteriorated, but if the job has been haphazardly done, the linings may have been badly damaged from accumulated damp. Certainly, if there are damp stains around the fireplace, the flue lining is probably in a bad state, and this is likely to involve costly work.

Forming a new flue involves cutting into the flue to insert insulating concrete liners in the chimney. It is not a DIY job. Additionally, if on opening a fireplace you discover major structural alterations, stop and call in an expert.

In any case, have the chimney professionally swept. You need to be reassured that it is free from birds' nests, the balls of newspaper which people use to stuff up the chimney in an attempt at dampening draughts and, of course, loads of soot. Don't try and do this yourself, it's a messy and expert business but be there all the same, to watch out for any falling rubble or mortar, which would certainly signal the possbility of structural weaknesses and the need for expert advice.

Chimney breasts have strong structural importance – don't touch them. Removing the breast on the ground floor will leave the chimney above it dangling and in need of structural support. Bodged work on chimneys in party walls of terraced or semi-detached houses could seriously weaken those walls. Chimney pots and stacks not in use can fall into disrepair; use binoculars to examine the brickwork, pointing, flashing and pots.

The next step is to ensure that the concrete hearth is present and in a sound state, otherwise your homely new fire could burn the home down by igniting the floorboards. This 'constructional hearth' is basically a slab foundation at least 5 in thick which will provide a non-combustible area reaching a minimum of 20 in into the room and 6 in either side of the 'builder's hole'. It will also take the weight of the chimney and fireplace. The 'constructional hearth' also bears the 'superimposed hearth' which is mainly decorative, but which must extend at least 12 in into the room and be an inch and seven-eighths thick.

Once the hearth has been checked, examine the state of the outer constructional lintel which supports the masonry above the fire opening, and then the 'throat lintel' which guides the entry of the fire into the flue. Cracks can be repaired with fire cement.

The fireback set into the 'builder's hole' is where the fire burns, and cracks in this can similarly be repaired, although new firebacks, in 16 inch and 18 in dimensions, are easily available.

If the existing opening is too big, then the space between it and the fireback can be filled with brickwork before the new prefabricated sections are put into place.

If the fireback has been removed, then you might consider one of the composite fireplaces available. These already include a ready-made fireback.

Remember that opening up a fireplace is a dirty job; even with care, the room will be flooded with dust, so carpets and as

many pieces of furniture as possible must be removed and the
door needs to be kept closed to prevent dust from seeping into
the rest of the house. Just one more thing: find a place to keep
the coal – before you start.

Water Purification Systems

The comfortable belief that Britain had the best drinking water in the world suffered something of a setback with the news that it also failed to meet the appropriate minimum standards set by the European Community. Recent events have shown that even some bottled waters cannot be trusted.

Domestic water treatment devices are relatively simple to install, requiring a section of the rising main to be cut out, with the water turned off. Fit two isolating stop valves before and after the device. Some come with a self-tapping connection, so that you don't have to turn off the mains, but I do recommend that stop valves are fitted, as they make servicing and the replacement of filters that much easier.

It's a bye-law requirement that cold water storage cisterns be covered and that prevents a lot of loft-borne dust falling in.

Current concern focuses on the number and levels of chemicals in water, particularly aluminium, lead and nitrates, although some, like chlorine, are deliberately added as part of the water treatment process.

There can also be sediment particles from the insides of old mains water pipes. Although these are largely harmless they don't make the water look or taste any better.

Then there's the problem of water hardness in some areas, mainly in the south-east, caused by a natural excess of magnesium and calcium compounds. Although hard water is generally thought to be good for you to drink, it requires more soap and detergent, produces scum marks around the bath and, when heated, produces damaging scale which is bad enough inside a kettle but can produce an expensive deterioration in performance in water heaters, hot water cylinders or boilers. This in turn results in higher fuel bills and eventually, in some cases, complete system failure. There are ways of descaling them, but it's a professional job.

A new water conditioner, scale reducer or softener will stop new scale from forming but will only slowly reduce existing scale.

Scale isn't a problem in central heating systems that use an indirect cylinder, where the same water circulates. Once this water has deposited its calcium and magnesium salts, no more will be produced unless fresh water is introduced into the system. The amount that comes in via the feed-and-expansion cylinder, which makes up for evaporation losses, is negligible.

Scale formation in water-heating equipment can largely be prevented by fitting scale reducers into the pipe supplying equipment such as combination boilers, gas water heaters, electric showers, washing machines and immersion heaters.

The result is that the hardness and the scales are modified at a cost of around £40, including a spare cartridge. Replacement cartridges, which will need to be fitted every two or three months, depending on usage, cost around £8.

One of the other simple ways to reduce scale is to use products such as Soffex or Micromet. These are simply suspended in a container in the cold water cistern and renewed every few months.

Unless they're specifically designed to do so, water filters do not affect the hardness or softness of the water. The way they work depends on what filter they use. A sediment filter will simply strain out particles of dirt or other unwelcome material, but will not affect its chemical composition.

A charcoal filter removes unpleasant tastes and odours such as those from chlorine. An activated carbon filter removes unpleasant tastes and smells and renders bacteria (not generally a problem except for babies and young children) inactive.

A water filter can be used for the whole house, in which case it is plumbed into the rising main, above the mains stopcock. To simply provide pure drinking water at the kitchen sink, it is connected into the pipe leading into that tap. Typical prices range around £75. A jug water filter producing two and a half pints per filling costs around £10, but *Which?* have found that while most will remove unpalatable substances, they do nothing about any water-borne odours. There are also filters which are fitted directly onto the cold water tap. These cost around £20.

It's worth remembering that most lead in water comes from lead pipes still found in some older houses. You may have changed the main pipes inside the house, but it's likely that the service pipe connecting your home is still made of lead. If you're worried about this, contact your local authority about getting it changed for a plastic one. You will have to pay for its installation.

A water conditioner, fitted to the incoming rising main so that it works on all water coming into the house, has the same effect as a scale reducer, but operates in a different way. In order to prevent the formation of scale, cold water in the rising main is either passed through a strong magnectic field, or is subject to a tiny electronic discharge. They cost from £75 to £100.

Water softeners remove the scale-forming calcium and magnesium salts from the water by a process known as 'ion exchange'. Incoming water is passed through a resin bed containing sodium salts. The calcium and magnesium salts are swapped for soldium salts which do not form scale, until the resin bed is saturated. The resin bed then needs to be regenerated by passing a solution of salt through it and washing the fluid down the drain. Modern water softeners are automatically controlled by an electric clock – all you do is add the salt.

The main snag with clock-operated water softeners is that they will only regenerate at fixed times, whether you want them to or not. Some are fitted with a meter control so that the regeneration will only take place at night when a fixed amount of water has been softened. They are generally fitted into the rising main after the branch to the the kitchen sink cold tap, leaving hard drinking water available.

Two connections, both fitted with isolating stopcocks, are required – one to take the water to the softener, the other to return it to the rising main. If a softened cold water supply is additionally required, a second cold tap can be added. A 'bypass' connection is also required in case the water softener needs to be removed, and the unit will also need a connection to the drains for flushing away the product of the regeneration process.

Most softeners will also require an electrical feed which drives the clock mechanism for automatic regeneration. They cost from around £350 for the smallest models.

You should tell your water authority if you intend fitting a filter, scale reducer or water softener – they may insist on you using one listed and approved by the Water Research Centre.

Working with Glass

Improving, rather than moving, must be the message to house-holders in the 1990s, and some of you will consider extending your homes with a conservatory, perhaps, or improving comfort with double-glazing. Adding a window can make a dramatic difference to an otherwise gloomy room. All these popular options, of course, involve glass.

Advanced technology and adventurous design have made available almost any kind of window, from the modest one in the kitchen which gives the washer-up a view of freedom beyond the sink, to banks of glass replacing part of a house wall.

But you need to know the right type to use in the right place, and there is a huge range of decorative glass available. With 27,000 domestic accidents a year involving glass, a large number of these involving small children running into panels and glazed doors, safety glazing is a priority issue. A large number of these accidents could have been avoided if safety glazing was used, and if you've ordinary 'float' glass panels anywhere, plan to replace them, but in the meantime fit protective rails in front of them. Do it now.

Nearly all plain glass is float glass, developed by a process which produces a smooth surface and uniform thickness of 3, 4, 5, 6, 10 and 12 mm. These correspond with the old sheet glass weights per sq ft of 24 and 32 oz and the old plate glass thicknesses, which ranged from three-sixteenths to half an inch.

The basic rule is that all windows need a minimum of 4 mm glass; only windows with a total area less than 6 sq ft (2.3 sq m) should be glazed in 3 mm, which is, incidentally, not the 3 mm horticultural glass used in greenhouses. Glass prices vary considerably – the basic price of 4 mm is around £15 per sq ft – shop around. Large picture windows, patio doors, conservatories and low-level glazing panels, partitions, shower and bath shower panels and outhouse roofs need safety glazing. This is the generic term for glass and certain plastics that do not break on impact, or if they do break, they break safely into harmless, tiny fragments rather than the dangerous slivers associated with normal glass. All safety glazing should be marked in the corner with British Safety standard BS 6206 A,B or C.

Toughened glass is formed by heat-treating float glass, and costs two to three times as much as it, but suffers the basic disadvantage that it cannot be cut once it has been toughened, so it must be ordered cut to size.

The second safety type, laminated, is a sandwich of two layers of glass with a strong plastic interlayer bonded between them and yet it is as clear as ordinary float glass. When it is broken by a burglar for instance, the outer layer will splinter but the whole pane will remain intact, making it particularly suitable as a security aid. There are no splinters flying about, and no exposed protrusions of glass, either. Laminated costs about the same as toughened, but it can be cut down to size, although this is a skilled operation and best done by a glass merchant.

Wired glass offers little more impact- protection than ordinary glass, but has distinct advantages in terms of fire protection because the wire holds it all together – it is often specified as the type of glass used in fire doors, and skylights, where it can take the weight of snow. Wired glass is difficult to cut and comes in 6 mm thickness. The cheapest is called roughcast, costing little more than float glass of the same thickness but you can also get polished clear glass, which is twice as expensive.

Differing types of plastic sheet safety-glazing materials are available that meet various classes of BS 6206 – the two best known examples are polycarbonate and polyvinyl (rigid PVC). They offer an inexpensive alternative which is easy to cut and, of course, much safer to have about and to handle. Polycarbonate is an ideal alternative to safety glass. The plastics are fine for fitting as an additional sheet of glazing inside a window, but they do scratch and can discolour after a time.

Modern homes with lots of big windows can suffer from radiant heat increasing room temperatures – passive solar gain. You can lessen this with solar control glass which is often tinted.

Conversely, keeping the heat in is best accomplished by double glazing, which should halve the heat loss, but you could achieve the effect of triple glazing, reducing heat loss by two-thirds, by reflecting back into the room a useful proportion of heat. Use a low-emissivity glass such as Pilkington K which is available in both toughened and laminated forms. It is offered as an option by some double-glazing companies.

Leaded lights are one of the most attractive types of glazing, as long as they suit the style and age of the house, and you don't have to clean the windows. These come in simple square or diamond forms, but stained glass versions are available. A similar, less authentic, but inexpensive, effect can be obtained with self-adhesive lead strips fixed to the outside surface of the glass. These have to be applied very carefully, on scrupulously clean glass, or they're likely to peel off in time. Artificial glass 'bulls' eyes' come in variously sized panes which fit windows and doors.

Large sheets of glass are unwieldly and and potentially dangerous to handle, so don't try. Get the glass merchant to deliver them on one of his specially-designed vehicles. If he breaks it on the way, then he'll have to pay. If you have a casement window to reglaze, remove it and take it with you when you buy the glass; that way you'll ensure the panes will be cut to the correct size. Take any broken glass with you to safely dispose of in his cullet container, the contents of which go back to a manufacturer for recycling. Don't put it in the dustbin.

Members of the Glass and Glazing Federation will give you advice on safety and what's available. Any work undertaken by a member is covered by safeguards provided in the Code of Ethical Practice, so you can be sure that the service you receive is reliable. This is particularly useful in avoiding double-glazing cowboys. A list of members in your area can be obtained from the Glass and Glazing Federation at 44–48 Borough High Street, London SE1 1XB.

Mirrors

Mirrors can work miracles in gloomy homes. They can bring the impression of added space and light to transform a dark room and make it look considerably bigger than it really is. Of course it's an illusion, but so too is much of a house's 'feel'. How different a newly-mortgaged place can seem, stripped of the furniture and bits and pieces that sold it to you.

Obviously the most imortant consideration in siting a mirror is what it will reflect. Placed opposite a window it will double the light and the view; opposite book shelves and you have an instant library; across the room to a shelf of indoor plants and there's the conservatory; but put in a dining room it will double the number of guests.

Most rooms will benefit from a mirror bouncing off light and adding life and interest, but the bathroom is the most likely of all to gain, as it's usually the smallest room in the house. Yet bathroom mirrors are generally confined to a mean little cabinet. Why are these invariably so expensive and tacky-looking? They can be made quite easily by anyone who can construct a box out of five pieces of chipboard or whatever, jointed together on the inside angles with plastic jointing blocks, with two sheets of mirror on runners forming the sliding doors. You could incorporate a striplight, with a shaver point too.

Solve the steaming-up problem by using the light-weight 'mirrors' made of plastic film on polystyrene sheets. They were originally made for aeroplane interiors where weight is crucial. They need minimal support and, being warm, will remain clear on the steamiest bathnights. Lighting is crucial in a bathroom, and you'd get lots of it by running a stark row of bulbs around the frame – Hollywood-style. It can be fun, although be warned, the light is very unflattering.

Consider using mirror tiles to effectively cover an entire wall. There's a wide selection of sizes and types; some are pre-drilled, others are self-adhesive. They are cheaper and easier to fix than sheet glass, but they must be put on a dry, level surface otherwise at best, you get a badly distorted reflection or worst, they won't even stick on properly.

They are built up in horizontal courses; some require a paper-thick gap to allow for movement, others are butted together, so check the instructions.

Wallpaper must be stripped, and plaster, emulsion paint, wood, chipboard or any other similarly porous surfaces must be sealed using gloss – not vinyl – paint, which should be allowed to dry for at least three days beforehand. Similarly, newly-plastered walls must be allowed to dry out to a whitish shade – this could take months! Don't try and stick mirror tiles on cold walls of unheated rooms before warming the wall first, so that temperature changes will not affect the adhesion of the fixing pads.

Large sheet glass mirrors are expensive and can be very heavy and difficult to handle and fix, but mirror magic doesn't involve using huge sheets of it. If you're not absolutely confident of your ability to fix a mirror safely on a wall, don't do it.

The rule is always to run it from floor to ceiling and right into a corner, which will give the illusion of floor and ceiling continuing around the corner – but of course extra care needs to be taken in the use of vacuum cleaners and brushes.

It's essential to leave a small air space (about 3 mm) between a sheet mirror and the wall in places of high humidity such as bathrooms and kitchens, and the space is also preferable in other rooms. Mirrors for bathrooms have a special backing to preserve the silvering, so don't fix any other type in these situations.

Again, the wall must be perfectly flat, otherwise you're likely to crack the glass as you secure it. You can overcome quite severe unevenness by first fixing a chipboard or plywood base-board onto the wall; if the surface is only slightly awry, use extra washers as a packing.

Glass is of course very brittle and great care needs to be taken when screwing through pre-drilled holes into the wall. The screw must be driven straight into the wall – the screw heads need soft washers behind them to prevent them binding or trapping the glass and exerting any pressure on it. Consequently the hole for the wall-plug must be drilled at right angles to the wall – if the plug isn't straight the screw will follow it, and almost certainly crack the glass.

You can frame fixed mirrors with a full four-sided frame, but a top and bottom strip made out of rebated wood would be quite sufficient in an alcove. Plug and screw the bottom support first, lift the mirror into place and mark the top edge. Fix plugs into the wall before lifting the mirror back and screwing the top rebated support into place.

Mirror clips are only safe to use on smaller, lighter pieces of glass. They come in sets of four adjustable and two fixed types. The latter are fixed first, using a spirit level, to support the base of the glass. Support the mirror on them and draw its outline on the wall as a guide to positioning the adjustable clips – one on each side and two on the top. All the clips are fixed with the metal washer against the wall and the soft, nylon washer next to the mirror backing. The screwheads are counter-sunk into the nylon washers to prevent any contact with the mirror back, and to hold the clip firmly, but also enable it to slide out and back on to the mirror, to hold it in place.

Traditionally, the living room mirror was placed over the fireplace; it's difficult to think of a more dangerous place, particularly if you have an open fire and young children around. Think about making better use of the alcoves each side of the chimney breast by covering them with mirrors and then fixing book shelves. You could use pre-drilled mirrors behind each shelf – the wood would hide the joins.

Mirrors can be fixed with great effect onto the doors of fitted wardrobes in bedrooms, taking away the heaviness of these large blank pieces of furniture and giving that illusion of space.

Fixings and Fastenings

*'Oh well, I was never really hooked on
those old pictures anyway . . .'*

Some people can't even put a picture up on a wall. For various,
often quite devious reasons, golf, fishing and football being only
three, this is an image some people are quite keen to promote.
But coming unstuck on even simple projects or repairs that
involve fixings and fastenings can ruin an otherwise reasonably
competent project or repair.

The difficulty is the enormous range of nails, screws, nuts
and bolts and quite specialist fixings and fastenings available.

Each has a particular and specific application, and they are rarely interchangeable. If you're not sure what to use, then go to a good hardware or tool shop and tell them what the job is. Don't go to one of the big DIY superstores where the young, well-meaning assistant is likely to recommend you get your collapsible anchor at the next Boat Show. And never buy special offer bulk assortments of screws, nails and plugs. It's a way some retailers have of getting rid of items that they can't otherwise sell, either because they're made of inferior materials or ones of such eccentric sizes they're very infrequently used.

Here, then, are a few guidelines about fixing things, particularly on walls, a simple job which nevertheless seems to defeat a lot of first timers. Man may have walked on the moon, but he hasn't yet invented a screw that will stick into masonry and stay there all by itself. So you've got to use one of a variety of plastic or fibre wall plugs or devices like the collapsible anchor for hollow, cavity walls.

More about these later, but first, how to make a hole in a solid piece of masonry. The easiest and most efficient way is with a hammer-action electric drill, switched to low speed and armed with a special, hard masonry bit. The method employed depends entirely on the the material being attacked. Traditional brick, and now blockwork, walls present no problem at all, and can be drilled with a non-hammer drill probably set on its slowest speed to prevent the tool overheating.

Shelves fall off walls because the fixer hasn't taken the trouble to match the plastic plug to the screw being used. A glance at the plug box, or the strip of plastic they come on will usually tell you that. These plastic strips frequently have gauges indicating the appropriate screw and plug sizes. But many of the newer-designed plugs will fit a range of screw sizes, for size six to ten, for example.

The other frustrating howler is to make the hole too deep, so that the plug disappears into it. Stick a piece of plastic tape around the bit to mark the appropriate depth. Many plastic plugs have collars which prevent them from being pushed in too far. These are fine for anything but fixing into tiles, when the plug must always be pushed through the tile into the hole, or the tile may crack. Stop the drill bit from initially skidding on the tile by drilling through a piece of transparent tape. Incidentally, it's best to start a screw into a plug with a couple of light hammer taps.

But things do go wrong, as the most boringly proficient DIY person will admit. If you've drilled a hole badly off-centre, it's no trouble to fill it with Polyfilla and start again. But usually, you *just* miss the right spot. You might be able to get around this by inserting the screw down the side. But it's always better to forget that hole, make another through the fitting and start again. So you've made a hole that's too big and the plug is turning within it. Put in a bigger plug and (only if the fixture will take it) use a bigger screw. It's also possible to put a smaller plug inside a bigger one.

Some walls, particularly those made of breeze block will crumble when you try and plug them. Try drilling out a large (say 25 mm) hole in them and hammering in an oversize piece of wooden dowelling, making good around it with quick-setting cement (Polycell make a good one) and later screw directly into the dowel.

But some walls seem to defeat the most persistent drilling – you usually discover this when you try and fix a curtain rail above a window because you'll be trying to drill into a reinforced concrete lintel. One solution is a 2 in by 1 in wooden batten fastened to the wall either side of the lintel and fixed in between with a good contact adhesive (put on the wall and not the wallpaper.) If you can make shallow holes in the lintel, then so much the better, but you'll have to cut the wall plugs down to size and use lots of smaller screws.

That's the elementary part. If you have a particularly heavy thing to put up on a wall, it's best to use a wall anchor. These work on the same principle as screw and plug, but of course are much more expensive and need at least a 10 mm hole. They're metal and expand as you screw in a bolt. Some of the lighter versions are called 'through bolts' because they will pass through the hole drilled into the cupboard or whatever – you of course use an ordinary high-speed steel bit to make a hole through the wood – and they have the advantage that you can drill the hole through that and into the wall, thus ensuring perfect alignment.

Some people expect a couple of wall plugs to do far more support than they're designed to, and really heavy fitments are best supported by an inconspicuous batten, preferably stained or painted to match the fitment, and fixed to the wall with masonry nails.

Heavy furniture can be fixed to hollow (cavity) walls by similarly bridging the studs – the cross-pieces in the internal structure – with a heavier batten. If the weight is really great, it's best to fix this with coach screws which are secured with a spanner.

It's really a matter of plain common sense which type of screw to use. You'll find that size 8 and 10 screws are used on countless occasions; less than 8 is really too slender for anything but the lightest fittings.

Employing Builders

Of course you can do it yourself. Just about anything is possible if you've got enough time, energy and determination. But if you're lacking in just one of these, then either cancel all plans or face the inevitable and hire a builder. There are a lot of good people around, but sifting the pros from the cons just isn't easy. It may be comforting to know that lots of money is by no means a key to success in hiring builders. One firm I know of botched a millionaire's house drainage so badly they managed to poison his ornamental carp. Another monstered another rich man's central heating system so dramatically that the innocent wife called in the gas board who were surprised to find an illegal but extremely economical meter had been installed.

The intention of many of these DIY pieces has been to indicate not only what's reasonably possible but also what's available, so I hope readers will already have a pretty clear idea of what to tell the builder to do without being too baffled by technical jargon. There is often an abyss of communication between the punter and the tradesman.

One of the safest ways of finding a good 'little man' is by recommendation; it's not infallible though – your friends might have vastly different standards of 'a smashing job' to your own, so go and see it and make your own judgement. Get a tradesman to produce written references – and check back on them.

The local council surveyor's department is an excellent source, but only if you can befriend one of the staff into telling you, totally unofficially of course, who in your area is good. There are dozens of professional bodies and organisations, covering almost every building activity, and their details are available in public libraries. Many will give free technical advice, most will recommend member firms, and will intervene in disputes. But such firms are likely to be pricey.

If you have real doubts about a builder's plans on a major project, for example an extension or an additional room, consult the local surveyor's department. The moment you do, you risk becoming involved in the bureaucratic machine. But the Building Regulations, which specify what you can and cannot do, are designed to set tenable standards of space, ventilation, light and so on. They're for your own good.

Planning permission for projects like extensions is essential; ignore them and the council have the right to knock everything down. But in getting such permission, you will also know the correct specifications for method and material. An informal, preliminary discussion with the planning department could also provide you with enough knowledge of the job to be done to provide a written specification which details the stages of work. The final line should always point out that all work complies with local authority requirements.

If you present a written specification to a builder it becomes the basis of a contract, so leave nothing to chance. Write down every step, including 'making good of decorations'. It doesn't have to be written in building language; just make sure everything you want done is included. Good builders will be able to put you in touch with qualified people who write complete specifications for the novice householders. It's a lot cheaper than an architect's fee, but of course you won't get the latter's training and experience in supervising the stages of a project and translating your particular needs into an actual structure.

Architects can be invaluable, though, if the project is complex and really beyond your fathoming. Many offer a 'partial service' which amounts to advice up to the planning stage, at a standard fee.

Always get at least three estimates before hiring a builder, and remember the most expensive will not necessarily be the best, nor the cheapest the worst. Difficult, isn't it?

The estimate should of course give a total cost, (including VAT and any offered guarantee) and establish an exact day on which work will start and how long the job will take. Failure to meet the start deadline could mean you have the right to cancel the job.

Unfortunately, many builders will begin work with great gusto, only to scale down considerably the operation as the work gets under way, when more manpower is needed for the next customer, so it's vital not to let the job slow up. No one likes a nag, but make your concern very clear immediately things look like slowing to a stop; if you don't, the next problem might be the builder not showing up at all for a couple of days, or even weeks. It happens, and there is very little you can do about it. Don't hang around when work is going on, but inspect the progress every evening, and if you think something is going wrong, tell the builder so as soon as possible. Much better a little loss of face at this stage than hiding your worries until the problem becomes more complex at a later stage of the work.

Never, ever, go away on holiday and leave a builder to get on with it. Chances are he won't.

One of the many causes for a builder's non-appearance, and also the sudden, dramatic rises in costs are 'the extras' that mess up his schedules. So, do not change your mind and have new ideas once the work has started. It's just not fair to the builder, and he'll make you pay for the aggravation. If you cannot avoid asking him to do extra work, agree a price at the time – in writing, from both sides.

Most builders will not want payment for jobs lasting two or three weeks until after the completion of the work, but it's reasonable that they should ask for interim payments on longer projects, in order to keep their own cash flowing. Never pay a lot of money in advance, but if you are really convinced a builder wants some cash for materials – unimpressive as these might be – then pay by cheque, so you will have a record of the money being passed over.

The building trade is unfortunately littered with bankruptcies; you can legally suspend your contract if the builder suddenly becomes insolvent or bankrupt. He is obliged by law to leave your premises and not receive further payment.

If you're dissatisfied with the finished product, then try a warning letter from a solicitor – the local library should have a copy of the Law Society's regional directory which will list solicitors familar with building contract disputes. But beware, most building firms have indemnity insurance covering court claims, and may simply bin a solicitor's letter, landing you with the cost of a court case you might not win and adding considerably to your grief. Consumer advice centres, Citizens' Advice Bureaus and the Trading Standards Offices may all be able to help in smaller claims. Claims of £500 and less can be dealt with by the Small Claims Court, where cases can proceed by documentation, only if both you and the tradesman agrees.

Removals

Moving home is claimed to be the third most stressful event in a family lifetime – after bereavement and divorce. It can also provide you with a huge bill at the very time when your finances are already busted, if you try and take the easy way out and employ professional removers. If you've lots of furniture and paraphernalia then you've really no option but to do this.

Contact one of the more than 800 firms belonging to the British Association of Removers, which says its members reach certain standards and offers to mediate between their members and customers if disputes about damage and loss cannot be be resolved in a more amicable fashion. In reality, the degree of some firms' willingness to settle such matters will be directly correlated with the amount of tip you give the 'Guvnor' as he and his team leave you depressed, bewildered and bone tired, sitting on a pile of unpacked boxes and wondering where the kettle is.

DIY moving is really only for flat-dwellers. Any bigger amounts of furniture make it into far too much of an enduro-marathon. And be realistic. Have you ever tried to lift a washing machine or a cooker?

First, time it right. DIY home removals, in fact any removals, are best done in the winter. The alleged 'urge' to move in the spring is strictly for the birds; they don't have solicitors who go on holiday on the eve of M-day, leaving your file and/or your seller's papers in the hands of an overworked colleague who seems invariably to have 'just gone to lunch'. That apart, DIY moving can be a pretty hectic, overheated business on a mid-summer's day, and former old friends and potential helpers who have not already made you well-aware of their suddenly 'very' bad backs are also less likely to be away enjoying themselves during the winter.

You really do need help, but not too much, otherwise the situation can quickly get very bad-tempered as eager bodies collide in the initial jokey enthusiasm. You should start your move two or three weeks before the actual day by reserving The Van. You can hire one from most car hire firms providing you are over 21 and have a clean driving license.

Some companies, like Ryder, have a pack-and-load option, and 20 ft box vans which will take an enormous amount of stuff, but generally a Ford Transit 35 cwt Luton-bodied van is ideal as it's reltively easy for a car driver to adapt to. A Luton will cost between £35 and £40 a day. A Luton-bodied van has that additional load space over the driver's cab, which really is invaluable for lightweight items. If you're moving between towns, where the big hire companies have branches, then it's possible that you can pay extra to 'drop-off' the van at your destination. This charge can be quite high, though.

It's absolutely esential to have some means of shifting heavy items around, and the best I've found is an extremely tough Black and Decker trolley, which can be used either flat as a furniture 'skate' under big bulky loads like beds, or easily converted into a more conventional porter's trolley. Either way, it will easily pay for itself. A rechargeable electric screw-driver will also relieve you of an enormous amount of wrist-aching dismantling of some pieces of furniture, as well as all the things you have to take off walls.

During your two weeks of nervous preparation you will of course have collected lots of strong, medium sized cardboard boxes. Start packing non-essential items almost immediately. Don't try and fill big boxes, you'll probably never be able to move them out of the room – particularly if they're filled with books. Tea chests are probably still best if you can get hold of a quantity of them, but as they're generally on hire you've got the hassle of returning them to recover deposits.

If you have any documents or valuables, consider puting them in the care of your bank during the time of the move. Fridges and freezers need to be defrosted before a move, so start depleting their contents as soon as you have the dreaded date for the completion of contracts.

Pack china, glass and crockery, heavily swathed in news-paper, no more than three layers deep, topping up each box with lightweight items like duvets, which will provide additional protection. Pack room by room, clearly labelling and colour coding the containers. This may seem tedious at the time, but may save months of frustrating searching in your new home.

When you load a van, remember that what goes on first comes off last. Distribute heavy items as evenly as possible on the floor of the vehicle, placing lighter furniture on top. Secure these lighter items down with rope – clothes line is ideal. If you don't it's possible that they will, in the course of the journey, all fall against the back door of the van, making it extremely difficult to open at a moment when you can well do without such extra challenges.

Gas and electricity boards need at least 48 hours' notice for disconnections, but it's worth paying to take your telephone number with you if you can, and worth paying a reasonable sum to have your mail redirected for three months, just in case your single Premium Savings Bond comes up.

Murphy's Law says that the washing machine connections will be different at your new address, and that your hot and cold filling machine will only have a cold-feed to be connected to. A device called a 'Y-connector' will solve this problem until you can get the machine properly plumbed in.

Check that your insurance policy covers breakages and damage during removals, and if it doesn't, consider taking temporary extra cover just for the move.

And make sure, in the maelstrom of a move, you remember where you packed the kettle, tea bags and mugs.

GREENGUIDE

for Weddings

written & edited by
Jen Marsden

GREENGUIDE

MARKHAM PUBLISHING • UNITED KINGDOM

Written & edited by Jen Marsden
Design & layout by Patricia Hennigs
Research by Gavin Markham, Freda

Green Guide Series Editor: Gavin Ma

This edition published October 200

ISBN 978-1-905731-49-7

Markham Publishing
31 Regal Road, Weasenham Lane Industrial Estate, Wisbech,
Cambridgeshire PE13 2RQ
United Kingdom
T: +44 (0) 1945 461 452
E: distribution@markhampublishing.co.uk
www.markhampublishing.co.uk

Printed and bound in the UK on FSC-certified, sustainable paper and board by Cambrian Printers Ltd,
Llanbadarn Road, Aberystwyth, Ceredigion SY23 3TN
T: +44 (0) 1970 613 000 E: info@cambrian-printers.co.uk W: www.cambrian-printers.co.uk

The views expressed in this guide are not necessarily those of the publishers.

Although we have tried to ensure the accuracy of the information provided in this book, the publishers
are not liable for any inaccuracies or inconvenience arising thereof.

Contents

Adam and Jill Vaughan, Regent's Park Bridge, July 2007

Deep peace of the running water to you
Deep peace of the flowing air to you
Deep peace of the quiet earth to you
Deep peace of the shining stars to you
And the love and care of us all to you

~ Celtic Blessing ~

Glam, Gorgeous and **Green**

I have a confession to make. I'm a guilty green bride. As founder of Ethical Weddings I feel I must 'fess up and admit that yes, my guests did have to travel between our ceremony and reception venue and that no, our wedding breakfast was not entirely organic.

It may seem a little odd to be sharing this revelation in a Green Guide for Weddings but whilst we're celebrating the growing enthusiasm for the green or ethical wedding (the latter to give a nod to social issues too), increasingly we are encountering brides for whom this extra element of tying the knot (on top of seating plans and family feuds) is leaving them in an ethical tangle.

Nowhere is this more evident than in our very own Ethical Weddings Forum where it seems an eco compromise can be cause for a crisis of conscience. The case that springs to mind was the bride who, attempting to navigate the green honeymoon minefield, had rejected one destination after another for reasons ranging from human rights records to carbon emissions. Having finally settled on a trip around Norway's fjords, the hapless bride was then left floundering when her uncle expressed surprise at her choice given Norway's stance on whaling.

Thankfully, another member of the Forum stepped in to commend her on her admirable planning thus far and to help her gain some perspective by asking whether on this reasoning we should avoid travel to Spain because of bull fighting.

To avoid turning a guilty shade of green whilst making your own wedding plans do remember that even thinking about the impact of your wedding is more than many will do. On a day that can all too often be about excessive consumption, waste, and 'me, me, me!', putting a little thought into how you can reduce, reuse and recycle on this biggest of big days could go a long way.

How successfully you can put your plans into action for what will in most cases be the biggest and most emotional party you ever throw depends on so many factors from the wishes of family and friends to budget and geographical location. Accept there will be compromises and cope with them creatively; get inspired by other ethical brides and green grooms who have gone up the aisle before you but don't compare and compete or the green guilt will be on top of you again!

As one of the latest comments in the 'Green Guilt' section of the Forum says: 'At the end of the day, it isn't a competition to be the greenest bride around. For me, it's about using the day to make a difference, and if we can make people think along the way, then all the better.'

Too often the headlines we see encourage this sense of competition, 'Is this Britain's greenest bride?', 'Who's the greenest of them all?', when really we should be helping each other. Chat in the forums, with your friends, share ideas, advice, confetti and even clothes! Be guided by what is important to you as a couple (rather than endlessly playing the fair trade versus local debate in your head); don't forget it's to celebrate your love that you're doing this in the first place!

Many of the brides interviewed for this Green Guide prefaced their comments with 'We tried to have a green wedding but...' But nothing. The more people try to plan green weddings, asking their chocolate fountain supplier for fair trade chocolate or their caterer for free range eggs, the more ethical choices will be available to future brides and grooms. If you've started to change the way people think about weddings with your questions – even in a small way – I think you can forgive yourself that glass of non-organic champagne... just this once mind! ■

Katie Fewings
Ethical Weddings Limited

Introduction

The big wedding day is coming. It's not everyday it happens – hopefully once in a lifetime for the lucky ones.

Author Jen Marsden © Squareink

The greatest advice I was ever given is, 'How do you eat an elephant?' Well although we don't want to eat an endangered species the answer is simple: 'Cut it up into little pieces'. This is exactly what this *Green Guide for Weddings* aims to do. Weddings can be costly events – not just to the bank balance, but also to the planet. A quarter of a million of us Brits do it every year – that's an awful lot of confetti and food scraps! Imagine if every single one of those weddings did one thing greener. It would make a huge influence on all the guests who attend, and in turn increase awareness of the positive aspects of our changing world. You can do the planet a favour with every choice you make!

In times of climate change and the huge media focus on going green, marriage is a good opportunity to consider your consumer action and its impact. It's also a fabulous time to find new eco companies, which you can use time and time again throughout your married life.

As a bride- and bridegroom-to-be you can be glam, gorgeous and green. We look at all the aspects to help you plan for your special day. There are challenging questions from all those involved in the preparations to overcome – the type of wedding ceremony you have, the outfits, gift lists and even honeymoon. You know you don't want a blood diamond on your finger – but what are the other options whilst keeping some bling?

Lesley Stratton-Hughes, a wedding planner and founder of company Getting Married from the Inside Out has noticed a change in people's values. 'The celebrity style inspired wedding still exists but awareness of the green wedding is on the rise. More and more people are using some, if not all eco friendly, eco chic ideas and on the whole this seems to bring about a much more thoughtful, fulfilling and enjoyable experience. The environmentally conscious bride tends to be less selfish, more open and aware and I think that can be extended to becoming more personally awake and aware too. I think times have changed so much and marriage means something different today. In order for it to work and fit in with these fast moving modern times it needs a different approach and understanding.'

> **She told me that if she had spent thousands and thousands of pounds, they wouldn't have been any happier. It was the first time I had come across an ethical wedding**

The first question to ask one another is 'what do we mean by green?' In this day and age of trendy environmentalism it sometimes seems that anything goes. People, planet, animals – everything seems to have a *cause célèbre*. Whilst it is a complex green world out there, the simplest answer is: what is most important to you and your partner. Green can mean animal friendly, fair trade, local, organic, recycled, seasonal, sustainable, vegetarian, vegan – the list is seemingly endless. We show you how each choice really does create a more sustainable world, offering the facts rather than a sermon.

Weddingchaos.co.uk conducted a recent poll and found that more than one in five brides (21.2 per cent) did consider the environment when planning their big day. It's easier than ever before to do, making planning that little bit easier.

Further inspiration comes from other couples who have greened their weddings with various case studies throughout the Guide. One recently wed bride, Becca Lush Blum said she had a green wedding as she 'wanted to start our married life the way we intended to go on – feeling optimistic that people can make a difference in the choices they make, and that a green future is possible.'

We have an array of experts offering their knowledge and opinion, guiding you down the aisle. Barbara Crowther, Communications Director for the Fairtrade Foundation tells us that even if your green passion is for other people, you can cover it on your day. 'Whether it's a fair trade rose in your buttonhole, the wine for your wedding toast, or the huge array of fair trade foods you could incorporate into your menu, the opportunities to make fair trade part of your wedding plans are many and varied. By choosing products carrying the FAIRTRADE Mark, you can ensure that your special day also helps poor communities move one step closer to a celebration of their own.'

To producers in developing countries your wedding budget is hugely supportive of all their sustainable visions. You can also have a greener wedding on a shoestring. Long time Oxfam volunteer Barbara Walmsely who established their bridal departments remembers how families didn't always spend so much dosh. 'My favourite customer was a girl who came back with her hired gown, enthused about her delightful wedding. With little money they asked all the guests to bring a plate of food to their home for the reception. I recall they even picked the flowers from their garden. She told me that if she had spent thousands and thousands of pounds, they wouldn't have been any happier. It was the first time I had come across an ethical wedding and I think it cuts a lot of the stress by keeping it simple.'

Katherine Cartlidge of Wedding Chaos adds, 'It may be a coincidence but three of the biggest costs of the typical wedding are also probably the most damaging to the environment; your venue, your food and your honeymoon. There is nothing worse than potatoes that have flown several thousand miles on an aeroplane ending up being served with your wedding breakfast…when the field next door is full of them!'

Clio Turton from the Soil Association agrees. 'Choosing seasonal, local and organic food and drink for your wedding will make it much more than a happy occasion for you and your friends and family – the choice will also benefit your local community, UK farmers, wildlife, farm animals, and the environment. You could even go for organic health and beauty products to get your skin glowing and fresh for the big day.'

When you are marrying what one bride to be describes as a 'reluctant environmentalist' it is better not to ram the eco aspects down their throat. If you are met with indifference then don't be so green-aspiring that it causes you to forget the reason you are getting married. The most important factor is to surround yourself by those you love to share your special day. Never feel disheartened as every small step you take is that first drop in the ocean and a blossoming seed of hope for the future.

May your wedding be joyfully green, however you choose to celebrate. And don't let those figurative elephants trample on your dreams! ■

Jen Marsden

The Wedding **Budget**

Being a little brash with your cash for your wedding is the one time you are likely to get away with it. Asking a friend what his budget was for his wedding, he gulped and looked a little sheepish. 'We didn't have one – we're paying for it now though'.

Having an eco wedding doesn't always necessarily mean that you are cutting back on luxury, but it can work out cheaper if you focus on the 'less is more' concept. A Sheik's son in Dubai spent over £22 million by getting a stadium purpose built for the venue. Now whilst that's not practical for the majority of marriages, it is worth putting your thoughts down on paper as to what you want realistically, and how much you can afford. As you attempt to green up your wedding, you may notice the savings through buying a second hand dress or choosing an outdoor venue, and not hiring a gas guzzling Rolls Royce.

Jenny Irwin, Marketing Manager of The Ecology Building Society has her top tip. 'Do not to get sucked in to the whole wedding market – prices seem to quadruple if the word wedding is involved. For example I bought my wedding shoes for £25 when the same pair at a wedding shop were over £100! You don't need to stick to tradition; it's your day so do what you want!'

Taking the time to plan a wedding will give you more time to save. The average engagement is fifteen months, which may help you bank the dreams you have for the day.

Traditionally, the bride's parents are expected to pay for wedding clothes for the bride and her attendants, flowers for the church and reception, transport, stationery, catering, the cake and the photography. This leaves the bridegroom to pay for the church or registry office fees, the bouquets, button holes and corsages for all the key players, outfits for himself and the best man, gifts for the attendants and best man, and the bride's rings and wedding present.

Brides if you think you've got off lightly by only having to pay for your fiancée's ring and wedding present then think again. In the words of Dylan, times they are a' changing. WeddingChaos.co.uk conducted a survey suggesting that a massive 64 per cent of bride and

grooms are now paying for their own wedding, whilst 13 per cent of couple's parents are joining forces to pay the burden. If your parents are giving you money towards the wedding then it might be worth mentioning to your relatives that they receive inheritance tax exemption. The taxman allows £5,000 tax free from your parents and £2,500 tax free from grandparents. Any other person can give you £1,000 tax free.

What the day is truly about: Andy and Niki Clarke, 2006 © Niki Clark

It may be that as a modern day couple you have more financial independence than days gone past; however it makes sense to put a reign on the spending before you begin.

Hearts of Gold

Whilst the classic wedding tends to cost more than £17,000 these days, if you don't want all the trimmings then you can get it for as little as £100 if you choose a simple civil wedding. You may have those secret wedding desires that you can't say no to, and if that's the case then prioritise before you snip the spending down. Having the wedding ceremony and reception in one venue is likely to cut

Have a wedding outdoors, naturally © lovleah

your costs considerably, by not having to worry about transport or to pay twice for venue fees. It's also worthwhile taking time to get various quotes rather than taking the word of one supplier. Checking the details thoroughly, such as whether VAT is included is crucial to keep a handle on your budget. Always put an 'Other' section in your budget to keep some money back for any unexpected costs.

Ensure your world doesn't get completely absorbed by wedding magazines – remember what the marriage is really all about.

Contract of Love

Don't appear too keen when dealing with suppliers, particularly if prices are quoted on an individual basis – they may hike it up if it looks like you've got your heart set on it. Ask whether discounts are offered if you confirm a booking straight away, or if you book at a particular time of year. Wedding businesses tends to be busier around Spring and Summer, so make sure you're not getting the prime time price.

When working with your suppliers, make sure you sign fool-proof contracts, stating date of delivery, quantities and correct delivery addresses. This will ensure the delivery of their products or services are on time. Ask for a clause for the worst case scenario if they don't deliver what you have agreed and ask to pay upon delivery – just in case anything happens to the company between the time of booking and the wedding.

Green Money

It might be that you decide to create a joint bank account for the purpose of the wedding. Why not give your two bob's worth by joining an ethical bank?

Financiers tend to invest in the arms trade, oppressive regimes and other unloving aspects, encouraging social exclusion by making the rich richer and the poor, well, broke. Whilst no bank is perfect, why not work with one who puts their support towards environmental, charitable and sustainable development projects?

As Will Ferguson from Triodos says, 'If you want your wedding day to be truly ethical, then the way you save for it should be as green as your bridesmaid's dresses.' You may buy organic flowers and splash out on a fair trade honeymoon, but you could undo some of your good work if you're saving for your big day with a bank that finances environmental destruction or social injustice in the developing

Considerable Costs...

By budgeting each aspect of the wedding you can get an idea of how much to save – or what to scrimp on.

Attire
Wedding rings
Wedding dress and alterations
Bride's head veil, shoes and
accessories
Bridesmaid gowns
Groom's suit, shoes and accessories
Bestman and usher suits
Hair and make up

Ceremony & Reception
Venue
Officiant
Registrar's Fees
Transport
Accommodation
Musicians
Photography and videography
Catering – food, crockery etc.
Table decoration
Bar and/or corkage
Other entertainment

Floral
Bouquets, buttons and corsages
Flowers for decoration

Gifts
Best man and usher gifts
Bridesmaid gifts
Guest's wedding favours and keepsakes

Stationery
Wedding Invitations
Order of services
Thank you letters

Afterthoughts
Honeymoon
Press announcements
Cleaning up (if DIY)

world. Triodos Bank only supports enterprises that benefit people and the planet, and has a range of actively ethical accounts for savers who want their nest egg to make a positive impact.

The Co-operative Bank also offer great savings and loans with a customer led ethical policy, and The Ecology Building Society have saving accounts that you could ask your guests to put money into rather than ask for gifts.

The Ethical Investment Research Services (EIRIS) website offers independent advice for the ethical performance of companies, including a directory of all the green and ethical funds in the UK.

Reassurance in Insurance

With the average cost of an engagement ring now in the region of £1,500, leading financial services provider Co-operative Insurance (CIS) is urging couples to make sure they have arranged adequate insurance to protect their bling. Research, carried out by CIS, has shown that only 35 per cent of us actually have the correct level of cover in the form of a personal possessions policy and, of those, only 12 per cent have specifically noted expensive items on their policy. James Hillon, CIS Head of Home Insurance, says, 'whilst not wanting to spoil the special occasion it's important that adequate insurance cover is taken out on these expensive pieces of jewellery. Unfortunately many people don't realise that they don't have personal possessions cover until it's too late.'

Currently there are no specific ethical wedding insurance options on the market, but you can get around it by adopting personal possessions insurance.

Naturesave offers contents insurance as one of its products. They pledge that 10 per cent of the premiums generated from the sale of all home buildings, contents and travel policies go to benefit environmental and conservationist organisations.

Borrowing

If you are borrowing money, then you want to be sure it's something that you can realistically pay back. Look at the loan repayment options carefully – it's not great starting married life with debt to endure.

If you are choosing a credit card, then make a plan for your repayments before you start the spending. A new credit card called 'think' by The Co-operative Bank is the world's first credit card aimed at rewarding ethical consumerism. It offers a lower rate of interest for designated ethical purchases, whilst at the same time helps the rain-forests. Not only are the cards made from PETg plastic – a greener material that doesn't involve vinyl-chloride, it offers a lower rate of interest for purchases made with ethical partners including Lush, IKEA, Co-operative Food Stores, Arriva, Raleigh, and thetrainline.com – perfect for the honeymoon. ■

Make your money float further with ethical investment © Shiyali

Wedding **Planner**

Are wedding planners a luxury, following in the throes of Hollywood super stars for something you can do on your own, or are they the fairy godmother coming along to help you for one of the biggest days of your life?

As their numbers increase every year, it looks like there are more individuals using the services of a wedding planner. In actual fact a Weddingchaos.co.uk survey suggested 51 per cent did not or would not use a wedding planner. Perhaps we just don't want to see Jennifer Lopez running off with our partner as in the motion picture...

So what does a wedding planner actually do? Some describe her (it is a predominantly female industry) as a financial controller, a mediator, facilitator and artisan. They certainly need negotiation skills both between the couple to be, the families and other individuals involved. On the day they can also act as the stage manager, manoeuvring the day with smooth success, however many are not required by this stage as all the preparations are usually complete. Wedding planners are only as involved as you wish them to be, and sourcing recommended suppliers is the first step to preventing a dose of hiccups.

Putting extra money into an already large budget can be a reason not to use a planner. The secret of wedding planners is that they often get discounts ranging from 10 – 20 per cent from the suppliers and whilst some planners understandably keep it for themselves, some pass it on to the client to show how much money is being saved. If they are professional planners from reputable sources then they are likely to save you some dosh anyway that can be put towards a solar panel on the roof of your new matrimonial house. If you're not the most organised individual, have a busy schedule or perhaps don't know where to begin when looking at your wedding strategy, then wedding planners do make financial sense. It's a good idea to have someone who is used to structuring action points and making all those calls to the suppliers for the big day. Wedding planners are used to the traditions that go with a wedding and are fully prepared for any seemingly stray emotions that may appear during this high pressure time, acting also as a spiritual guide.

A wedding planner will help you relax on the day itself © Graham Clark

Lesley of Getting Married from the Inside Out says that her own wedding seven years ago had a huge impact on her. 'I had an epiphany as I was about to say my vows that will stay with me forever.

'I was calm, confident, vibrant, and knew that whatever the outcome further down the line I was meant to be getting married then to the man I had chosen to be with. It was an incredible, spiritual experience and I think it happened because I was prepared for it.

'I made a conscious effort to prepare myself both emotionally and psychologically in the months before we got married – I really got to know myself.' Her own experience is the driving force behind the service that she provides. 'As I watch weddings mutate into something purely commercial – style over substance – with an alarming loss of meaning and focus I feel that I have something to offer and share by helping to change how getting married is seen today, through reinforcing the core values but also putting a contemporary 21st century slant on it. I want to help people be mindful and conscious as they make this transition because so often it is done on autopilot, blindly following a template or formula.' As a trained life coach she also helps her couples get to the root of their nerves, doubts or anxiety and ultimately be free enough to be in the moment on their wedding day.

Jill Satin, a celebrant from the British Humanist Association gives an insight into a humanist ceremony

For humanists, the fundamental truth is that we have one life and that life on earth is all we have, but that makes it all the more precious and we treasure it and nurture it without recourse to religion. Because we have faith in the spirit of life, meaning and purpose in our lives can be created by living life abundantly and ethically. Marriage is one way to achieve that.

Couples who choose humanist weddings are usually political and socially aware, have environmental and green concerns, and value freedom of thought and action. Many couples from mixed ethnic and cultural backgrounds choose a humanist ceremony because it allows them the freedom to explore and celebrate their individual family heritage. What the couple want to say and do in their wedding is of paramount importance and so the ceremonies are co-created, often over several months, between the couple and the celebrant. All humanist ceremonies celebrants are trained to the highest standards in ceremonies work including research, writing, and delivery and many have complementary skills in event planning and even catering.

We don't advise couples how to have their wedding. One wedding last year was held on Dartmoor. The couple arranged transport to the road nearest the site by minibus and the guests then had a procession, carrying homemade banners to the place of the wedding. The reception was held in the local parish hall and the food was organic, locally sourced and provided by a local catering firm.

Another was on a beach. The couple each took a small cup of sand from by their feet and mixed it together (to represent a joining that couldn't be broken) and then guests each added something they found (such as a feather or pebble) to make a memento of the day. As the phrase has it – take away only memories and leave no footprints. ■

Humanist ceremonies – the ceremonies arm of the BHA – has 135 accredited wedding celebrants who conduct weddings in England and around the world. Fees vary across the country from £350 – £650. Humanist wedding ceremonies currently do not have any legal status in English law and therefore most couples choose to undertake a legal civil ceremony before or after their humanist wedding ceremony. If you live in Scotland then since 2005 BHA Scottish celebrants are licensed to conduct legal wedding ceremonies. Contact the BHA website at www.humanism.org to find a Humanist Ceremonies accredited celebrant in your area.

'Greening up your wedding is easier than you might think,' says eco wedding planner Bridget Stott. As a professional party and wedding planner for her own company Piece of Cake, she actively encourages couples to use local suppliers and has all the tips for the occasion. She's also aware that a bit of creativity goes a long way. 'One couple wanted to grow organic vegetables, and rented an allotment. They asked friends and family to offer some time working on the site or to buy gardening equipment or plants for it, instead of a typical wedding gift list.'

Rosie Ames is the founder of eco chic wedding and celebration website GreenUnion.co.uk and also runs her own wedding planning service, Dream Weddings & Celebrations, from her home in North Devon. Her passion is creating gorgeous, stylish and sustainable celebrations whatever the budget and she agrees that it is easy to do. 'We are now seeing a return to beautiful, meaningful and sustainable celebrations. Couples are less interested in excessive over-spending and over-consumption and smaller events are becoming more popular. The main thing to remember when planning a green or ethical wedding is that none of us are perfect. What's important is that you take small steps to do your bit, balancing sustainability with fabulous details. Just understanding this rule will ensure you have a wedding day to remember.'

> **Wedding planners are only as involved as you wish them to be, and sourcing recommended suppliers is the first step to preventing a dose of hiccups**

Young, passionate Charlie Burton always wished to be a wedding planner, yet found it difficult to justify the huge amount of waste involved in conventional weddings and so instead set up The Natural Wedding Company as another green website directory. 'I like to think of my green wedding directory as a sort of Yellow Pages. One of the most important things to me when it comes to weddings is getting away from this glossy super expensive image that people have of what a wedding should be. I want people to forget all the conventional, media produced ideas of what a wedding should be, and to really think about what their wedding day means to them, and deep down what they really want to get from it.'

Like most wedding planners, EcoMoon aid the design of the wedding, from colour schemes to table decorations, stationery, unusual favours, sourcing and co-ordinating all aspects, yet with an ethical twist.

They can also offer guest management, invitation advice, dress shopping and a 'Help Me' service for any worries or concerns you, your wedding party or your guests may have.

For similar services, Boutique Weddings charge 15 per cent of the overall cost of the wedding. They work with the Woodland Trust, the UK's leading woodland conservation charity by dedicating a tree for every couple they work with, and investing one per cent of their annual pre tax profit to them.

The Unexpected Wedding Planners

You may find wedding planners in all forms. One bride to be said her sister was put in charge of everything as the couple themselves were too busy and they knew her green tastes would be exactly what they were after. Getting your friends and family involved when they offer to help often makes the whole experience more inclusive – as long as they have similar ideas to you! Using everyone's skill sets can assist you in ensuring the wedding is less expensive or cheaper.

If you are getting married in a church, you may find that you receive a lot of support from the vicar and fellow parishioners – they are certainly used to the celebrations!

If you choose to have a humanist wedding, you may find that your chosen celebrant acts as a green guide for you too.

Online Organisation

If you do decide to use a wedding planner you don't necessarily need one in the flesh and bones, as is the glory of our interconnected information highway. There are an increasing number of websites that do the planning work for you. Amy Rucco, CEO of American company Wedding Window finds they also make the day easier. 'Engaged couples can share all of the details of their wedding with friends and family members conveniently and easily. That way all of the wedding guests can become more familiarised with both the bride and the groom prior to arriving at the actual event. Couples can also dramatically reduce the amount of snail mail correspondence that they would typically need to send out to inform guests of upcoming events if they have a wedding website. They can simply upload all of their planning information for their wedding guests on their website and then advise their guests of their website address via a Save the Date eCard.' Some couples find benefits from being able to look up the directions to the wedding on their mobile phones en route to the wedding itself therefore eliminating the need for printed directions. A low-cost and tailored service, this idea has been so successful that they have clients in over 85 countries.

Green Wedding Guru by wedding supplier Dee Grismond is a new blog that provides brides and groom to be with lots of useful information on how to make their wedding that little bit greener. They never lecture but try to offer examples of what you can do depending on what shade of green you want your wedding to be. They have a host of wedding and environmental experts giving useful advice and fielding your questions online. ■

Let the love float over your day © liebesspiel von schwänen

The **Venue**

How many people should we invite? How many people can we afford to invite? Why not turn this dilemma on its head by asking the question: What kind of venue do we want to get married in – and how many does it fit?

Wedding venues. We all have an idea of where we would like to get married. Certainly the diversity and choice of green wedding venues will make you want to say 'I do' all over the country if you're not careful.

It's important to get the wedding venue right – once you've ticked this box you'll find that other aspects will fall into place, as the venue can often dictate the theme. In the presence of so many friends, proving your eco ways is tough when your primary concern is saying your vows at the appropriate time. The largest wedding attendance was a Jewish wedding in Jerusalem in 1993 where 30,000 people attended – imagine the paper cup wastage on that one!

The venues that do your eco worrying for you can make life that little bit easier. One of the key factors in choosing your venue is location. Do you stay close to home where your friends can all attend? Do you go back to the roots of where your family are based – and if yes, can you fight it out as to whose family if you're not from the same region? Do you dare elope and make it a very small scale affair, merging your wedding with your honeymoon?

If you want to have a truly green occasion you will be considering transport options as well. How are you going to get your guests to the venue for the ceremony, and then on to the reception if that takes place elsewehere?

Weddingchaos.co.uk conducted a survey of 1,200 people asking couples what their preferred venues were. Whilst less than 48 per cent opted for a traditional church wedding there is still interest out there from couples. It's the flexibility of the venue that is making 26 per cent of couples go to licensed venues who can offer the 'all-inclusive', hassle free option. It's also perhaps due to the fact that couples are still required to regularly worship in the church they wish to wed in that is discouraging them. Registry offices account for 12 per cent of marriages, with the remaining 14 per cent going

abroad to marry – the latter is possibly not the most economic or ecological option.

The George in Rye is a wonderful green wedding venue who will even provide the organic wedding cake © The George in Rye

The Green Church

If you want a more conventional wedding with church bells involved but want to keep it eco friendly then you can! While civil ceremonies and partnerships are not accepted in your more traditional wedding service, there are a number of churches who have led the way with the green movement.

Aside from offering fair trade refreshments and organically certified biccies in the adjoining church halls, there are many churches that are heavens above the rest. Now the churches have gained their fair trade status, they are looking at the whole green cycle – from procurement, to combating climate change.

Churches and their church halls are wonderful venues for DIY weddings © David Hughes

The Greenest Churches...

North England
St Chad's, Far Headingley, Leeds
St John the Evangelist, Hurst Green, Lancashire

South England
Holy Trinity, Cleeve, Somerset
St Barnabas's, Queen Camel, Yeovil, Somerset
St Bartholomew's, Great Barrow, Chester
St Mary's, Welwyn, Hertfordshire
St Peter's, Spixworth, Norwich
Bramford Road Methodist Church, Ipswich

St Mary and St John, Cowley, Oxford
Mill Road Baptist Church, Cambridge

London
St Andrew's, Fulham, London
St Peter's, Bexhill
St Aldhelm's, Edmonton, north London
St James's, Piccadilly, London

Overseas
St John and St Philip, The Hague, The Netherlands

Source: 2007 Green Church Awards, Church Times

There are now over 100 churches in the UK that promise to include environmental considerations daily into their prayers, as set out by the organisation, Eco Congregation. With activists amongst its clergy, The Green Church of the Year (awarded by Church Times) went to the Holy Trinity in Cleeve, Somerset.

Most churches have an adjoining church hall, minimising the stress of getting from A-B, and making it easier for you to make the arrangements.

Considerations

If you want a green wedding and plan to have a venue do it all for you, then why not have some fun going beyond the glossy brochures and getting the green truth? Sometimes you may be faced with blank or perplexed faces but with a bit of explanation of your requirements you will likely get some answers, even if they are a bit airy fairy.

Certification

Good locations will have an accreditation of some sort – perhaps a few green awards for tourism or sustainability. Responsible Tourism Awards, Green Tourism Awards and Green Apple are just a few to look out for. This is handy for when you want to put the finer points in the hands of someone else. It's easier than having to do your own research and point out local eco suppliers. You can grin with pride when you tell your guests that there is a hippo in the venue's toilet (a water-saving device rather than a wild animal, that is).

If you want a green awarded wedding overlooking the Cornish sea then Bedruthan Steps Hotel is a lovely option. A family run hotel, it was founded in 1959 by the Whittington's. They've won awards including Gold in the Green Tourism Business Scheme and also a highly commended in the First Choice Responsible Tourism Awards. They actively promote a greener wedding to the 30 weddings held there each year. Approximately

A wedding in the vaults of The RSA, one of the greenest venues in the country who waste nothing in their green detail © The RSA

70 per cent of all the food is sourced locally and based on seasonal produce. Because of the hotel's rural location it is not possible to get a train direct however their nearest station is Bodmin Parkway and they can arrange a 30 minute biofuel taxi ride to the venue. They also offer a tree planting carbon offsetting scheme.

There's also the ISO14001 that is an independent audit ticking many boxes for the green stuff – it shows commitment to get accredited and is reviewed every year.

Check if the venue has a written ethical and/or environmental policy in place, stating what it does do and what their aspirations are. You may be surprised.

Knowing full well that a client is always right, if you ask for the green option, the venue are likely to bend over backwards to meet your requirements. Whilst it may seem like hard work, the benefit of this is that you are helping pave the path for the next couple that come along asking for a touch of the emerald-esque. Some venues across the larger cities have already got it sussed. One that noticeably makes a huge effort in its written policies is The RSA, located just off the Strand in London. What's great about this venue is that if you're a city slicker you don't have to hop on a train to wed. The RSA provides colourful graphs on all their environmental reporting on their website. They produce on average 120 bags of rubbish every week of which around 75 per cent are recycled and what's left is mainly food waste which cannot be recycled due to health and safety restrictions. Their linen has been specifically chosen to be more durable and uses less of their eco considerate detergent and energy when being cleaned. Even their branded water bottles are re-used due to an investment in an onsite water purification system.

Energy
More and more venues are taking steps to go green. Those that know their energy usage deserve a gold star! You can look out for the solar panels and wind turbines or folks on bicycles (pedal power) on site, but even if you don't see any signs don't give up. Ask where their energy is sourced from. Hopefully the answer will be through a renewable source supplier such as Ecotricity, Good Energy or Green Energy – or using some of the more mainstream energy companies' green tariffs – folks such as npower, British Gas and EDF energy offer them. Energy efficient light bulbs and installing devices that minimise energy usage – light sensor devices and automatic power timeouts on bar fridges overnight – should be applauded.

Waste
There tends to be a lot of waste after weddings, and we're not just talking about your uncle's false teeth under the table after a few too many reception brandies.

> It's important to get the wedding venue right – once you've ticked this box you'll find that other aspects will fall into place, as the venue can often dictate the theme

The venues that buy from local sources thus minimising the need for additional packaging are always good places to seek out. Buying in products that have recyclable packaging – in particular glass, some plastics (for example those that have the 'PET' symbol on them) and cardboard are good, or biodegradable packaging as long as there are means to compost. It's worth outlining to your wedding guests (without going overboard with the preaching) about your aims to reduce the environmental eyesore. Whilst you may not want your guests picking up after themselves, it's a good idea to check out the recycling facilities that are offered by the venue. Cooked food waste is usually the big green issue as it's hard to do much with it unless there are a few animals about to help. Minimise this yourself by having really tasty food that all gets eaten up and knowing what your guests will eat. Or ask the venue if they compost.

There are a lot of nasty chemicals out there... why not go the whole hog and ask them to switch to greener cleaning products for the clear up? You can even get reasonably inexpensive compostable bin bags to stick the scraps in.

If you fancy going across the sea to Ireland to seek out a readymade green option, then there's The Brooklodge Hotel in Macreddin Village, founded in December 1999 by three brothers Evan, Eoin and Bernard Doyle. They had a vision of creating a village-type environment encompassing a resort of high class accommodation with a homely country house feel, a retreat destination by way of spa treatments combined with the tranquillity of the environment. The Strawberry Tree restaurant, Ireland's only certified organic restaurant serves organic and wild foods. The Brooklodge Hotel holds on average 130 weddings a year. They recently bought a biodigester to gobble up the dry food waste, preventing it from going to landfill, and turn the wet waste into biofuel for electricity generation. Almost everything is recycled and they have their own sewage treatment system. If that's not enough, the heating comes from an on-site wood chip plant plus geothermal heat sourced from underground springs.

Types of venues

The Au Naturale
So the great outdoors affair. If you don't mind whether the weather is temperamental or you want something a little different then this is definitely a lovely, low cost option. You don't need to worry about decorations as you've got nature setting the scene for you.

You could have your wedding in your own back garden if it is big enough. Or why not get permission from your nearest Botanical Gardens or local park? If you're fond of water, then by the side of a lake or river could be rather special (surely the fish will be delighted, as long as they're not part of the planned feast). On the top of a moor, in the garden of a stately home, in a forest, in a field on a farm – the choice is entirely yours.

Have your wedding au naturale in a traditional environmentally thoughtful yurt
© World Inspired Tents

Supporting conservation work, one outdoors venue is Woodland Weddings. Founded three years ago, the Forestry Commission in Fort William, Scotland decided that by offering wedding ceremonies in the national forest would highlight the versatility of the woodlands. Set in a remote area it's not the easiest place to get to – after reaching Fort William by public transport or car you would either have to take a car or a horse and carriage (which could take some time) to reach the actual spot the ceremonies take place on. Woodland Weddings only have about eight weddings a year making it quite a special place, particularly as groups can be no larger than 20 people. Waste is kept to a minimum as no confetti is allowed, and with no need for energy, having a wedding outdoors like this is probably the greenest option out there.

The New Forest Tourism Association has set up an initiative called the Green Leaf Scheme, and all their establishments have signed up to the system which you can identify with a little green oak leaf on their section of the website. There is also a New Forest Marque that identifies that most ingredients will have travelled no more than a few miles to reach the plate, and for extra incentives they even offer discounts for guests arriving by rail!

Staff from New Forest suggest avoiding all that electricity by conducting a very quick official ceremony in the certified room before going to a glorious location in the forest or to a local garden, beach, under a tree or on a cliff top to conduct a full ceremony.

As a winner of the Responsible Tourism Awards 2007, there are many options in the New Forest offering a 'green' approach, including options for tight budgets such as self-catering.

Having a wedding on a farm brings the rustic effect into a wedding theme – and there's often plenty of space to roam about. You will also be bringing revenue into the countryside, helping to protect the natural diversity. Huntstile Organic Farm in Somerset is accommodating, whether you feel like camping out with your guests, in a bed and breakfast setting, or in self catering accommodation. They can offer organic catering from their working organic vegetable farm, set in the foothills of the Quantocks between Bridgwater and Taunton.

With no guarantee to the weather it would be foolish not to look at shelter options. Whilst there are many marquee companies out there that are relatively eco friendly in their own right and having minimal environmental impact, it's good to look for companies who have their roots in green or are local. The classic 'yurt' that has recently gained much attention at Summer festivals across the land is an innovative solution. One such supplier is Yurtopia, who can deliver across the UK. A little like tee-pees they are based on structures that nomadic peoples of central Asia have been using as their homes for thousands of years. You can either rent or buy them – or if you are feeling particularly hands on, go on a yurt building course and learn how to make them yourself. The wood is cut by hand, generally carried from the woodland to the workshop by hand and then stripped, worked, shaped and steamed (yes, you guessed it) by hand. The only machinery used is a cordless drill that runs off a 12 volt car battery and a sander that runs off a generator. Other fantastical tipi style tents are from Papakåta, a company set up because the founders wanted something for their own wedding for their friends to wow at. The tents are wonderfully flexible as the sides go up and down in minutes – perfect for Britain's weather and more aesthetically pleasing than the plastic window style marquees that always tend to look a little grubby. The Papakåta folks are looking at using rainwater for cleaning equipment and sourcing biodiesel generators for the electricity.

One bride told us that her husband built what is known as a 'chuppah' which is a traditional Jewish structure to get married under. 'We cut some local hazel poles, and made the structure, and then decorated it with lovely foliage, flowers and berries from the garden. We chose a lovely spot under some mature trees, in dappled shade at the bottom of a large garden. At the end my husband smashed a glass underfoot (another Jewish tradition), starting the festivities.' With a do it yourself hubbie like that, before you know it he will be building romantic showers a deux to save water at bath time!

You can always shelter your wedding against the elements naturally and go underground – literally – by having your wedding in a cave. There are a couple of caves that can host a party of even 400 people. One example is Carnglaze Caverns. You won't totally end up in the dark either by being wed amidst a very romantic setting of candlelight.

The Country House
The benefit of hosting a wedding in a country house is the gardens that surround them. Often they are special sites of historic interest that truly benefit from a small cash injection. There are plenty of options across the UK. 'Preparing for your wedding is an exciting time and there is lots to think about,' says Jayne McDonald of Historic Scotland. 'We have a professional and knowledgeable planning team that can advise on different aspects of your wedding. Our wide range of castles, palaces and abbeys will provide the ideal setting to maximise the venue for your perfect day.'

A beautiful high visual, low environmental impact wedding inside a Papakåta yurt © Papakåta

© Nicki Clark

In the last year Historic Scotland has helped over 700 couples plan the wedding of their dreams and cares for 345 outstanding historic properties and sites throughout Scotland – including Edinburgh Castle! Jayne also adds that 75 per cent of the couples who wed in their sites are from Scotland, keeping it quite a local effort, and that they are members of the Green Tourism Business Scheme.

If you've ever dreamt of having a wedding in a beautiful country manor then The National Trust offers some of the most beautiful, ecologically conscious venues. The National Trust has been recognised for many of its green initiatives including the Green Business Award, the Green Apple Award and the IVCA Clarion Award (which celebrates responsible communication on Sustainable Development, Cultural Aspiration, Social Inclusion and Corporate Social Responsibility). Founded in 1895 by three Victorian philanthropists who were concerned about the impact of uncontrolled development and industrialisation, they set up the Trust to act as a guardian for the nation in the acquisition and protection of threatened coastline, countryside and buildings. The National Trust offers beautiful and unusual wedding venues for couples seeking a truly breathtaking backdrop for their special day, hosting approximately 850 weddings a year, in over 100 historical venues throughout England, Wales and

Northern Ireland. There are several ways to reach a National Trust property, with most properties accessible via train or bus route. Their annual handbook clearly explains the different travel options to each property, outlining the bus services, train, cycle and road routes. They are aiming to reduce car borne visits from a level of 90 per cent to 60 per cent by 2020 by working on various initiatives, such as better access to public transport and fuel efficient staff vehicles. Their garden waste is composted, and efforts are being made to minimise kitchen waste. They are also harvesting rainwater for garden use, fitting low water consumption appliances, waterless urinals and dry compost toilets, to name but a few. All new buildings (such as visitor centres) are designed to be as 'environmentally benign as possible by making use of passive solar design, super efficient insulation, water and energy saving appliances'. The Trust tries to use materials that are from as ecologically kind a source as possible. The building department holds stocks of reclaimed materials for reuse.

> **On the top of a moor, in the garden of a stately home, in a forest, in a field on a farm – the choice is entirely yours**

They also have installed about 13,000 low energy light bulbs and are monitoring their energy for further efficiency.

Another green venue with extensive organic gardens, having planted over 4,000 trees of 108 species in the last 20 years is The Longhouse. This encourages masses of different birds to nest and various other rare species of animals. They have won a few awards for their efforts including a Gold Sustainability Award from South West Tourism in 2006 and a Green Apple Gold award for environmental construction. Built in 2005, The Longhouse is part of Mill on the Brue which is a family-run business started by the current owner's parents 26 years ago. They always wanted to make the venue as sustainable as possible and it made sense to encourage wedding couples to try and make their wedding as green as possible too.

The Longhouse was designed in an extremely environmental way – rainwater harvesting, passive solar gain and super insulation. Wedding guests can stay in the bunks and have a fair trade, locally sourced breakfast in the morning. The centre as a whole has very high standards in environmental practices including energy usage, sourcing as locally as possible and using minimal transport. Catering at The Longhouse is all local and can be organic if specified, with the food waste going to compost. Their heating is through gas central heating and geothermic with a top up heat source of a large wood burner. They also have a small wind turbine and source their electricity from a renewable energy supplier. To get there, it is a ten minute walk from the local train station at Bruton.

Daphne Lambert of Penrhos Court on her green vision

We bought Penrhos in 1975 as a set of medieval buildings about to be bull-dozed down. As we renovated each building we found a new use for it. The first to be renovated was an 18th century cow byre and we started a restaurant, the next building became the first of the small brewery revival. I kept pigs that ate the spent grain from the brewery, manured the ground for the vegetables we grew for the restaurant, and we cured the hams in beer. From these days came my understanding of the connection between the health of the soil and our own. At about this time I studied and became a medicinal nutritionist.

When we completed the manor house and the bedrooms in around 1990 we started eco friendly weddings. We were the first restaurant to be certified as organic by the Soil Association in 1995 and probably the first venue to call our weddings 'green weddings'. We have about 25 of them each year.

We can create menus for all tastes with the criteria being organic, local, wild and seasonal. As a nutritionist as well as a chef I can make food for all sorts of special diets. 'You' magazine voted us Best Organic Restaurant in 2002. We have chickens, four compost heaps and a wormery for all organic matter as well as a bottle bank. We use our paper in a variety of ways – animal bedding, compost and cardboard is used for mulching.

Respect of nature is intrinsic to everything we do. It's not necessarily obvious to all our guests as we do not spell it out, we are just aware we have addressed these issues. It's pretty hard to compare different venues. I wouldn't say we were sophisticated, it is friendly – almost like having a party in your own house but not having to do any of the work. We won a millennium marquee award for environmental excellence in 2000.

To reach us you can get a train to Hereford direct from Paddington or Manchester or the South West. You can then get a bus, however most people arrive by taxi. Our next step is thinking about getting an environmentally friendly courtesy car! ∎

Hazelwood House is another beautiful estate on 67 acres whose owners do not like interfering with the land, ensuring wildlife is abundant. With a 16 bedroomed early Victorian house, seven cottages, a former Chapel and a boathouse there is plenty to choose from for the couple to be. Rather than a 'package' deal they work closely to ensure you get what you want, including organic champagne. About 12 couples a year choose to wed there. All the catering is organic, locally sourced and cooked with a no microwave policy, and they will even list the suppliers on the wedding menu! If you fancy a post-wedding congregation around an open log fire in Winter, then this is place to do it! You can get a train from Paddington to Totnes, and then it's a 25 minute taxi drive to Hazelwood.

Florence House on the brow of Seaford Head, Sussex is another option just one and a half hours away from London and close to a train station. Bought in the 1920s by a local merchant as a wedding present for his daughter, the current owners decided to focus on eco friendly weddings five years ago to fit in with their personal environmental ethos. The gardens are a divine sanctuary, popular with yoga and meditation retreats. The beautiful house in its area of natural beauty can be utilised for both informal and formal wedding receptions and civil ceremonies without distractions from other visitors like most wedding venues.

Buckland House also offers exclusive occupancy for your wedding day ensuring no one else but your wedding party on the premises. With four rooms to choose from, the largest being the Grand Lounge that seats 200 people, and close to central London, Birmingham and Cardiff, you're sure to have a fun bash! The venue is set in the Brecon Beacons National Park, surrounded by mountains and overlooking the River Usk. It may be worth sticking around with the four poster bed and two person whirlpool bath in the Bridal Suite. It's also ideal for vegetarians with a gourmet vegetarian menu.

Nottinghamshire based manor house Beesthorpe Hall offers a tranquil, English country atmosphere for civil wedding ceremonies. The venue's electricity is supplied from renewable sources, all the suppliers are kept local, including the food, the gardens are managed organically and all the cleaning products are eco considerate. They are also offering yurts and composting toilets if you want to hold the wedding outside. They can cater for up to 60 people with their in-house chef.

The Village Vibe

Perhaps you want to wed in a quaint village full of charm and oodles of history?

For a do it yourself wedding there's the timeless community hall option. If you're keen to roll your sleeves up it will certainly support the local community and give you plenty of choice to decide how you want your wedding reception to look. Get all your friends involved in the decorating and you're sorted. All that you require is knowledge of your friends' strengths and delegating tasks appropriately – including someone to manage all the activities to give you a stress free day. This is the perfect role for the best man, if he is what it says on the tin. You can actually have this option anywhere, but for a bit of excitement why not consider somewhere like a remote Scottish island like one couple? Their advice is, 'As long as you're happy to include the locals, then they will be happy to welcome you – and you're likely to get some good, traditional music out of it too!'

Rather than be stifled by the formality of a typical English country house, you could choose The George in Rye, East Sussex. It was first opened in 1575 and was taken over by Alex and Katie Clarke who bought the hotel in 2004, when it was in a rather dilapidated state. That's when they decided to restore it in an ecologically conscious manner, making the most of the traditional features. The ballroom with its antique chandeliers and hand painted wallpaper dates from the regency period. Part of its friendly charm is that it's right in the heart of Rye, which is a magical and romantic small town of medieval rooftops and cobbled passages – a perfect place to keep the wedding guests occupied! Connected by train to London and Brighton, it's a good opportunity to get out of the city. Food is sourced locally – everything from Romney Marsh Lamb to local vegetables and fish from Rye Bay. They have an ethical fish sourcing policy and serve varieties accredited by the Marine Stewardship Council. They are supporters of local English sparkling wines from the likes of Biddenden and Chapel Down, and really encourage wedding parties to try these instead of Champagne. Hosting

© Papakâta

about 50 weddings a year they are strong on their recycling which covers all glass, card and cooking oil and they act responsibly with their energy conservation, even though due to the age of the listed building they're prevented from installing solar panels or turbines.

If you fancy a low key wedding tucked away from the world, then the 1860s Polhawn Fort in Cornwall is a venue that comfortably sleeps 20 people. You could make a few days of it, and if you like sailing you can even hire their yacht, the 'Polhawn Whisper' and cruise around the idyllic Plymouth Sound.

Modern Venues
The perk of some modern or newly renovated venues is that they may just have all the environmental features of a good, green venue: highly insulated, with the latest technologies for water and energy efficiency.

The Pines Calyx on the coast of Kent, is a purpose built, site-specific venue with a six acre organically managed garden, within a designated Area of Outstanding Natural Beauty. Its environmental architecture, rather than being an eyesore, actively promotes the landscape. The building is also known for its 'nutritious' design, in that it works along the natural systems with healthy interiors. Alongside their seasonal, Kent produced organic grub they offer a Real-Health catering option that has been designed and co-ordinated by nutritional therapists to incorporate specific foods and food groups!

Sheepdrove Eco Centre in Berkshire is another purpose built building that offers absolutely magnificent natural light, with the idyllic backdrop of an organic farm. Much of your food can be supplied from their abundant gardens and fields. Their Oak Room is a spectacular cathedral-like space with high walls and vaulted ceilings, perfect for flexibility. You can also look upon a spectacular spiral staircase in the dining room that encloses the bread oven, or enjoy photographing memories amidst the herbal bliss of the Physic Garden. ■

The **Transport**

'**G**et me to the church on time!' Don't allow nightmares of arriving late on the day get to you. Let it be one of the first things you organise so that it's out of the way.

According to Climate Care, an organisation that offsets harmful carbon dioxide emissions by funding sustainable energy projects, the average wedding emits around 14.5 tonnes of CO_2, a staggering amount compared with the 12 tonnes emitted by the average person during an entire year.

For couples trying to plan a greener wedding, one of the most crucial and obvious considerations is transport. Not just for the big day, but for all the organising and fretting time too. The sad news is that there just aren't many eco options out there as it's still a relatively underdeveloped area of not just the wedding market but also of the transport industry in general.

Wheel in the Wheelin'
The more minimal your wedding is, the less need there is to drive around from supplier to supplier and thus you'll have a lower environmental footprint. Use the internet to source services – you can probably do most of your organisation over email and telephone. Try to keep your wedding suppliers local, so that you reduce the necessity for travelling around. If everywhere is on your local bus route, it will certainly make life a lot easier.

If you do need to visit your wedding suppliers, and you don't think taking your three-tiered cake on the bus with you during rush hour is a good idea, then perhaps one option is to join a car club scheme. The general idea behind these is that there is a fixed membership fee that you pay annually or monthly, and then you only pay for the day or weekend hire of the car when you actually require it. It's perfect for occasional car usage instead of finding out your car battery has imploded. By being part of a scheme like this you need to have a good, clean driving license and ensure that all the people who will be driving the car are members. Who knows, you could even hire one of the fancier options in the fleet for the day itself, so that you don't get your clothes too rumpled.

Let a happy horse and cart get you to the church on time
© Raimonds Spakovskis

Not ignoring the fact that much organising has to fit around employment hours, try to arrange appointments that you have outside of peak congestion periods. That way you won't be sitting in traffic for ages whilst your exhaust emits carbon dioxide. Many wedding suppliers are small family-run businesses who are happy to have meetings during evenings and weekends as it suits their own needs with childcare.

If you're off in a group to the dressmakers for a fitting, then make an effort to arrange to share cars and taxis together. It's still surprising how many people make solo journeys when there are others going in the same direction!

Purchasing Power

Now that you've got that wedding ring on your finger, perhaps you're thinking of buying your own wheels. If that's the case then it's worth investigating the green car options out there. The Environmental Transport Association produces an annual top ten best and worst cars list for you to mull over. For hybrid cars, the best manufacturers are Honda and Toyota. For biofuel cars (although there are concerns that certain biofuels are contributing to a world food crisis) then try Saab or Ford. If you're feeling daring, why not consider electrical choices, such as GoinGreen and NICE cars? For the open air

Environmental journalist, Jo Moulds talks through her plans of having a geographically-diverse wedding, in one location

We're having our wedding in Lancashire – my roots, although my fiancé Tom is from Gloucestershire. I've lived in London for twelve years now, so we're keen to bring all the locations we care about together for our wedding day. I'm the greener one – Tom's friends knew it was love when he started buying recycled toilet paper in bulk when we first dated. Now all I need to do is convince him that a seasonal roof on our shed would be a good idea. It can be a bit of a struggle organising a wedding with a reluctant environmentalist.

The wedding's going to be the classic church wedding. We'll have our reception in my parent's back garden and we're getting a marquee from a family friend for that. A large scale yet local company will cater for us, although it was funny when I asked them to source local, seasonal and organic food as they looked a bit shell-shocked, saying 'We've never been asked that before'. So as we organise the wedding I'm trying to put green suppliers in touch with local suppliers to try and rub a bit of the green-thinking about. Our flowers are from a local shop called Going Dutch, who have promised to source seasonal flowers for us.

We've got about 160 people attending. I'm trying to keep the numbers down but it's either all or nothing sometimes. We're trying to get the friends coming from London to car share – and quite a few have promised to use the train.

Our honeymoon was another aspect I just couldn't change Tom's mind about. He wanted to get away and was hoping for somewhere exotic like Brazil, whereas I would have been happy to go somewhere romantic in the UK. We settled on Italy. Now of course I'm planning how to get there by train… ∎

feeling then electric scooters by Verteci and Vectrix aren't bad ideas at all, and the Powabyke does exactly what it says on the tin. You can then show off your new car/scooter/bike on the day!

The Carriage du Jour
So the special day arrives and you want to have the unique experience of stepping out into your crowds of friends. Whilst a Rolls-Royce isn't the greenest mode of transport, there are a few better choices.

If you live in London you're particularly lucky as you can hire chauffeur driven eco taxis. Ecoigo has a fantastic fleet of executive cars with smartly dressed drivers taking you in their Toyota Prius hybrid cars. It's not overly expensive and they offer Belu water to the pas-

sengers. Then there is Radio Taxis whose 3,000-strong fleet of cars are now fuelled with biofuel, which improves the mileage per gallon and reduces CO_2 emissions. It has also driven down their costs. The new taxis can be distinguished by a green high visibility reflector on their front window screen. If that's not enough, then Green Tomato Cars and Go Green Cars can also whizz you down to the awaiting aisle.

It just shows that brides who bike are sexy! © Fotosmurf

If you live in Devon then perhaps you can try a hint of the East by using zero emission rickshaws. Lilypeds dress your carriage up in flowers and even include some confetti and a bottle of bubbly.

Horses and carriages could be seen as a reasonably environmental option as, after all, it's the horses providing the power. We're not going to start measuring the tonnes of straw the horses eat as to the carbon they emit compared to cars, but the green world does have shades of grey, and there is a complicity of ethics if you see yourself as a Dr Doolittle type. It's important when going on a horse and carriage hunt that you get testimonies from couples who have used the company before, and it's worth asking to see the stables to ensure the horses are in good health, clean and happy. ■

The **Attire**

It's likely to get the fear into you. 'What on earth do I wear?' For the brides, there are endless opportunities for looking like a green goddess on the day. A quick search on the internet and you may find the more bizarre options out there, which is great if you want to be distinctive. If you don't then you can still relax.

Theming a Wedding

If you have themed your wedding (perhaps you have been inspired by your venue) then start early on to ensure you get the appropriate attire. Depending on the theme this can make your fashion buying harder or easier, but it's best to leave plenty of time in case you decide to get something bespoke.

Consider whether you want the bridesmaids to wear the same, sometimes it's simpler to let them choose their own, particularly if you've got different ages, shapes and sizes in the principal wedding party.

Make Your Own Wedding Dress

The wedding dress is seen as the biggest important fashion purchase of your life – so don't be afraid to be meticulous to your needs. Is it something you want to cherish forever? Wear again? Turn into a Christening gown for future kids? Once you have realised what you would like to do with it, then you can decide how to go about getting the ideal outfit.

You'll want to feel unique on your wedding day. If you're a dab hand with your needle and thread (and that includes the men out there), you may want to take on the task of making your own outfit – it will certainly have a touch of the individual about it. As the saying 'if you want something done properly, do it yourself' goes, it will have the right level of quality you desire and you might even find yourself minimising your carbon footprint as you save all those trips for dress fittings.

Pop into your local haberdashery shop, or any good department store to get ideas for patterns. There are three particular patterns that are common for wedding dresses: the basic A-line wedding

*Allison's natural
fabric dresses are all
made in England
© Allison Blake*

dress which suits most figures; figure hugging silhouettes suitable for the more athletic bodies but also can restrict your movement if you want to bust a groove on the dance floor; or the ball gown, fitted with a bodice and suitable for the curvier figures. Looking through wedding magazines can also give you an idea of what would suit your body, complexion and colourings. It's also best to go on a window shop and try a few wedding dresses on to know what style will look best. Make sure you practise the construction of the wedding dress by creating a fitting muslin and testing out the patterns on yourself, having fittings at every stage of the process.

It's worth investing in fabric shears, a hemming gauge to ensure you have the measurements correct, and a seam ripper for undoing any mistakes. Try to buy all the required material at one time; including spare material for mistakes and alterations in case the fabric runs out or another roll produces a slightly different colour.

Taking Measurements...

When making your own wedding dress you need to know your own body type.

It's worthwhile taking time to get the measurements correct to minimise the need for complex adjustments. Only wear simple underwear when making these measurements.

Neck
Measure around fullest part of neck.

Back Waist Length
Measure from the nape at the base of the neck down to the natural waistline.

Bust
Measure straight across widest part of back, under arms and across fullest part of bust, not underneath the bust.

Waist
Measure around natural waistline.

Hips
Measure around fullest part – usually 17.7cm-22.8cm (7"-9") below waist. Make a note of the distance between waist and hips.

Skirt Length
Measure from floor (wearing shoes with appropriate height heel) to your required skirt length.

Your local haberdashery shop may be able to help you if you struggle with taking correct measurements.

The Knitted Wedding

Joining a knitting group or sewing class is a great way to find the skills you need to make your own garments – ideal if you have lots of time to prepare for your wedding.

Across the country there are plenty of evening and weekend classes, and it's a great place to meet fun individuals who may be willing to help out, and you'll automatically be setting time aside to work on the outfits, something that couples often don't do enough of, leaving a last minute panic run to the shops. Needles are usually supplied – all you need is the wool – and it can be great fun over a drink or two.

Rather than make your own wedding dress why not go slightly oddball and… make your own wedding? The Cast Off knitting group based in London had a very successful knit fest. If everything is made out of wool then your environmental impact will be limited – although you may end up with hungry guests!

As one member of the knitting group reveals, 'Completely knitted weddings are entirely possible and in some ways less hassle than conventional ones. If your sandwiches are knitted, people will bring their own lunch, and if your bouquet is knitted, you can keep it forever! The best part of a knitted wedding however is the atmosphere. Imagine a ceremony, where everyone in the room had made something. Experienced knitters can work on cakes, cameras, corsages, and champagne and everyone else can work on flowers, sandwich fillings and of course, confetti. If you want to be in control of your wedding then a completely knitted one is probably not for you!'

> **Try to buy all the required material at one time; including spare material for mistakes and alterations in case the fabric runs out or another roll produces a slightly different colour**

The completely knitted wedding can be seen at www.castoff.info and for patterns, yarns and advice on how to knit a wedding then visit Prick Your Finger.

Even if you don't want to knit your whole wedding, it's perfect for creating your own trimmings. For socially conscious, luxurious yarns, then visit the Be Sweet website. The enterprise supports three job creation programs in South Africa that help empower female artisans and villagers by giving them confidence and the means to

Fabric Fabulous...

There are lots of eco fabrics out there; here are just a small selection of the more readily available ones

Cotton

Pesticides damage not only the environment, but the people working and living amongst the crop. Let's gloss over the gloomy stories of children who die or get sick from the spillages of dumped barrels of chemicals and do something positive. If you want to go with the run off the mill stuff, then try to make it organic. There are plenty of fair trade options out there too, but they are far more difficult to get your hands on if you're making your own.

Bamboo

Fast growing, It doesn't need the chemicals cotton requires, and it's beautifully smooth on the skin.

Hemp

Contrary to popular concern, you won't get high off this cannabis-derived fibre. It's a very strong, durable material and although it can be a bit rough around the edges in its raw form, mixed with a bit of (peace) silk, you'd be amazed how sexy and soft it can be. No need for the chemicals, it aerates the soil as it grows.

If hemp replaced cotton globally, the increased fibre yield would reduce toxic pesticides by 94,000 tonnes.

Peace Silk

If you love the world, (even the worms) then peace silk is the way to go. It uses the cocoon of the silk worm once it has spread its wings and vacated. Whilst the silk fibres are shorter lengths than conventional silk it is the perfect vegan option.

Linen

Perfect for the Summer events, this is a lovely fabric to keep you cool. It is particularly strong, but wrinkles like silk.

Merino Wool

As long as the sheep of New Zealand don't need it then this fabric can be a lovely, luxury option for Winter weddings. Just make sure it has a 'Zque certification' to ensure the animal hasn't been harmed.

Vintage / Antique

The perfect opportunity for eco-chic, particularly if you like rummaging for a good bargain – and you can make your outfit the 'something old'. There are plenty of options for getting high quality, enchanting fabrics that have already been loved. You never know, you may get something ready-made for the altar!

Recycled

You really can make your wedding garment out of anything as we show later on in this chapter – and there are plenty of places you can go to pick up the bits and pieces you need.

Natural Dyes

If you fancy adding some natural colour touches to your creation, then

Try to find vintage suit or hire one for the bridegroom and his best man © Ksurrr

various websites such as Fibrecrafts.com offer natural dye starter kits with detailed instructions on how to use turmeric, indigo and other pure colours.

Little Extras

Sequins, ribbons and special extras you buy from haberdashery shops may have some questionable ethics. With the majority of them made in India and China, the likelihood is that they are made through sweatshop labour conditions. Perhaps if you are going all DIY on your wedding then the best thing is to make embellishments for sewing onto your dress yourself.

Tastefully done, you could use old glass beads from broken jewellery, small shells from the beach and discarded birds' feathers to sew onto the dress. If you're wedding is an autumnal affair, then why not go raiding through the park for dried leaves or use dried flower heads to garnish yourself! You can also use all your little extras to spice up shoes or make your own jewellery.

If you're having a wedding in the Winter or need a sophisticated shawl, then you can get all the fake furs in the world from Maison de la fausse fouree.

Corsages

If you're going for the classic morning suit or kilted look then why not make your own corsage? It's very simple to do. All you need is some twine and some small shrubbery such as fern leaves or heather which you can then tie together. Acquire some thin black tape and wrap this around, hiding it by wrapping some ribbon around it if need be. Then affix a large safety pin through the tape or ribbon and you're done! ∎

The Cast Off Knitting club enjoy their Completely Knitted Wedding with couple Freddie Robins and Ben Coode Adams in Battersea, London

support themselves and their families in an otherwise economically depressed region. The programs have grown to include over 80 women villagers and female members of the Xhosa Tribe who live in Cape Town and the Eastern Cape region respectively. South Africa is the biggest producer of luxury mohair, providing 65 per cent of the world's supply. All Be Sweet's yarn is hand dyed and hand spun, and many are offered in over 60 solid colours and 15 hand painted colours. Select balls are accented with delicate ribbons, metallic strands and African beads. South Africa's baby mohair yarn comes from the fleece of Angora goats that are the descendants of a breed originally from Tibet.

Buying Organic...

Organic cotton standards were developed by UK certification organisation the Soil Association when it was found that around 150 grams of pesticides are used to grow the cotton for one t-shirt, the equivalent of one cup of sugar, some of which can be deadly to the farmers who produce them. Their research suggested that 20,000 people die each year as a result of sprays used on non organic cotton. 8,000 chemicals which can cause human allergies and are harmful to nature are said to be used to produce textiles.

A report entitled 'Deadly Chemicals in Cotton' by the Environmental Justice Foundation (EJF) a UK based non-governmental organisation, in collaboration with Pesticide Action Network (PAN) UK believe that a million people worldwide are hospitalised due to pesticide poisoning. The symptoms include 'burning eyes, breathlessness, excessive salivation, vomiting, nausea, dizziness...' The list goes on. With 99 per cent of cotton farmers living in developing countries, it is the poorest that suffer most.

By buying organic cotton you can cut the risk not just to people but also to the environment. Organic farming encourages a more sustainable method of balancing the soil naturally through encouraging natural diversity. Even the tiniest soil organism is important to ensure a good crop yield – and pesticide usage is a threat.

With the Soil Association symbol present you can be assured that no GM or dangerous chemicals are used, and that the dyes are natural and probably safer. According to PAN UK, there are now over 80 brands that offer organic cotton. The current organic cotton market is estimated to be £107 million (2008).

On the High Street

There's a bit of a dilemma when it comes to clothes shopping on the high street: the convenience and variety is certainly great. And it's true – you can be relatively green and shop at Top Shop, H&M, Debenhams, Tesco and M&S who are nowadays stocking organic or fair trade certified garments.

Even Gap are shaping up their act, being active members in organisations such as the Ethical Trading Initiative (ETI) to ensure factories are not exploiting workers, checking suppliers do not use child labour whilst actively campaigning for fairer wages and increasing

Buying Fair Trade...

Cotton has always had its history attached to slavery. Even today with over 100 million rural households involved in the crop's production there are still victims to vulnerability due to unfair trading processes and a dominating global market.

Look out for the FAIRTRADE Mark, an independent consumer label licensed by the Fairtrade Foundation, which was developed for certifying Fairtrade cotton in 2004. The label acts as a guarantee that disadvantaged producers in the developing world are getting a better deal, and smaller farmers are able to develop a more powerful position in the global market. Only smallholder cotton producer organisations, rather than plantations, can be certified. They are involved in democratic decision making and local, sustainable development. All products with the FAIRTRADE Mark meet the international certification body called the Fairtrade Labelling Organisations International (FLO). Whilst some Fairtrade certified cotton is also certified organic, the two standards do not always go hand in hand. Yet Fairtrade certified cotton does expect implementation of integrated crop management to ensure better environmental protection, are not permitted to use genetically modified seeds and, as they are normally smaller holdings, farmers tend to use more traditional and holistic means to acquire their yield.

Some migrant workers earn just 22 pence an hour sewing clothes together for the British market, which falls below the breadline of a living wage.

Whilst fair trade cotton does not extend to the textile and garment manufacturing industry, other organisations such as Labour Behind the Label, War on Want, The Clean Clothes campaign and No Sweat are challenging the poor wages that garment workers receive, often in exploited circumstances. These groups are campaigning for safer working conditions and an increase in independent trade unions and want to confront evident injustice.

their rights. The potential positive impact these popular shops can have on the garment industry if their organic and fair trade lines and ethical trading aspirations develop is huge.

The high street shops do not tend to have a lot to offer when it comes to finding your top hat or veil, but there may be bits and bobs you can pick up. The best place to try out is Monsoon, which is also a member of the ETI and usually has a luxury yet affordable wedding range for both brides and bridesmaids alike. Not only are they building on their Fairtrade certified cotton range, they fund the Monsoon Accessorize Trust that supports projects helping street children around Delhi railway station, education and training for women and children in Delhi's slums, an immunisation programme in the remote villages of Rajasthan and a specialist education project for deaf children in a Jaipur slum. It's worth asking about eco thinking designer collections in the department stores as well, such as

© Dominiq

Katharine Hamnett or Stella McCartney. Edun, the socially conscious clothing company set up by Bono and his wife Ali Hewson with the designs of New Yorker Rogan Gregory is also in a department store near you, with their dresses ranging from £100 to £250.

The negative aspect of high street shopping is that some unknown entity will end up with your hard earned pennies, rather than supporting local, independent shops. The thought that our high streets across the country are all carbon copies of one another may not be appealing either. By shopping at independent clothing companies who work directly with small scale producers you can shift a bit of your heart to sustainable development amongst the rural poor. Garment workers won't need to migrate to cities in hope of earning a living working in the unpredictable factories that high street retailers utilise.

Instead they can focus on developing better healthcare, education systems and additional income revenues locally, providing support not just for the worker but for the local community as a whole. Sounds better than lining the pockets of fat cats, eh?

Fair trade fashion pioneer People Tree is one of the brands both independent and on the high street with a presence in Top Shop. They have some beautiful dresses that are ideal for a simpler wedding if you don't want to go down the classical white gown route.

There are various sophisticated ethical retailers online such as Adili, Fashion Conscience and Devidoll who offer a wide range of ethical fashion brands on their online shopping sites. As you can't always judge the sizes perfectly, it's worth ordering in plenty of time in case a return or exchange is needed.

Romanticism comes alive with silk, hemp and cashmere blends © Virids Luxe

Emerging company Amana marry beautiful design with ethical production practices. Working with female artisans in the Middle Atlas Mountains in Morocco, the young designers Helen Wood and Erin Tabrar behind the brand have been forging long term partnerships (so much so that they sleep on the floor of the women's houses when they visit) to create fairly traded pieces of organic cotton, organic silks and sumptuous hemp mixes. Whilst they do not offer wedding dresses, there are some beautiful skirts and tops for the bridesmaids.

New fair trade, carbon neutral company FIN have very elegant wild silk or organic cotton dresses. With prices at around £400 it is a relatively cheap wedding dress option compared to the usual average £6,000 cost. If you are getting married outdoors or in Winter then check out their incredibly luxurious 100 per cent lamb's wool coat.

For something new and a little bit different including patterned fair trade organic materials then try the Wildlife Works brand that has just arrived from an 80,000 acre eco-sanctuary in Kenya. Winner of best fashion retail brand at the RSPCA awards, these clothes are available through Equa and Natural Collection online. 'Clothing was not originally part of our plan' says founder Mike Korchinsky. He realised that providing a sustainable income to the local community would help prevent poaching of endangered species by engaging them in the process. The plan is that for each £5 million turnover of the company, another wildlife sanctuary will be founded. Uniquely inspired by indigenous African plants and imagery, almost all of the organic garments are crafted by hand at the Rukinga eco sanctuary. Mischa Barton has already been spotted wearing the collection.

Viridis Luxe is fresh faced on the British fashion scene, offering beautiful hemp, silk and cashmere blends. Whilst they don't offer particular wedding dresses either, their Summer collections have the most beautiful white evening dresses screening style, elegance and romanticism. Coming over from the designers in the USA where hemp cultivation is legal, it is now available at Fashion Conscience and Devidoll.

Fin offer great options for simple contemporary organic bridesmaid dresses © Fin

Slow and Steady Wins the Race, a new lower-priced clothing label in New York are preparing to challenge H&M and Gap with their collection and are about to launch a wedding dress to add to their existing range of less formal clothing and lingerie. Currently they are only

Adam Vaughan, editor of SmartPlanet.com wed his fiancée Jill in July 2007

I'd be over-egging it to call the whole thing a green wedding, but it was a 'wedding with green elements'. We had it for the usual reasons really: trying to make a small difference on climate change, and trying to pass on a bit of awareness to friends and family who usually avoid my green soapbox.

When it comes to green issues I'm a bit of a Johnny-come-lately, having only made serious changes to my outlook and lifestyle in the past five years.

It took bloody ages to plan the wedding, well actually only about four months, but that seemed like long enough. I actually hated the planning. We sent all the invites via email. We decided to have the wedding over two days as we got married in a registry office in Lambeth so we were a bit anxious over space – but it had a surprisingly pretty marble room at the Town Hall. There were 20 guests and we all went to a vegetarian restaurant afterwards called Manna in Primrose Hill. We travelled from the ceremony to the reception in five hybrid cars (Toyota Priuses) that were carbon offset.

The next day we invited 100 guests to Brockwell Park in South London. We walked there and encouraged our guests to travel via public transport.

In an attempt to be green we asked for no gifts, but got some nonetheless!

I shopped around for a suit with some eco or ethical aspect – made in a style that I'd want to wear on a regular basis. The high street was rubbish, including M&S, which had no decent fair trade and/or organic suits.

I ended up getting fitted by Junky Styling who 'upcycled' an old suit they found secondhand, and added frills and details as they do. As I ride my bike everywhere, I put it on straight away and cycled home. Jill wasn't too impressed. My advice is don't buy clothes that you'll only wear once.

For our honeymoon we went to Brighton for a few days in a boutique hotel. ∎

stocked in The Victoria and Albert Museum Gift Shop in London – but watch this space.

Something Borrowed, Something New

Clothing and textiles amount for over two million tonnes of waste in the UK. That's an awful lot of bowties. Whilst the temptation to go out and get something new for your special day may be fervent, perhaps there is something out there already? You never know until you look…

Secondhand clothing has with it a rather painful image, perhaps reclaimed or revived are more suitable expressions. Although the urge to think of mouldy, stained clothing amidst eagle eyed little old ladies in knitted cardigans awaiting a sale is still rife, you would be surprised how funky charity shops are. Conveniently placed they tend to behave more like high end boutiques these days.

The big name wonders such as Oxfam and Barnardos are setting a precedent in their retail outlets. Not only are they bringing in brand-spanking new ethical gift ranges, they have been branching out into specialist areas.

Barbara Walmsely, Volunteer Bridal Coordinator of Oxfam started the bridal department concept in 1985 by hiring out bridal gowns from her back bedroom to make money for the organisation. Eleven years later, after two more bridal departments had been established on the first floors of Oxfam shops, Barbara and her long suffering family got their home to themselves again. She had made a profit of over £65,000 and proved her idea had worked. Barbara explains, 'I decided on sup-porting Oxfam as I have been a passionate supporter since I was old enough to rattle a tin (in those days the age was 16 years), now over 50 years on, I'm so excited seeing my bridal vision grow. We depend on bridal shops that pass on their unsold dresses. With donor shops sometimes selling gowns for thousands of pounds, we appreciate their kindness and thoughtfulness very much. If we didn't take them they would be thrown away. One shop I know actually shreds brand new dresses because they want to keep their prices up.'

In the UK Oxfam now has twelve stores which house departments purely dedicated to weddings, in Bracknell, Bradford, Cambridge, Chippenham, Coventry, Eastbourne, Heswall in the Wirral, Leicester, Poole, Southampton, Dublin and Bangor.

Barbara Walmsley puts the finishing touches to another Oxfam bride © Oxfam

Single-handedly Barbara has constant contact with all the different departments and describes herself as chief beggar – asking bridal shops to donate dresses, arranging for carriers to pick them up to take them to the warehouse, value them and send to the branch she thinks will have most success selling them. She does all this for no monetary gain, getting her motivation purely from a constant awareness of the suffering and injustice in so many parts of the world. 'We also depend on gown donations from individuals. It's a shame that people don't give them away more, but understandably girls place a sentimental value on their dresses. Tucked in a loft somewhere the dress may rot, and if it is silk and packed in polythene it will turn yellow. I was pleased to hear one lady made her daughter-in-law's dress into lampshades, at least that way it was being used. It's just frustrating if no one does anything with their gown, it's such a wicked, wicked waste.' The average Oxfam wedding gown price tag is £250 – although one customer bought a particularly chic outfit, which retailed at £4,500, for £800. Barbara adds, 'What a bargain and what a wonderful way of changing the world!'

Whilst it may not have the glow of green or charitable credentials that other sites have, The Dressmarket is a fabulous website for dress purchasing. It was founded in 2004 by Stuart Teadley after his sister expended a 'carbon footprint the size of Peru' driving round the country looking for her wedding dress. It's helped hundred of couples find revived wedding dresses and offers one central place where people can find exactly the right dress, be it new or once-worn. Stuart says that the majority of dresses survive the day in perfect or near perfect condition and after professional dry cleaning are practically indistinguishable from new. His opinion is that most brides are more interested in getting the dress rather than the newness of it. So how green is the website? Well certainly brides can avoid expensive and polluting journeys looking for dresses that may not be there. The perfect Dressmarket transaction is done either entirely on line or with a single visit made between buyer and seller. The prices range from a couple of hundred up to a few thousand, with the lowest price offered at £75 and the highest at £4,000. It's certainly another afford-able place to look – they did have one at £8,000 a couple of years ago, but that didn't sell!

You could also hire your wedding attire – if you are only going to wear it once then it makes financial sense, with prices starting at £100. Just Pleats offers a dress hire service if you want something a little hippyish and 1970s but want to give it back along with the flowers in your hair once you are wed. From Here to Eternity near Taunton is just one place you can sort out all the bridal party's out-fits – including the cravats, rouches, veils, handkerchiefs, gloves and top hats. To ensure men's prying eyes don't get a glimpse, they could always go to a service just for homme, such as Simply Suits. The key to hiring is to shop around as if you were buying an outfit to keep!

The Retro Wedding

The planet is groaning, and fashion is a big culprit of our throwaway society as it's never just about the new. A quick flick through the the-saurus and we know it's all about the latest style, craze, fad. And right now one of our saving graces is retro mania.

> ‘ Tucked in a loft somewhere the dress may rot, and if it is silk and packed in polythene it will turn yellow. I was pleased to hear one lady made her daughter-in-law's dress into lampshades, at least that way it was being used ’

When 900,000 million items of perfectly good clothing, shoes and accessories, are thrown away these days, it makes sense keeping the stuff that will become popular again in our vogue-tastic cycle. Whilst not suggesting that the bridegroom wears his 1980s hideously pat-terned shell suit to the altar there are some classic pieces from the 1950s that are something to smile about. Think Sinatra, Martin and the crooners – if their style still looks good then so can yours.

Vintage doesn't have to be expensive. Beyond Retro opened in 2000 in a warehouse in East London where they sell a wide range of vintage clothing and accessories for men and women. Their vintage wedding items are available from £18 to £120 and they sell vintage veils, silk flowers, headpieces and shoes which would be perfect for weddings.

Junky Styling has an inspirational range of thoughtful design for both bride and groom to be. Offering a bespoke service from Brick Lane in

London they can create chic and unique suits starting from £400, and wedding dresses starting from £1,000. Some of their pre-made collection offers some quite risqué yet intriguing designs that will certainly be a talking piece. Then there is Jailhouse Frock, a funky girlish site for women marrying a Cary Grant type and want an outfit and all the accessories to match. Remember that the pleated look regularly comes in (and out) of fashion. To step further back in time then

Fair Trade Wedding Dressmaker Joanna Mackin of Wholly Jo's, West London

Wholly Jo's was born out of a desire to do something useful with my time when my youngest started school. I learnt dress making from my mother and from school. The rest is self taught and a flare! It has proved impossible to make Wholly Jo's completely fair trade but we try our best. Our customers can be assured that their dress is not made in a sweat shop in the Far East, but just by me in Uxbridge.

It took nearly six months to locate enough suitable fabrics to start Wholly Jo's. We have a selection of organic, fair trade, bio sustainable and peace products. We rely on trust a lot, as to get certified is prohibitively expensive for a lot of my producers. I have yet to find fabrics of a suitable quality that are all of the above so for now people need to chose what aspect of ethical is most important to them. Standard high street designs are nearly all strapless and a-line skirts in various guises. The beauty of what I do is the bride can have whatever she desires. I only make up to six or so dresses a year, so it's a very personal service.

My husband Neil and I got married in the late 80s as students. Friends from our church and college did virtually everything. Some of the guests even did the washing up. I got married in a blue and white dress from Laura Ashley (it was the 1980s) the most expensive dress I had ever had at that point but no white meringue. The mythical Auntie Flo may have questioned the lack of 'white' as it was still felt important then but I knew where I stood and so did the people that mattered so that was fine. The whole thing cost around £750 and is still one of the most special days of my life. Low cost means that you skip some of the unnecessary items, and often means you have focused on who and what is really important to you. But if it means you have shaved a few hundred pounds off at the expense of using slave labour, thousands of product miles and those employed are getting minimum wages then that's not green, its exploitation. ■

Vintage Modes offers affordable 1920s wedding gowns, and often original pieces that will only set you back about £300. There are several other online vintage shops in varying degrees of simplicity and style.

The Debbi Little Parachute Dress, stocked at Equa Boutique, took the world by storm for its innovation. Made from 1950s parachutes, each one is slightly different because the fabric dictates how the dress can be made. The dress size is dictated by your bust size due to the built in corset bra. Perfect for bridesmaids, this dress is available in a variety of colours. Based in Islington's Camden Passage, Equa is one of a kind in that it is the only ethically dedicated boutique in Central London.

Eco Dressmakers

When you pick a dressmaker, find out how much time it will take for fittings and visits and the costs involved before you make a decision to hire someone. It goes without saying that you will want to see the quality of the dress not just the designs, as they do of course vary. You may be taking an already existing dress to a dressmaker to adapt or you may be asking for something from scratch. Either way there are a growing number of green conscious designers out there. Joy from Utani set her ethical fashion company up to support fair trade projects around the world. 'I use mainly 100 per cent organic and fair trade cotton, hand woven in India. They are ethically produced because I get them from Bishopston Trading Company which has FAIRTRADE certi-fication. I also use vintage and recycled fabrics in order to be envi-ronmentally conscious and they are fun to work with!' She can offer a serv-ice to couples across the UK as long as they are willing to make at least three visits to her studio for consultations and fittings. Dependant on the cost of the fabric and detail of work, a simple design could start at £150.

Conscious Elegance offers the more traditional looking bridal gowns, cut and sewn to order by local seam-stresses. As a green hearted business they offer certified organic dresses (by Central Union Certification, formerly

Debbie Little's iconic silk 1950s parachute dresses, available from Equa Boutique © Equa

known as SKAL, an international group of companies that quality manages the process), biodegradable packaging and eco friendly couriers to get it to you.

Julia Paramour is another dressmaker that you can sit down and help sketch designs with and who enjoys turning your vintage fabrics into suitable apparel.

London based Allison Blake uses all natural fabrics as she hates the synthetic fabrics on the market. Every year she sends a box full of samples to a specialist Oxfam shop; these dresses are usually unusual samples and early prototypes that don't get put into production. She also recycles all leftover fabric rather than throwing it away.

Mark Liu's designer zero waste dress © Mark Liu

Another London based designer is refreshing Lucy Tammam. With her own fashion label Tammam she has three years experience of creating wedding dresses. Not only does she source eco fabrics, she works with fair trade organisations that can do beading and embroidery. All of her off the peg collection is made to order from fairly traded units in India and Nepal, whilst her bespoke options are made by the eco chic chick herself.

Gaiahouse offers a full design consultation for bespoke bridal wear from ethically produced materials such as peace silk and they pride themselves on boycotting chemically rich or exploitative fabrics. Gaiahouse also refuse to use materials that are produced using child labour or require toxic chemicals in the cleaning and dying process.

Ruth Singer's dressmaking abilities extend also to accessories suitable for weddings including bags, scarves, corsages and textile jewellery from sustainable and recycled fabrics including vintage lace, all of which can be made to order. Her wedding dresses prices start at £750.

Renowned designer Tara Lynn develops a relationship with each bridal customer to design them the perfect wedding dress and grooms attire. She thinks it's important that the groom's attire coordinates with the bride's gown and promises to offer a fulfilment of fantasies, whether it is a fairytale embellished castle wedding or a beach air reception. She is living the epitomy of a green wedding dress designer with a solar powered studio in 92 acres of land surrounded by the mountains in Vermont. Whilst she accepts international orders, it may be worth a thought to the carbon footprint before you decide!

Designers

Gary Harvey, formerly the creative director of Levi's Europe has a delicious range of outspoken dresses all using recycled materials. You can get a wedding dress made out of newspapers, or even out of…wedding dresses. Some of his designs have a touch of the cheeky nudity, whilst others are just enchanting.

For beautifully designed high end dresses then Mark Liu's revolutionary 'Zero Waste Design' offers a waste free design unlike most new garments that waste some 15 per cent of the materials during the cutting process. Liu's jigsaw-esque dresses offer an elegant yet funky edge on textile design, and he has some beautiful white and cream fabric designs such as his 100 per cent silk organza snow dress that retails for around £690, or through combining a skirt and top in wool and metallic fabrics. Each piece can be ordered by commission in organic fabrics.

Taught by her mother from a young age, Gracie Burnett in Dorset uses all natural pigments from indigo, lac, weld, woad, majistra, madder, and pomegranate to produce collaborative, bespoke wedding dresses and accompanying jackets starting from £1,500. She sources all the fabric herself from organic farmers and craft co-operatives in Europe, Bangladesh, China and India.

Celebrated designer Pearl Lowe has a new 1970 screen sirens inspired collection, blended with her signature 1940s influence. Handmade with recycled antique lace that is sourced from vintage outlets and custom dyed, Lowe's dressmaking talent stands out from the crowd. Her collections of dresses start at £695, and are available in Liberty, The Cross, and online at Ecobtq.

Motasem offers fabulous classic and contemporary cocktail style wedding dresses from a designer who has worked on brands such as Jigsaw and M&S. Made to order in the UK, they are launching organic silk fabric dresses, with prices from £565.

If you want to have an outlandish outfit for your wedding then From Somewhere provides the look. Their collections are made up of (get you hankies ready) unloved and unwanted garments. To avoid the incinerators and challenging the wasteful fashion industry, these panelled designs are a fabulous fusion of reclaimed fabrics, including tweeds, woven and cashmere for some contemporary temptation.

To get the men involved in the designer spirit, why not acquire some fine tailoring from the quintessential British tailor Timothy Everest, who was taught by tailor to the Beatles and The Rolling Stones. His own starry customers include handsome hunk Ed Spellers. His eccentric grandeur with a modern twist comes in the form of a made to measure or bespoke service.

Accessories

Undergarments
So what if your underwear can't be seen by the guests? They will be by the bridegroom! If you fancy some ethical wedding panties made of a luxurious 60 per cent hemp and 40 per cent silk mix with an organic cotton gusset, whilst getting your something old, something new, something borrowed and something blue all in there, then Green Knickers has the answer. Their wedding knickers come with blue roses, a hook to attach a borrowed trinket for the day and a bow made from reclaimed textiles to ensure the bride is blessed by this time-honoured motto. Sultry Enamore offer beautiful lingerie for your big wedding day using mixes of organic silk, hemp, soya and hand selected vintage fabrics. You can get ruffled knickers, garters, camisoles and even matching eye masks! Alternatively, American Apparel offer some more yoga-tastic organic cotton knickers and undergarments whilst Mossberry, an ethical boutique in Leicester have 100 per cent organic cotton and lace bra and panty sets from French ethical designers Les Fees de Bengale.

Enamore's sexy range of wedding lingerie © David Betteridge

Shoes

Put your feet on show with some fabulous ethical footwear. Most shoes are made of animal leather, an energy consuming and highly toxic chemical procedure that is non biodegradable due to the tanning agents used. But you can don something gentler. Beyond Skin produces glamorously green shoes that are stitched, lasted and finished by hand in a small, family-run factory in East London. All the shoes are manmade materials including suedes, satins and organic cottons for a vegan friendly option. Their satins are made from polyester rather than viscose (known for using lots of acid chemicals that seep into water systems, damaging the environment). Their synthetically made leathers are produced from cotton-backed polyurethane. PU (polyurethane) looks like PVC leatherette, but unlike PVC it doesn't contain chlorine which produces dioxin during manufacturing. Sadie Frapp and Alison Goldfrapp amongst other A-listers have been spotting wear Beyond Skin's Sui Generis bespoke service.

Charmoné's Wildflower Collection is ideal for weddings, characterised by sculpted heels and romantic expression. With a European design, the shoes are made with Italian microfibres that are water

Terra Plana's vegetable tanned leather eco soles with recycled quilt heels in all their glory © Terra Plana

resistant and animal friendly. Whilst synthetic, like Beyond Skin's range, they also argue that polyurethane is kinder to the planet. These shoes are produced sweatshop free in Italy and Brazil, and they donate 5 per cent of profits to environmental and development charities. The Flying Cow similarly avoids the fur and leather faux pas of the fashion industry, using eco friendly leathers and linen, hemp and cotton synthetics instead.

Terra Plana, (Latin for 'flat land') use classic shoemaking practices combined with vegetable tanned leather which results in beautiful flat or three-inch heel chic shoes. These boast recycled quilt uppers all locally sourced in a range of colours and design elegance.

Elegant Wedding Shoes offer vegan/vegetarian friendly shoes, hand-made using satin or silk in the UK. As they are fully dyeable, you can ensure they match your dress. Vegetarian Shoes also have a range of dressy, fashion footwear amidst their more informal assortment.

You can save a pair of unloved shoes through buying brand new, unworn and secondhand bridal shoes and accessories from website Sellmyweddingdress.co.uk.

Jackets
If you get excited shivers at the sight of your love, you can warm up with Ciel's hip, sumptuous quilted jackets with faux fur trims and cer-tified organic hemp silks, cottons and muslins. These are made from a variety of sources in the UK, Europe and South America under Labour Behind the Label law complying factories. As Vice Chair of the Ethical Fashion Forum, Ciel's founder Sarah Ratty knows all the ins and outs of the ethical fashion industry, offering an exciting array of accessories.

The Makepiece label was founded in 2004 by designer Nicola Sherlock and farmer Beate Kubitz. Whilst loving her knitwear design degree, Nicola had become disillusioned with the fashion industry working in New York and couldn't see the point of good design for society's throwaway passion. With Beate's background in campaigning they found it difficult to buy clothes they were ethically comfortable wearing. After moving to the North of England, Nicola started a small flock of sheep to keep some land in order and realised that wool is a sustainable fibre which can be turned into clothing on a very local scale – without conflicting on principles. 'Recently, a bride asked us to design the dress as separates so that she could wear them for special occasions. Another asked for a Winter cape made from British angora – something she could wear whenever she needed something warm and glamorous.'

Yorkshire business Izzy Lane was created by Isobel Davies when she saw the demise of the British wool industry. So she also raised her own flock of soft wool Wensleydale and Shetland sheep and lovingly uses their wool to home spin into weaved masterpieces, before using natural dyes. Cashmere from the Scottish Highlands is also used in her collection, as well as handmade shoes approved by the Vegetarian Society.

For Asian influence, then Sari Couture offers beautiful quilted jackets made out of recycled saris. Initially started to raise money for children in developing countries, the use of unique sari material gives the design some edge whilst giving back ten per cent of its sales to a children's charity. Matching evening bags made out of remnants of your wedding dress can also be produced.

Bags

Ethical bags are everywhere in all shapes and forms – but sometimes it's hard to find the ideal one for a wedding. Matt & Nat have a particularly virginal offering by way of the Jorja Small Streamline, made with white pebble vegan leather, antique silver hardware and screw rivets, faux suede lining, all stitched together in grey. ■

The Jewels

So you've got the outfits sorted, but what about obtaining the dazzle? Leo DiCaprio did a pretty good job of persuading us that diamonds were immoral, but how ethical is it to put that ring on your finger?

Society's expectations, even amongst the most jewel encrusted hands, have changed. We all want some transparency in businesses that were never really thought about deeply before. Traditionally the golden rule to diamond buying is 'The Four Cs' – cut, colour, clarity and carat – but let's add another: consideration. The worry isn't just about diamonds, it's about the sourcing of the gold and silver and other precious gems. Whilst there are alternatives to mined jewellery, it may be hard to budge the idea of having the perfect ring on your finger.

Whilst the traditional industry remains, emerging ethical businesses able to attain consumer's high level, luxurious jewellery expectations are fast becoming the movers and shakers of the jewellery world. Greg Valerio, founder of Chichester based Cred Jewellery says he does what he does simply 'because it's the right thing to do. We are trying to demonstrate that creating beautiful jewellery does not mean you have to exploit people or the planet in the process. The average £10,000 wedding ring will create three tonnes of toxic waste such as cyanide or mercury, and that's just the environmental impact.'

As corporate social responsibility becomes the heart of business, individuals in the jewellery industry are taking heed of the issues, and coming together to adopt good working practice. The Council for Responsible Jewellery Practice was set up as a not for profit organisation in May 2006 to address the importance of responsibility and accountability for maintaining standards of ethical, social and environmental performance. The Council cover all areas of the industry from mine to retail, both large and small scale. The hope is that it will give consumers confidence when they buy jewellery from the High Street. With advocacy work amongst the industry as well as using the Council as a sphere for networking and information sharing, this is a fantastic opportunity for the jewellery industry to make a commitment to sound business practice.

© Hansich

Jewel Jargon

As interest in ethical jewellery increases, so does the awareness, although we often get misled by the jargon. So what really is a blood free diamond?

Conflict Diamonds are rough diamonds used by rebel movements or their allies to finance conflict aimed at undermining legal governments, such as Sierra Leone in the 1990s.

The Kimberley Process is a governmental, industry and civil society initiative that ensures rough diamonds have been legitimately purchased and are conflict free. The Kimberley Process certifies diamonds for export and import purposes, and guarantees they are conflict free. The good news is that 99 per cent of diamonds sold in the UK are now conflict free, and human rights NGO's Amnesty International and Global Witness published a shopper's guide entitled, 'Are you looking for the perfect diamond?' to help people use their consumer power wisely.

Conflict free diamonds whilst assuring they are mined lawfully does not necessarily mean they were mined fairly. Valerio adds, 'It's a politically constructed process designed to illuminate illegal trade and to that end it has by and large being a success. Yet it hasn't demonstrated the social and environmental aspects, it doesn't look at the dollar a day economy in Sierra Leone with rampant exploitation where individuals are hoping to find the perfect diamond in order to make them a millionaire – it's all poverty driven.' An estimated 65 per cent of the world's diamonds come from Africa, with countries like Nambia gaining 40 per cent of its annual export earnings from diamond trading.

Issues of forced and/or child labour and environmental damage still occur, and the International Labour Organisation

Dejoria rings offer conflict free diamonds which you can create your own designs with © Dejoria

deems mining as the most dangerous activity for child labourers. Fifi Bijoux founder Vivien Johnston is aware that children are 'highly prized' in some of these workshops. 'Their good eyesight and deft little fingers are useful tools.' There is also an issue in enhancing the colour in gemstones. 'Irradiation, (exposing the gem to nuclear radiation) is sometimes used and if not properly controlled, these can remain radioactive for years. As a result, employees may not be the only ones at risk. Anyone buying one of these stones could be inadvertently buying a radioactive blue topaz. We need to stop being so naive about the supply chain and be able to trace and check on all gems in the supply chain, not only diamonds.'

Whilst there is currently no certification for fairly trading the components of a ring, various businesses are practising the concept in developing countries where raw minerals are mined. With an estimated 10 million people globally who are directly or indirectly supported by the diamond industry, a call for change is essential.

John Paul DeJoria (who also co-founded Paul Mitchell hair and beauty products) founded online company Dejoria jewellery in his own personal crusade to combat conflict free diamonds. He believes that love should never be tarnished and insists that all DeJoria diamonds

> **The average £10,000 wedding ring will create three tonnes of toxic waste such as cyanide or mercury, and that's just the environmental impact**

are sourced with this ethical background. 'We will be ploughing back some of the revenue we generate into highly worthwhile and needed health related projects across the world.' That doesn't mean the diamonds are more expensive though and it's estimated that buying online saves you 30–40 per cent off High Street prices.

When it comes to mining ethics you've got two choices. You either attempt to clean up the industry in the country you are working in. This is a little tricky when working with countries that accept backhanders and are prepared to exploit the environment in an opportunity for short term financial gain. So the other option is you look for countries that are already set up with political stability, standards and transparency. That is why a lot of ethical jewellers are turning to Canada who have the same natural raw minerals yet without the qualms. One example is Belgium company Nenoir diamonds, who are supplied by BHP Billiton. This company mine under strict regulations imposed by the government of the Northwest Territories, and are cut and polished according to guidelines established by the Council for Responsible Jewellery Practices. With the government they have also created an independent environmental monitoring agency to ensure that the land is protected, and a strict sustainable development policy. Each one is then engraved with a unique 'CanadaMark' inscription on its girdle, allowing the retailers to trace their origin.

Green Gold

For those wishing to purchase their gold from responsible sources then it is worth looking at the pioneering Certified Oro Verde (Latin for 'Green Gold') Program in Colombia. The first programme of its kind, it seeks to reverse the devastating damage caused to the unique native ecosystem by out of control large scale mining. Currently the initiative is being implemented in co-operation with 12 Afro-Colombian communities, in the municipalities of Condoto and Tadó.

The Oro Verde Corporation was created in 2001 as an alliance between two community councils in Chocó and two NGOs. Having established an Analogue Forestry Program as an alternative method of rehabilitating the forest and restoring the biodiversity of the region, their focus is to empower the communities and to allow them to use natural resources sustainably. What has arisen is the first environmentally certified and socially responsible gold and platinum. Once the Green

Gold metals are bought from certified miners (who are of course paid a fair price) they then sell it to jewellers across the world, charging a 10 per cent premium over the international price of gold and a five per cent premium over the international price of platinum to help finance their community projects. The jeweller receives a certificate guaranteeing the origin and extraction methods. Based on the success of this project they have expanded the model to other regions under the creation of an Association for Responsible Mining (ARM). This network of independent organisations that boast fair trade standards are

The Helen Ring with Green Gold, core to the design with Fifi Bijoux, British luxury ethical jeweller © Fifi Bijoux

now working in a global scale effort to promote responsible standards and criteria for artisanal and small scale mining, ensuring good gold for your bling. Cred Jewellery sell this green gold in the form of 18ct gold, platinum and diamond wedding rings in the UK, and are looking forward to having independent third party certification by ARM. With pilot testing taking place with six gold mine co-operatives in Colombia, Peru, Ecuador and Bolivia, they are planning to launch a fair trade gold certification standard by mid-2009, hopefully with backing from fair trade labelling organisations such as the UK's Fairtrade Foundation.

From Mine to You

A lot of the jewellery we buy on the High Street is usually rather inexpensive – often cheaper than the two month's salary a man should traditionally pay for his fiancée's engagement ring. Vivien Johnston is a vivacious character who was working in the mainstream industry until she got distressed by careless mining. 'I got sick of photographs of sumps building up after mining had occurred. Stagnant water is a breeding ground for mosquitoes which meant that malaria and tuberculosis were rife in areas already often struggling with extreme poverty and disease. The methods of chemical extraction are also horrific. They leach into the land and water ways. The toxic effect on the land, maritime life and of course the people who live in the vicinity cause long term damage.' That is why she set up Fifi Bijoux Luxury Jewellery in September 2006 and her eyes sparkles with passion when she talks about how she does it differently.

Whilst there are responsible mining practises that manage chemical use or employ alternative Ph neutral, non toxic methods, Fifi Bijoux source their gold from mines which simply pan for gold, replacing the topsoil afterwards. Johnston adds, 'The mines I work with respect the land and the miners. The land is not left for dead but is actively regenerated. Some of the precious minerals I use have organic farming and seed bank projects attached'.

Similarly, Jane Kellas of Silverchilli started her business after working in Mexico for a fair trade company. 'I was troubled to see that lots of support for artisans in the form of fair trade or specialist promotion was arranged upon ethnic lines, as the emphasis seemed to be on anthropological grounds and preserving culture. I noticed that the silversmiths seemed to be having just as hard a time, but could not find an organisation to support them. I guessed this was because they did not fall into a specific ethnic or cultural group. We made a

Tim Ingle and David Rhode talk about setting up Ingle & Rhode, The Ethical Jeweller in 2007

We met at university back in 1994 and always had the idea of doing business together one day in spite of taking two very different directions in our careers.

Last year David decided to take the plunge and propose to his girlfriend with an ethical ring. It took a lot of time and research to find one that had been sourced and manufactured in a socially and environmentally responsible way. We got talking, and realised a lot of other people must want ethical engagement rings and have the same problems finding them. That's how Ingle and Rhode was born. Our supply chain is totally transparent and we always state who our collaborators are; each component of any piece that we sell can be traced back to the mine. We mostly work with diamonds, 18ct gold, and platinum and collaborate with top designers. As well as a range of classic designs, we also offer a bespoke service. Our larger white diamonds are premium gems from Nenoir. Our rubies, sapphires and smaller white diamonds are mined in Madagascar, Tanzania and Lesotho respectively by small scale co-operatives. This means the wealth generated by mining is directly retained by the local communities, which is fantastic considering that small scale artisanal miners often receive only a fraction of the local market value of their gemstones, as traders and exporters collude to rip them off. Consumers also tend to forget the importance of the metals – gems are only one part of the problem. Our casting gold comes from the EcoAndina Foundation in the north-west of Argentina. Small scale mining communities work there under carefully regulated conditions to produce metals that are both environmentally friendly and socially beneficial. The miners have the right to bargain collectively, child labour is strictly prohibited, and prices are set on a fair trade basis. Most of our sheet and wire comes from the same source. Our platinum comes from a refinery in the US and is 100 per cent recycled. Some of our gold sheet and wire is also recycled. ■

Management Consultant Hywel Sloman decided to surprise his now fiancée Maire with an Ingle and Rhode engagement ring. 'We just don't want our wedding plans to cause any harm. I knew I wanted an ethical ring, and found them on the internet. When I phoned them, they were very helpful so I made an appointment for a consultation. They were very informative and totally transparent. More importantly, Maire was delighted. If I ever buy an eternity ring, I'll definitely go back to them!'

conscious effort to design mainstream products which were very affordable.' Making the shells of wedding rings since 2004 her company suggest that you source and get rings set in the UK. Not for profit, Silverchilli has a working model that allows their silversmiths to choose the community projects that they feel deserve investment.

Sarah Sheridan's designer conflict free diamond engagement and wedding band rings © Ingle & Rhode

Johnston believes that the jewellery industry has a huge opportunity to make a positive contribution to the lives of people who have historically been exploited and seen their land ravaged. 'I resent the millions of dollars spent by diamond companies on PR spin around the time the film 'Blood Diamond' screened. They should have been investing that money in finding sustainable solutions to the problems we all know exist, instead of embarking on a campaign of denial.' Johnston is happy to pass on her experience of establishing a set of ethical criteria for her supply chain, having presented to an industry conference of delegates including De Beers, Cartier and the mining giant Rio Tinto amongst others. 'The response was pretty good, I am working to improve the jewellery supply chain in general though as I hope that in five years all jewellers will be able to offer some degree of ethical assurance. To me it's about creating a movement and a real shift in expectations of the meaning of 'luxury'. It doesn't matter if someone is spending £100, a £1,000 or £10,000. They buy Fifi Bijoux because they appreciate the contribution they are making to small scale artisan miners' lives, to the work that the miners carry out to make their activities as sustainable as possible.'

Most of the Fifi Bijoux gems come from South America, such as topaz and aquamarine, although the rutile quartz that are used in limited edition items comes from a small rural mine in Bahia, Brazil. This particular mine has a lifespan of approximately five years, so developing a sustainability programme was a priority. The profits from the cutting and polishing of the gems are reinvested in organic farming of vanilla and recently in citrus and mango plantations.

Johnston is now working with Laban of Dragons Den fame, who had visited a gold mine in Ghana and was appalled by what he saw. Whilst they set up a mine there, they are supporting The Entebbe Women's Association for women in Uganda. Together they have

Penny Gray's blue earrings made from recycled jewellery parts © Penny Gray

launched a pendant called 'From Little Acorns' in which 10 per cent of the profits to go build water towers, invest in piglet farming – a considerable safer business than mining – and sending local children to school.

Mounds of Gems

If you wish for a large variety of precious jewellery to choose from all in one place, then why not visit the website Jewel Garden? Like a lot of new ethical jewellery businesses, Hertfordshire businesswoman and passionate jewellery collector Charlotte Pritchard wanted to know where to shop on the High Street but found little inspiration. Since launching in November 2006, Charlotte has succeeded in creating a collection of desirable and affordable handcrafted jewellery which includes designs from up and coming talent such as Ashiana, Nannapas, Hendrikka Waage, Babette Wasserman and LA Jewellery. When choosing designers to add to the Jewel Garden collection, Charlotte has to not only like their designs but also their ethical policy. 'We ask each potential new designer where they source their materials from as a lot of the jewellery we sell is handcrafted. The jewellery trade is fragmented but we will look along the supply chain to see where things have come from and source responsibly as best we can.' They give one per cent of their annual profits to chosen charities each year.

There is something satisfying about knowing the individuals behind the art creation on your finger. If you intend to pass your rings down as a family heirloom, then you have more than your own story of love to go with it. Louise Power of Adila jewellery makes a special point of describing her designers and producers in detail with her online company, in such a way that you feel you know them personally. Working to support a small care home for infants diagnosed with HIV/AIDS she acknowledges that 'they are more than just a name and statistics – we feel much more connected.' That's not something you would get in your local Argos.

Beads Bonanza

You don't have to go down the mining route to adorn yourself. Contemporary jewellery designer Karina Anne who describes her business as a result of a hobby that got a bit out of hand uses a wild array of beads. 'When I started making jewellery, I didn't really think about where gemstones come from and I just used to buy what I thought was pretty and would work well with a particular design. I think that is how most people buy jewellery and other accessories – it probably doesn't occur to most of us (or at least it didn't a few years ago) to think about where things came from or who made them. It's not just the mining. When gemstones are ground to shape them into beads there can be dangerous and sometimes lethal consequences for those workers who do not have access to the necessary safety equipment.' Instead she uses glass and crystal beads which she believes have greater beauty, and finds lampwork beads fascinating. 'I have my favourite bead artists in England and Canada. The beads can be quite expensive, and very often are one-offs, but each one is handmade and their uniqueness makes them all the more desirable. I think they should be treasured as little works of art! You can buy inexpensive lampwork beads from China, but these are really very different from the ones I am talking about.' She has also started using Venetian glass beads from Murano in Italy. 'Gemstones seem so unnecessary when there are so many lovely, handmade alternatives available.'

Pippa Small, a deity of ethical jewellery and renowned for collaborations with Gucci, Nicole Farhi, and Chloé is a classic example of keeping it simple whilst also working on craft initiatives with indigenous people in the Kalahari, Rwanda, and Panama. She helps them to research their traditional designs to generate self sufficiency and income. She prefers to minimise metal in her designs, allowing the

© Vladislav Gajic

stones to have their 'natural organic form'. She has designed work for the boutique range of new company Made. Training local artisans in Kenya the products are created using long established materials such as horn and recycled brass and even tin metal. You can get similar fairly traded jewels from Tearcraft, who have been selling jewellery for over thirty years. The Shared Earth shops also offer a delightful variety of jewellery created by individual artisans from across the world dependent on this income.

Recycled, salvaged, vintage jewellery is available from companies such as The Bird In the Meadow, who have a 'Love is the key' necklace adorned with pearls and an old fashioned key.

If you want a hedonistic headdress then you can even get a conscientious tiara for the day, hand fashioned from sterling silver, recycled glass and feathers from jewellery designer Caroline J. A Janganant, or one created from sea glass and sea plastic by Sarah Drew Tiaras.

Natural Adornment
There are many unusual but charming pieces on the ethical market that are naturally green for you to exchange on your wedding day. We're not talking daisy chains either. Sea glass is one enchanting hidden treasure that is made by the meeting of water and land over time that wears the glass down. Nina Cowen, who makes jewellery out of sea glass she found from a Victorian glass factory that had dumped their leftovers at sea, describes the process. 'Sea glass may be the perfect medium for our consumer society awakening to the impact of recycling. For me, sea glass is as precious as a diamond and its creation nicely contrasts that of the traditional wedding gemstone. With diamonds, the tough natural rock is cut and reshaped by man into sparkling stones; with sea glass, rough shards of manmade glass are tumbled and reshaped by nature into luminous, frosted stones. No item can ever be repeated exactly, making each one unique and individual. Settings and clasps are in hand forged silver or gold. Sea glass looks best against bare skin or muted colours and complements natural fabrics such as cotton, linen, or silk.' You can get a wide variety of colours with sea glass. Welsh company Green Beach have also combed the coast for shells to add to their faux pearl, recycled glass and fair trade bead range, offering a bespoke facility in addition to a restringing service of any of your lovingly snapped jewellery. Swansea based business Goose Island offer chunky wooden and glass beads, or dainty shell and ceramic pendants.

Blue lampwork bracelet by contemporary jewellery designer Karina Anne © Paul Coghlin Photography

If you want something with some forest roots, then you could get a beautiful ring by designer Stephen Einhorn who uses 2,000 year old petrified oak from the Thames. Einhorn has developed a unique impregnation and sealing technique to protect and waterproof the rare Thames Wood that is then set into silver. All his jewellery can be customised to suit a particular style.

For a bit of the Brazilian Amazon in your necklaces, Jungleberry offer up natural remnants from the forests such as colourful tento, acai and jarina seeds, and coconut shell, which are all handmade. Just Trade retail some similarly lively red seed necklaces, as well as crotched wire pieces.

Or you could try the knotted look by buying unique, rare Turkish lacework (also known as Needle Lace Oya). Arzu Keles who has brought it into the UK explained, 'I was brought up with needle lace around me and it is valued in Turkey. The villages where the products are made are appreciating the value of the UK customer. Each piece is handmade and so we want people to know that every piece is made with love.'

The real gem in natural jewellery is that it doesn't need to blow your budget – the average price is usually £20. ■

The **Beautification**

You want to be the blushing bride – the photographs will be around for generations to come. Yet how green is it to beautify yourself for the special day? What are the ethics within the cosmetics industry?

Beauty comes from within. If you're not confident with that statement and want to slap on the war paint then it makes far more sense – both for your own health needs and to respect the environment – that you use small scale, plant derived ingredients rather than wait for the lab to come up with another brew. If you are what you eat, then you are also what you put on your face and body, as toxins from chemicals in your beauty products can seep into your skin. You're likely to be buying new make up for the wedding, so this is the perfect time to make some changes within your cosmetics bag.

A Cocktail of Chemicals
Some perfumes contain up to 100 different ingredients and over 9,000 chemicals are used to concoct the toiletries we use to make ourselves clean and fresh. But can you explain the ingredient list?

Parabens
Parabens are the preservatives put in chemicals, and whilst you can get them from nature (for example in fruit shrubs), the majority in commercial products are synthetically produced. They have been linked to skin irritation and controversially, studies at the University of Reading suggest high doses of parabens have been found in breast tumours, suggesting they are getting into our bloodstream and major organs.

Sodium Lauryl Sulphate
Sodium Lauryl Sulphate, also known as SLS, is an inexpensive ingredient that forms the foam for much of your bath bubbles or shampoo. The issue with a lot of SLS's is that they cause skin inflammation, particularly for those with skin conditions such as eczema and dermatitis, as they dry out the skin. Connections to mouth ulcers if you use toothpaste with SLS in it have been suggested, as well as carcinogenic properties that have been linked to cancer.

Have relaxation time in a Fired Earth painted bathroom © Fired Earth

Phthalates
Phthalates are solvents and fixatives used in beauty products. A Greenpeace research report called 'The Chemical Home' revealed that they can reduce male and female fertility.

Artificial Musks
Musks provide the fragrance for a lot of toiletries, and those made artificially have been linked with reproductive toxicity. Not so comforting for a future of bouncing babies.

Chemicals are used to keep costs down, ironic really considering UK consumers spent £15.6 billion on their products last year (source: Euromonitor). Their other argument is that it would take resources to seek an alternative. With little research it is tricky to know what occurs when chemicals are mixed together (this is known as 'the cocktail effect'). Whilst nothing damaging has been substantially proven, the cosmetics industry are applying a principle of precaution and are attempting to shift towards more natural ingredients, however this shift will take time.

Animal Action

The big cause de celebre of the 1980s was an increased awareness of animal welfare. Things haven't changed a great deal with skin and eye irritancy tests as well as toxicity tests still being carried out, even though there are alternatives to animal testing, such as human volunteers and computer modelling. The Naturewatch Compassionate Shopping Guide shows where consumers can choose beauty, personal care and household products that have not been tested on animals. Dawn Lewis, the Editor explains. 'Though numerous companies produce outstanding cruelty free products, just as many still use ingredients that necessitate further animal testing. Although in the UK animal testing of cosmetic ingredients ended in 1998, testing of newly developed ingredients destined for use in personal care products continues elsewhere in the world, and in Europe alone continues to cost the lives of thousands of animals per year. Invariably products containing animal tested ingredients still turn up on beauty counters nationwide.'

The BUAV has been campaigning for 100 years against animal experimentation and predict that over three million animals are used for experiments in the UK every year, which results in an animal dying in British laboratories every 12 seconds. The BUAV were instrumental in bringing about the UK ban and run the only internationally recognised Cruelty Free accreditation programme, which audits and approves cosmetic and household product brands and retailers. BUAV chief executive Michelle Thew says, 'Companies from The Body Shop to Dermalogica to The Co-op to M&S have shown it is possible to go cruelty free and run successful national and multinational businesses. They know that the vast majority of consumers do not want animals to suffer for a longer lash defining mascara. However, many are being misled by unsubstantiated claims on products.'

Ingredients...
The cosmetics industry is renowned for using various animal derivatives within their products.

Gelatine: from bones

Keratin: protein from hair, horn, hoof, feather

Lanolin: the grease from wool

Musk: from deer

Shellac: crushed insects

If you don't want any animal by products in your lippy, then it's worth looking for the Vegan Society symbol.

PETA also have a comprehensive cruelty free products list that can guide your marriage titivation.

The RSPCA Good Business Awards prize companies attempting to step away from animal testing. In 2007 Lush won the award, with M&S being noted as the most progressive company in the field for supporting the Fund for the Replacement of Animals in Medical Experiments (FRAME), an organisation seeking alternatives to animal testing. US company Urban Decay came highly commended for making inroads to bypass animal testing through in vitro testing, skin patch testing and practical application. Another highly commended British company, Liz Earle Cosmetics also regularly donates to FRAME, with their suppliers moni-

Find some natural minerals © Liv Friis-larsen

tored independently on an annual basis. Even beauty giant L'Oreal have started growing artificial human skin cells in their labs to avoid animal testing, although you may feel this is a little 'Frankenstein' for vanity. With new legislation on its way, animal testing in cosmetics is due to be banned throughout the EU in 2009.

The Natural Way

Preserving ingredients can be difficult and this is the reason that a lot of chemicals are stuck in products: to keep them fresh and prevent bacteria spreading. By using heat treatments and minimising water and oxygen from the product all helps prevent bacterial development and therefore means the products need fewer preservatives. Natural antibacterial ingredients that have been used for centuries can aid the cleanliness of the skin. Tea tree oil, for example, is a far better bet.

There are lots of others too, such as honey, sugar and alcohol. If you go to certain parts of the world you will still see these being used as the primary ingredients of local beauty goods. Honey has been getting more attention recently for its healing properties, and whilst it is not deemed ethical by the Vegan Society (it's stealing bee's food),

Lula Lewis, of organic apothecary Lovelula.com is getting married to fiancée Caspar

We chose to get married in our back garden which borders a beautiful forest, a place which is really special to us and which we both love. We wanted the occasion to be in tune with the environment around us. I've always been passionate about nature and the great outdoors – I'm most at home in amidst nature. And I've always used natural skin and body care products and sourced local food.

Getting married in our back garden in a marquee has cut down on lots of travel for guests (many of our friends and family live close by) and we're not using a venue which uses lots of power and resources (the power for lights in the marquee will run off our mains source which is renewable electricity and little heat is needed). We're taking ten months to plan the wedding – I am one of five children and my fiancé Caspar is one of seven children, so it was never going to be a small wedding! We're aiming for around 120 guests altogether and there is such excitement of looking forward to a day spent with all the people we love most in the world.

For catering, we're hiring a local chef and waitresses so they don't have to travel miles to be here, the catering equipment hire company is just four miles down the road and I'm sourcing food locally – for example sustainably-reared venison from Tatton Park which has just been culled from their free roaming herd.

Our gift list includes sustainable items such as organic bedding. We will have local and in season flowers – which means leaving things to chance a little but my Mum and I will be popping down to a local grower a couple of weeks before to pick out what would work.

Our wedding invitations were handmade and printed on recycled, non bleached card. The guys are hiring their outfits which means a special suit isn't being bought that will sit unworn in a wardrobe, and for the bridesmaids we're buying dresses they'll hopefully be able to wear again.

Obviously all our beauty products will be organic and chemical free products from LoveLula.com! For our honeymoon we're going to an eco health spa in Austria. ∎

there was one case where a hospital patient had severe burns that couldn't be healed by skin grafts, yet miraculously made a recovery when an unorthodox doctor spread honey on the wounds.

Essential oils are a great way of getting full, natural aromas as are plant extracts such as calendula and rose. Beware though of plant based chemicals passing themselves off as natural.

One ingredient that is causing problematic clearing of the rainforests is palm oil. With one in ten supermarket products using palm oil, this has damaging effects on endangered orangutans and other inhabiting species of Sumatra and Borneo. The large scale palm oil plantations encroach upon indigenous tribe's lands, causing displacement and conflict. Many High Street companies such as Lush and The Body Shop are looking to offer alternatives, however soap ingredient Sodium Laurel Sulphate often contains palm oil. In 2007 over 200 natural beauty products were launched in the UK – leading the way for Europe – and this is expected to grow.

Too Many Standards

Don't let the men in white coats with their synthetic ingredients get you down. The obvious option to cut out chemicals is to use only organic products. Unfortunately there is no legal definition for what organic is when it comes to health and beauty – you only need a tiny organic dribble in the ingredients for a company to be able to describe a product as organic on the label. With no strict regulator, the beauty industry is a cheeky business. Mainstream beauty columns or magazines are paid for by the companies advertising, therefore it's rare that beauty editors are willing to speak out about the potential hazards involved in the ingredients or point out that a company's product is far less organic than it actually promotes.

What's more is that there are a lot more organic certification programmes springing up, supported by big businesses who don't necessarily speak true of our organic expectations.

Spiezia Organics skincare commissioned an independent survey to see what consumer knowledge of pure, natural and organic beauty was. Nearly half (49 per cent) of the respondents thought pure, organic and natural statements on packaging meant that these products did not contain any chemicals, and a further 11 per cent were unsure. They were appalled that even their defined eco savvy consumers were unable to differentiate. Actually, pure or natural

©Liv Friis-Larsen

products need only contain two per cent of natural ingredients. Spiezia's post-survey recommendations were that you look at the ingredients listed on the products carefully.

The most trustworthy standard for organic certification for the beauty industry in the UK is the Soil Association. These beauty standards were launched in 2002 after much consultation with industry experts. Following the same certification process as organic food, products with this stamp of approval aspire to be as natural as possible, as minimal as possible and without petrochemicals or GM ingredients. Petrochemically derived mineral oils, whilst feeling good initially, are known to asphyxiate the skin and block pores. For the Soil Association symbol to be present on the beauty product it must contain a minimum of 70 per cent organic ingredients, not including water.

The Soil Association are encouraging companies to find other processes to increase the quantity of organically certified and safe products on the market.

Outside of the UK there are other trustworthy certification bodies – and whilst standards differ a little due to the variety of governmental regulations from country to country – the French Ecocert label, the United States Department of Agriculture (USDA) and the Australian Certified Organic (ACO) labels should also be looked out for.

The Biodynamic Agricultural Association (BDAA) is another organisation inspired by Rudolph Steiner whose members seek to produce ecological diversity and sustainability. With over 120 biodynamic farms in the UK, it is different from organic in that it uses astronomical calendars to determine timing for planting, with every biodynamic farm aiming to become self sufficient in compost, manures and animal feeds. Herb based preparations that include some animal organs are also used. The Demeter symbol guarantees products have been produced biodynamically.

On some natural cosmetics you may also see a symbol with the letters 'BDIH'. These stand for the Federation of German Industries and Trading Firms for pharmaceuticals, health care goods, dietary supplements and personal hygiene products and ensure products are certified natural under their guidelines. This means that producers who have the 'Certified Natural Cosmetics' seal on their products use natural raw material such as plant oils, fats and waxes, herbal extracts, essential oils and aromatic materials from certified organic or wild harvested plants. Under this seal, ingredients from fair trade projects and the ecological impact is also considered significant.

Currently there are no fair trade certified products for health and beauty; therefore it might be an idea to keep it local as well as organic, to ensure no humans have been exploited for the contents of your bathroom cabinet.

Spa Days & Treatments

Before and after your special day it's pleasurable to get that pampering treatment – it may be the one lifetime opportunity for you to do this and perhaps loved ones want to give you this gift to relax.

There are many opportunities to have organic spa treatments, both in external spas, as well as buying products that you can use in the comfort of your own home or with friends. You could get organic, ethically sourced essential oils from companies like NHR Organic Oils and make your own bridal countdown regime. BAFTS registered Far East Trade have a Thai-inspired range of Yonjai Spa products including body scrubs that are fairly traded from the Suan Plu Women's Co-operative in Bangkok. Green People have another fabulous organic facial spa range that includes a hydrating cleanser, firming gel and rejuvenating serum and oil, with 10 per cent of their profits being donated to environmental charities. A new brand on the block, vegan approved company No Cow offer spa day kits that also include organic cotton bath robes and soya candles to complete the pleasurable experience.

> **Essential oils are a great way of getting full, natural aromas as are plant extracts such as calendula and rose. Beware though of the plant based chemicals passing themselves off as natural**

Have a de-stress session at Titanic Spa's swimming pool, the UK's largest eco health resort
© Titanic Spa

The reputable, 25 year old company Neal's Yard Remedies suggests that you embark on relaxing treatments such as massage and aromatherapy, as well as a facial several days before the wedding day, in case of any blemishes as a result of cleansing. A reflexology session will help release stress and revitalise. Neal's Yard Remedies is the perfect just off the High Street option that have plenty of qualified, experienced therapists who are not only knowledgeable of their products but can also offer general advice.

Genene Edwards of Exhale agrees that it is important to get a first rate massage. 'We only work with the best therapists who give something extra to their massage. Having two or three qualifications is not enough... it has to feel fantastic!' If you are in the London area, you can get their therapists around to work on your tummy knots in the comfort of your own home or at work.

Pukka Herbs now offer fantastic organic massage oils that are produced by farmers in India and Sri Lanka.

For home treatments it may be worth checking out the Alternative Spa Company, who present a range of organic wedding ideas and gifts using Australian brand Miessence skin care, who are independently certified by the Australian Certified Organic (ACO) organisation. They offer a free wedding consultation and pre wedding preparation for the bride and groom, and products from hair to body care are offered in natural jute bags. If you fancy a DIY skincare service then Chery Lin Skin Therapy, based in Gloucestershire is focused on treating the skin, body and senses where you can choose your ingredients (pure and organic of course) and make your own. For that perfect manicure or pedicure, Green Hands can recommend a range of home care products to get your green goddess's nails into fabulous condition in time for your wedding, without the use of formaldehyde that is a notorious allergen.

For a bit of the ooh lala on your day you can always try some Ecocert products by French company Naturetis who offer camomile oil that has a calming effect for the skin, and prevents redness – perfect for blushing brides! Willow Beauty have an organic skin care range, certified by the Soil Association which includes an exfoliator with argan seeds and face masks fragranced with bitter orange blossom, lime and cedarwood oil. You can either buy online or go for a hydrating facial at Senspa in the New Forest.

If you fancy making the most of your wedding preparations and you want the true spa experience, then as Blue Fish Spa Manager, Alyson Staines declares, 'Not all spas are the same'. Some of them are environmentally extravagant!

The Titanic Spa in Yorkshire is worth a visit. Titanic was launched at the beginning of 2006, with £1.5 million invested to create a truly unique, carbon neutral building. Titanic's eco credentials now include a CHP (combined heat and power) unit to provide heat and electricity, a chlorine free, salt regulated swimming pool, photovoltaic solar panels to catch the daylight all year round and a private borehole 100m below the earth's surface that provides vast quantities of pure Yorkshire water to the spa. Guests to the spa can choose from a wide choice of Elemis and Decleor treatments, alternative therapies, Hamman and mud chamber offerings. For brides to be, Titanic's new hassle free Bridal Makeover promises to alleviate any of that pre-wedding stress. This costs £125, which includes a pre-wedding consultation with hair and make up on the day as well as complimentary refreshments and a glass of champagne. There is also a hen party option.

For somewhere further down south then Scin Boutique Spa in the heart of Notting Hill provides simple natural and organic products and treatments for men and women. You can choose from deep cleansing facials and back treatments to relaxing massage, manicures, pedicures, waxing and spray tanning. Scin can put together tailor made pre-wedding pamper packages for the bride to prepare herself in the lead up to the big day and can also organise hen parties for up to ten people. They also sell quite a few different ranges, including organic certified products from great brands such as Pai, Circaroma, Jo Wood, Taer, Green People, as well as non certified yet highly concentrated organic and natural ingredients brands such as Laidbare, Suki, MOP, Apivita and This Works.

The Angel Therapy Rooms in Islington is another green alternative. They are against using corporate laundry services to clean towels and robes, use minimal electricity due to maximising the use of natural light and candles, their oils are 100 per cent natural and organic, and all their retail products are locally sourced and certified by the Soil Association. All their refreshments are seasonal and local and even their Zoya nail varnish is chemical free which is used in all their holistic pedicures and manicures, so your nails can get an eco makeover too.

> **Rather than being a rash eco warrior by not washing your hair months before the wedding day and then receiving gasps from your guests, why not try a few of the companies out there who have done all the head scratching for you?**

Blue Fish Spas in the Lake District have taken a truly organic approach with their choice of brand Li'Tya from Australia that incorporates Aboriginal healing techniques, native plants and clays designed to relax, ground and uplift. They have also joined forces with Mother Earth who produce natural and organic skincare products close by in the village of Coniston. They offer alternative therapies such as Hopi Ear Candling so that you can hear when to say your vows, Vichy wet room treatments and traditional gents wet shaves.

It's a little dubious, the dieting game. However if you want to get away to detox or are worried about your weight then Dao at Sura Detox in Devon can offer a greener way to slim, using Miessence products. The venue has planted 40,000 trees in neighbouring fields to do what they can to offset their carbon emissions and they donate half an acre of primary rainforest in Brazil, to a charity underwritten by David Attenborough.

Hair

That glossy look from your conventional hair care pays its price. It is in fact often stripping your hair of its natural merits, being covered over by the gloop of PVC-like properties (that's the silicone added to make your hair deceptively shine). Products that work in harmony with your hair are far better for your hair's health, keeping it stronger without making you look like Worzel Gummidge.

Have a girlie morning and get ready with your friends and family at your local hairdresser
© Squareink

Rather than being a rash eco warrior by not washing your hair months before the wedding day and then receiving gasps from your guests, why not try a few of the companies out there who have done all the head scratching for you? Headonism is a company that offers the most incredible shampoos and conditioners that are naturally scented with oodles of essential oils such as exotic vetiver, patchouli and ylang-ylang. Using amber glass and a natural cork top, the products are preserved from the sunlight, locking in their pure properties. Similarly, Soil Association certified Tints of Nature offer lovely fruity whiffs. For a gentler approach then the Herb shampoo from Essential Care is available – with this green gloop look you can tell it isn't chemically enhanced, yet it is incredibly effective. Weleda introduced a new entirely free from additives hair care range in early 2008, using natural cleansing properties from sugar and coconut. Scottish company Faith in Nature uses exceptional raw materials including hemp oil, ginkgo biloba, neem, and even chocolate in their BUAV approved and Vegan Society accredited products, including naturally coloured shampoo and conditioners.

If the bleach-like stench of regular hair dyes doesn't put you off changing your hair colour, then complicatedly named chemicals such as phenylenediamine should. Yes the alarm bells go off again.

You could instead try one of the few products on the market from the Naturatint product range or you can always consider getting a pampering appointment at an organic salon such as Karine Jackson in London's Covent Garden.

Simple Stuff

If you are on a mission for big business to go green then the main players are already jumping on the bandwagon in the beauty world. L'Oreal now own The Body Shop, Estee Lauder own Aveda – it really is one after the other. Even Waitrose supermarket has their own Soil Association organic body and bath range. Rather than deliberating over increasing ethical dilemmas, it may be worth heading down to one of a few organic apothecaries on the internet such as Lovelula.com, theorganicsalon.com or Pure Organics to give you a range of completely environmentally conscious products from some of the best true, independently owned beauty brands. Local wholefood stores also stock the lesser known organic health and beauty products.

If you fancy giving your key bridal party a little something to spoil themselves with then the Beyond Organic Skincare, which is certified organic by the BDAA have a great Weekender range, including moisturising day creams and fragrant serums in attractive tubs. They are a small, family business in Cornwall that has just started using an organic citrus extract, cutting out the need for a preservative. With a committed staff, even their walls are decorated with organic and solvent free paints.

Nude, founded by Fresh and Wild's Bryan Meehan is a new natural skin care range free from the chemical nasties. It even has post industrial recycled plastic for its packaging.

There are plenty of soaps available to scrub up clean from small companies such as La Belle Plante, Caurnie Soaperie, Simply Soaps, Visionary Soap Company (now sold in Oxfam shops) and Cornwall Soap Box. Some of them offer personalised options that can be fantastic wedding favours for your guests.

Winner of The Soil Association Organic Industry Awards 2007 is small tub company Balm Balm. It's the ethical 'petroleum jelly' of our time, mainly as it's simple concoction of organic wax and oil can be used all over your body.

Cosmetics

With so many companies giving themselves natural credentials without having any certification standards to support their stance, it can be tricky to know where to glam up. And the potential health menaces that come with using cosmetics aren't particularly positive. Did you know that the average lipstick wearer consumes 1kg over her lifetime? On your big day you can paint your face a little more naturally. If you fancy having a celebrity endorsed lippy then Cargo cosmetics have arrived with their PlantLove range that boasts a 100 per cent compostable lipstick tube (it's made from corn), and contains no mineral oils or petroleum in the ingredients, instead opting for essential oils. If that's not enough, the price includes a donation to charity and the range is available at a Sainsbury's near you.

If you have a desire for a bit of colourful dazzle then you can try B Never Too Busy To Be Beautiful's range of glitter pots and vibrant make up. Sister brand to Lush the company aims to be green using fairly traded containers, and is the only UK company to carry an entire colour cosmetics line that is suitable for vegans. Whilst the cosmetics range contains no SLS's, they may have up to one per cent of parabens in their ingredients. The bejewelled cases, fairly traded by local artisans in India and Morocco through a number of grass-roots projects helping displaced people, are also perfect little wedding favours. Charlotte Matheson – B's Head Make Up Artist notes that 'Every bride should have an emergency kit of make up life savers up her sleeve for the big day. These products can help save the lady of the moment from any potential cosmetic disasters. I always carry some Love hair perfume and Cocktail body lustre with me for bridal makeovers. The body lustre gives a gorgeous luminosity to the skin which adds to the radiance and flawlessness of the skin's texture, especially in the photographs.'

Miessence offer great base foundations to hide the blush and New Zealand company Living Nature who use their native plants (such as Harakeke Flax) has possibly the best ethical mascara stick about. Green People offer organically certified lipstick in four natural shades, as do Korres. Jane Iredale cosmetics are described as 'skin care make up' that uses a blend of minerals and pigments through technology which does not allow bacteria to form unlike many cosmetics. A bridal makeover service is available at Compton Villas (also a popular wedding venue) in Dorset. Other companies you may want to look for are So Organic, Fresh Face Cosmetics, Beauty Naturals and for the more high-end brand, Dr Hauschka (which won 'Best Organic Range' in the 2007 Natural Health beauty awards).

For the Men

Surprisingly, men use approximately seven grooming and styling products a day, cashing up a staggering annual £519 million for the industry. Simon Duffy, one of the Bulldog co-founders mentions that 'We need to turn our attention now to what we put on our bodies, as ingredients in grooming products can be absorbed through the skin.' Blokes – you can ditch the Brylcreem and go natural. Bulldog is a male grooming range produced in the UK available exclusively in over 320 Sainsbury's stores, making it far more accessible than a lot of other brands (that is if you don't like internet shopping). Animal friendly and steering clear of manmade chemicals, Bulldog products are packed with essential oils and a host of natural ingredients.

Trevarno's male range of products is also great for grooms to get their skin in shape for the big day (the selection includes facial moisturiser, aftershave oil and bath and body oil). Made on a beautiful country estate in Cornwall where peacocks roam, Trevarno works hard in sourcing the highest quality, socially just and ecologically responsible suppliers of ingredients for their skincare range. Just a few examples of these practices includes buying locally grown Westcountry herbs and obtaining sustainable palm oil from a producer

who works closely with the Worldwide Fund for Nature. Trevarno are also the first beauty company to meet The Organic Farmers and Growers strict standards to gain organic certification.

If you want to have some choice then Male Organics is one company entirely dedicated to offering the full male health and beauty service – and that includes the natural toothbrush!. With an environmental policy through to carbon offsetting the deliveries and using 100 per cent recyclable packaging, they are ethical at their core, offering over fifteen well respected brands.

For the Honeymoon

It's perfectly natural that you will have some pillow play after the first dance and if you don't want a brood quite yet then you can get fairly traded condoms from The French Letter Company.

Beware of chemicals Polyethylene Glycol (also known as PEG) and Propylene Glycol which are known carcinogens within penetration enhancers. Both these chemicals are ingredients in less than sexy products such as oven cleaners and antifreeze, so it may be worth avoiding it. Instead, try Yes! products for some truly organic lubrication. For something more risqué then try the Forestry Stewardship Council (FSC) certified spanking paddles (from Sam Roddick's shop Coco de Mer). Eco Boudoir has a wide range of ethically exciting products for further honeymoon escapades. ■

Make sure you take time out during the wedding preparations © Arsat

The **Catering**

Food glorious food! A full day of festivities and your guests will be hungering for a delicious range of green grub at the wedding feast. If you keep it local, let it be slow, give it some love, nutrition and careful consideration then your guests will be in cuisine paradise.

Seasonal Fayre

Eating in season is the obvious green effort for your catering. Every food whether it is fruit, vegetables or meat has a life cycle, when it is plentiful and matured for the palate. When you eat out of season you're likely to end up eating food that has been either frozen (not such a big issue but you don't always end up with the freshest of flavours) or created using technology to grow at times when it wouldn't normally in nature. Chemically enhanced, air conditioned and artificially lit are not the most appealing descriptions for grub going into your belly. The other blunder is that non seasonal food is often shipped in from overseas, adding to climate change craziness.

Eat the Seasons, a website declaring which food is in season locally in Britain suggests the benefits of seasonal food as 'reducing energy needed to grow and transport the food we eat, avoiding paying a premium for food that is scarcer or has travelled a long way, supporting the local economy and reconnecting with nature's cycles and the passing of time.' Sounds tempting, doesn't it?

If you've ever had an organic vegetable box delivery you'll see how much more authentic your carrots and spuds look when they're splattered with a bit of earth having been freshly dug up. And you will notice the distinct taste of vegetables not robbed of their worth by being bundled in plastic. Eating seasonally is also often more financially beneficial – as it's just the farmer in the nearest field who is being paid, rather than all the middle men and profit margins that supermarkets thrive on for business. Instead you can support local producers in building a more sustainable food industry locally, endorsing local biodiversity and supporting the local economy.

When choosing your venue consider the catering options it provides or is willing to supply carefully. One example of good practice is The National Trust. Where their properties provide a wedding

Simple decoration can be just as luxurious – remember that it's about quality not quantity © Mrorangeoo

catering service, they employ their food policy of looking first to each property for produce, and then to the county and then the region before finally from around the UK. With over fifty working kitchen gardens across England, Wales and Northern Ireland providing local and seasonal produce to The National Trust restaurants, wedding clients are able to work with a designated Catering Manager or liaise with external caterers to develop a menu that is truly local and seasonal as well as delicious.

Farmer's markets are the perfect place to buy seasonally in the city – and you will be amazed at the variety on offer, regardless of the time of year. There are over 500 farmer's markets in the UK and the best thing is that they never have too many of the same type of stallholder so you don't have to whimper around looking at yet another bunch of turnips. In fact the seasonal variety is incessant, and can be far more exciting than the brightly lit, predictability of the supermarket, where you depend upon a product aisle switch to prevent monotonous autopilot habits. You may also find that your wedding guests get ingredients they have not tried before, but are enjoyably edible.

If you're not aware of your local food suppliers, then Big Barn is a handy website providing you with the information as it includes a location map and postcode search facility. Big Barn believe that buying local shouldn't be a once-in-a-while thing but for every day. 'We

Seek nutritious foods that will sustain your guests © bgraphic

don't believe in shopping locally just for the sake of an argument against the supermarkets. A lot of what they do, they do very well. We just believe that the best food comes from local sources, where shelf life and cheapness are not the only priorities.' They've got a point. We do need to slow down and enjoy food for not just the nutritional benefit but for the love of it!

Slow Food

Taking on board a simpler eco gastronomic approach is The Slow Food Movement, in a 'convivium' (local branch) near you. The wise spark behind Slow Food was Carlo Petrini, an Italian journalist who was horrified when he saw a brand new branch of McDonalds opened at the foot of the Spanish Steps in Rome. He realised that fast life was disrupting what we should hold true. A manifesto of slowing down was born, suggesting that sensual pleasure, enjoying food for what it's worth and rediscovering the flavours and savours of regional cooking were a far better way of preserving a culture of enjoyment rather than frenzy. Slow Food doesn't always mean you will keep your wedding guests drooling at the mouth in long anticipation either. It's more about the approach to food cultivation and compensating for the 75 per cent of European food product diversity that has been lost since the 1900s. Other cheerless facts are that 33 per cent of livestock varieties have disappeared or are near disappearing, and that 30,000 vegetable varieties have been lost in the last century, with one more being lost every six hours!

Collectively Slow Food has initiatives designed to identify, preserve and protect threatened food and drink products, rare breeds or species. Small firms, including one man bands that have passed quality and traditional food production down the generations have been closing up their shops due to our ever increasing over-centralisation and industrialised methods. Slow Food challenges this aggressive obliteration by reviving foods such as cheddar cheese handmade in Somerset from unpasteurised milk, Three Counties Perry, and Cornish Sardines and Pilchards which are all appetising wedding feast fayre.

There are over forty branches of the Slow Food Movement in the UK to inspire you with ingredients for a perfectly laidback day.

Organic

Organic food and drink is now worth £2 billion in the UK, but why get your guests to eat organic at your reception? With so much speculation surrounding organic food and drink it's not always easy to understand the benefits it can bring. Yet according to Mintel research, over half of us are buying organic food – so there's definitely something in it.

Naturally Good

Like with the seasonal food movement, organic is generally more focused on small family-run farmers, promoting the local economy and using less energy by supplying people in the vicinity. These methods are also better for the sustainability of land, aiding soil quality (preferable to soil erosion in intensive farming) and water retention. When supplying the demands of today we forget that the monocultural landscapes in conventional farming could affect production for the future. Whilst critics say you can't harvest as much food with organic foods compared to conventional food production, the organic movement believe you can, arguing its long term sustainability. The Soil Association report 'Organic works' demonstrates that organic farming is helping to reverse the decline in the UK's agricultural workforce, which has fallen by 80 per cent in the last 50 years. Changes to farm practises have replaced skilled labour with agrochemicals and larger machinery, and have been coupled with the increased size and simplification of farms.

You get a greater sense of connection of where your food is from if you are buying directly from an organic farmer as they are three times as likely to market their products locally or directly as non organic farmers in the UK.

Clio Turton of the Soil Association expands. 'On average UK organic farming uses 26 per cent less energy per tonne of food produced. This is mainly due to the non use of fertilisers, which are the largest source of carbon dioxide emissions in agriculture and the single largest source of nitrous oxide emissions in the world.'

Tougher standards by the Soil Association are being introduced for the small number of air-freighted organic fruit and veg that ensure there is a market for organic farmers in developing countries and alternatives for transportation from overseas are being sought to combat carbon issues. They are even looking at introducing a carbon labelling method for existing certified products.

Potential Toxins

Like with organic beauty products, food is free from pesticides, potentially preventing health problems from cocktail effects. A 1993 study into pesticides exposure amongst children suggested that diet was a main cause, and you can assume that exposure through diet is the same for adults. There are legal limits set for pesticide use in conventional farming, however no one really knows if these limits have been established at the right level so they could still affect the health of producers. Pesticides also have high levels of toxicity to aquatic life, flora and fauna. Around 31,000 tonnes of chemicals are used in farming in the UK each year to kill weeds, insects and other pests that attack crops. Organic farming standards accept only a minimal amount of pesticides that are of natural origin (plant derived) or simple chemical products that leave no residue on food, although most organic arable farming have no need for them at all. Studies have shown there are more birds, butterflies, beetles, bats and wildflowers on organic farms.

Use berries to add natural colour to your table decor © Lwzfoto

Nutritional Gain

Sadly even to this day green fingered enthusiasts are arguing across the allotment fences as to whether organic food is more beneficial in providing the essential stuff for our bodies. And sadly, not enough research has been done on the subject, mainly due to the fact that it's only the large multinationals who can afford to fund research of this scale. However, early results from a European Union funded study that began in 2004 called 'Quality Low Impact Food' suggest that organic food contains 40 per cent more antioxidants than non organic. A review of other studies suggested that organic crops had higher levels of vitamin C, magnesium and phosphorus, chromium, iron and calcium. A 2001 taste test study from Washington State University noted that organic apples were firmer and tasted sweeter. Omega 3 levels in organic milk have also been proven higher in other recent investigations. As Turton says, 'With organic food you get higher dry matter content – meaning you get more carrot for your carrot!'

One thing you won't get in Soil Association certified grub is food additives that are usually put in to change the look or taste of food, or to preserve it. These include artificial sweeteners such as aspartame or monosodium glutamate, (an additive banned for children specific foods but seemingly acceptable to be added for us adults). There are 313 additives in the UK, which are government regulated and accepted for consumption after testing. Yet additives have been under fire for links between health problems such as asthma, hyperactivity, toxicity to nerve cells and even cancer.

The True Cost

Most studies suggest that organic food is more expensive – however this is not always the case if you are buying directly from local farms. Another reason for a seemingly inflated price is because of government subsidies that lower the price of intensively farmed foods below what they cost to produce. Then there are costs which aren't considered when comparing conventional with organic, such as tackling water pollution caused by artificial fertilisers which is taken off your pay check in tax or through paying for your water amenities.

Carnivore Care

Another area that comes under the green dilemma wing is meat. As a nation which supports animal charities more than people based charities, it is sometimes surprising we don't always connect our love of animals to the ethical issues in eating them. The first consideration, as the Department for Environment, Food and Rural Affairs mentions on its website, is that 'Maintaining high standards for animal health and welfare on the farm is essential for efficient production, establishing consumer confidence and managing risk of disease to both humans and animals.' The guidelines follow welfare in all areas of meat production: from on the farm to transporting to markets and finally, to slaughter. There are welfare codes covering stockmanship, health, feeding, accommodation and management, as well as specific requirements for breeding for each type of animal. So whether it is pigs or chickens, farmers have to adhere to the codes and are checked up on by inspectors. Farming news today is plagued by animal diseases such as MRSA, bovine spongiform encephalopathy (BSE), foot and mouth disease and bovine tuberculosis (bTB), and intensive livestock farming is often the culprit of these growing scares.

A report produced by the Soil Association indicates that 70 per cent of the 29 million eggs laying hens in Britain are battery farmed, plucking and pecking at one another in their own faeces, crammed so much so that they have difficulty standing. Then there are the pigs that never go outdoors (70-75 per cent, in fact) or the dairy cows that are culled early because they are all milked out.

As the RSPB indicates, there is an intrinsic link between livestock and the management of biodiversity on farmland, for example, 'Extensive beef production – suckler cows on low input grassland – that is crucial to the maintenance of many hill and upland habitats'. Dairy farming is notably the worst for environmental damage causing 'water pollution, ammonia emissions and declining bird populations'. The RSPB set up Freedom Foods in 1994 specifically looking at animal welfare. This is also another guarantee, independently verified by researchers that animals are loved a little more before they are prepared for the plate.

In general, farming livestock organically prevents these unpleasant images by allowing the animals to live outdoors. Farmers are also 'encouraged to choose breeds which are well adapted to local conditions and capable of resisting disease.' Joyce d'Silva of respected animal welfare group Compassion in World Farming acknowledges this. 'Organic farming has the potential to offer the very highest standards of animal welfare. We believe the Soil Association's welfare standards are leaders in the field.'

Organic livestock requires organic feed which is currently in short supply in the UK – and with more cereals being set aside for biofuel production it is going to be interesting how this market adapts.

Without preaching organic from the rooftops, even if you decide not to eat organic, then do consider a UK meat supplier, who have more stringent animal welfare standards and are put under more thorough contamination examination than imported meat. And don't be afraid to grill your local butcher about where your meat came from before you stick it under the noses of your loved ones.

Fishy Feasts

The seafood industry is a global market and a valued commodity, with a trading value greater than tea, coffee and sugar commodities combined. If you fancy serving up some fish then ensure you buy it from a responsible source that is dedicated to sustainability. 52 per cent of fish stocks are fully exploited, which means that they are being fished at their maximum biological capacity, with 24 per cent of stocks being overexploited, depleted or recovering from depletion. That means there may not be fish for future generations, affecting the ocean's eco systems. It has potential to damage the income of the 200 million people working globally in the fishing industry too. The Marine Stewardship Council (MSC) was first established by Unilever (the world's largest buyer of seafood), and WWF in 1997 to reverse the decline in the world's fisheries. MSC now operates independently and not for profit and they have developed an environmental standard for sustainable and well-managed fisheries. If you are concerned about overfishing and its environmental and social consequences, you can choose seafood products that have the MSC Standard label on them. James Simpson from the Marine Stewardship Council mentions, 'If you want to know where your fish comes from then you'd need a lot of time to read through the reports and a few marine biology degrees! With MSC, all the hard science is done for you; it is peer reviewed and open to consultation.' This standard applies the principles of annually auditing the condition of fish stocks, the impact of the fishery on the marine environment (regardless of whether it is large or small scale) as well as ensuring management systems minimise environmental impact.

You can get a wide variety (with over 1,000 products certified worldwide and over 200 in the UK) from salmon, hake, herring, pollock, to cod and albacore tuna. The major supermarkets have signed up to the scheme, as well as Young's Seafood and British Seafood. Simpson explains further. 'When you're eating wild caught fish, the local food rule of thumb doesn't apply. It is much more important to have sustainably caught fish than to eat local fish – which normally have no assurance of sustainability – unless you are lucky enough to live near

Verity Hunt-Sheppard who works for The Vegan Society had her green, vegan wedding in 2007

Our wedding was very much a traditional one: a church service followed by a reception. At the time of our engagement my husband and I had been vegan for just under a year. We ummed and ahhed over how vegan our wedding should be and whether we should provide mixed catering or not. In the end we decided to stick to our beliefs, confident that those who loved us and valued our friendship would understand and probably expect nothing less! It was the best decision we made. Initially we wanted a local caterer, but the ones we contacted weren't confident in providing vegan food or were outside our budget so we contacted vegan caterers 'Veggies' who are based in Nottingham. We had both eaten Veggies food before as they cater for many of the vegan fairs and festival and are famous for their burgers! As ours was an afternoon wedding we decided on an afternoon buffet, comprising of samosas, baajis, savoury rolls, pasties, sandwiches, various salads and a selection of cakes. Veggies price's were excellent and well within budget.

Our three tier wedding cake was homemade and decorated by my mother and we just adapted a traditional fruit cake recipe and hired a professional cake stand to display it on. Once the food was fully vegan, 'veganising' the rest of the wedding was easy. Some main brand beers such as Budweiser and Grolsch are vegan so our vegan guests didn't miss out at the bar, and the bar where we had an evening disco provided a list of their wines and details of the suppliers in advance so we could check for vegan ones before the big day.

I avoided silk in the clothing of the flower girls and page boy. My dress was a beautiful secondhand non silk garment from a theatre department, which I wore with my mother's original wedding veil.

My wedding day was – hand on heart – the best day of my life. I still cannot believe how well everything went and what a wonderful time we had. Our decision to have vegan catering was not only respected but praised by our impressed guests. Many couldn't believe that vegan food could be so delicious and I know some of our friends are now eating more vegan food as a result. One guest told me that she had never felt so satisfied at a buffet.

The response to our vegan wedding was definitely positive and I don't believe it was much more difficult to arrange than any other wedding. And thanks to various family members donating their skills from floristry to professional make up, our wedding and honeymoon cost just £3,000 in total. ■

an MSC certified fishery. However you can get certified mackerel from Cornwall and North Sea herring in supermarkets such as Waitrose and Sainsbury's.' Simpson adds that they are just beginning to get the few British, independently run fishmongers left on board, but that it is a slow process. 'Going through the chain of custody traceability certification isn't the cheapest thing but there are ways of keeping costs down by grouping together with other businesses. Several people have reported better prices for MSC certified fish, which is good for the industry and for sustainability. Having said that, you could serve MSC certified fish fingers at a buffet for less than 20 pence per pack. I would recommend asking the fish counter at your local supermarket for MSC wild Alaskan salmon – their vivid pink colour is completely natural due to their diets in the wild, containing less white strips of fat in them than farmed salmon. Most supermarkets also stock smoked wild Alaskan salmon as well – it's fantastic. If you ask in advance then they may even provide you with a whole fish and cut it up for you.'

The Soil Association have organically certified farmed salmon, and are adopting responsible fish farming under their scheme.

Vegetarian and Vegan Ventures

If you aren't keen on the idea of serving a breast of broiler chicken or some piteous pork at your wedding and want to keep it simple by cutting out the meat and fish ethical dilemmas then you could make your reception dinner completely vegetarian. You may find that a number of guests are vegetarian, which reduces the fuss of having to make two separate dishes. Catering for solely vegetarian dishes can also bring the costs down substantially. There is still a mainstream view that vegetarianism causes nutritional deficiency, a myth that needs to be brought to a halt as vegetarians are often proven to have a healthier diet! Most foods contain a mixture of nutrients, yet meat is known for being high in protein. This can be substituted for other high protein foodstuffs such as nuts, seeds, pulses, grains and cereals, soya products, dairy products and free range eggs. There is also a skill to mixing proteins to ensure you get essential 'amino acids' – this happens quite naturally when we cook, such as making macaroni cheese or quiche (a great post-nuptial buffet dish). Vegetarians often have a good diet because they aren't so dependent on processed foods, and tend to cook more with fresh veg. And you don't have to worry that all your guests are going to get on their plate are chickpeas and tofu – the variety and flavours to be had with vegetarian food is endless.

Far from being a food fad, veganism is increasing as an eco chic and considerate lifestyle, yet it is a term often confused with being a vegetarian. Vegans, unlike vegetarians, choose not to eat any foods derived from living or dead animals, which includes meat (from red meat to white meat and fish), animal milks (cows, sheep and goats dairy products), eggs, honey, and any other animal products such as gelatine, cochineal and shellac. If you have vegan guests attending your wedding, then make sure you don't cook in butter, using instead soya butter or oils and try to serve dairy options (such as cream or cheese) separately to keep everyone happy. For more information on vegan cookery, including recipe ideas, then visit the Vegan Society website.

Fair Trade

Seasonal delightful desserts with wedding catering at Bedruthan Steps Hotel © Bedruthan

Just like your wedding attire, look out for the FAIRTRADE Mark when it comes to sourcing your ingredients or making your green requests from your caterer. Whether it is honey, bananas, or tidbits such as sweeties, shortbread or dried fruits for decoration, you can do your bit to support producers in developing countries. Globally, consumers worldwide spent £1.1bn on Fairtrade certified products in 2006. This income directly benefits over seven million people including farmers, workers and their families. It's not just about the money either but the community development of health care, education and local amenities that you can support with your purchasing choices. With large companies getting involved (such as Tate & Lyle whose sugar will be completely Fairtrade certified in 2009), there is a great opportunity for you to have some ecolicious fair trade fayre on the tables.

Caterers

An increasing number of caterers are able to supply local, organic and seasonal food but be aware of those hitching the prices up for a bit of additional profit as it really doesn't have to be more expensive.

Nutritional and catering consultancy Food for Life's Tony Bishop-Weston, whose company offers 'Health MOT' gift vouchers with TV Nutritionist Yvonne Bishop-Weston in Harley Street, suggests you consider the nutritional benefits of the food that you serve at your wedding reception. 'It's a cliché that people drink too much at weddings but all too often a sad reality too. By insuring there are

Favourite Caterers...
From the North and South of England

North

York based El Piano whose wedding menus are as organic as possible and changed to suit the seasons suggest you prepare for hungry guests. 'People often travel long distances for weddings, arrive peckish and end up cranky. After travelling, the ceremony and then receptions that last for more than four hours are a long time to only have one meal, so it's worth considering a second set of simple eats.' They also encourage all wedding groups to spend their money on the food and not on staff or service. 'Paying catering staff makes catering wildly expensive and is poor value for money. For a 'home style' or 'community style' wedding, food presentation and clear up is something that can be provided by supporters to the wedding party.' Not only are their buffet style menus completely vegan and gluten free, with prices at roughly £10 per head; they also provide reusable or 100 per cent biodegradable disposable table and service ware. Another Yorkshire company is Org who can cater for up to 150 people with local and organic food, including meat options, as well as organic and Fairtrade wines and beers, starting from £8 per head.

South

If you'd like to keep things simple, with a London Summer picnic in the park wedding reception then 'fresh!' can supply organic sandwiches, wraps and salads, with platters of crudités, falafels, houmous, dips and fruit kebabs. Their minimum order is £100 but they can cater for up to a thousand people, costing approximately £7.95-£10.95 per head. Organic Express Caterers in London were the first catering company to be accredited with the Soil Association, and are carbon neutral through supporting a renewable energy project in Eritrea. They also recycle all glass packaging and use an electric vehicle to move goods. Nomad Food and Design, also in London, offers organic, local and Fairtrade fusion and modern cuisine. Ethical catering company Skye Cooks are based in East London, but can travel anywhere. Their wedding services can vary from cold buffets for £20 per head to luscious barbecues and three course meals for a higher budget for up to 500 people.

adequate and interesting supplies of protein rich foods you can provide a modicum of protection to people's bodies. There is a wide selection of protein rich foods available even for super green vegans. Try to avoid the temptation to load people up with simple starchy white carbohydrates such as white French style garlic bread. The potential for driving people's blood sugar up only to come crashing down and risk getting fractious and argumentative may be avoided by using wholegrain, wholemeal versions served with adequate protein. For example choose buckwheat pasta and include tofu and pine nuts in the dish. Choose desserts carefully and try to use agave syrup rather than sugar or honey. Dark chocolate with dates and ground almonds and hazelnuts make great nutritious truffles – roll them in shelled hempseeds for even more nutrients.'

Put your caterers in touch with your local organic box scheme or farm and see if you or your wedding planner can come to some green and nutritious arrangement. Or why not go with a green caterer from the offset? There are many across the country that offer a whole service, even organic cocktails, without you having to slave over a stove.

Cakes

Let's get onto the crumbly stuff. Cake is always a tantalising taste-bud of conversation at the reception, and it is on record in the photo albums for years to come as the two of you cut it together. Do you make the wedding cake yourself, ask a talented friend, or order it in? If you want an extravagant six tiered wedding cake then it will make more sense to hire the job out to a local patisserie, or else you'll be all caked out by the time the day arrives.

The popularity of the traditional wedding cake with its sugar icing, marzipan and fruit concoction is declining. Some couples instead prefer to offer an alternative such as sponge cake for their fussy guests or just go the whole hog with a succulent chocolate cake. Like with all the catering, think of guests with allergies or specific diets when planning the perfect celebratory bake. Alison Biddle of Fancy That! Wedding Cakes has noticed a huge surge in demand for organic and eco friendly wedding cakes over the past eighteen months, and as a result has tried to make all of their cakes as environmentally friendly as possible. 'I am yet to speak to a bride who doesn't want an eco friendly cake if it is an option.' She admits that it is tricky getting organic ingredients from the main wholesalers, which is where the prices increase for couples wanting to use solely fair trade and organic ingredients. 'It is easy for us to make 'pro-organic' choices – a cake which utilises organic products and ingredients wherever possible. Typically this would mean using fair trade, organic chocolate and organic cream on our signature chocolate glazed cake, with fresh locally picked fruit, and flowers to decorate. We go as far as keeping our own free range hens on the farm.' They also offer alternatives, such as their cheese wedding cakes, made entirely from organic cheeses, decorated with organic fruit and vegetables, on a reuseable yew board.

Another company that can deliver cakes personally and nationwide is Cakes by Ann, who often have to double the price of cakes to match the cost of sourcing organic cake ingredients. 'I worked for eighteen years as a wedding and celebration cake designer for a company who decided to cater for large supermarkets with orders of 50,000 cakes at a time. These sorts of cakes have to be able to be mass produced so don't give much scope for personalisation. With our cakes no two are ever the same.' Bristol based company, The Organic Chocolate Cake Company offers Soil Association certified wedding cakes that come in up to three tier designs. The tasty cakes can be arranged in American style, with the tiers directly on top of each other, or separated with pillars which allow flowers or material to be placed between them. Cake Couture can provide 100 per cent organic cakes as well – even if it's mouthwatering Belgian chocolate that you are after. Their specialities include lemon cake and orange and poppy seed. Cakes can cost up to a £1,000, depending on the number of portions you require – although typically you can expect to buy one for £300. To keep your wedding to budget, you can always buy a cake readymade, from companies such as Daylesford Organics, or pile up tasty organic bakery tidbits from The Village Bakery.

Gorgeous art in the form of an organic chocolate cake © The Organic Chocolate Cake Company

Drinks

It's best not to leave your guests thirsty! If you are serving water (which is advisable if lots of alcohol is being slurped), then try to avoid unnecessary plastic or glass bottled options. Studies have shown that tap water is just as healthy for you, often tastes better and minimises waste from packaging as well as energy from production and transportation.

You may want to offer some juicy jubilation from organic, local companies, perfect to keep the kids content whilst you toast with the bubbly stuff. You can get absolutely delicious juices ranging from orchard fruits from companies such as James White, Lumscombe Organics and Chegworth Valley, to delicious organic cordials from Rocks Organics. If you want to supply fair trade juice, then look no further than Fruit Passion who supplies orange and tropical juices in one litre packs as well as in mini cartons. The Natural Beverage Company can also keep your guests feeling fruity with their refreshing Fairtrade certified smoothies, perfect to serve at breakfast the next day for those aching heads.

Celebrate with some organic fizz © Organic-champagnes.com

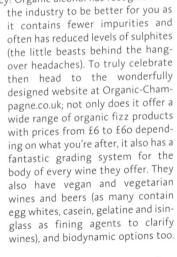

For the grownups then the green vino market is massive, all you've got to decide is what you fancy! Organic alcohol has recognition in the industry to be better for you as it contains fewer impurities and often has reduced levels of sulphites (the little beasts behind the hangover headaches). To truly celebrate then head to the wonderfully designed website at Organic-Champagne.co.uk; not only does it offer a wide range of organic fizz products with prices from £6 to £60 depending on what you're after, it also has a fantastic grading system for the body of every wine they offer. They also have vegan and vegetarian wines and beers (as many contain egg whites, casein, gelatine and isinglass as fining agents to clarify wines), and biodynamic options too.

If you are after organic wines then there is an array of companies specialising in the UK.

What about wines from the finest vineyards in countries such as South Africa and South America? The Fairtrade wine industry is now worth £8.2 million in the UK – with so many shops offering it. You can nip into your local Thresher's or Wine Rack and buy cases of Origin's Fairtrade wine from South Africa or Argentina, or go to the Traidcraft website. Supermarkets offer their Fairtrade brands too, such as M&S, Waitrose, Sainsbury's and The Co-op who also offer their Fairtrade range in wine boxes. The choice is endless – just look out for the FAIRTRADE Mark.

Bottom's up! The organic beer bonanza is all over the country. You can get the stuff from Black Isle Brewery in the heart of the Scottish Highlands to the vegan brewery of Marble Beers in Manchester, before working your way to the Atlantic Brewery in Newquay. Now there's a thought for a fizz-fested honeymoon!

If you're more of a cider-drinking duo, then you can pick from the Ciderstore, which has a wide variety from various organic cider suppliers, Weston's Cider, and The Cyder House, who were founder members of the Soil Association.

For treasured tipples, The Organic Spirits Company offer Juniper Green Organic Gin, Organic Vodka, Highland Harvest Organic Scotch Whisky, Papagayo Organic Spiced Rum, Papagayo Organic White Rum and Utkins Fairtrade White Rum. The Sussex Wine Company offer organic cognac and Armagnac.

Getting The Right Balance

Different guests will eat and drink different quantities, so keeping it regular and in small quantities rather than one big meal and drink fest at the end of the reception is the answer to keeping everybody happy. One way of doing this is the traditional French wedding way by having a conscious break in between each course to allow conversation to flow and for guests to partake in snippets of entertainment, whether it is the speeches, music or a dance-off – just allow the stomach to settle properly for the latter! ■

The Dreamy **Details**

The magical touch. These thoughtful considerations are literally the icing on the cake for all your wedding guests. It's likely that you will want your wedding ceremony and reception to glow. You can also give it that green hue by finding suppliers who care as much about their ethics as their earnings.

The number of small businesses set up with ecological thinking at their core is escalating, and whilst many don't necessarily market themselves within the wedding industry, you can enjoy seeking out some unique items.

Stationery

So what do you do to minimise the impact when you're inviting your guests? There is the option of using an online service, however this can have its own green queries – what about the servers that are online all day and night to power the website? Do they offer green hosting (i.e. solar powered through companies like Athenaeum)? These little factors are challenges that can impress your dutifully green friends. One couple who had a wedding received quibbles from older relatives who felt that the RSVP of an email address was inappropriate for those without internet access, so it may make more sense to go down the traditional snail mail route for some guests.

If you do decide to send out paper invites, then one option is to make your own. It will certainly cut costs – and you can use recycled paper and unused materials that you have got kicking around the house. Or you could use one of the many companies out there that offer ready made wedding invitations and RSVP cards. Dee Grismond of Cherrygorgeous says that, 'Wedding stationery really helps set the scene for your wedding, showing your guests straight away what type of wedding you are having. It's a great way to show your eco friendly values right from the start'. Grismond's service includes a carbon zero delivery.

One fantastically named company, Ellie Poo Paper, provide – you guessed it – paper made from dung. They can offer a bespoke service where you can choose everything from the colour of the rose petals moulded into the paper to the ribbons for scrolling. If that's

Wedding favours can come in all shapes and sizes © Surpasspro

not enough then they have the rather innovative option of hand-made 'plantable/growable' paper that is mixed with wildflower seeds from the UK, which should give your guests a little bit of Summer meadow if you plant it.

You could do what some extreme pairs have done with company Creative Paper Wales and help collect droppings to create sheep poo paper. That's not all, this company once made paper from the pairs of jeans a couple were wearing when they met – apparently it was very durable paper indeed. Now where did those Levis go...?

Another company is SEED who offer hand screen printed stationery on recycled paper and card. They also produce handbound and printed photo albums, to match the invite design. Each one is very beautiful, recycled and individual, far better than the usual leather albums flown from Australia!

Vinati's Paper, an accredited wedding stationer for both the Four Seasons Hotel and the Commonwealth Club in London offers bespoke hand blockprinted, handmade and recycled paper. It is manufactured by individuals being paid a fair wage in Indian villages using old cotton rags or waste paper. All the workers involved have their children's school education paid for by the business, and there is a strong emphasis on developing the worker's skills. Inspired by Indian, Persian and Oriental motifs, some papers are made from regenerating plant bark. Other natural fibres like jute, straw, banana, husk, silk, wool and herbs are then blended with the primary fibres for a decorative effect.

Flowers

If the average person in the UK spends £28 on flowers each year, then you can imagine what the costs are like are for weddings. You've got the floral bouquet, the headdress, the bridesmaid's posies, the corsages and button holes, the flowers for the church, the reception and on top of the cake to consider!

Britain has a £2.2 billion market for flowers, with a lot of debate over where we source our flowers. With the industry being a global affair you've got environmentalists versus the people-ists. Whilst deciding what to do about the flowers you want for your day it's best not to get too much of a complex over the green decisions you make.

There are some individuals showing off their green flower power. Caroline Ede who grows and arranges flowers for weddings across the UK describes flowers as a very creative industry. 'As a fine artist who paints and prints, I find making up the composition and choosing the colours of the flowers very similar to painting a picture. I try and live my whole life as ethically as possible: non consuming, recycling and loving the planet. I think weddings are greener if the flowers are UK sourced. This means they can be more expensive than factory farmed ones from abroad. Very green low cost weddings can be achieved using lots of greenery and flowers in season.'

Seasonal

If you want to buy local, then specifically ask the florist you choose to plan your flowers by season. There are many flowers still grown in the UK, particularly in the Channel Islands, where freesias, irises and roses are grown. In Cornwall, Lincolnshire and Scotland bulb flowers such as daffodils tend to grow successfully. In Summer you can expect to see UK grown chrysanthemums, delphiniums and pinks.

Carole Stewart for the Growers of Scented Narcissi on the Isles of Scilly is aware of an increase in demand for local flowers, with their flowers blooming in the Winter months from October through to

March. 'We knew that people wanted to buy our British grown narcissi but we had no means of reaching them. Our flowers were inclined to be hidden under the more exotic imported blooms on flower stalls, in florist shops and at the supermarkets – or mixed into bouquets of imported flowers. So we decided to take matters into our own hands and set up a website and a direct delivery service.'

Once ordered they are hand picked from where they are grown in the open air. After being sent by ship 28 miles across the sea they then get couriered to the customers. 'Of course there are some flower miles, but very few compared to most imported flowers.'

© mrorange00

It's not just the environmental aspects of flower growers in the UK, but also the livelihood. 'We are a very important part of the social framework of the islands. Many of those who help us out with harvesting and packing in the Winter months work in the tourism industry in the Summer months. This little cottage industry helps to maintain the way of life of the islands as well as its landscape. The Isles of Scilly are shaped in many ways by the tiny fields the flowers are grown in, dotted around all five of the inhabited islands in this beautiful archipelago. Most of our growers are members of the Countryside Stewardship Scheme. Amongst many other things this helps to preserve the flora and fauna in the hedgerows surrounding the little flower fields.'

For Autumn weddings why not add seasonal fruits, such as apples, corn and berries and hops, and for Winter affairs why not add some holly and ivy into the equation? If you want to search for flowers by month, then visit the Flowers & Plants Association website.

Consult a local florist for guidance on availability and give them ample time to source flowers for you. By visiting local shops you can see their flower arrangements and what is on offer. At certain busy times of year you may need to give the florist four month's notice, and you should give them at least a month to match the colour scheme of outfits.

Lincolnshire based company, Catkin Flowers began when founder Rachel Petheram got married in 2002 and wanted country flowers such as sweet peas, herbs, marigolds and cornflowers but couldn't find a supplier so instead grew her own. 'There's something romantic and whimsical about flowers in jam jars on the table.' After friends asked her to do their weddings too, Rachel and her garden designer husband rented a walled garden in a former National Trust property's kitchen garden. As weddings are usually planned a year in advance, she is able to sow the seeds and tailor posies individually and to any budget – 'even a fiver if that's all that someone has.' Petheram is aware of the myth that green and organic is still a bit hippyish. 'It can be gorgeous and girly and ridiculous if you want it to be, and far more imaginative than carnations.' She thinks it is easy to grow your own flowers, as long as you continue cutting them to encourage them to produce more flowers, and sowing them successionally in sets over a period so that you get the timing spot on.

> **Often carbon emissions are higher in the energy guzzling greenhouses of Holland than in imported flowers from Kenya – so just because it's this side of Europe doesn't always mean it is more ecological**

It's also worth looking at the organically grown option as flowers are known to contain chemical nasties within their fertilisers and foreign-sounding names that aren't particularly sweet, such as insecticides, nematocides, fungicides and plant growth regulators.

Jane Lindsey of Snapdragon Flowers, who set up her company growing organic flowers because she thought it was ridiculous she couldn't buy Scottish grown flowers, thinks the ideal solution is to use a network of

Seasonal and local blooms from the Isle of Scilly. You can get these particular petals from October to March
© Scented Narcissi

local growers. She won't deliver outside of Central Scotland for that reason. She grows a wide range of flowers and has a couple of local gardens growing greenery such as dogwood and holly. 'As flower blooming times are unpredictable to some degree we often leave the precise choice of flowers until a couple of weeks before the wedding. I do not buy in flowers apart from when a bride wants roses which is when I source British grown roses.'

Sue Harper who runs Sweet Loving Flowers in Dyfi Valley, Wales started her business because she really loved people's expressions of delight. Rather than allowing pesticides to harm the earth, she has restored what once was a sheep field to one full of wildlife with many bees and birds. She says that as an organic flower business she would be happy to take her flowers up to four or five hours away

Half oranges with cloves hollowed out give colour, light and fragrance
© Niki Clark

(this includes London, Birmingham, Liverpool and Cardiff), understanding that although it would be ideal to keep the miles down, there are still few organic flower growers in the UK. 'At least they're not air miles so it would be up to the customer to decide how they feel about the distance'.

Heather Gorringe of Wiggly Wigglers, who has sourced flowers from her own fields and hedgerows for nearly twenty years, agrees. 'When we are so able to grow gorgeous flowers in the UK with less environmental impact it seems a shame that we have managed to wreck much of the UK flower business for the sake of cheap imports. From a cost perspective our bouquets are pretty competitive with other florists but probably not if you go and get flowers from Tesco.'

Fair Trade

We could all get on our soapbox and scream 'buy local' but the fact is that when it comes to flowers, 85 per cent of them still come from abroad – and a shift in attitude will take time. So do we shrug our shoulders, twiddle our thumbs and wait?

Flowers certified with the FAIRTRADE Mark have fast become popular with mainstream shops. They are also rather convenient with M&S, John Lewis, Sainsbury's and Tesco all offering fair trade alternatives. This is an obvious choice for expediency. Waitrose have seen a 40 per cent increase in their fair trade sales since last year and their flower buyer Louise Motala is happy. 'Our customers are demonstrating a real desire to help growers and their communities in the developing world. These flowers don't just look good, they do good too.' One in four of Waitrose's bunches are now Fairtrade certified.

Nearly 95 per cent of Kenya's cut flower production is exported, 15 per cent of which already comes into the UK. Whilst there is controversy in importing flowers into the UK, there are a couple of arguments for it. Often carbon emissions are higher in the energy guzzling greenhouses of Holland than in imported flowers from Kenya – so just because it's this side of Europe doesn't always mean it is more ecological. Rather than putting on additional flights for the industry, importers try to use returning cargo planes that usually supply food and aid to Africa.

By buying fair trade flowers you are providing employment opportunities to people who may not otherwise acquire work. You are empowering individuals to stand up and challenge this global industry, allowing them the opportunity to join trade unions and aid community development. The sad fact is that the majority of the flower industry doesn't care about its ecological impact – whether their decision to use pesticides is putting worker's health at risk or making their employees work exploitative hours. Whilst there is controversy that the companies behind the fair trade flowers which we buy from our supermarket are by no means small, at least they are trying to push the existing standards up and address the issues – every petal helps.

If you are hesitant about buying from the supermarket then why not try Moyses Stevens, Imogen Stone or Arena Flowers as alternatives for your blooming buds.

Katie Fewings of ethicalweddings.com provides some history. 'The UK went into developing countries and started using the large flower farms, trading down the prices and exploiting the people working there. Whilst the temptation is to go green by buying local flowers, at least by purchasing fair trade flowers we're sorting out the mess already made'.

If you aren't going to buy local, seasonal flowers then it's worth buying fair trade flowers rather than cheap cut flowers with no clear ethical principles attached. And eventually the industry will come up smelling like roses – just the way they should.

Avoiding The Thorns
You don't necessarily have to have fresh flowers for your day. Some

Angie Gough of Share the Feeling's Little Gift range

Share the Feeling was founded after I completed a long stint working at the BBC on the Special Olympics. I really missed the day to day interaction I had with people with learning disabilities and I wanted to show that you can run a successful, profitable business employing people, and that their talent and skills would add value to the product. The Chain Gang was formed and they are the most loyal, fun, talented group of employees I could've hoped for.

We try to be as green as possible, using vegetable inks and sustainably produced papers and cards and recycling paper in creative ways – like making reminder cards and confetti with leftover paper and card.

We've created wedding invitations for over 50 couples. We keep the numbers low, because it's quite an intensive process and we like to get to know the people we're working with. When our couples come back for baby announcement cards, we really know that they were happy first time round.

Sometimes being green means spending a bit more because, for example, materials that are handmade or locally sourced are usually more expensive than imported mass produced products. But doing things yourself is a really good place to start.

We've just sewn little gift bags for a couple who found gorgeous vintage cotton at home – they saved time and money by getting us to do half the job and doing the rest themselves, creating a really personal touch. ■

Share the Feeling's Little Gifts range includes items like stars and symbols, old coins, pieces of string, post office elastic bands and all kinds of stuff that otherwise would be chucked out, as well as sweeties, marbles and feathers sourced locally in Hackney.

couples find dried or silk flowers (checking how violent the silk is first of course) make a realistic option that can be used as a keep-sake – or donated to a local hospice who appreciate cheerful blossoms around.

Confetti and Candles

The ritual of throwing confetti originated in Italy where rice and nuts were thrown at the bride to bestow prosperity and fertility to the couple. The Czechs have their own green tradition and instead throw peas at the newlyweds, which you can even sweep up and stick on the compost heap afterwards!

A lot of the greener venues have banned confetti because of its inability to decay and because it scars their sites. If your venue does accept confetti, then it may be worth providing your guests with something that has an eco touch. One inventive couple spent some time in Autumn out in parks collecting big earthy coloured leaves, storing them in tubs until their Spring wedding. You may also con-sider using onion peel, dried fruit peel or seeds as other ideas. Guests could also blow bubbles made out of a natural, plant based washing up liquid at the couple.

There are several companies who offer manmade colourful yet biodegradable confetti. Charles Hudson offers real delphinium flower petal confetti produced with sunshine and fresh air, stored in hand-made paper cones. Loves Me Loves Me Knot offers freeze dried petal confetti too.

Most candles are petroleum based, which you can see from the black soot they emit, which is known to be a carcinogen. Instead you could use a healthier, natural alternative such as soy wax. London based Timothy Han offers luxurious soy candles flavoured with fruits and herbs such as fig, lavender, sage and lemongrass rather than artifi-cial fragrances, whilst using a metal free, unbleached cotton wick. Similarly, Hapi Bean Soy Candles is a small, highly ethical business based in Hertfordshire offering hand poured candles to suit every need. All their candles are scent free and contain vegan, GM and pes-ticide free soy wax from a long established American soy bean plantation that has no impact whatsoever on rainforests. Each Hapi Bean tealight burns cooler than other waxes which means the can-dles last longer, burning for 4-5 hours and use up every single bit of the wax. The wicks are also made of natural unbleached fibres. So Organic also offers organic plant wax based candles in various natu-ral fragrances which you can light up your new married life with.

You can acquire organic hemp candles, which can fill the room with pure fragrances of coconut, pineapple, orange or mango – these are available from The Hemp Shop. The candle is long burning and comes in a recycled metal tin which can be used again once the candle's flavour has run its course.

Moorlands Candles provide a range of tall vegetable oil and beeswax based candles. Mandala Aroma also offers vegetable wax candles, such as the Love Nurturing & Balancing Aromatherapy Candle that will burn for 40 hours in its glass container. If you want unique and yummy looking bakery cake candles then Scottish

Complement the day with traditional Scottish mini shortbread hearts ©Daylesford Organics

company Aromanca offer Ecosoya wax melts in fragrances such as lemon meringue pie and strawberry cheesecake that promise to lighten the mood amongst your guests!

If you don't want candles, then you could also consider fairy lights. Designer Oliver Heath's range of solar powered colour changing beaded crystal lights give off that romantic glow, with varying speeds too. You can also get simple, amorous white light solar star lights from Earthwhile for a similar price.

The Sunjar is another colourful option from designer Tobias Wong. It looks like a jam jar, but it's jammed full of solar cells, batteries and LEDs that can then power it in the evenings. It's available from Nigel's Eco Store.

LEDS have been used since the 1960s for powering our alarm clocks, but it's only recently that researchers discovered a method for them to produce white light that they have proven popular for an energy efficient alternative illumination, using nearly six times less wattage for light output than an incandescent light bulb. If you want a really stylish large portable lantern, then The Luau from Love Eco is a more expensive option but provides a strong soft white LED light, glowing for up to ten hours.

If you have a Summer wedding you are likely to minimise energy consumption, particularly if it's outdoors.

Wedding Favours

Ahh, the tiny gifts to thank your guests for coming. Too many options and so many decisions to make. Why not plan them around your wedding theme or the season of the year? You could as with the tradition of favours (dare it be said again) make your own, as long as you don't run out of time and resources. Visit your local BAFTS shop to see what they have, or visit wedding websites like Green Union and Ethical Weddings for inspiration. One wedding couple managed to source all their wedding favours at their local farmer's market when they were busy finding their local meats and brew for the feast.

Snapdragon flowers also offer keepsakes such as bespoke embroidered notebooks, scented sachets and mirrors. As well as handmade mulberry paper flowers, Angie Davey at Invitations for Occasions specialises in handmade soaps and candles that can be personalised.

You could give all your guests a cute British tree seedling that they can plant to remind them of your special day with Wedding Tree Favours, who offer holly, scots pine, yew, oak, beech, hornbeam, crab apple, ash, birch, chestnut, willow, alder and field maple.

How about a bit of chocolate character? There are many fair trade and organic companies who can offer something a little sweet. As Montezuma's articulate with their cocoa embellished tongues, 'Chocolate is always a crowd pleaser'.

Organically delectable Montezuma's provide single truffle favours online where you can choose the flavour and ribbon to match the day's colour scheme. Similarly you can have individually wrapped personalised favours from Ubuntu Chocolate (Zulu for 'humanity to others') who offer handmade, high cocoa content chocolate using natural ingredients and flavours such as cardamom, marzipan and lime chilli.

Chocolala offers luxury Fairtrade certified handmade truffles. Their wedding favours come in a trio of flavours with a lala lemon, a light praline and a milk chocolate truffle. You can buy them in packs of seven. If you prefer, they can inscribe initials, hearts or kisses into the chocolates with different foils and have the boxes printed specially for you.

Berry Scrumptious is an Aberdeenshire based company that offers luxury chocolate dipped, organic, seasonal strawberries in little themed boxes for each guest. They also offer strawberry 'fountains' that can have up to six tiers – a less messy and more interesting option to the popular chocolate fountains.

Staffordshire based Daylesford Organics have a delightful, affordable range of chocolate and biscuit items, including mini boxes of covered goji berries or white chocolate covered cranberries that come in lovely little boxes with a heart shape cut out, as well mini shortbread hearts.

For a tipple, Just Miniatures boast organic miniatures such as Paraguay Spiced Rum, Juniper Green Gin, Casal Dos Jordoes Port and Cognac in packs of twelve. Or you could give some baby boxes of Love tea from The Green Apple Store.

For a crafty keepsake, The Heartfelt Project offer hand sewn traditional beaded crafts from women in South Africa.

If you want to use your own wedding favours then you can buy exquisite mini box and mini bag favours from Kolkata Weddings at The Natural Store. Or try Little Cherry and Eco Party Bags 100 per cent biodegradable bags in a range of colours and style. All the online eco stores have tidbits you can dazzle your wedding guests with.

The other option is you don't leave anything for your guests – except a note on each table stating that you have donated some money to charity in lieu of favours. Even with this you can still get very creative like Chris and Claire Gill who had the great idea of producing a jigsaw puzzle with the image of the Oxfam Unwrapped presents they bought for each table, using jigsaw pieces with each guest's name on as place settings!

Photography

According to Weddingchaos.co.uk, only 50 per cent of couples hire a professional photographer for their weddings. However, if you are going down teh professional route. can you be green with your photos too? It appears you can. For example, at the RSA venue in London their 'Say Cheese' man, photographer Liam Bailey has started offering 'Pixie Shoot', a greener alternative to the ever popular disposable cameras used on dining tables. They offer reusable digital cameras that guests can use throughout the dinner which are then collected afterwards so that images can go online immediately.

There is even a Green Photographic website, which strives to 'provide a service that is as respectful to the environment as possible'. All their stationery is printed on recycled paper and all the electricity and fuel used in conjunction with photographic commissions is offset with an annual donation to an offsetting organisation.

Alternatively you could use a service such as MyWeddingStory. All their commercial printing is prepared on FSC managed or recycled stock using vegetable inks for those that want hard copies; however the idea is for wedding guests to upload all the pictures onto a web-site, recording the images electronically. Again they are carbon neutral and only use rechargeable batteries. Unlike a lot of photographers who use the classic style cameras, digital photography ensures there is no use of gelatine in the film base and no chemicals in the developing laboratory. Jonathan who runs the business even has built a gallery out of FSC managed timber using local craftsmen, which is lit with ultra low energy LED lighting. 'Last year three of my weddings were booked entirely by email, so I didn't need to travel at all'.

Many couples find that capturing the day in stills rather than using a videographer is far less obtrusive – and you're likely to have more of the little details banked in your memory, which can be with you forever. Some photographers such as Olivia Brabbs who covers the whole of Yorkshire with her photography prefers to observe rather than direct the day – yet it's completely up to you how much control you want the photographer to have.

Entertainment

Choosing the music and activities at your wedding is a very personal choice – and nobody can dictate this to you. However if you have musical friends, then why not go easy on the pocket and get them involved? Multimillionaire Peter Shalson and his wife Pauline paid £2 million pounds to get Elton John to sing a song at their wedding, which does seem a bit extravagant. Find out what the local talent is like. Do you want something original or someone to sing cover songs? Rather than hire a DJ or an electric band, acoustic is very green with its lack of electricity usage – just ensure to place hard of hearing guests at the front of the venue. Or you could hire classical musicians for another off the grid option.

Table Décor

If you're outside or away from an official venue that offers crockery, then you may need to source an alternative yourself. There are various companies that offer eco friendly options, including degradable, biodegradable and compostable.

Degradable

A product that will naturally break down over time, such as tin that weathers and oxidises.

Biodegradable

A product compiled of natural materials that can be broken down into simple compounds and absorbed back into the eco system without harm if it has moisture, heat, and micro organisms. Biodegradability is certified by The International Standards Organization (ISO) 14855, which requires 60 per cent biodegradation in 180 days.

Silly Jokes offers biodegradable crockery in packs of 100. Made from reed pulp fibre these microwave and heat resistant plates returns to nature in weeks when mixed with soil, water or compost. Party Plastics also boast biodegradable bowls, plates and PLA plastic glasses, which are manufactured from renewable resources (plant based instead of oil). To biodegrade, you must dispose of them with green waste which is sent to a commercial composter. It's best not to stick them in an ordinary litter bin or recycle with ordinary plastic though as they won't degrade any faster.

The personal touch with bespoke hand screen printed invites on recycled card © Seed

Compostable

A product that breaks down speedily when in contact with oxygen and converts to carbon dioxide, water, inorganic compounds and biomass. Compostability is certified by the European Norm EN13432, which requires 90 per cent biodegradation in 90 days.

You can get hold of compostable tableware from the very green credentialled Karma cups, which use an ethical business bank account, renewable energy and use biofuel vehicles from locally collected waste vegetable oil.

Edinburgh based company Vegware has a technologically driven, environmentally sustainable range of cutlery and tableware and a bespoke packaging service. These bioplastics are made from vegetable starches such as potato or corn that are used in place of oil based plastics. Vegware's natural starch cutlery has a natural flex which means that it is less prone to snapping than standard plastic cutlery.

Bamboo, one of the world's fastest growing plants that doesn't need to be replanted, makes good outdoor crockery for its lightweight yet hard wearing properties. Greener Style offer plates and cutlery sets made from 100 per cent organically grown bamboo, and Natural Collection offer mini bamboo bowls, perfect for table decorations and snacks. For something a little more designer (and pricey) then Hen & Hammock sell Tom Dixon's range of bamboo picnic sets including four cups, four bowls and – you guessed it – four plates.

Palm leaf crockery is a 100 per cent natural product from sustainable and renewable resources that can be used again or composted with food waste. Biobags offer a fantastic range of Areca palm leaf products including plates, trays and baskets in several shapes and sizes and their customer service has been applauded. Similarly, Biopac also offer 'quirky' palm leaf presentation crockery.

If you want to hire in some crockery for the day and you are based in Devon or Cornwall, then why not try The Vintage Cook? It's perfect if you're having a vintage themed wedding! They offer fantastic local and sustainable wedding catering, specialising in a vintage china hire service which they take away to wash up with Ecover washing up liquid, enhanced with organic essential oil. They also offer venue styling using eco friendly props such as fairy light covered Cornish Willow frames, Chinese paper lanterns and reuseable fabric bunting. Idyllic Days, based in Surrey offer a similar china hire and venue styling service for up to 300 wedding guests.

Instead of place cards, you could write your guests names on pebbles, leaves and other natural objects. Or you could use Kent 'Inspirational Environmental Business Award' winner Charlie Artingstoll's wedding 'Timber Tags' made from recycled wood sources. He can also produce natural napkin rings and coasters for the occasion.

Bridget Stott of Piece of Cake Party Planners suggests using nasturtiums and violas to decorate salads – not only beautiful as table decorations but edible too. Plant pots full of herbs can add some bucolic charm.

You may want decorations around the seating to add more colour to your day. Rather than throwaway garlands, traditional bunting (the type that reminds you of a village fête) is a greener consideration. Zig Zag bunting use 100 per cent natural cotton. All their offcuts are either sent to the local school for craft projects or composted. They offer padded hearts as another accessory available as wedding favours, which use offcuts from a local business, natural jute ties and reclaimed buttons. ■

Seasonal Flowers...

Spring	Summer	Autumn
Amaryllis	Aster	Chrysanthemum
Apple blossom	Azalea	Dahlia
Azalea	Carnation	Iris
Bluebell	Chrysanthemum	Daisy
Broom	Cornflower	Freesia
Camellia	Daisy	Gladioli
Carnation	Delphinium	Gypsophila
Cherry Blossom	Freesia	Hydrangea
Chrysanthemum	Fuschia	Lily
Clematis	Gardenia	Love-lies-bleeding
Crocus	Gladioli	Micklemas Daisy
Daffodil	Heather	Morning Glory
Daisy	Hollyhock	Orchid
Forsythia	Iris	Rose
Freesia	Jasmine	
Gladioli	Larkspur	**Winter**
Heather	Lilac	Carnation
Honeysuckle	Lily-of-the-valley	Chrysanthemum
Iris	Lupin	Forsythia
Jasmine	Marigold	Freesia
Lilac	Orchid	Gentian
Lily	Peony	Gypsophila
Mimosa	Rhododendron	Holly Berries
Orchid	Rose	Iris
Polyanthus	Stock	Lily
Primrose	Sweatpea	Orchid
Rhododendron	Sweet William	Rose
Stephanotis	Tiger Lily	Snowdrop
Tulip		Stephanotis
Waxflower		Winter Jasmine

The Gift **List**

It's a time when you can go consumerist mad, as all your friends and family rally around with their purses brimming to congratulate you for getting hitched. There must be something in the jokes about getting three toasters and two sets of knives as more people are turning to wedding gift list options managed by the professionals.

Traditionally Finnish brides went door-to-door collecting gifts in a pillowcase as luck for a long marriage. However, how much more stuff do you need more? And is there an alternative?

According to Weddingchaos.co.uk people are a little more picky these days, with a huge 54 per cent of couples asking for money or vouchers as a gift, preferring understandably to pick and choose what they need when they want it, rather than having a house brimming with brand-spanking new objects that they weren't particularly keen on. Money helps, especially when you're spending cash for the event. It is standard procedure to give money to couples in Asian countries, and in some geographical spots such as Poland, Cyprus, Greece, and the Philippines there is a whole 'money dance' involved at the ceremony where guests are expected to pin money to the bride's wedding dress or veil.

The Green Choice

If you are going to buy a gift, why not make it green – something sustainable, long lasting and showing your support to the people that have made it. There are plenty of green gifts out there and some of the online eco retailers offer wedding gift list services. So you want the new towels for the laundry cupboard? When processing textiles, hazardous substances are often used and have reported to leach chemicals out of the products. Whilst conventional cotton uses 24 per cent of all insecticides and 11 per cent of all pesticides in the world, buying organic is the more wholesome option. Whilst a lot of craft products are still unable to be certified by the Fairtrade Foundation, it is worth finding out where your local British Association of Fairtrade (BAFTS) shop is. Due to the independent nature of them you are likely to get a wonderful personal service.

Eco Retail Therapy

Online there are tons of ethical products. The Natural Store recently launched an Ethical Wedding Services section including a Wedding Gift List for any of their 3,500 featured products. Their products range from furniture to food, fashion to interiors and garden to beauty. They offer free delivery if the couple decide to have everything delivered to them on a particular date.

Eco department store Natural Collection (which was awarded Online Retailer of the Year by The Observer Ethical Awards in 2007 and 2008) offers another robust developed wedding list for green nuptials. Kitting out a home in eco style together can be very exciting. The minimalist less is more approach will certainly save you a few hours in years to come when you're squabbling about the junk you've accumulated.

If you are buying new items then look at the longevity of it. Perhaps slapping some eco paints (such as Earthborn or EcoPaints) or wall paper (from a company like Graham & Brown) will give you a fresh start together. Oliver Heath's range at Ecocentric is particularly lavish, and they even offer Ecocentric gift vouchers with their wedding gift list so you don't need to decide what to buy immediately. You can interior decorate with hip companies such as USE-UK who have a range of retro and/or recycled products. By Nature is also promising a new wedding list including recycled and fair trade dining ware – and they will match 10 per cent of the total amount spent and give it to your chosen charity. Ethical Home Boutique is another new pretty website just opened that will have an expanding number of products.

If you're wanting matrimonial bliss in the bedroom then So Organic have also just launched a wedding list that includes SKAL-certified organic bedding and linen, often the softer option. Green Fibres also have a wedding range where several people can contribute to more expensive gifts or sets so your guests don't feel that their pockets have been burned. They even offer smooth luxury with a silk filled duvet.

And if a pristine bed is on your hit list, then consider FSC certified bed frames from Warren Evans with an organic certified mattress. You may wish to get some bespoke furniture. Hendel-Blackford Fine Furniture or Ryan Frank are just two of the eco gurus in this field.

Green & Easy is a perfect web option if you're looking to develop your green fingers, as they've got lots of sustainable gardening products.

Charity Begins at Home

A few years ago some of the larger charities cottoned on to the fact that some bride and bridegrooms were using their 'buy a goat' catalogues for their wedding gift list as an altruistic alternative. World Vision were one of the first and ended up managing over 200 wedding gift lists manually after supporters asked to 'donate' their gifts to the charity. With friends of the happy couple calling up to place the order at all times of the day, David Thompson, Marketing Manager at World Vision was staggered at their generosity and selflessness. 'It is a great honour for us. For people to do that for a charity and off their own backs is amazing.' So they spent a bit of time developing their website and setting up facilities whereby the couple in question could email their friends and declare whether they wanted to donate gifts like a cow pat stove for a family in the Himalayas or a sewing kit to women in Albania.

Ask for a goat for your wedding from Oxfam Unwrapped. © oxfam

Although the charities received some opposition to gifts of buying animals, David adds that it isn't about unnecessary gifts. 'If we're working with a country we wouldn't consider dumping goats on the local people unless there was a need and if we had a system in place to handle any potential danger of degradation of the local landscape. That's why we have a lama project in Bolivia as they have big wide feet that tread lightly without damaging the environment. We do our best to find solutions that are relevant, sustainable and don't actually harm the environment but give the community what they need whether it is protein or a livelihood. World Vision can spend ten to fifteen years in a project to ensure everything runs smoothly and effectively.'

Of course you may still want a wedding list and run a charitable option on the side – great for when good, affordable presents on your product gift list run out. Newlywed Clare Oakley recently received £6,000 from her 200 wedding guests who thought her wish to receive contributions towards Alternative Gifts was a fantastic idea. Whilst this amount isn't the norm, any monetary donations have significance.

Christina Aguilera was reported to have spent $2 million on her unrestrained wedding but then asked guests to donate to any charities supporting the victims of the New Orleans tragedy, rather than buy her a wedding present. If it's good enough for her then it's good enough for the rest of us.

Another newly launched charitable wedding gift list from Save the Children is The Wish Service. Here you can choose from 30 gifts all of which are desperately needed by communities Save the Children work with around the world. Christian Aid's Present Aid offers over 40 presents that go to fund projects supporting agriculture and livestock, emergency and disaster preparedness, healthcare, power and energy, training and education and water and environment. Similarly, Oxfam Unwrapped offer up virtual presents funding their international projects. FARM Africa offer what they describe as an 'African Dowry' list, which provides livestock, seeds, training and other support, tailored specifically to the needs of a local African community.

If you don't have a particular charity affiliation, then why don't you

do a bit of surfing on websites that cover them all, such as Weddinglistgiving.com? Set up in 2004 the scheme was established by two cousins, Holly and Hannah, both of whom have a background in fundraising for charity. Hannah came up with the idea when she merged homes and got married in 2004. You can either choose a charity to support by categories that are important to you – be it animals, conservation, children, or by region, thus supporting work in your local area.

Another similar site is provided by Give It, who provide a range of online gift list services, including The Alternative Wedding List, The Green Gift List (which supports a variety of environmental charities), The Scottish Wedding List and The London Wedding List (featuring a wide range of Scottish and London based charities).

How green do you want to go? Sazzy and Stardust from the band Naked got a tree planted in their name by a wedding guest © Trees for Cities

There are no toasters and kettles or pots and pans. Couples select a group of charities, or make up their own choice. Everything is simple and online and couples receive a final certificate confirming total donations to each charity. Give It mention that 'Websites are usually all about supporting one charity. Most marrying couples won't have a favourite charity as that tends to come later in life. Your guests are likely to support a whole range of different types of causes. As we're a not for profit organisation there are no corresponding downsides such as anyone trying to make a profit from the charities.' Good Gifts offers another wedding list service with over 200 virtual charity gifts available, which doesn't get spent on anything other than the gift itself.

A very innovative website has been launched called Buy Once Give Twice. Generally when a charity holds an auction a supporter pays thousands of pounds for a luxurious and often unique prize who then fails to collect their item. Instead, the purchaser can contact the site and re-auction the lot for the charity. The original charity will receive 60 per cent of the resale value and once re-sold, the new purchaser nominates their favourite charity to receive the other 30 per cent. Major charities have already signed up. Perhaps you could ask your guests to bid online for a surprise? You can always combine the charitable and still get a sustainable present. Trees for Cities give guests the opportunity to buy a pair of Hawthorn Trees, representing love and partnership and you can get a dedicated plaque too.

> **The couple in question could email their friends and declare whether they wanted to donate gifts like a cow pat stove for a family in the Himalayas or a sewing kit to women in Albania.**

Shop for Change, launched by Mercy Corps offers unique products from the 35 countries the charity works in. One example are beautifully moulded Sri Lankan brass wedding sets, as according to tradition, when a Sri Lankan bride marries she is given five brass items: an oil lamp, a water jug, a tray, a spittoon, and a pot.

There are plenty of ideas for green gifts out there. When compiling your own wedding lists do remember it's the thought that counts. After all, by attending your wedding your guests have already given you the greatest gift you could ever have – memories. And as cheesy folks say, presence is more important than presents! ∎

The **Honeymoon**

As the wedding celebrations gradually fade away you hope to curl up somewhere hidden as a newly married couple. Can you have a burden and guilt free green honeymoon?

The Eco Boudoir

The honeymoon time used to be a period to get away from it all, but as we take for granted all the travelling around we do today for business and pleasure in our information thirsty, no borders society, perhaps we can turn the honeymoon on its head and stay at home! There is something whimsical about using your home as your post-wedding love nest, rather than dashing through it on your way to work (with half a slice of toast in your hands). You can spend time together as a couple making your house the welcoming home you always dreamed of. These days it's not something we do enough. Use the wedding relics of your soy candles and luxurious fair trade chocolates to enjoy one another's company in an uncomplicated form. Make your bedroom an eco boudoir, your bathroom an organic spa and your kitchen the green cuisine restaurant of your local area

Jamie and Katie Fewings relax on a Cornish beach © Lisa McMahon

for a week. Switch off your phone and log off your computer and – just be! Discover the local community, take walks in the park or venture into the countryside and make friends with your neighbours as the new Mr and Mrs. Do you really need to lie on a beach to replenish your souls together? Or can it all be done by creating a sanctuary in your own street?

Making it Local

You don't need to move into your neighbour's house down the road to keep your honeymoon local. Plenty of people have got it sussed as to how to enjoy leisure time locally, and it's one of the largest industries in the UK. You've worked tirelessly to make the wedding green, so why not let someone do the vetting work for you this time? There's a whopping £61 billion expenditure on tourism, employing approximately two million people, directly or indirectly. That's an overwhelming amount of places to go on our little island!

The first place to look for inspiration on green and local honeymoons is ecoescape. These handy guides to eco friendly places to stay and visit in the UK, Ireland and beyond are helping travellers to discover new forms of responsible escapism closer to home. And the good news is that honeymooners don't have to stay in a tipi (unless you'd like to of course!) as the ideas in the books and on the website cover lots of budgets including luxury eco chic getaways. You could stay in a secluded lodge that enjoys uninterrupted views across the Yorkshire Dales, or a B&B that offers nothing but comfort and good homecooked food from the local region.

The government are big fans of the sustainable development of tourism in order to safeguard the local countryside, heritage and culture for future generations and with them on board there are plenty of green accredited places to visit and rest your wedding weary heads.

The Green Tourism Business Scheme (GTBS) is the UK's leading sustainable tourism certification scheme, assessing business and grading them with 'rigorous criteria', awarding them a bronze, silver or gold standard if they are up to eco expectations. With over 1,400 members including accommodation providers and visitor attractions they have flexible indicators for environmental performance. The obvious one is they should be compliant with environmental legislation and be keen to improve their green tinted halos. They have built in good environmental management including staff awareness, specialist training and monitoring, waste and transport minimisation, and energy and water efficiency. It doesn't stop there. Ethical purchasing of recycled materials, local food and drink and FSC certified wood, whilst encouraging biodiversity are also expected. In the ecoescape series you can see which businesses have achieved a GTBS award.

Amy Carter, founder of eco haven Guludo Lodge in Mozambique tied the knot in November 2007

We had a green wedding as it completely reflected our lives – we have dedicated the last five years to relieving poverty and environmental conservation through our business and charity so there wasn't really a decision to be made. After three months of planning – mostly from Mozambique – we had a Christian ceremony in a small, local 11th Century church close to my parent's house, although we used a friend's fifty year old Moris 10-4 for moving the key bridal party around. The reception took place in my parent's garden with two adjoining giant hat katas from Beautiful World Tents.

About 120 people attended and we used fair trade or locally sourced ingredients that had an Indian and Mozambican twist from Word of Mouth Catering by Margaret Wingham. It was highly professional and very reasonably priced. We also bought fair trade and organic wines, beers and champagnes online.

For our gift list, people gave to Nema Foundation, the charity that we set up, operating in Mozambique, working with poor, rural communities. In fact our invitations were made by a new craft group set up by Nema in the local village; they were absolutely stunning, and everyone loved them! Our flowers were minimal and were either fair trade or locally sourced.

We got the bridesmaid dresses from eBay which they had already tried on in Debenhams to know what size they wanted. My dress was made by Fabio Gritti, bought secondhand from Deja Vu in Albury near Guildford. My cosmetics were from Nutrimetics which use only natural ingredients for all their products and my hair was done by Sanrizz. The favourite part of all the planning though was writing our vows!

We had an initial honeymoon up in the Scottish Highlands which we continued on the white, tropical sands of our lodge in northern Mozambique. ∎

Carbon Chaos

Wherever you decide to honeymoon, it's worth watching your flight intake. Aviation is a substantial problem due to the hefty numbers of us wanting to fly these days. There are environmental concerns over potentially harmful chemicals used for deicing wings, such as glycol and potassium acetate and understandably, noise pollution. The biggest issue is each individual's carbon footprint, which is the quantity of CO_2 emissions that you produce when you travel, creating an increased number of greenhouse gases into the atmosphere. Contrary to popular belief, short haul flights are unnecessary and contribute to around 120 million of us passing through the airports of Heathrow, Gatwick and Manchester alone! Airports guzzle energy and resources like a large music festival – yet this is not just one weekend of the year, it's every day. With more developments and amenities required to fuel our own flying demands, a simple promise to fly less would make a substantial difference to the environmental pitfalls of aviation. It has also been suggested that carbon release at high altitude is worse than the chugging of motors on the British motorways. A typical plane releases approximately 35kg of carbon dioxide per kilometre. Long haul flights can sometimes be more fuel efficient as they have fuller capacity and the fact that the majority of fuel is used during takeoff and landing.

Taking it Slowly

If you want to get out of Britain, then you can quite possibly choo choo to Europe quicker than your daily commute to work. With Eurostar boasting the UK's first high speed line with 186mph trains cutting journey times between London, Paris and Brussels, the environmental advantages are eternal. Like all old romantic movies, there's something special about sharing a carriage together as you daydream out of the window at the passing settlements. You'll also be reducing ten times your carbon emissions than if you were to go on a short haul flight – 10.9kg of CO_2 compared to 122kg. It's not an overly expensive way to travel either.

ecoescape is also all about travelling slowly. Laura Burgess of ecoescape explains further. 'Travelling slowly overland anywhere in the world is becoming a way of harnessing the journey so that what we see on the way is as important as what we do when we arrive. And that's why in ecoescape there are details of public transport and ways to arrive without using a car or a plane. Taking its inspiration from the Slow Food Movement, ecoescape can help you plan a slow and memorable honeymoon.'

Honeymoon with a difference and have a bush dinner at sunset © Aim4Africa

Good Globetrotting

Amidst the climate concerns, globetrotting is increasing and the World Travel and Tourism Council (WTTC) estimate that over 660 million trips are made every year, contributing towards 11 per cent of the global GDP.

We don't live in a utopian world of slow or carbon free travel just yet. If you just can't say no to a little sunshine or the opportunity of a lifetime and it's a logistical nightmare to arrange by train then be considerate when planning who you book with, where you stay and whether you can make a positive impact whilst in the lovebird cage.

When you book your honeymoon also be aware of other potential conflicts of travelling overseas – and don't be fooled by the green washing of the companies who don't have any accreditation to back themselves up. Much of the industry is still unregulated, devastating environments, degrading cultures and destroying traditional livelihoods. Tourism Concern campaigns for fairly traded and ethical forms of tourism. As an independent, non industry based UK charity it lobbies governments and the industry to be more accountable, and provides tourists with information on how to ensure a holiday is rewarding for everybody and not exploitative. Currently it strongly advises against visiting Burma due to the human rights abuses of forced labour and displacement arising directly from the tourism development industry. The tourism income also funds the illegal military regime that prevents Burma from being a democratic country. There are other locations to be aware of when booking a honeymoon as well, including The Maldives, and the Bimini Bay Resort in the Bahamas. More information about these campaigns and others is on the Tourism Concern website.

Krissy Pemberton of Responsible Travel, an organisation promoting ethical companies, gives her top tips to having a honeymoon with a heart abroad. 'If you are going to fly, it is more important than ever that you holiday responsibly upon arrival. And whilst you're at it, remember to offset the carbon emissions from your flight. It isn't a magic wand by any stretch of the imagination but it all helps. Make your honeymoon count. Make sure when you get to your destination that your holiday is really investing in the local economy and people rather than just another all-inclusive honeymoon package. These packages all too often provide scant opportunity to experience the local culture and interact with the local community whilst the residents themselves see little economic benefit, or worse, have been sidelined to make way for a resort draining precious resources, damaging the environment and giving nothing in return. Choose a honeymoon where you get the chance to stay in locally owned accommodation, enjoy organic and locally produced food (cutting down on food miles) and where you can be sure the owners are making every effort to minimise their environmental impact, using renewable energy, conserving water, and recycling and reusing wherever possible.'

The International Ecotourism Society (TIES) is a not for profit organisation facilitating a global network of eco tourism professionals and travellers who are aiming to make tourism a viable tool for conservation, poverty alleviation, protection of culture and biodiversity, sustainable development and education. Sparking the debate and solving the issues, they have members in more than 90 countries representing various fields including academics, consultants, conservation professionals and organisations, governments, architects, tour operators, lodge owners and managers. TIES indicate that whilst many projects around the world have striven to establish eco tourism projects, they often lack adequate access to the markets and are economically fragile.

© Paulus Rusyanto

Picture Postcard

Enjoy Europe

If you fancy going a little more local, then you could visit Long Travel's renovated 'trulli', conical shaped stone houses only found in the region of Puglia in Southern Italy. They have been lovingly restored by Pugliese craftsmen to a high standard, with stone floors and stone cones and sympathetic use of local and traditional materials. These have then been decorated with unusual and attractive ceramics from Caltagirone in Sicily and paintings from local artists. There are exciting adventures for you to have in the unspoilt UNESCO World Heritage Site of Itria Valley, amongst rolling hills, drystone walls and vineyards. The trulli are close to very beautiful, historic towns such as Cisternino, Martina Franca and Ostuni, with their fantastic local trattoria (often 'agritourist' restaurants with only local, authentic cuisine), their independent shops and traditional festivals. This destination is not far from lovely, sandy beaches of the Adriatic, and many share a swimming pool in the grounds planted with olives, figs and pomegranates and many other native trees.

Safari in Style

Tribes travel offer a safari at a luxury eco camp in the remote West Kilimanjaro area of Tanzania that brings financial benefit to the local Maasai, whilst viewing the Big Five of Africa. They suggest you link this with time on the tiny island of Chole, south of Zanzibar and next to Mafia Island. Chole Mjini offers wonderfully rustic

and very romantic accommodation in tree houses. It has impeccable eco credentials, but also offers a truly wonderful way to relax and enjoy the Indian Ocean.

Trail Time

If you like walking then Treasure Discoverer's Trek in Bhutan, booked through Himalayan Kingdom offers a guide to take you through remote villages for a relaxed and fascinating experience. Supporting the local community and with strictly controlled groups to prevent negative effects to the environment, they provide you with guides, porters and food. You can also buy locally produced handicrafts to remind you of your honeymoon for years to come. They also recommend the Dwarikas Hotel in Kathmandu. Having been built by a man obsessed with restoring Kathmandu's architectural heritage the accommodation itself is a work of art.

Cram Cruising

For variety on your honeymoon then Bushbaby Travel have a solution. You can fly to South Africa and stay at the Thakadu River Camp, Madikwe Game Reserve, which is wholly owned by the local Molatedi Village. There are options for honeymooners to volunteer in the village too. After some rewarding time there you can then fly to Dubai directly to the aptly named Evason Hideaway and Spa at Zighy Bay in Oman. With the beach a short stroll from the village you can also support the ecological footprint here by fol-

©Mphoto

lowing their 'Little Green Book' to respect the local eco system. All Bushbaby Travel options have the future in mind as all their destinations are 'malaria free' – perfect if you are planning on starting a family soon after your marriage, as you can't try for a baby for at least six months after taking anti-malarial tablets.

Barefoot Luxury

Guludo Beach Lodge is an understated, uncomplicated tropical beach paradise. The award winning eco lodge is situated in the north of the Quirimbas National Park, Mozambique on an absolutely deserted white sand beach. The perfection of Guludo is sealed in its design, ensuring the presence of each guest actively benefits the local community and environment, just by being there. Each of their nine bandas is positioned along the beach and offer dazzling veranda views of the Indian Ocean, with king-sized beds, en-suite alfresco bathrooms and a private path to the beach. You can also learn

to dive through the PADI accredited dive centre and qualified instructors. They are keen to treat honeymooners as VIPs without hitching up the prices – from special touches of gourmet cuisine candlelit dinners on the beach, romantic picnics, sunset cruises on their traditional dhow sailboat, or even sunset drinks at the lookout point where couples can spot wildlife whilst watching the sun go down. A growing percentage of their revenue goes directly back into the area, through their associated charity, Nema Foundation, which supports school feeding programs, malaria alleviation programs, providing student scholarships, coral reef monitoring, enterprise development, humpback whale research, and the building of a primary school, to name just a few! For those concerned about their carbon footprint, Nema will be launching its own carbon offsetting project aimed to increase livelihood development and conservation within the area. ∎

The Association of Independent Tour Operators (AITO) is the first tourist industry association to have incorporated green tourism and responsible travel into their business charter. Each potential member's sustainable tourism credentials are examined before they can join to ensure sustainability and that local cultures and the environment are treated with the utmost care and respect. All members must protect the environment, respect local cultures, benefit local communities (both economically and socially), conserve natural resources and minimise pollution. They also have a Responsible Tourism Committee which award members with up to three stars for tour companies that are truly green. There are currently 29 companies in this category.

Whilst responsible travel often conjures up tropical jungles and fevers to match backpacking and bugs there are in fact many luxurious options for you to lay back and simply relax in.

Pre-honeymoon familiarisation is also advised by Pemberton. 'Prepare yourself by reading up on local cultures before you go and learn a few words of the local language – travelling with respect earns you respect.'

When you go shopping in local markets, don't over haggle as you may be exploiting the person driven by poverty into an unfair price – and avoid souvenirs that use local endangered species, such as exotic woods or animal hides. A moral dilemma for most is people (especially children) who are begging. It should not be encouraged with money as it increases a handout dependency and offers no sustainable solution in the long term. Instead give through reputable charitable organisations that help support the roots of poverty.

Pemberton also suggests that you think about your packing carefully. 'Planning for a honeymoon shouldn't be an excuse to stuff your case full of cosmetic bottles and boxes. Get rid of unwanted packaging at home or avoid it in the first place as it is often more difficult to dispose of waste responsibly in developing country destinations.'

Good green travel websites like Responsible Travel will offer transparency on how the holiday makes a difference, whether it is contributing to social development and conservation efforts within the community or providing a sustainable source of income and a reason for the local people to conserve their natural environment and protect their native wildlife. ■

Green Guide
Wedding
Directory

© Mat Hayward

Your Toolkit for a
Green Wedding

When looking at the options for your green wedding you will find that there are many suppliers all across the UK rattling for your business. The most important part of wedding planning is ensuring the process is as smooth as possible by finding the right people to work with from scratch so that you don't end up being a Bridezilla on the day. In practical terms, the best suppliers – and by that we mean both the cheapest and planet-friendly – will be local. By choosing local suppliers you are likely to prevent the classic stress of to-ing and fro-ing that occurs during the wedding planning process. Go on other recommendations from brides to be, and don't rush into any agreements until you have looked around at all the options.

In this section of the guide we have provided a useful toolkit with some of our favourite wedding suppliers in the UK. Over the next few pages you will find over 330 listings with a short blurb on each company and their contact details to get you started. These are businesses with good green credentials and which will allow you to look and feel glam and gorgeous on your day. All these companies have been vetted by us to ensure they are reducing their impact on the environment and are operating fairly with the people they work with. From our experience, they also seem like lovely people to work with too!

As a starting point we've provided some very useful resources, from websites that allow you to speak to other green brides-to-be, to places where you can get your ethical wedding gift list set up. There are also ideas and suggestions for eco friendly venues, caterers, florists, photographers, stationery and beauty pampering prior to the day and even the honeymoon. Each section is organised by chapter category so that you can systematically tick each section off on your wedding planning list. You will find, however, that many of the companies overlap on different services for the day – for example your chosen venue could also provide your catering or be your honeymoon getaway, or your beauty pampering could also provide your wedding favours.

This is by no means a definitive list of all the suppliers. Please visit the Green Guide directory online to access over 15,000 companies and services at **www.greenguide.co.uk** ■

Weddings with
The National Trust

A beautiful and unusual venue can offer a breathtaking backdrop for your wedding day.

The National Trust offers hundreds of properties from clifftop temples and beachside settings, picturesque ruins and extravagant interiors, ancient fortresses and intimate halls, glorious gardens and sweeping driveways, for a day to remember.

Not only are these stunning locations, but they also offer a very 'green' option. As one of Europe's leading conservation charities, the Trust is concerned about its environmental performance. Set up in 1895 to protect Britain's threatened coastline, countryside and buildings, you can be sure that by booking your wedding at one of our properties, you are helping in all sorts of ways.

Ethical food sourcing – with over 50 working kitchen gardens, wedding couples can work with our Catering Managers to develop a menu that is truly local and seasonal as well as delicious.

Eco friendly travel – why not encourage your guests to come by train or bus! Most of our properties are accessible this way, and our policy is to reduce car borne visits from a level of 90 per cent to 60 per cent by 2020.

Control of waste – we minimise kitchen and package waste and often don't provide litter bins as we ask our visitors to be responsible for their own waste, and with over 4,000 septic tanks and private sewage treatment systems, even our toilets are green!

Saving water – we are reducing consumption and protecting supplies, so don't be surprised if your guests see waterless urinals or dry compost toilets!

Saving energy – with over 13,000 low energy light bulbs installed, your wedding will be glittering as well as eco-friendly.

So, with over 850 weddings a year at our properties, you can be sure that your chosen venue with the National Trust is as green as it can get! ■

To chose the right venue for your wedding, visit our website www.nationaltrust.org.uk/weddings, email functions@nationaltrust.org.uk or ring our enquiry line 0870 458 4000.

THE
NATIONAL
TRUST

GREEN GUIDE WEDDING LISTINGS

THE WEDDING BUDGET

Ecology Building Society
7 Belton Road, Silsden, Keighley,
West Yorkshire BD20 0EE
T: 0845 674 5566
E: info@ecology.co.uk
W: www.ecology.co.uk
Specialises in lending on run-down, derelict
properties in need of renovation or conversion and
for the construction of ecological new builds.
Mortgages are advanced against the value of the
land or the unimproved value of the property, and
funds can be released in stages as the project
progresses. Mortgages are also available across the
UK for: properties with non-standard constructions
such as timber, straw bale, rammed earth, wattle
and daub, etc; the purchase of woodland; buy-to-let
properties in need of renovation; organic
smallholdings; and housing co-operatives. Ecology's
range of green savings accounts supports its
unique lending programme.

The Co-operative Bank
PO Box 101, 1 Balloon Street,
Manchester M60 4EP
T: 0161 832 3456
E: customerservice@co-operativebank.co.uk
W: www.co-operativebank.co.uk
The UK high street bank that gives customers a say
in how their money is invested and encourages their
input into the ongoing development of its Ethical
Policy. The Policy contains statements which
stipulate who the Bank will and will not finance.
Offers armchair banking 24 hours a day, access to
LINK cash machines and a national network of
outlets. smile is a part of the Co-operative Bank,
and was the UK's first full service internet bank.

Triodos Bank
Brunel House, 11 The Promenade, Clifton,
Bristol BS8 3NN
T: 0500 008 720
W: www.triodos.co.uk
Triodos Bank only lends money to enterprises that
create social, environmental or cultural value.

Personal customers are offered a range of ethical
savings and investments, including accounts in
partnership with organisations like the Soil
Association and Amnesty. Loan finance, current and
deposit accounts are available to ethical
businesses, as well as the assurance that you'll be
working with an organisation that shares your
values, and that your money will only be working
for positive change.

THE WEDDING PLANNERS

Online Directories & Planning

Eco-Friendly Weddings
13 West Cairn Crescent, Penicuik,
Midlothian EH26 0AP
T: 01968 677 501
E: info@eco-friendlyweddings.co.uk
W: www.eco-friendlyweddings.co.uk
E-zine with advice, info and articles for couples
looking for green and ethical wedding alternatives
and promoting companies which offer eco friendly
and ethical services or products.

Ethical Weddings
30 Westcourt Road, Worthing,
West Sussex BN14 7DJ
E: katie@ethicalweddings.com
W: www.ethicalweddings.com
Ethical Weddings, set up by Katie and Jamie Fewings
in May 2006 following their own wedding in 2005, is
an online wedding magazine and directory that helps
couples plan the wedding or civil partnership of their
dreams, without compromising their values. It acts
as a meeting place for couples, suppliers and experts
to exchange ideas and give advice and
encouragement, whilst the Ethical Weddings
directory brings together wedding suppliers who are
striving to make a difference to our world, both
socially and environmentally.

Green Guide
31 Regal Road,
Weasenham Lane Industrial Estate,
Wisbech, Cambridgeshire PE13 2RQ
T: 01945 461 452
E: info@greenguide.co.uk
W: www.greenguide.co.uk
The Green Guide is the longest established practical
guide to ethical living in the UK and was first
published in 1994. Not only is it the oldest, it is also
the most comprehensive, with over 15,000 entries
– of which thousands are available online – making

it the UK's most diverse source of intelligence for anything organic, natural, fairly traded and ethical. The information is constantly updated. The ethos of the Green Guide is simple. It is about changing our patterns of consumption and seeking out greener, natural and ethical alternatives to every conceivable type of product and service. It's about buying more wisely, consuming less, wasting less, thinking through the consequences of our purchases.

GreenUnion

Catsheys, Romansleigh, South Molton,
Devon EX36 4JW
T: *01769 550 580*
E: *info@greenunion.co.uk*
W: *www.greenunion.co.uk*

An online wedding directory for people planning eco-chic weddings and celebrations.This eco friendly wedding website will help with everything you need to know about planning stylish, sustainable and ethical weddings and celebrations without compromising on quality or design. The comprehensive resource of products and services from hats to honeymoons, and cakes to carriages will help every couple plan a healthy, happy and ethical wedding day.

The Natural Wedding Company

E: *charlie@thenaturalweddingcompany.co.uk*
W: *www.thenaturalweddingcompany.co.uk*

An online directory and resource for couples looking to create a more natural, ethical and intimate wedding, encouraging smaller more intimate weddings that are not only gentle on the planet but also celebrate the coming together of families and friends. As well as providing a comprehensive directory of primarily UK companies and suppliers, the site also has an ever-growing 'ideas' section which offers do-it-yourself suggestions for your wedding. In addition, there are a number of interviews with the inspirational people behind some of the best green businesses, such as Linda Moss of Organic Holidays, April Doubleday an ethical jewellery designer, and Nora Sotamaa a budding designer of ecological menswear.

Ceremonies

British Humanist Association

1 Gower Street, London WC1E 6HD
T: *020 7079 3580*
E: *info@humanism.org.uk*
W: *www.humanism.org.uk*

Provides humanist (non-religious) weddings, funerals, gay affirmations and baby namings,

through a network of trained and accredited officiants and celebrants. All ceremonies are prepared and scripted individually according to the needs and wishes of the individuals and families.

Light on Life

18 Lansdown Place, Lewes,
East Sussex BN7 2JT
T: *01273 476 696*
E: *info@lightonlife.co.uk*
W: *www.lightonlife.co.uk*

Creates and conducts ceremonies for all life events – baby namings, weddings, civil partnerships, funerals, birthdays, house warmings and more. Strives to be ethical, local, eco, and above all beautiful and unique. Works with Arka Original Funerals in gently taking care of all funeral arrangements. Arranges workshops and talks, and is passionate about ceremony and ritual. Also has a shop in Lewes.

THE VENUES

County Loos

Hill Croft, Bradeley Green, Whitchurch,
Shropshire SY13 4HE
T: *01948 666 396*
E: *countyloos@hotmail.com*
W: *www.countyloos.com*

Environmentally friendly toilet hire. Serviced daily or weekly as required, no mains needed. Loos also available for those with physical disabilities.

Geodesum-Reshaping Marquees

10 Lansdown Road, Bude,
Cornwall EX23 8BH
T: *01288 356 077*
E: *info@geodesum.co.uk*
W: *www.geodesum.co.uk*

Reshape your big day with the Cornish company that's reshaping marquees. Like smaller versions of the Eden Project, Geodesum uses modular geodesic domes to break the mould set by standard marquees, so creating stunning bespoke spaces from 500 to over 3,000 square feet and catering for up to 250 seated guests. Natural, high quality canvas covers allow light and air to pass through which creates a warm and welcoming atmosphere. No internal poles and removable side canvases makes for an irresistible alternative to the norm. Geodesum is happy to work with brides and grooms to create a unique venue, which will stun and surprise wedding guests with its genuine 'wow' factor.

New Forest

Forestry Commission, The Queen's House,
Lyndhurst, Hampshire SO43 7NH

T: *023 8028 3141*

E: *enquiries.new.forest@forestry.gsi.gov.uk*

W: *www.forestry.gov.uk/newforest*

The New Forest lies to the west of Southampton Water in south-west Hampshire. It is internationally recognised as one of the largest areas of heathland in Europe (18,000 hectares). It has over 3,500 hectares of ancient and ornamental woodlands and about 1,400 hectares of valley mire, and is home to a huge diversity of wildlife. The forest enjoys protection under the European Directives as a Natura 2000 site and is designated a Special Area of Conservation and a Special Protected Area. Under the previously recognised protection designations, the whole forest is a Site of Special Scientific Interest. This large area of woods, heaths and mires has been shaped over the centuries by the grazing animals and forestry activities. It is an oasis of 'wilderness' set amongst the surrounding conurbations.

Historic Scotland

Longmore House,
Salisbury Place,
Edinburgh EH9 1SH

T: *0131 668 8600*

E: *Hs.education@scotland.gsi.gov.uk*

W: *www.historic-scotland.gov.uk/*

Organisation looking after over 300 sites representing Scotland's history from prehistoric sites and stone circles to castles, cathedrals and palaces. Becoming a Friend costs £38 per year with half price admission to English Heritage and Welsh Cadw sites. Special rates for families and OAPs.

National Trust, The

Heelis, Kemble Drive, Swindon,
Wiltshire SN2 2NA

T: *01793 817 400*

E: *enquiries@thenationaltrust.org.uk*

W: *www.nationaltrust.org.uk*

Created in 1895, the National Trust is the UK's largest membership organisation with 3.5 million subscribing members and 47,000 volunteers. The Trust cares for over 300 houses and gardens that are open to the public. It also protects over 700 miles of coastline. The Trust welcomes 500,000 school visits every year, whilst in the countryside, it works with many tenant farmers.

Over the Moon Tents

48 Chapel Street, Yaxley, Peterborough,
Cambridgeshire PE7 3LN

T: *07983 969 826*

E: *info@overthemoontents.com*

W: *www.overthemoontents.com*

Supplies yurts, tipis, historic tents and awesome intents for stylish, special occasions and offers a range of tent, decor, music and lighting hire services. Also specialises in providing music and lighting to go with their tents and can service events with up to 500 guests. Operates ethically as a business to reduce their impact on the environment, promoting bio-diesel-powered generators and natural plant and fabric decor, using ethically sourced tents and decor, and recycling and reusing what they can.

Penrhos Court Hotel & Restaurant

Penrhos, Kington, Herefordshire HR5 3LH

T: *01544 230 720*

E: *info@penrhos.co.uk*

W: *www.penrhos.co.uk*

Penrhos Court is a 700-year-old manor farm on the border of Herefordshire and Wales. It has been rebuilt and is now devoted to food, health and ecology. It is home to the Greencuisine School of Food and Health which runs nutritional based courses. Penrhos is also available to hire for green weddings, celebrations and company meetings.

RSA House

Royal Society for the Encouragement of Arts,
Manufactures & Commerce, 8 John Adam
Street, London WC2N 6EZ

T: *020 7930 5115*

Located in the heart of London, the RSA House occupies a unique setting for your special day. From the grandeur of the Great Room to the intimacy of a candlelit ceremony in the subterranean vaults, the RSA's talented and dedicated team will create a perfect day in a truly memorable setting. For those hoping to tread lightly down the aisle the RSA is offering a special Footprint Wedding Package incorporating fair trade wines and sustainably sourced ingredients. They will even plant a tree in your name as part of the RSA's trees initiatives.

Woodland Weddings

Forestry Commission Scotland, Lochaber Forest
District, Torlundy, Fort William PH33 6SW

T: *01397 702 184*

E: *kirsty.mann@forestry.gsi.gov.uk*

W: *www.forestholidays.co.uk*

Woodland Weddings puts the forest at your service with a beautiful registered site right next to the Caig Waterfalls and Witches Pool. The old stone bridge is also featured in the film Rob Roy and makes a lovely feature in any photographs. Ideal for a small outdoor civil ceremony (maximum party size is 20). The fee includes the hire of the site plus exclusive use of the car park. Details of other service providers such as hotels and catering on request. A site inspection is definitely recommended to appreciate the true beauty of this spot. Other areas in the district could also be available.

World Tents

Redfield, Buckingham Road, Winslow, Buckinghamshire MK18 3LZ

T: 01296 714 555

E: info@worldtents.co.uk

W: www.worldtents.co.uk

Supplies yurts, marquees, geo-domes, historical tents tipis and more, all made of natural canvas and wood from sustainable sources.

THE TRANSPORT

Public Transport

PlusBus

CPT, 3rd Floor, Drury House, 34-43 Russell Street, London WC2B 5HA

E: feedback@plusbus.info

W: www.plusbus.info

PlusBus is a great way of getting to and from over 230 of Britains' busiest rail stations and is a ticket (like a bus pass) that you buy at the same time as your train ticket at the station, or by phone. It gives you unlimited bus travel on participating bus services around the origin or destination town of your rail journey at a discount price. Tickets start from £1.50 a day with most prices between £2 and £3 a day. Holders of railcards also get one-third off the adult PlusBus ticket price – making it even better value-for-money. The website contains details of prices for all towns and cities served by PlusBus. It also has PDF maps of the zone for each town within which bus travel is available.

Coach Hire

Coach Hire Connections

Kings Ferry Ltd, The Travel Centre, Gillingham, Kent ME8 6HW

T: 01634 377 577

E: sales@coachhireconnections.com

W: www.coachhireconnections.co.uk

Coach Hire Connections offer carbon neutral private coach hire for group tours, family outings, school trips and airport transfers.

Car Clubs & Car Sharing

Carplus

Suite C17 Joseph's Well, Hanover Walk, Leeds LS3 1AB

T: 0113 234 9299

E: info@carplus.org.uk

W: www.carplus.org.uk

Carplus is the national charity promoting responsible car use. It works with local authorities, developers, employers and community groups to support the development of a national network of car clubs and car sharing schemes to complement other sustainable transport solutions.

CityCarClub

Smart Moves Ltd, 7 Northumberland Street, Huddersfield, Yorkshire HD1 1RL

T: 01484 483 061

E: enquiries@citycarclub.co.uk

W: www.citycarclub.co.uk

Offers a pay-as-you-go way of driving a car without all the cost and hassle of owning one. And by limiting car ownership, it's the greener way to drive too. For under £5 an hour, you can rent cars by the hour, day or as long as you like. Choose from 100's of new cars conveniently parked near to where you live or work – check online to see your nearest location in London, Bath, Bristol, Brighton, Birmingham, Edinburgh and Norwich. Cars are booked online or by phone and your membership card, with smartcard technology, acts as your keys to any of the cars.

Freewheelers

E: web.info@freewheelers.co.uk

W: www.freewheelers.co.uk

Matches passengers with drivers going the same way in the UK and on the continent, providing an economical and sociable form of transport whilst utilising the planet's limited resources more effectively. Car-sharing is commonplace in many other countries – in Germany over a million people use a similar service each year. Online service only.

Streetcar

Park House, 8 Lombard Road, Wimbledon, London SW19 3TZ

T: 0845 644 8475

E: services@streetcar.co.uk

W: www.streetcar.co.uk

Offers self-service cars for rent by the hour, day, week or month, with all the convenience of owning a car. The cars are parked in a dense network of dedicated spaces in several UK cities. A new

Volkswagen Golf can be booked for as little as 30 minutes or as long as 6 months. They are reserved online or by phone, and can be collected and returned 24/7 using high-tech smartcards and a PIN number. Usage charges are based on how long you have the car, and how far you drive. You will be billed once per month. A annual membership fee is £49.50 including a break down recovery service for the year and third party insurance cover with a £500 excess.

WhizzGo

T: *08444 779 966*

W: *www.whizzgo.co.uk*

Operates the leading national pay-by-the-hour car network across the UK. It is cheap, simple and green with a city-wide fleet of pool cars that are located in designated on-street bays across city centres within easy walking distance of wherever you are in the city. This provides hassle free access to cars at a more cost-effective price than pool, leased or privately-owned cars and conventional car hire. WhizzGo organises the insurance, tax, cleaning and other vehicle maintenance issues so you do not have to. The fleet consists of new Citroën cars chosen for their lower carbon dioxide emissions and the Toyota Prius. The company is also pioneering the use of various new alternative technologies and fuels.

THE ATTIRE

Vintage & Recycled

From Somewhere

341 Portobello Road, London W10 5SA

T: *020 8960 9995*

E: *info@fromsomewhere.co.uk*

W: *www.fromsomewhere.co.uk*

Collections that are entirely made up of reclaimed pre-consumer waste materials, unwanted and discarded, done-with, but still perfectly useable, still beautiful, still functional. Each piece is individually cut from high quality reclaimed fabrics including cashmere, cotton, silk, jersey, tweeds and wovens. So the singular beauty of each garment lies in its uncompromising balance between a contemporary approach to fashion design and a poetic and ethical solution to borrowing from past treasures for our modern needs.

Hellish Cheeky

15a Wind Street, Ammanford,
Carmathenshire SA18 3DN

T: *01269 591 967*

E: *info@hellishcheeky.co.uk*

W: *www.hellishcheeky.co.uk*

Each piece of Hellish Cheeky clothing is individually designed and handmade from recycled or vintage textiles. They are driven by the idea that they can rework items into one-off individual pieces that are not only functional and look fab but also raise awareness of recycling and environmental issues. So, fashion with a social conscience.

Junky Styling

12 Dray Walk, The Old Truman Brewery,
91 Brick Lane, London E1 6RF

T: *020 7247 1883*

E: *shop@junkystyling.co.uk*

W: *www.junkystyling.co.uk*

Junky styling was the perfect tag to attach to this unique style of clothing which specialises in secondhand suiting as twisted, tailored garments. Now 11 years on, with their well-established shop in London's Brick Lane and in-house production studio, nothing is holding this company back. Anni and Kerry are still best friends and the same multi-talented crew are putting out new clothing ranges in every direction. See the website for further details or give them a call.

The Dressmarket

10 The Square, Torphichen,
Edinburgh EH48 4LY

T: *0800 052 1465*

E: *info@thedressmarket.net*

W: *www.thedressmarket.net*

Offers brides-to-be an opportunity to find once worn and never worn wedding gowns from private sales, boutique overstocks or designer samples as well as bridesmaids dresses and other wedding items for a fraction of their original cost.

Charity Shops

Cancer Research UK

PO Box 123, Lincoln's Inn Fields,
London WC2A 3PX

T: *020 7242 0200*

E: *supporter.services@cancer.org.uk*

W: *www.cancerresearchuk.org*

Head office for the Cancer Research UK which has over 600 charity shops across the UK. The income it generates through these shops is vital to funding its research. The shops sell a variety of goods, mostly donated and the majority also carry a selection of new goods.

Oxfam GB Shops Support

Oxfam House, John Smith Drive, Cowley,
Oxford, Oxfordshire OX4 2JY

T: *0845 300 0311*
E: *enquiries@oxfam.org.uk*
W: *www.oxfam.org.uk*

Oxfam works with others to overcome poverty and suffering. Over 750 shops across the country raise money to support Oxfam's work around the world, selling a huge range of quality, donated goods at reasonable prices, including clothing, books, music and houseware. Some shops also stock a selection of fairly traded foods and other ethically-sourced gifts. For details of your local branch call or visit the website.

Salvation Army Trading Co Ltd

66-78 Denington Road, Denington Industrial
Estate, Wellingborough, Northamptonshire
NN8 2QH

T: *01933 441 086*
E: *office@satradingco.org*
W: *www.satradingco.org*

Head office for Salvation Army stores and clothing collections. Call for details of your nearest store or visit the website to find your nearest clothing bank.

Scope

Scope Response, PO Box 833,
Milton Keynes MK12 5NY

T: *0808 800 3333*
E: *response@scope.org.uk*
W: *www.scope.org.uk*

Scope is a national disability charity with a focus on cerebral palsy. The aim is that all disabled people achieve equality. Scope has over 250 affiliated local groups. The Helpline provides in-depth information and advice on all aspects of cerebral palsy and disability issues as well as information about and referral to Scope services as appropriate. Scope has a free text messaging service. To use it you need to text SCOPE plus your message to 80039. Also has over 300 charity shops and recycling bins across the country plus a toner doner and mobile phone donation schemes. Call or email for further information.

Dressmakers & Designers

Allison Blake Designs

Tel: 020 7821 7000
Email: allison@allisonblake.com
Web: www.allisonblake.com

Allison Blake provides a specialist couture service to create the perfect wedding dress. Make an appointment with her for a personal consultation where designs and ideas can be discussed to create the perfect dress. The couture service involves making a made to measure pattern which will be made as a calico toile and then fitted perfectly to your body. At your next visit the real silk dress will be fitted and this will be followed by a final fitting closer to your wedding date.

Ana Cristache

365 Fulham Road, London SW10 9TN

T: *020 7352 2038*
E: *office@anacristache.co.uk*
W: *www.anacristache.co.uk*

Supplies bespoke and made-to-measure bridal wear, bridesmaids dresses and mother-of-the-bride wear.

Conscious Elegance Ltd

48 Hallgarth Street, Durham,
County Durham DH1 3AT

T: *0191 383 9263*
E: *info@consciouselegance.co.uk*
W: *www.consciouselegance.co.uk*

Designs and supplies eco friendly gowns, which are individually hand-sewn in the UK, and made using only organic and sustainable materials and methods. The packaging is fully biodegradable and the shipping is carbon neutral. You can even recycle your gown with their free Christening Gown/Naming ceremony service for your future little ones.

Gaia House

T: *01273 777 752*
E: *lynnesalvage@yahoo.co.uk*
W: *www.gaiahouse.uk.com*

Eco and ethical dress designers, creating individually designed bridal wear and occasion wear created from eco fabrics for the bride with a conscience. The wedding dress collection is made in 100 per cent organic 'peace' silk and mixes. Offers a bespoke couture service including design consultation which ensures that the fabric, cut and colouring are absolutely right for you.

Motasem

Haysmacintyre, Fairfax House, 15 Fulwood
Place, London N1 5ER

T: *07788 713 714*
E: *mail@motasem.co.uk*
W: *www.motasem.co.uk*

A luxury label from Sabina Motasem Ali, offering classic and contemporary cocktail and wedding dresses, which could also be worn after the big day is over. Oozing simplicity and elegance, the dresses are timeless and trans-seasonal, making them great investment pieces for any women looking for sexy and comfortable dresses. The range includes day to evening dresses and organic options. The dresses are available to purchase online and through appointments in Islington, London on a 'made-to-order' basis from a sample collection of set designs and sizes (8-16). Prices start from £300 and have a four-week delivery. All dresses are ethically produced in the UK and Europe.

Tammam

T: 07815 774 759
E: info@tammam.co.uk
W: www.tammam.co.uk

A luxury fashion label selling top end ethical (fair trade, natural fibre, eco, vegetarian) clothing, specialising in womanswear and outerwear with a vintage influence. The collections combine high fashion, quality craftsmanship and an ethical policy. Tammam also offers bespoke (and off the peg soon) wedding dresses. There is also a range of charity T-shirts designed for the breastfeeding manifesto (100 per cent profits go to children's health charities). They strive to support workers and factories in developing countries under fair trade terms. Nothing produced under the label will cause harm to any human or animal at any part of the production process. They also take environmental impact into consideration.

The Frockery

8 Sparrowcroft, Forfar, Angus DD8 2AP
T: 01307 468 509
E: info@frockery.co.uk
W: www.frockery.co.uk/catalog

A family-run online boutique and dress agency based in North East Scotland specialising in the sale of quality pre-owned, vintage and recycled fashion which doesn't cost the earth.

Wholly Jo's

13 Cleveland Road, Uxbridge, London UB8 2DW
T: 01895 905 527
E: Joanne@wholly-jo.co.uk
W: www.wholly-jo.co.uk

A wedding gown designer and dressmaker based in Uxbridge, West London. You can have the dress of your dreams, made to fit exactly and designed to your own unique specifications, all with the peace of mind that you are not damaging the environment. The gowns are made from organic, fair trade and cruelty free products. Also uses vegetarian peace silks, organic cotton and hemp fabrics.

Adili.com

Blandford Hill,
Milborne Business Park,
Milborne St. Andrew, Blandford Forum,
Dorset DT11 0HZ
T: 01258 837 437
E: info@adili.com
W: www.adili.com

The ultimate online eco fashion and lifestyle store stocking the widest range of ethical fashion in the UK. With over 80 of the top brands for women, men and children you can look beautiful as well as ethical. All brands stocked are evaluated against an ethical matrix so you can be sure that every product is purely ethical.

BoBelle

174 Woodstock Road, Yarnton,
Oxford OX5 1PW
T: 01865 375 114
E: sales@bobelle.co.uk
W: www.bobelle.co.uk

BoBelle is an online boutique specialising in fair trade and handmade fashion accessories and gifts. The wide range of products available include wonderful handbags and purses which are made using eel skin; a by-product of the food industry in Korea. This leather is wonderfully soft and extremely strong and does not 'crack' like other leathers can. There is a wide selection of colours to choose from. Additionally, BoBelle supplies handmade and recycled photo albums and frames, handmade jewellery, organic cotton baby wear and locally produced organic cotton lavender bags. All gifts are carefully wrapped at no extra charge in acid free tissue paper and tied with raffia. Parcels are then sent in a 100 per cent recyclable box/envelope with 100 per cent bio-degradable protective filler, with no profit being made on postage

Bourgeois Boheme

Hydrex House, Garden Road, Richmond,
Surrey GW9 4NR
T: 0208 8788 388
E: info@bboheme.com
W: www.bboheme.com

A hip online boutique offering a range of ethical fashion accessories for both men and women. The range is all free from animal ingredients (all the products are vegan), and includes footwear, bags, wallets, belts, cosmetics, and more.

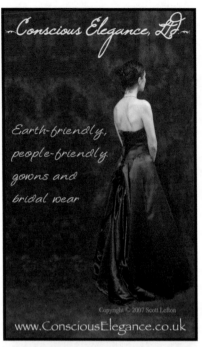

Ciel

45 Church Road, Hove, East Sussex BN3 2BE

T: 01273 900 880

E: sales@ciel.ltd.uk

W: www.ciel.ltd.uk

Hip, luxurious and organic, Ciel is a design-led eco fashion womenswear label that designs from the inside-out – choose from beautiful, vintage look organic cotton lingerie, the Ciel Spa collection of organic plant wax candles, and body and bath products. The range includes a line of glamorous hemp silk separates, in edgy but romantic contemporary designs using artisan hand block prints on silk, the Ciel signature coats and jackets, and sumptuous knitwear in organic alpaca. Ciel were the inaugural winners of UKFE Award for Ethical Fashion 2007-2008 and a finalist in The Observer Ethical Awards 2007-2008. 'Ciel continues to raise the bar for ethical fashion,' according to the Evening Standard. 'Having ethics just got glamorous with Ciel!' said UK Vogue.

Deploy Workshop

148a St John Street, London EC1V 4PR

T: 020 7377 2000

E: mail@deployworkshop.com

W: www.deployworkshop.com

A women's fashion label with a genuine point of difference. A pioneer in the design world, DePLOY reinvents the idea of mass customisation in fashion as each piece is adaptable – a dress becomes a skirt, or a blouse becomes a dress – all with the snap of an imperceptible fastening! The upshot for customers is the fabulous and real notion of the largest wardrobe fitting into the smallest suitcase. As such, it accommodates the diversity of modern life and answers the needs of busy, active yet stylish woman. From the boardroom, to a gallery or out to dinner, there is one outfit with numerous possibilities. Each garment's multi-functionality enables customers to make more out of less, and replace new fashion garment 'parts' – thus engaging in a recyclable design and manufacturing process. 'My aim is to make the fashion process less wasteful, more sustainable, and more interactive with the end-customer,' says Bernice Pan, DePLOY's creative director, who has a PhD in Fashion Innovation and leads a team of eight.

Devidoll.com Ltd

PO Box 59315, London NW8 1DF

T: 0845 362 6273

E: contact@devidoll.com

W: www.devidoll.com

An online boutique that sells chic, up-to-the minute fashion, pure products for the body and exquisite soft furnishings for the home. DeviDoll also only stocks things that, in some way, benefit the planet and its people so choose something from DeviDoll's collection and you contribute to a wiser use of human and natural resources. Every label at DeviDoll is made from organic fabric or made from alternative, sustainable fabrics, or provides especial benefit to women and/or children in production, or helps revive ancient handicrafts amongst local populations, or is made from vintage/reused materials. The instinct to look good is in all of us. So is the instinct to do good. DeviDoll brings these two important impulses together – making it possible to look fabulous on the outside and feel spectacular on the inside, in one go.

Enamore

207 Catherine Way, Bath, Somerset BA1 7PA

T: 01225 851 004

E: info@enamore.co.uk

W: www.enamore.co.uk

A creative fashion label producing beautiful clothing, lingerie and accessories from organic and sustainable fabrics. The collections are currently produced in the UK from the finest organic hemp, soya, cotton, silk and hand selected vintage fabrics.

Fashion-Conscience.com

6 Bromar Road, London SE5 8DL

T: 0871 384 1180

E: customerservice@fashion-conscience.com

W: www.fashion-conscience.com

Based in London but shipping worldwide Fashion-conscience.com keeps an eye on the main fashion trends and picks from the best and most stylish ethical labels and eco-luxury items. They stock labels from all over the world, from the established such as Terra Plana, Ciel and Stewart + Brown, to the hip and emerging, such as Camilla Norrback and Doucette Duvall. All the packaging is recycled or biodegradable, and they use 100 per cent sustainable energy in the business.

Frank & Faith

Longbarn House, Spadger Lane, Stafford, Dorchester, Dorset DT2 8UB

T: 01305 266 899

E: info@frankandfaith.com

W: www.frankandfaith.com

Frank & Faith is a Dorset based, socially conscious clothing label launched in Autumn 2006 by fashion designer and buyer, Faith, and her Chartered Accountant husband, Frank. The founding philosophy is that the clothes should look beautiful and be fashionable but are manufactured in an ethical and sustainable way. Will always use organic, recycled or sustainable yarns and fabrics and be made ethically – the aim is to produce clothing ethically by manufacturing in Britain. The usage of their 'Made in Britain' label further promotes locally produced goods and industries. This enables them to be sure their garments are made fairly, as all manufacturing falls under UK labour laws (including the minimum wage), EU labour directives and International Labour Organization conventions. In addition they can easily visit their factories to assess working conditions on a regular basis, thus protecting the brand from 'Sweat Shop' manufacturing.

Gossypium

Unit 1 Shepherd Industrial Estate,
Brooks Road, Lewes,
East Sussex BN7 2BY

T: *0870 850 9953*

E: *info@gossypium.co.uk*

W: *www.gossypium.co.uk;*
www.thecottonstore.co.uk

An organic and fairly traded cotton brand. Products include casualwear, baby and childrenswear and a yoga collection. Available by mail order, online, from their shop in Lewes and soon to be stocked at selected stores nationwide.

Greenfibres Eco Goods & Garments

99 High Street, Totnes, Devon TQ9 5PF

T: *01803 868 001*

E: *mail@greenfibres.com*

W: *www.greenfibres.com*

Sells certified organic and natural clothes and textiles bedding for adults and children. Materials used include organic cotton, organic linen, organic wool, and natural hemp and silk. Products range from Demeter certified organic wool baby blankets to organic cotton bras, and organic cotton bedding made in Devon. A line of mattresses for adults and children are made from materials such as organic wool, organic cotton, coconut fibres, natural latex, horsehair and organic linen. Call or email for a free A5 colour catalogue or drop into their store in Totnes, Devon. Their aim is to offer you options that support a healthy and organic lifestyle.

GreenKnickers Ltd

51 St Julians Farm Road, London SE27 0RJ

T: *020 3241 2035*

E: *info@greenknickers.org*

W: *www.greenknickers.org*

GreenKnickers make fair trade and organic underwear to make you smile and make you think, designing beautiful fun undies which make perfect green gifts. Their supply chain is green and fair from the growing of raw fibres right along to the customer.

Keep & Share Company

Lugwardine Court, Lugwardine, Hereford,
Herefordshire HR1 4AE

T: *01432 851 162*

E: *amy@keepandshare.co.uk*

W: *www.keepandshare.co.uk*

Keep & Share is an alternative luxury label, offering seasonal collections of unconventional – yet infinitely wearable – knitwear for both men and women. Each piece is designed to satisfy over time, and is knitted in the UK by the designer, Amy Twigger Holroyd, and her small team of makers. They seek to reverse the effects of throwaway fashion by encouraging their customers to buy fewer, more special pieces, and to keep their items in use for longer. True to their name, they create quality pieces that will transcend short lived trends and age gracefully; versatile products that can be worn in different ways and by different people over their lifetimes. Committed to reducing the environmental and human impacts of their business, the manufacturing is small scale and most of the machines are human-powered. Uses locally-sourced, naturally-coloured and organic yarns for their Eco Edition line.

Monsoon Accessorize Ltd

Monsoon Building, 1 Nicholas Road,
London W11 4AN

T: *020 3372 3000*

E: *generalenquiries@monsoon.co.uk*

W: *www.monsoon.co.uk*

Monsoon Accessorize has developed a strong brand with a highly distinctive identity. The intrinsic beauty of fabric, colour and technique so evident in the early sourcing of Monsoon's products from the Far East continues to exercise a strong influence. The stores carry a Fairtrade-certified cotton range, sourced from small scale, disadvantaged farmers, ensuring a better deal for local communities. The company is committed to being an environmentally responsible retailer, reducing the carbon footprint across the business. As part of an ethical trading policy all suppliers are asked to commit to minimum standards of pay and working conditions across the company's whole supply chain. The Monsoon Accessorize Trust is a registered charity that funds education, healthcare and income generation projects for disadvantaged women and children in Asia. See the website for further details.

Mossberry

3 Church Lane, Rearsby, Leicestershire LE7 4YE

T: *07742 934 407*

E: *fran@mossberry.co.uk*

W: *www.mossberry.co.uk*

Mossberry was the first ethical boutique in London selling 100 per cent fair trade fashion for women and children. They are now based in the Leicester area and trade exclusively through the website. The idea behind Mossberry is to deliver unique designs from all over the world whilst making sure the products are ethically and environmentally sound. They try to visit some of the manufacturers each year and keep customers informed through founder Francesca's blog. They stock goods from recognised fair trade manufacturers and suppliers and the cotton is, wherever possible, organic. The packaging is either recycled, recyclable or biodegradable. They also stock fair trade gifts and soft furnishings.

People Tree Ltd

91-93 Great Eastern Street, London EC2A 3HZ

T: *020 7739 9659*

E: *people@peopletree.co.uk*

W: *www.peopletree.co.uk*

A pioneering fair trade fashion and eco friendly mail order company, offering dynamic fashion for men, women, children and babies. The range features organic cotton, natural materials and low-impact dyes, and promotes traditional skills and organic farming, creating much needed income to rural areas and protecting the health of farmers and the environment. People Tree works with groups in 18 countries in Asia, Africa and Latin America, helping marginalised producers improve their lives and using fair trade as a route out of poverty. Also supplies jute storage items and organic cotton bed linen, as well as organic cotton clothing for babies and children. See the website for further information.

Quail by Mail Ethical Fashion

56 Higher Street, Brixham, Devon TQ5 8HW

T: *07966 876 539*

E: *contact@quailbymail.co.uk*

W: *www.quailbymail.co.uk*

A ladies fashion label based in the south-west of England. Quail is different because they design for themselves, using small, rural manufacturers in England and specialising in organic and fair trade fabrics. Offers stylish clothing with true ethical provenance and quality.

Beyond Skin

34 Westbourne Gardens, Hove,
East Sussex BN3 5PP

T: *0845 373 3648*

E: *info@beyondskin.co.uk*

W: *www.beyondskin.co.uk*

An exclusive ethical footwear label producing classic handmade shoes. All the footwear is made in England and Spain is produced in a way that is non-exploitative to animals or humans and – wherever possible – the wider environment. The company was created in response to the challenging predicament of combining style and fashion with a cruelty free lifestyle. The trans-seasonal, made-to-order footwear is produced from a variety of different materials, ranging from luxurious satins and soft synthetic suedes to organic cottons, recycled bottle tops and hemp.

Freerangers

87 Derwent Street, Chopwell,
Newcastle-upon-Tyne, Tyne & Wear NE17 7HZ

T: *01207 565 957*

E: *info@freerangers.co.uk*

W: *www.freerangers.co.uk*

Wonderfully comfortable animal free footwear and more. Shoes, sandals, court shoes, boots and clogs all made from Lorica – a revolutionary breathable material. Ladies and gents sizes up to 14. All styles are created with care in UK, by craftspeople who take a pride in their work. Range includes footwear, bags, purse, wallets, sporrans, belts, guitar straps, soaps, pamper products, fleece jackets and snuggles, T-shirts and zip tops. All totally animal free and licensed by the Vegan Society. Mail order only.

Green Shoes

Dart Mills, Old Totnes Road, Totnes,
Devon TQ11 ONF

T: *01364 644 036*

E: *info@greenshoes.co.uk*

W: *www.greenshoes.co.uk*

Supplies handmade footwear for men, women and children in leather and non-leather, from shoes and boots to Summer sandals, in a large range of full and half sizes and a choice of width fittings. Also supplies a range of bags, belts and accessories, and a new eco tan leather range made from pure plant leather. Voted 'Best Buys' for leather and vegan shoes by Ethical Consumer Magazine in 2006 and were given the highest star rating for ethical footwear by Permaculture Magazine in August 2008. Full resoling and repair service for their own products available. Order online or by mail.

Muks

3 The Lycee, 1 Stannary Street,
London SE11 4AD

T: 020 7587 0139

E: muks@muklukstore.com

W: www.muklukstore.co.uk

Muks is a footwear and accessories brand worn by international celebrities including Kate Moss, Chloe Sevigny, Katherine Heigl, Kate Hudson and Milla Jovovich. Muks was introduced to the UK in 2004 by Canadian-born Jaime Cooke with the Mukluk, a stylish and warm boot traditionally worn by Canadian Aboriginals for hundreds of years, and the Muks collection has expanded each year. Muks prides itself on using 85 per cent biodegradable materials and its links with Canadian Aboriginal culture, working closely with its Aboriginally-owned manufacturer in Canada. All the beadwork is hand-sewn on a fair trade basis at First Nations Reserves, helping to preserve the traditional craftsmanship of Canadian Aboriginals. Muks also donates a percentage of its profits to CAHRD, a non-profit organisation that benefits Canadian Aboriginals. Introducing a fur free range in its Autumn/Winter 2008/09 collection.

Terra Plana

64 Neal Street, London WCH2 OPQ

T: 0207 407 3758

E: 64nealstreet@terraplana.com

W: www.terraplana.com

Aims to be the most innovative and ecological friendly designer shoe brand in the world. The goal is to create sustainable products and be a sustainable company in all dimensions: people, process, product, place and profits by the end of year 2010. Terra Plana design and produce beautiful, fashionable artisan footwear using the most ethical products and process possible, such as chrome free leather tanning, recycled EVA rubber, recycled PU mid-soles, vegetable tanned leathers, recycled materials, including quilts, coffee bags and old t-shirts. The soles of the 99 per cent recycled trainers (Worn Again) are made from regurgitated rubber for the shoe mould shop floors, and all of the sock liners/foot-beds, are made from 100 per cent recycled foam scraps.

Vegetarian Shoes

27 Foundry Street, Brighton,
East Sussex BN1 4AT

T: 01273 691 913

E: information@vegetarian-shoes.co.uk

W: www.vegetarian-shoes.co.uk

Supplies quality leather free footwear made in England and other European countries and made with hi-tech breathable materials. Range includes birkenstocks, their own brand para boots, walking boots, dress and casual shoes, jackets, belts and bags. Free mail order brochure available or order direct online. Also has a shop at 12 Gardner Street, Brighton, BN1 1UP. **T:** 01273 685 685.

Design by Jana Reinhardt © Ingle & Rhode

Made

Suite 15, 97 Mortimer Stereet,
London W 1W 7SU

T: *020 7927 8310*

E: *enquiries@made.uk.com*

W: *www.made.uk.com*

Made accessories incorporate fair trade elements into their materials, craftsmanship or the entire piece. The original designs are sourced in developing African countries, before being re-worked by influential UK designers – Sam Ubhi, Olivia Morris, Pippa Small, Natalie Dissel, Hayley Mardon or Beatrix Ong. The final co-designed Made accessories have the crucial contemporary element needed to make them desirable for the British market. These final designs are then handmade by the original developing country producers using sustainable, local resources – precious metals, stones and indigenous materials that are familiar to the craftsmen – creating distinctive and original jewellery, bags, belts and shoes.

Hennumi

34 Thayer Street, Marylebone,
London W 1U 2QX

T: *020 7377 2000*

E: *mail@deployworkshop.com*

W: *www.hennumi.co.uk*

Hennumi specialises in bridal and special occasion hair accessories, combining recycled and off-cut fabric with fresh water pearls, Swarovski crystals, feathers and vintage mother of pearl buttons. Tosin Trim, Hennumi's designer, aims to promote an appreciation for the value of unwanted fabric and clothing by re-using such material in the creation of desirable accessories. A small range of cushions and handbags is also available. Subtle hints of previous uses of fabrics can occasionally be seen, such as the reuse of buttons and button holes from men's shirts on the cushions. Hennumi sources material from Deploy demi-couture womenswear and beyond, making use of its off-cut fabrics to create complementary accessories, often customisable to serve multi-functional purposes. Hennumi and Deploy collaborative design and production approach allows for more efficient usage of both material and human resources and offers a complete palette for the style and ethically conscious customers.

THE JEWELS

April Doubleday

Monkswillow, Monkleigh,
Near Bideford, Devon EX39 5JS

T: *01805 624 305*

E: *aprildoubleday@hotmail.com*

W: *www.aprildoubleday.com*

A designer and maker of ethical jewellery. The designs are big and bold using the coastline and sea as inspiration. April uses recycled wood from musical instruments in her work, as ebony and rosewood are precious woods today. She sources most of her stones from labs until she can visit mines to see if human rights are in place. She uses some gold plate inside the folds of etched silver as minimal gold is used and fair trade green gold from the west coast of Columbia (choco) where the communities run the mines and where the miners have mining rights. No chemicals or poisons are used in the extraction or the cleaning process.

Chocolate Couture Ltd

T: *0800 6349 182*

E: *gina@chocolate-couture.com*

W: *www.chocolate-couture.com*

Step into Chocolate Couture's online boutique and choose from a gorgeous collection of ethical jewellery and gifts, with a focus on high standards and ethics. From sumptuous handcrafted jewellery to beautiful ethically sourced gifts there is a wide choice. Feel free to contact them to discuss your wedding or commitment celebration requirements or ring designs. Choose something unique or handcrafted today and maintain your ethical focus.

Cred Jewellery

Cred Studios, The Sanderson Centre, Lees Lane,
Gosport, Hampshire PO12 3UL

T: *023 9252 9139*

E: *info@cred.tv*

W: *www.cred.tv*

Produces wedding bands and commissioned pieces using ethically sourced metals. Cred believe truly stunning jewellery needs inner beauty, which can only come from an ethical foundation.

Dejoria Diamonds

ROK House, Kingswood Business Park,
Holyhead Road, Albrighton,
Staffordshire WV7 3AU

T: *01902 376 106*

E: *simon.wiser@dejoria.co.uk*

W: *www.dejoria.co.uk*

Supplies conflict free diamonds for engagement

rings and other rings, earrings, pendants, bracelets and necklaces. The engagement rings are certified and they also provide an independent insurance valuation dossier for your complete peace of mind. They assure that the diamonds are conflict free, as after all, diamonds are a token of love, and love should never be tarnished.

Fifi Bijoux

T: *0141 339 8943*
E: *admin@fifibijoux.com*
W: *www.fifibijoux.com*

Fifi Bijoux is a luxury ethical jewellery company, specialising in offering design-led, contemporary jewellery made from precious materials which come from socially and environmentally responsible mining programmes and which have been fairly traded. The products are designed and made in the UK and are available in 9ct and 18ct gold for ready-to-wear items and in platinum for individual bespoke items. See the website for stockist details or contact them for more information.

Glamourkitten

10 Boundstone Road, Farnham,
Surrey GU10 4TQ
T: *020 7625 1981*
E: *lucy@glamourkitten.com*
W: *www.glamourkitten.com*

Offers a fine range of stylish, unusual vintage, reused and recycled jewellery. Give or wear strikingly original necklaces, brooches, earrings and bracelets, or the company's gift tokens. Their Seraglia Collection reuses antique, reclaimed and unexpected materials to create lasting heirloom pieces. They can also repair or reuse your own treasures, believing that reuse and repair are a great way to respect the Earth's limited resources. See also www.weallreuse.com.

Ingle & Rhode

211 Piccadilly,
London W1J 9HF
T: *020 7917 9515*
E: *enquiries@ingleandrhode.com*
W: *www.ingleandrhode.com*

Beautiful jewellery produced in a socially and environmentally responsible way. At Ingle & Rhode, they work with leading designers, using only the highest quality materials, and making all of their jewellery by hand in the UK. But what makes them really special is that they only use ethically sourced precious metals and gemstones, and are able to tell their clients exactly where and how each piece of their jewellery was created.

Jungle Berry

Flat 3, 5 Haycroft Road, London SW2 5HY
T: *020 7095 9225*
E: *info@jungleberry.co.uk*
W: *www.jungleberry.co.uk*

A fair trade enterprise specialising in design-led fair trade jewellery made with natural materials sustainably sourced from the Amazon rainforest. Their expanding range also includes stylish and original fair trade fashion and home accessories from Brazil and Mexico.They have been certified by the British Association for Fair Trade Shops (BAFTS) since 2005.

Karina Anne Design

T: *07847 504 116*
E: *info@karinaanne.co.uk*
W: *www.karinaanne.co.uk*

A jewellery design business based in Suffolk, using premium quality materials in all designs, including Thai Karen sterling silver, Swarovski crystal, freshwater pearls and lampwork glass beads to make beautiful wedding jewellery. They don't use gemstones, as they believe these cannot be ethically sourced. Some of the silver is fair trade and the lampwork beads are handmade in small batches from their favourite glass artisans in England and Canada. Designs are modern and fresh and suitable for all types of weddings from a simple country wedding to a more lavish occasion. There are even some fun pebble designs for beach weddings. Commissions are very welcome – they love making bespoke jewellery for that special day, so contact them to discuss ideas. They also have a range of jewellery and gift items for bridesmaids and other members of the wedding party, and a small selection of everyday jewellery which is perfect for the honeymoon.

Leju

82 Downhills Way, London N17 6BD
T: *0208 245 7570*
E: *info@lejudesigns.com*
W: *www.lejudesigns.com*

LeJu jewellery is an explosion of colour. Sustainable, plant based materials are the key to their stylishly playful designs found in a rainbow of colours, contrasted with the natural earth-toned hues of the 'vegetable ivory' – their primary component. Vegetable ivory is a palm seed from South America that is carved and dyed using plant extracts and oils. It is the only 100 per cent sustainable alternative to animal ivory and helps stop cruelty to elephants for their tusks. LeJu is based in London, where the jewellery is handcrafted with elements of suede and sterling silver.

Penny Gray Jewellery

11 Taroveor Terrace, Penzance,
Cornwall TR18 2SY
T: *01736 874 422/ 07870 759 544*
E: *penzancepen@hotmail.com*
W: *www.pennygray.co.uk*

Produces jewellery from found sea glass, shells, recycled glass bead necklaces and pearl necklaces and reworks them into objects of desire once more. There is an element of recycling to the work. Penny looks for vintage necklaces that are no longer fashionable, buttons that are no longer en-vogue and reworks them into modern designs.

Sarah Drew

64 Gover Road, St Austell, Cornwall PL25 5NF
T: *01726 68433*
E: *sarah@sarahdrew.com*
W: *www.sarahdrew.com*

Recycled jewellery handmade in Cornwall using antique brooches, vintage beads and found objects from Cornish beaches, such as driftwood, sea-glass and sea-plastic, combined with hammered chain and chunky semi-precious stones to create new contemporary pieces of jewellery to keep. An extensive bridal range includes tiaras, head-dresses, chokers and necklaces made from antique brooches and crystals. Buy online or comission a special piece.

Sea Glass Jewellery

Studio 1, Island Tower, Folly Bridge,
Oxford, Oxfordshire OX1 4JU
T: *01865 202 443*
E: *gina@seaglass.co.uk*
W: *www.seaglass.co.uk*

Sea glass, beach glass, marine gems, sea sapphires, mermaids tears, Atlantic amber... these shoreline sea-jewels are created from discarded glass worn down to smooth organic forms by sea water and the constant surge and ebb of the tide. When you pick up a rounded pebble of sea glass glowing in the shingle or left on sheer, wet sand from a receding wave, it can feel like hidden treasure found in a dream, yet incredibly, still in your possession when you wake. No wonder children love to collect sea glass: they know this state of affairs is rare and precious. Much of the glass Gina Cowen uses comes from the cullets (discarded off cuts) from Victorian glass factories by the north east coast, where many tons of glass must have been dumped at sea, in a recycling process, that the producers could not have imagined would be so mysteriously redemptive. A process of chemistry between sea water and glass, and the

physics of weather, and passage of time has transformed the product of industrial negligence into gems of enchantment and beauty. For Gina, a piece of sea glass is as precious as a diamond and its creation nicely contrasts that of the traditional wedding gemstone. Settings and clasps are in hand forged silver or gold. Sea glass looks best against bare skin or muted colours (cream, white, stone, ecru, grey, black) and complements natural fabrics such as cotton, linen, or silk.

Silverchilli.com

E: *customerservices@silverchilli.com*
W: *www.silverchilli.com*

Fresh, funky fair trade silver jewellery.

THE BEAUTIFICATION

Hair

Tints of Nature

Herb UK Ltd, 310 Ampress Lane, Ampress Park,
Lymington, Hampshire SO41 8JX
T: *01590 613 490*
E: *office@herbuk.com*
W: *www.tintsofnature.co.uk*

High performance hair products, which maximise the use of gentle, natural ingredients, whilst minimising the necessity for harsh or damaging chemicals. Tints of Nature permanent hair colour is ammonia, resorcinol and parabens free, with the lowest possible percentage of PPDs. Using certified organic extracts, it is one of the kindest ways to colour hair effectively, including grey. Tints of Nature is supported by a range of shampoos and conditioners and a highly effective scalp treatment. There is also a selection of semi-permanent colours called Changes. Organic Colour Systems is the first range of long lasting, permanent hair colours containing certified organic extracts and natural ingredients. Contact for further information or for details of your local stockist.

Nails & Manicures

Green Hands

53 Etnam Street, Leominster,
Herefordshire HR6 8AE
T: *01568 612 426*
E: *webshop@greenhands.co.uk*
W: *www.greenhands.co.uk*

Supplies products for natural manicures and pedicures. Specialists in natural nail care, organic hand creams, organic cuticle treatments, water based and low toxicity nail polishes, non-toxic polish removers and glass nail files.

AlternateStyle

London N17 6AA
T: 020 8352 0910
E: info@alternatestyle.co.uk
W: www.alternatestyle.co.uk

For herbal, organic and natural alternatives to beauty, skincare, and lifestyle products that are made to the highest standards, sourced ethically and not tested on animals. The range includes exotic products such as African black soap for all kinds of dermatitis, unrefined shea butter for healthy smooth skin, natural emu oil products from Australia and other premium healthy alternatives. Use altgrgd08 for free postage on first order.

Alternative Spa Company

16 The Hawthorns, Long Riston, Hull, East Yorkshire HU11 5GA
T: 07777 638 646
E: info@alternativespacompany.co.uk
W: www.alternativespacompany.co.uk

Independent organic beauty consultants offering a wide range of products and services such as organic spa takeaway treatments, organic weddings and organic gift packs. Provides advice to ensure customers get exactly what they are looking for via phone and email, or consultations can be arranged in the East Yorkshire area. They also offer advice, support and products to businesses looking to sell or use organic products in their business.

Aveda UK Ltd

3rd Floor, Holborn Hall, 193-197 High Holborn, London WC1V 7BD
T: 0870 034 2380
E: consumercare@gcc.aveda.co.uk
W: www.aveda.co.uk

Aveda is the first beauty company manufacturing with 100 per cent certified wind power and is one of the largest purchasers of organic ingredients in the personal care industry. It fulfills its mission by providing high-performing products that are good for professionals, customers and the earth. The range has over 700 products including hair care, skincare, make up and candles. Available at selected stores and hairdressing salons nationwide.

Balm Balm

PO Box 830A, Thames Ditton, Surrey KT1 9BB
T: 020 8339 0696
E: info@balmbalm.com
W: www.balmbalm.com

A 100 per cent natural and organic skincare range, winning the Soil Association's Best Organic Skincare Award for 2007. There are only four products to choose from but they believe that they have all your moisturising needs covered as they are multi-functional. The face balms can be used on legs or the lip balms on the face. The products, based around a simple wax and oil formulation, are so gentle that the Fragrance Free ones, in particular, are gentle enough to use on even new-born babies.

Beauty Naturals

11 Kingsmead, Station Road, Kings Cliffe, Peterborough, Cambridgeshire PE8 6YH
T: 0845 094 0400
E: damian@beautynaturals.com
W: www.beautynaturals.com

Natural, cruelty free health and beauty since the 1970s. Inspired by the late herbal skincare specialist Martha Hill, the Beauty Naturals catalogue includes a comprehensive and affordable collection of high quality, cruelty free, natural health and beauty products. The range is diverse and incorporates traditional formulations along with new, organic, natural alternatives. Generous discounts and free postage with all orders. Call for a free brochure or visit the website.

Bert & Daisy

PO Box 297, Wisborough Green, West Sussex RH14 0WP
E: happiness@bertanddaisy.co.uk
W: www.bertanddaisy.co.uk

Offers over 24 different brands of natural and organic skincare, beauty, body care and baby care products. Delivery is only £1.95 or free if you spend over £35. Every product is vegetarian and fulfills their strict ingredient criteria of no parabens, petrochemicals, SLS, synthetic fragrances or colours, PEGs, phthalates, DEA, TEA and absolutely no animal-tested ingredients. They reuse suppliers packaging and pack all orders with 100 per cent compostable chips.

Beyond Organic Skincare

Tremanda, Gillan, Helston, Cornwall TR12 6HG
T: 0845 500 3550
E: info@beyondskincare.co.uk
W: www.beyondskincare.co.uk

100 per cent natural and certified organic skincare,

with absolutely no parabens or other harsh chemicals. Their range is packed with vitamins, anti-oxidants and omegas 3,6,7 and 9. The products contain more than 190 biologically-active compounds which makes them effective, naturally.

Borealis Products

Roseburn, Fenton Terrace, Pitlochry, Highlands PH16 5DP

T: 01796 473 030
E: customercare@borealisskincare.co.uk
W: www.borealisskincare.co.uk

Established on the Isle of Skye in 1985, Borealis Products has now moved to Pitlochry. They continue to produce the range of quality skincare and toiletries as always. Freshly made in small batches the ingredients are high quality, chemical free and cruelty free. Log on to their website to see their products or phone and request their mail order catalogue. Based on ancient formulas it really is a unique range.

Chery Lin Skin Therapy

PO Box 64, Tetbury, Gloucestershire GL8 8LW
T: 07879 615 680
E: info@cherylinskintherapy.co.uk
W: www.cherylinskintherapy.co.uk

For fresh, organic original skin and body care that is nourishing, active and eco friendly. Using only highly nutritious ingredients, all products are freshly handmade to ensure maximum vibrancy and therapeutic value and are designed to work on the senses so that optimum enjoyment is gained through use. The products are unique as each one is made only when an order is received. It is important that every product has maximum therapeutic value, freshness and aroma.

Dr. Hauschka Natural Skin Care

Elysia Natural Skin Care, 27 Stockwood Business Park, Stockwood, Redditch, Worcestershire B96 6SX
T: 01386 792 622
E: enquiries@drhauschka.co.uk
W: www.drhauschka.co.uk

Elysia is passionate about providing consumer solutions for sustainable living without any compromise, offering a range of ethical products including Dr.Hauschka Skin Care. These are natural products for face, body, bath, shower and hair care, sun protection and a complete make up line. Wherever possible, ingredients are grown using biodynamic or organic methods and the range is Certified Natural by the German association BDIH. Also supplies Holle, Demeter-certified, biodynamically-produced baby foods and milk

formulas; Speick, Certified Natural men's grooming products; and Walter Rau natural soaps.

Earthbound Organics

The Toll House, Dolau, Llandrindod Wells, Powys LD1 5TL
T: 01597 851 157
E: sales@earthbound.co.uk
W: www.earthbound.co.uk

A Welsh manufacturer of handmade, organic facial creams, soaps, body oils and skin toners. Earthbound Organics was created by Jo Ordoñez who believes that what we put on our body can also be put in our body. All the ingredients are researched and are local where possible. Each cream, oil or soap has specially chosen herbs and cold pressed plant oils to help nourish and soothe skin. There are no 'nasties', preservatives, emulsifiers, colours, etc. Jo's background is one of biology and aromatherapy. Also offers a new range called Young Skins for 13-18-year-olds.

Funk Bubble

25 The Gardens, Southwick, West Sussex BN42 4AP
T: 07775 898 889
E: info@funkbubble.co.uk
W: www.funkbubble.co.uk

100 per cent natural toiletries and body care products – all of which are suitable for vegans. Uses no synthetics, artificial colours, perfumes or preservatives and uses only the best essential oils, fruit and plant extracts. The products are biodegradable and the packaging is recyclable.

Great Elm Physick Garden

Rock House, Great Elm, Frome, Somerset BA11 3NY
T: 01373 814 607
E: info@great-elm.com
W: www.great-elm.com

Great Elm Physick Garden's award winning organic skincare uses the power of herbs and plants from the traditional English country garden to heal, nourish and nurture your skin. In their organic garden in Somerset they grow as many of their ingredients as possible. What they cannot grow, they source very carefully and as ethically and locally as is feasible so as to preserve natural goodness and save transport miles. The physicks are based on the old herbalists' principle of 'simples': use the best ingredients you can find and the fewest possible; each in sufficient quantity to do its job. They do not use lanolin, petrochemicals, synthetic colourants or chemical preservatives or any other 'skin nasties'. They test only on willing human beings.

Green People Company

Pondtail Farm, Coolham Road, West Grinstead,
West Sussex RH13 8LN

T: 01403 740 350
E: organic@greenpeople.co.uk
W: www.greenpeople.co.uk

Manufacturers and suppliers of organic health and
beauty products for all the family, ranging from
baby products to shampoos, sun lotions and a
herbal cleansing/detox tonic. Does not use sodium
lauryl sulphate, parabens, ethyl alcohol or any
unnecessary synthetic additives. Does use 100 per
cent pure, gentle ingredients, including organic
plant oils, organic herbal infusions and essential
oils. 10 per cent of profits are donated to charity.
Registered or certified by the Vegan Society, the
Soil Association and the Organic Food Federation.
Recommended by Good Shopping Guide and
Ethical Consumer. Call for further information and
a free catalogue.

iloveorganics

13 Wainwrights Yard, Kendal,
Cumbria LA9 4DP

T: 01539 721 100
E: info@iloveorganics.co.uk
W: www.iloveorganics.co.uk

The very best in organic and natural health and
beauty products, including names such as Dr.
Hauschka, REN skincare, Organic Pharmacy, Green
People, Jason, Lavera and many more. Also runs an
organic beauty salon with cutting edge organic
treatments and holistic therapies.

Inika Cosmetics

PO Box 1382, Kingston-Upon-Thames KT1 9JB
T: 0845 450 664
E: info@inikacosmetics.co.uk
W: www.inikacosmetics.co.uk

Inika is an Australian brand with a mission to
introduce the world to a new era of cosmetics, one
where you don't have to compromise colour and
performance to be kind to your skin and gentle to
the earth. They capture Mother Nature's richest
and most flamboyant hues to create make up made
with crushed minerals from the earth. They
guarantee never to use harsh chemicals, bismuth
oxychloride, parabens, talc, fragrance or GM
ingredients. The boxes, paper stock and brochures
are made from recycled or sustainable forestry
stock. Carbon emissions on staff and product travel
and transport overseas are offset. The cosmetics
and brushes are all certified vegan and cruelty free.

Jo Wood Organics

2nd Floor Godfree Court, 29 Long Lane,
London SE1 4PL

T: 0845 607 6614
E: info@jowoodorganics.com
W: www.jowoodorganics.com

Combining glamour, rock 'n roll and a healthy
organic lifestyle was never going to be easy, but for
ex-model Jo Wood, wife of Rolling Stones guitarist
and artist Ronnie Wood, it was a choice 18 years
ago that was to define her as a pioneer and
committed supporter of all things natural and
organic. Following the successful international
launch of her first organic body care range Jo Wood
Organics in 2005, Jo has now turned her attention
to the mainstream market with her second range,
Everyday. A range of affordable and widely
accessible organic beauty products, Everyday is
designed to be used and enjoyed 'everyday'. The
range includes an exfoliating salt scrub, cleansing
body mousse and nourishing body cream in two
new fragrances, Tula and Langa. Officially certified
organic by ECOCERT, each product within the range
contains 99 per cent natural ingredients from
accredited and audited sources.

Jurlique

Holly House, 300-302 Chiswick High Road,
London W4 1NP

T: 0870 7700 980
E: sales@jurlique.co.uk
W: www.jurlique.co.uk

An alternative beauty company, tending and
sustaining the earth on its certified organic and
biodynamic farms where the company has been
growing herbs and flowers for over 20 years.
Jurlique's ethos is that beauty emerges from
naturally-balanced skin and that the environment
and the seasons challenge our skin's ability to
maintain balance. The products provide a natural
rebalancing solution for every skin by combining the
living energy of specially selected plants to treat
oiliness, dryness and sensitivity and so maintain a
natural balance. Available online and at Jurlique Day
Spa, SpaceNK, Selfridges, Whole Foods, Fresh & Wild
and Planet Organic.

Lavera

Conchieton Business Centre, Kirkcudbright,
Dumfries & Galloway DG6 4TA

T: 01557 870 567
E: info@lavera.co.uk
W: www.lavera.co.uk

Lavera offers over 230 natural and organic body
care products, suitable for all the family and all skin
types. They haven't just stopped using parabens,

nor petroleum, nor synthetic aromas, nor synthetic preservatives because they have never used them in the 20 years they have been producing genuinely natural body care products. Neither have they ever tested on animals – they use real people for their tests! Find their quality but sensibly priced ranges in good health food and organic shops or visit the website.

LoveLula.com

Ellament Limited, Unit 6e, Barrowmore Enterprise Estate, Great Barrow, Chester, Cheshire CH3 7JS

T: *0870 242 6995*

E: *lula@lovelula.com*

W: *www.lovelula.com*

An organic skincare and beauty specialist, this organic apothecary is certified by the Soil Association and all of the 500 hand-picked skincare, beauty and cosmetic products are free from SLS, parabens and petrochemicals. Choose from well known brands such as Lavera, Spiezia, Balm Balm and Trilogy or exclusive organic brands such as Kimberly Sayer, Alquimia and Bod.

Lucy Rose

PO Box 136, Ross-on-Wye, Herefordshire HR9 7LE

T: *01989 750 354*

E: *sarah@lucyrose.biz*

W: *www.lucyrose.biz*

Organic and natural beauty products without parabens, petrochemicals, synthetic fragrances, SLS/SLES or any other harmful ingredients. Certified organic and approved by the Vegetarian and Vegan Societies and offering free postage and packaging on all orders. Lucy Rose is a family run business which was formed in 2006 and is named after the owners' two daughters. Like many people they became increasingly aware of how their everyday lifestyle and the products they used were having a negative effect on the environment and their health. So they decided to set about the task of finding kinder, safer and more environmentally aware products which were affordable and still made them feel great. They created Lucy Rose to share these natural and organic products and help protect our precious planet for all our children and future generations.

Mandala Aroma Organics

14 Chapel Street, Chorley, Lancashire PR6 8QD

T: *01254 831 629*

E: *sales@mandala-aroma.com*

W: *www.mandala-aroma.com*

A range of organic products for bath, body and home, with no SLS, parabens, colourings, synthetics, and not tested on animals, just made with love and care in the UK with organic ingredients by qualified aromatherapist Gillian Kavanagh. Also supplies natural wax candles with essential oils to create a romantic room.

Neal's Yard Remedies

Head Office, Peacemarsh, Gillingham, Dorset SP8 4EU

T: *01747 834 634*

E: *mail@nealsyardremedies.com*

W: *www.nealsyardremedies.com*

Manufactures and retails a complete range of high quality toiletries based on pure essential oils and organically grown herbs. Also supplies certified organic essential oils and a complete range of natural medicines. Has an organic, non-GMO ingredient and minimal packaging policy.

No Cows

45 Betham Road, Greenford, Middlesex UB6 8SA

T: *07806 702 758*

E: *info@nocows.com*

W: *www.nocows.com*

An online ethical shopping brand which was established to offer a fabulous yet ethical shopping experience for consumers with products specially selected because they are great to own and use, but are also all animal and cruelty free, organic wherever possible and have minimum impact on the environment. Offers cosmetics, soy wax candles and organic wines, all of which are registered with the UK Vegan Society.

Organic Botanics

PO Box 5043, Brighton, East Sussex BN50 9LR

T: *01273 573 825*

E: *info@organicbotanics.com*

W: *www.organicbotanics.com*

A gorgeous range of vegetarian organic skin care, baby care and ointments made with certified organic ingredients including unrefined cold-pressed oils which are highly nutritious and have anti-ageing properties. The entire range is cruelty free and paraben free and is approved by The Vegetarian Society. Many products are approved by The Vegan Society and The Soil Association. Made in the UK.

Pai

PO Box 54147, London W5 2EQ

T: *020 7193 3607*

E: *info@paiskincare.com*

W: *www.paiskincare.com*

Pai is a luxury organic skincare range that comes

beautifully packaged. Pai products are made from Soil Association-certified organic ingredients and are chemical free. They are hand-mixed in small batches and are so fresh a 'Best Before' date is stamped on every bottle. Pai was recently rated the No.1 organic skincare product in Grazia magazine and has received other glowing reviews in The Sunday Times, Telegraph Magazine, Daily Express, Tatler, Marie-Claire and Organic Life. Pai products are available to buy online and through selected stockists.

Peachykeen

4th Floor, 59 Piccadilly, Manchester M1 2AQ
T: 0845 070 7282
E: info@peachykeenorganics.co.uk
W: www.peachykeenorganics.co.uk

Peachykeen make natural products for an organic lifestyle. They love creating natural skin care using organic ingredients and their motto is 'keep it simple' so you'll find everything natural and nothing synthetic. The products are made by hand and with care, and use minimum packaging, fair trade ingredients when possible, and locally grown and extracted essential oils.

Raw Gaia

8 Southdown Place, Brighton,
East Sussex BN1 6FP
T: 01273 311 476
E: info@rawgaia.com
W: www.rawgaia.com

Raw Gaia is the world's first range of living skin care products made using only cold-pressed, organic and vegan ingredients, infused with essential oils and floral waters of the finest quality. The products have skin moisturising and uplifting qualities because they are absolutely pure, alive and made with the Earth's most nourishing and beautifying skin care ingredients, which are far more effective than any chemical or artificial moisturisers. Handmade through a special low temperature process, Raw Gaia's skin care products retain the antioxidants, vitamins, minerals and essential fatty acids of the ingredients, which help to moisturise, heal and revitalise all types of skin. The ingredients are organic, vegan, cruelty- and chemical free, and as much as possible, fair trade.

Simply Soaps & Hedgerow Herbals

PO Box 331, Salhouse, Norwich,
Norfolk NR13 6LP
T: 01603 720 869
E: enquiries2@simplysoaps.com
W: www.simplysoaps.com &
www.hedgerowherbals.com

A skincare and body care company set up in answer

to the growing number of people who want to know what it is they are putting on their skin. The company aims to create the finest soap in the world with a philosophy of producing beautiful soaps with honesty and integrity, maintaining quality by sourcing the finest ingredients from around the world and, where possible, using organics. Products are handmade using traditional methods, which means the glycerine remains in the soap and not extracted as a lucrative by-product. Caters for vegetarians and vegans and uses a low energy manufacturing process. Online mail order for retail and wholesale deliveries worldwide.

Skincare Café

8 High Street, Windsor SL4 1LD
T: 0870 443 2744
E: customercomments @skincarecafe.com
W: www.skincarecafe.com

Supplies organic products that are specially formulated using a unique blend of plants, vitamins and pure organic essential oils. All products are made by hand in the UK, and effective in helping restore your skin's natural balance and radiance. Certified organic, and Vegan and Vegetarian Society-registered, these products are not tested on animals. They are 100 per cent free from nasty chemicals including synthetic perfumes and colourants.

Sorrells Naturally

26 Uplands Way, Winchmore Hill,
London N21 1DT
T: 020 8360 7427
E: shop@sorrellsnaturally.co.uk
W: www.sorrellsnaturally.co.uk

Provides unique hand-blended, natural, organic and wild-crafted body and bath products, all made in the UK. A family run business dedicated to discovering and sharing the countryside's most naturally-made bath and body products. They sell beautifully made soaps, facial creams and serum, facial oils, hand creams and body butters, as well as shampoo and conditioners, naturally made linen and bamboo towels, and crystal deodorants. The range is increasing as they discover more and more of what the UK has to offer!

Spiezia Organics Ltd

Gear Farm, St Martin, Helston,
Cornwall GR12 6DE
T: 0870 850 8851
E: info@spieziaorganics.com
W: www.spieziaorganics.com

One of the first cosmetics company in the UK to have Soil Association-certification. The products are made on an organic farm in Cornwall under the strict criteria laid down by the Soil Association. There are absolutly no chemicals in any of the products, nor any added water and their unique production methods use only the preservatives that occur naturally in the herbs and oils. The products are not tested on animals and are suitable for vegetarians. All the packaging is recyclable, and the production methods are environmentally friendly.

Suvarna

31 Heversham, Skelmersdale,
Lancashire WN8 6QQ

T: 01695 728 286

E: info@suvarna.co.uk

W: www.suvarna.co.uk

Offers a wide range of quality organic cosmetics, including their own brand skincare range which is made by hand from mostly organic plant oils, herbal extracts and pure essential oils. Also sells a range of very pure, BDIH certified cosmetics from Logona, Sante and Weleda, including organic skincare, organic makeup, organic shampoo, organic hair dyes, and oral hygiene. All the cosmetics contain certified organic ingredients wherever possible, and are free of GMOs, parabens, artificial perfume or colour, mineral oils and waxes, formaldehyde and phthalates.

Tær Icelandic

Pure Icelandic Ltd, 10 John Street,
London WC1N 2EB

T: 01753 759 720

E: info@taer.com

W: www.taer.com

Tær, meaning pure in Icelandic, is a natural, luxury skincare range. The unique blends combine ancient wisdom with modern cosmetic science, and are bursting with active ingredients including potent Icelandic organic herbs, essential oils, powerful sources of vitamins and minerals and the very latest humectants. Brides-to-be can feel truly pampered and enjoy the benefits of purer, more luminous skin with this range of skin and body care. The beautiful, recyclable, pastel coloured glassware make it an ideal gift for any new bride. Honeymoon skin can be kept in prime condition with the new Tær Icelandic Essential Travel Kit.

Visionary Soap Company

32 St. Thomas' Road, Hastings,
East Sussex TN34 3LQ

T: 01424 460 022

E: info@visionarysoap.co.uk

W: www.visionarysoap.co.uk

The UK's only fair trade-dedicated body care

company which handcrafts its own range of soaps and body care products. All products are free from synthetic perfumes and dyes, petrochemicals, sodium laureth sulfate, parabens, alcohol and animal ingredients. The company sources its ingredients and accessories from a combination of Fairtrade Foundation UK, BAFTS and IFAT certified producers in Palestine, Madagascar, The Comoros, Ghana, Bali, The Philippines, India and Sri Lanka. All products are also organic and certified by the Vegan Society. The vision of the company is to produce the finest quality natural products whilst also incorporating their values of social responsibility, environmental sustainability and holistic wellbeing.

Weleda (UK) Ltd

Heanor Road, Ilkeston, Derbyshire DE7 8DR

T: 0115 944 8200

E: info@weleda.co.uk

W: www.weleda.co.uk

Skin and hair care products, toothpaste, sun protection and aftershave sold through health food stores and chemists. Call for details of your local stockists.

WuChi by Maks

24 Ambler Road, London N4 2QU

T: 0870 413 2685

E: info@wuchi.co.uk

W: www.wuchi.co.uk

WuChi is a range of luxury handmade, natural and organic skincare products designed to create a home spa experience. Using a heady mix of essential oils and active plant extracts, Wuchi aims to make your bathing ritual a therapeutic and rewarding experience.

You're Gorgeous Handmade Soap

1 The Cottage, Tan y Bryn, Bryn Pydew Road,
Llandudno Junction LL31 9JZ

T: 01492 543 394

E: mail@youre-gorgeous.co.uk

W: www.youre-gorgeous.co.uk

Supplies luxury soaps that are created entirely by hand in North Wales using fine natural ingredients from all over the world and the cold process soapmaking method which retains all the natural skin conditioning glycerine normally removed from commercial soaps. The soaps are made with plant oils and extracts, botanicals, organic ingredients, aromatherapy blends and essential oils and then hand cut, finished and wrapped.

Bulldog Natural Grooming

E: *thebulldog@meetthebulldog.com*
W: *www.meetthebulldog.com*

Bulldog's grooming products are perfect for helping the groom, the best man, and the father of the bride to look and feel great for the big day. As the first mainstream natural male grooming range, Bulldog's natural formulations are industry leading. Each product is packed with at least seven essential oils and a host of amazing natural ingredients. None of the products contain parabens, sodium laureth sulfate, artificial colours and synthetic fragrances. The prices (ranging from £2.99 to £5.99) make the range easily accessible to all. In 2007 Bulldog won Pure Beauty Magazines' award for Best Male Grooming Launch of the year. Bulldog is also the official grooming supplier to the London Wasps Rugby Union team. Available nationwide in Sainsbury's, Debenhams, and other selected stores.

Male Organics Ltd

15 Holywell Row, London EC2A 4JB
T: *020 7684 5471*
E: *hello@male-organics.com*
W: *www.male-organics.com*

The UK's one-stop shop for men's natural and organic grooming products, helping blokes live in a more chemical free, sustainable and eco friendly way. The aim is to raise awareness about the chemicals in everyday grooming products and to let you know that there is an alternative which is better for you and the environment. Having had difficulty in finding a dedicated organic webshop for men on the internet, they've created their own.

Titanic Spa

Low Westwood Lane, Linthwaite, Huddersfield HD7 5UN
T: *0845 410 3333*
E: *enquiries@titanicspa.com*
W: *www.titanicspa.co.uk*

Titanic Spa, the UK's first eco spa, has been created within a traditional textile mill. Favoured for its seclusion on the edge of the Pennines, this intimate spa has gone beyond the organic philosophy, offering exceptional results-driven spa treatments, creating spa therapies that work in natural synergy with skin, body and mind. Spa breaks start at £99 per person.

Dolma Vegan Perfumes

19 Royce Avenue, Hucknall, Nottingham, Nottinghamshire NG15 6FU
T: *0115 963 4237*
E: *info@dolma-perfumes.co.uk*
W: *www.dolma-perfumes.co.uk*

Entirely vegan, BUAV and Vegan Society-approved company producing an exclusive range of vegan perfumes, aftershaves, skin care and toiletries based on pure essential oils, herbal extracts and floral waters. Does not use any animal-derived materials and neither the products nor the materials from which they are made are tested on animals. The fixed cut-off date of 1976 applies. Send SAE (1st class stamp) for free mail order catalogue. The set of eleven trial-sized perfumes at £21.00 (postage paid) makes an ideal gift. Cheques/postal orders should be made payable to Dolma.

Enata Bespoke Perfume

PO Box 830A, Thames Ditton, Surrey KT1 9BB
T: *020 8339 0696*
E: *info@enata.co.uk*
W: *www.enata.co.uk*

Passionate about fragrance, Enata supply everything you could want to fragrance your self, your home and your life. The products are all made by hand in small batches with care. Packaging is exquisite, unique and personal. Your sense of smell is uniquely personal and fragrances to a perfumer are like colours to an artist, capable of reflecting and enhancing mood and style.

Janita Haan – Natural Perfume

Long Barn, Felindre, Brecon, Powys LD3 0TE
T: *01497 847 788*
E: *janita@janitahaan.com*

Inspired by the beautiful essences found all over the world and honouring ancient perfumery practices, Janita creates perfumes redolent with flowers, spices, resins and seeds from land and sea. Single note solid perfumes are offered in beautiful, hand painted ceramic, silver or shell containers – an exquisite way to enjoy subtle nuances such as jasmine, mimosa, boronia, rose and narcissus. There is also an exclusive range of eco packaged, traditional, boxed, milled and naturally dyed perfumed soaps. Choose from wood, floral, fruit, herb and incense. A member of the Natural Perfumers Guild, Janita provides a personalised service for those looking for a unique and individual scent with their own signature perfume.

THE CATERING

Eco Cuisine

Penlee, 4 Hedge Lane, Palmers Green,
London N13 5SH

T: 020 8882 0350

W: www.eco-cuisine.co.uk

Using organic, free-range, sustainable, non-GM and British produce, Eco Cuisine caters for private and corporate clients. From dinner for two to a party for 200, each event is sourced individually to give you confidence in where your food comes from. Has become carbon neutral in 2008 and can also now offer clients 100 per cent recycled, compostable and edible crockery, trays and drinking cups from sustainable and renewable sources.

Organic Buffet

18 Benson Close, Reading, Berkshire RG2 7LP

T: 0118 9524 799

E: vincent@organicbuffet.co.uk

W: www.organicbuffet.co.uk

Organic Buffet is registered to the Soil Association foodservice and catering code of practice and specialises in corporate and private events and weddings. They have had a real success with the start of their organic hog roast and organic spit roast, alongside buffet menu.

Passion Organic

177 Ferndale Road, London SW9 8BA

T: 020 7501 9933

E: info@passionorganic.com

W: www.passionorganic.com

Soil Association-accredited organic catering service, providing delicious, nutritious, quality organic food and drink for events, conferences and special occasions. Supports local producers and purchases organic fair trade products whenever possible. Also provides venue sourcing and styling services, deli lunches and breakfast, and in the summer season, barbecue parties using sustainable charcoal and the finest organic meats. The chefs recycle and compost as much as possible and the company also supports a carbon neutral tree planting scheme in Mexico.

The Green Kitchen

46 Springwood Drive, Braintree, Essex CM7 2YN

T: 01376 553 096

E: hello@thegreen-kitchen.co.uk

W: www.thegreen-kitchen.co.uk

An organic and wholefood catering company delivering a diverse range of fresh, homemade food for birthdays, celebrations, weddings, funerals, children's parties, picnics and corporate events. Can create bespoke menus to suit the occasion whilst balancing flavour and artistry with good health and 'well-bellies' in mind, serving alternatives for food allergies and specific diets. All ingredients are seasonal, natural and unprocessed. To tread lightly on the earth the kitchen is supplied by registered organic farmers from the local area and they work hard to recycle and compost all waste produced. The Green Kitchen also attends farmers markets in Essex and surrounding areas with a unique range of foods, including vegan and gluten free products.

Veg-Out

Brockmead, Littlington, East Sussex BN27 1HY

T: 01323 871 619

E: info@veg-out-sussex.com

W: www.veg-out-sussex.com

Exclusively vegetarian and vegan caterers and function organisers for all occasions. The service is designed to meet their clients personal requirements, whether catering for a small group of people or a larger event where they deal with all the organisation. The chefs have trained at the prestigious Cordon Vert cookery school of the Vegetarian Society and can cater for special diets. Menus are as imaginative as you wish – from canapes to wedding breakfasts, from buffet lunches to sit-down meals – they can suggest and recommend dishes to suit most requirements including vegan, gluten free and sugar free. Their experienced events organiser can help with such things as venue location, room decorations, gifts, flowers, entertainment, photographers and specialist cakes.

Angus Organics

Airlie Estate Office, Cortachy, Kirriemuir,
Angus DD8 4LY

T: 01307 860 737

E: sales@angusorganics.com

W: www.angusorganics.com

Established in 1998, this was the first organic farm in Angus, situated on the Airlie Estates, a family run estate since the 14th-century. The commitment is to produce the highest quality Aberdeen Angus beef within a mixed organic farm, and to concentrate all efforts on traditional methods of production. During the summer the home-bred cattle are grazed on clover-rich organic grass in the foothills of the magnificent Angus Glen and organic cereals and grass silage in the Winter. Conservation is a very important aspect of the estate: buildings are maintained using traditional materials, controlled heather burning is carried out, deer numbers are kept to a sustainable level and a fly-only policy is adopted on the rivers South Esk and Prosen.

Fletchers of Auchtermuchty

Reediehill, Auchtermuchty, Fife KY14 7HS
T: 0800 083 6476
E: fletchers.scotland@virgin.net
W: www.seriouslygoodvenison.co.uk

30 years' experience means seriously good venison. Nominations for Slow Food Awards, BBC Food & Farming Awards, and Local Food Hero Awards speak for themselves. Their deer are free-ranging, fed naturally, and field shot for perfect, stress free venison. They offer traditional hanging of carcasses, a Master butcher, additive and wheat free products, and free cooking advice. Order by phone or online. Also sells from their farm shop and farmers' markets.

Gilcombe Farm Shop

Gilcombe Farm, Bruton, Somerset BA10 0QE
T: 01749 813 825
E: info@gilcombefarm.com
W: www.gilcombefarm.com

The UK's largest supplier of rare breed organic meats offering a 24-hour delivery service. All the animals are from family farms in the West Country and include Tamworth & Berkshire Pork, Hebridean Lamb, Aberdeen Angus/Longhorn Cattle. Nationwide delivery of just £7.50 per order over £40. For any orders under £40 the delivery charge is £10. Also runs a farm shop, open Monday-Saturday.

Graig Farm Organics

Dolau, Llandrindod Wells, Powys LD1 5TL
T: 01597 851 655
E: sales@graigfarm.co.uk
W: www.graigfarm.co.uk

From the heart of mid-Wales, Graig Farm Organics, the winners or finalists of Organic Food Awards every year since 1993, offers probably the widest range of organic meats and other produce by mail order. The range includes all the usual meats, as well as specialities such as Welsh Mountain mutton and lamb, wild and organic farmed fish and award-winning ready meals. The mail order range also includes groceries, fruit and vegetables, alcohol, books and skin care. Working with a group of organic farmers, they have complete traceability on each piece of meat. A unique labelling system enables the consumer to see the farm and breed of animal on each pack. Also available from their farm shop and selected retail outlets nationwide, as well as online.

Hawkshead Organic Trout

The Boathouse, Hawkshead, Cumbria LA22 0QF
T: 015394 36541
E: trout@hawkshead.demon.co.uk
W: www.hawksheadtrout.com

Grown to Soil Association standard, with no artificial colour, these lake trout are supplied nationwide, whole, filleted, fresh or smoked, to retailers, box schemes, mail order companies and caterers. Also supplies organic salmon steaks and fillets and smoked salmon. Operates an environmental action and animal welfare plan.

Heal Farm Meats

Kings Nympton, Umberleigh, Devon EX37 9TB
T: 01769 574 341
E: enquiries@healfarm.co.uk
W: www.healfarm.co.uk

Heal Farm Meats pioneered the high welfare production of meat animals, reared without additives, over 30 years ago out of a strongly held conviction that intensive farming with its heavy reliance on chemicals could not be justified. At the time it was a revolutionary concept, but recent food scares have proved them right. Convictions are still as strong today and Heal Farm are proud to have been influential in shaping attitudes towards responsible meat eating. Meat available from old-fashioned breeds, including hams, sausages and poultry, ready-cooked recipe dishes, multi-bird roasts and seasonal specialities such as mutton, homemade desserts and cakes, local cheeses and much more are all supplied by mail order nationwide.

Heritage Prime

Foxholes Farm, Little Bredy,
Dorchester, Dorset DT2 9HJ
T: 01308 482 688
E: heritageprime@aol.com
W: www.HeritagePrime.co.uk

Biodynamic rearing and production of meats to Demeter standards and nationwide mail order of pork, lamb, beef, and occasionally poultry. Specialises in the purity of meat with the finest eating quality, consistently. Pioneers in homoeopathy for livestock.

House of Rhug

Rhug Estate Office, Corwen,
Denbighshire LL21 0EH
T: 01490 413 000
E: philiphughes@rhug.co.uk
W: www.rhug.co.uk

Soil Association-registered organic café, farm butchery and shop selling a range of produce including the farm's award-winning meat. Operates a national mail order service for the farm shop goods including organic meat and pies, which are all produced to the highest quality and welfare standards. Also supplies bronze organic Christmas turkeys.

Jolly's Fish and Farm Produce

Scotts Road, Hatston, Kirkwall,
Orkney KW15 1GR

T: 01856 872 417
E: info@jollyfish.co.uk
W: www.jollyfish.co.uk

Suppliers of superb organic grass-fed beef and lamb, and organic sausages, bacon, and pork, all from their own Orkney farm, and also fish, including organic salmon and organic gravadlax. They smoke salmon, mackerel, and kippers over oak in a traditional kiln. All the products are available by nationwide mail order, their shop, and via a monthly box scheme. They describe their Kirkwall shop, with its great range of local foods, as being 'like a farmer's market everyday'.

Loch Fyne Oysters

Clachan, Cairndow, Argyll PA26 8BL

T: 01499 600 264
E: info@lochfyne.com
W: www.lochfyne.com

Based in Argyll, at the head of Loch Fyne, the longest sea loch in Scotland. The original Loch Fyne oyster bar, shop and smokehouse are housed in a former cattle byre beside the Inveraray Road. A mile across the water at Ardkinglas lies the mussel and oyster fishery. From here Loch Fyne Oysters specialises in producing and supplying quality fresh and smoked seafood, shellfish, meat and game to individual and trade customers around the world and to the Loch Fyne restaurants throughout the UK. The business is based on enterprise with respect for animals, people and ecology. They are committed to independent producers using sustainable methods to produce high quality foods. The salmon is carefully sourced from Freedom Food-accredited or organic fisheries. 3 per cent of the value of all home delivery orders is donated to the Loch Fyne Trust to protect the marine life of Loch Fyne and its coastal communities.

Sheepdrove Organic Farm

Warren Farm, Lambourn, Berkshire RG17 7UU

T: 01488 674 747
E: sales@sheepdrove.com
W: www.sheepdrove.com

Poultry, beef, lamb, mutton and pork are reared on the farm and processed to high standards in terms of welfare and meat quality. Soil Association-registered.

Swaddles Organic

Royal Oak, Daventry,
Northamptonshire NN11 8QY

T: 0845 456 1768
E: info@swaddles.co.uk
W: www.swaddles.co.uk

One of the pioneers of organic home delivery of meat and meat products, winning numerous awards for a variety of products and committed to maintaining both total organic integrity and excellence of product. Offers a huge range of organic produce, including simple cuts of meat, special dinner party joints, ready cooked meals, pies, sausages, bacon (without nitriates & nitrites), dairy produce, groceries and fruit juices to customers throughout the UK.

Groceries & Provisions

Abel & Cole

16 Waterside Way, Wimbledon, London,
London SW17 0HB

T: 0845 262 62 62
E: organics@abelandcole.co.uk
W: www.abelandcole.co.uk

Abel & Cole deliver boxes of delicious, fresh organic fruit and vegetables, organic meat, sustainably sourced fish and loads of other ethically produced foods. They deliver to most of the UK. The company thinks carefully about everything they do: buying as much as possible from UK farms, and ensuring all their growers get a fair price, so taking care of the environment and giving customers a fantastic, friendly service.

BigBarn

College Farm, Great Barford, Bedford,
Bedfordshire MK44 3JJ

T: 01234 871 005
E: matt@bigbarn.co.uk
W: www.bigbarn.co.uk

The virtual Farmers' Market to help you find and buy fresh local produce. Simply visit www.bigbarn.co.uk and type in your postcode to see a map of your local area showing different icons, each representing a producer and the type of goods they sell with further information attached. BigBarn and its 6,500 producers want to make buying local more convenient and get a local food section in every supermarket where the farmers get 75 per cent of the retail price. To help this happen register and you will be emailed occasional special offers from your local producers and local 'foody' news in BigBarn's post code specific newsletter.

Daily Bread Co-Operative Ltd
The Old Laundry, Bedford Road, Northampton,
Northamptonshire NN4 7AD
T: *01604 621 531*
E: *orders@dailybread.co.uk*
W: *www.dailybread.co.uk*
One of the biggest suppliers of wholefoods and
related products to the public in the UK with over
2,000 products from beans to herbal remedies.
Runs a mail order service and an online store
offering nationwide delivery to the UK.

Daylesford Organic Home Delivery
Unit 14 Threshers Yard, West Street, Kingham,
Oxfordshire OX7 6YF
T: *0800 083 1233*
E: *mailorder@daylesfordorganic.com*
W: *www.daylesfordorganic.com*
Specialises in what is organic, fresh, seasonal and
local: vegetables, fresh from their kitchen gardens;
award winning handmade cheeses from their
organic creamery; breads, pastries, cakes and
biscuits from their organic bakery; foods from the
chefs in their kitchens; fresh meat from their
organic estate in Staffordshire. Visitors to the farm
shop, where you will find everything under one
roof, can also dine at the restaurant and café. There
are several other outlets in London.

Ethical Food Company
Units 4-5 Verney Junction Business Park,
Verney Junction, Buckingham,
Buckinghamshire MK18 2LB
T: *01296 733 737*
E: *enquiries@ethicalfoods.co.uk*
W: *www.ethicalfoods.co.uk*
Online food and grocery supplier, delivering
nationwide. Supplies organic, local, fair trade and
animal welfare farmed sustainable food and drink,
with online and telephone ordering.

Everybody Organic
26-27 Caxton Hill, Hertford,
Hertfordshire SG13 7NE
T: *0845 345 5054*
E: *everybody@everybodyorganic.com*
W: *www.everybodyorganic.com*
Delivery of organic fruit, vegetables, and groceries
direct to your door, offering a convenient and
ethical way to shop. Order as little as £6.50 with
free delivery. Go to the website and enter your
postcode to find out the day they deliver to your
area, or call for help putting your order together.
Delivery nationwide.

GoodnessDirect
South March, Daventry,
Northamptonshire NN11 4PH
T: *0871 871 6611*
E: *info@goodnessdirect.co.uk*
W: *www.goodnessdirect.co.uk*
Healthy shopping made easy, with thousands of
ecologically sound products to choose from, and
delivery throughout the UK. Supplies
environmentally friendly household products,
cruelty free cosmetics, vegetarian and vegan foods,
organic foods of every kind, seafresh fish, foods for
special diets and so much more. It's worth taking a
look at their website.

Loch Arthur Creamery
Camphill Village Trust, Beeswing,
Dumfries DG2 8JQ
T: *01387 760 296*
E: *creamery@locharthur.org.uk*
W: *www.locharthur.org.uk*
Part of the Camphill Village Trust which
encompasses several communities whose life and
work incorporate adults with special needs. The work
at Loch Arthur centres around the agricultural life of
the community with 450 acres farmed under
Demeter certification and produces organic dairy
foods including hard and soft cheeses, yoghurts,
cream cheese and butter. Also sells organic meat,
fruit, vegetables and bakery products plus an
extensive range of local and organic foods from their
own farm shop. National mail order service available.

Natoora
London SW8 4AS
T: *020 7627 1600*
E: *contact@natoora.co.uk*
W: *www.natoora.co.uk*
Natoora is an online service for some of the best
and freshest local, French and Italian food and
supports 150 farmers across Britain, France and
Italy. Delivery across Britain six days a week during
selected time slots. Products include fruit,
vegetables, charcuterie, cheese, meat, fish and
bread – and some are organic.

Organic Connections International
Riverdale, Town Street, Upwell, Wisbech,
Cambridgeshire PE14 9AF
T: *01945 773 374*
E: *sales@organic-connections.co.uk*
W: *www.organic-connections.co.uk*
Organically grown fruit and vegetables delivered
direct to your door. Delivers free to CB and PE
postcodes, with other areas nationwide at a small

charge. The organic produce is supplied from their own farm or that of various selected local growers. Choose from a wide range of organic products, including fruit and vegetable boxes, pasta boxes, salad boxes, cheese, eggs, bread, groceries and much more. For organic growers, they also offer a complete marketing service to make the most of all your crop, supplying the complete range of fruit and vegetables to wholesalers, pre-packers, processors and other box schemes nationwide.

Planet Organic

42 Westbourne Grove,
London W2 5SH
T: 020 7727 2227
E: deliveries@planetorganic.com
W: www.planetorganic.com

The perfect place for those seeking everything for a healthy lifestyle with thousands of organic products: fresh fruit and vegetables, groceries, meat and fish, natural body care lines, vitamins, supplements and household cleaning products. The kitchens prepare daily seasonal dishes made from organic ingredients to eat in the in-store café or to take home. Also stocks an extensive range for those on special diets, sells books and magazines and runs a juice bar.

Westcountry Organics Ltd

Oak Farm, Tedburn St. Mary, Exeter,
Devon EX6 6AW
T: 01392 833 833
E: enquiries@westcountryorganics.com
W: www.westcountryorganics.co.uk
Nationwide delivery of organic vegetable boxes containing a wide range of seasonal and additional organic vegetables and fruit.

Tea, Coffee & Chocolate

Booja Booja Company, The

Howe Pit, Norwich Road, Brooke,
Norfolk NR15 1HJ
T: 01508 558 888
E: info@boojabooja.com
W: www.boojabooja.com
Manufacturer of delicious organic, dairy free confections such as chocolate truffles, Criollo cacao nibs and beans and a delicious alternative to dairy ice-cream called Stuff in a Tub. The entire range is free from gluten and wheat and is suitable for vegans and vegetarians. Winners of 29 awards including five Gold Great Taste Awards for the Chocolate truffles and most recently winners of the Best Organic Food Product 2007 for the new 'ice-cream', at The Natural and Organic Awards. Certified with the Soil Association and Vegan Society. Available in good independent wholefood shops, fine food retailers throughout the UK and never sold in supermarkets.

Chocolala Limited

W: www.chocolala.co.uk
Suppliers of fresh, fair trade chocolates, made and packed by hand so each tin has a quality that's special and personal. Also tries to work to their Quaker principles. In practical terms this means trying to make a quality product as well as they can, without ripping anyone off or dumping on the planet!

Coco Chocolate

174 Bruntsfield Place, Bruntsfield,
Edinburgh EH10 4ER
T: 0131 228 4526
E: info@cocochocolate.co.uk
W: www.cocochocolate.co.uk
Organic handmade chocolatier based in Edinburgh. Special events, including weddings, corporate events and chocolate tasting evenings, are warmly welcomed and catered for. They can create bespoke chocolates for special occasions or supply their best selling favourites. The range includes an

Aphrodisiac Collection and the Coco Siren Box – 18 of their best selling infusions in the one box, each adorned with its own beautiful cocoa butter artwork. New infusions include organic dark chocolate with lime and coconut, organic milk chocolate with caramel, seasalt and pinenut, and organic white hot chocolate infused with cardamom and cinnamon.

Divine Chocolate

4 Gainsford Street, London SE1 2NE
T: 020 7378 6550
E: info@divinechocolate.com
W: www.divinechocolate.com;
www.dubble.co.uk
Purveyors of the leading UK fair trade chocolate brands Divine and Dubble. Divine now comes in six flavours: milk, dark, white, hazelnut, orange and coffee, and also Divine Cocoa and Drinking Chocolate. Divine After Dinner Mints and Divine Delights are wonderful gifts whilst seasonal offerings include Advent Calendars and Easter eggs. Available in Co-op, Tesco, Sainsbury's, Asda and Waitrose, plus Oxfam and many independent stores. Dubble is at Sainsbury's and Oxfam and Dubble Easter Eggs at Tesco and Oxfam.

Montezuma's Chocolates

Birdham Business Park, Birdham Road,
Chichester PO20 7BT
T: 0845 450 6304
E: simon.pattinson@montezumas.co.uk
W: www.montezumas.co.uk
At Montezuma's they take great satisfaction in the accolades and acclaim they have received in the few years since the company was founded. They pride themselves as the most innovative chocolate maker in the UK with a reputation far wider than their Southern roots and a handful of shops, and they aren't shy about thrusting into the limelight to shout about their principles. These principles haven't been bolted on or constructed to join a bandwagon. They are really passionate about their impact on the planet and that means the environment, their partners, their customers, and, of course, the societies they touch.

Natural Coffee Company, The

Arabica House, Ebberns Road, Hemel
Hempstead, Hertfordshire HP3 9RD
T: 01442 256 625
E: sales@naturalcoffee.co.uk
W: www.naturalcoffee.co.uk
Coffee roasters of speciality coffees, stocking twelve fair trade and Soil Association-certified organic retail blends. Also roasts organic coffees

for the catering trade. Coffees hand packed to order. The range of coffees include blends for a specific usage – filter, cafetiere and espresso, and specific origins, from Colombia, Costa Rica, Peru, Sumatra, Ethiopia and Papua New Guinea. The Swiss Water Process decaffeinated from Sumatra is an excellent coffee meeting all ethical and Kosha certifications. Also supplies coffee from Guatemala and El Salvador in the Rainforest Alliance range. Also has a new line in natural tea which is organic and fair trade. They are always pleased to discuss their range of ancillary products including coffee machines, sugars, cups and speciality hampers.

Origin Coffee

Trewardreva Mill, Constantine, Falmouth, Cornwall TR11 5QD

T: 01326 340 320

E: info@origincoffee.co.uk

W: www.origincoffee.co.uk

It's all about a bean – 42 to be exact. Picked by hand, roasted to perfection. That's the essence of Origin. The important thing about Origin beans is that they know where they come from. They also know that the beans in their blends have been grown in a way that preserves and protects the natural environment and that benefits local communities and the farmers growing them. Based in Cornwall, Origin sell fair trade, organic or Rainforest Alliance-certified coffees, because only these make sense to them. They believe that any one of their coffees will be amongst the most flavoursome you have ever tasted, because, working with nature, without the chemicals and with a contented workforce tends to bring out the best in the bean! Origin also work closely with talented local artists and have produced a range of unusual coffee gifts including limited edition cup collections.

Tea & Coffee Plant, The

180 Portobello Road, London W11 2EB

T: 020 8453 1144

E: gateway@coffee.uk.com

W: www.coffee.uk.com

Coffee roasters, blenders and tea packers, supplying thirteen origins of organic coffee, most of which are also Fairtrade-certified, via mail order and online. Also runs a large wholesale business supplying organic restaurants and coffee bars, as well as own-label coffee packs to retailers such as Wholefoods. Particular favorites are House Blend or organic Italian Roast coffee, Ginzing organic herb teabags and their own organic breakfast teabags. Check the website for more details on the gourmet, Fairtrade and economy lines.

Cheese & Speciality Foods

Bath Soft Cheese

Park Farm, Kelston, Bath, Somerset BA1 9AG

T: 01225 331 601

E: bathsoftcheese@hotmail.com

W: www.parkfarm.co.uk

Makes a range of handmade hard and soft cheeses from their own herd of organic cows. Available by mail order. Also offers B&B in the farmhouse.

Caws Cenarth

Fferm Glyneithinog, Lancych, Boncath, Pembrokeshire SA37 0LH

T: 01239 710 432

E: sales@cawscenarth.co.uk

W: www.cawscenarth.co.uk

Soil Association-registered organic farmhouse cheeses available on the farm, via nationwide mail order and at local markets.

Fine Cheese Co, The

29 & 31 Walcot Street, Bath, Somerset BA1 5BN

T: 01225 448 748

E: sales@finecheese.co.uk

W: www.finecheese.co.uk

Specialist in artisan, unpasteurised cheeses including over a hundred from the British Isles. Offers a selection of wines, charcuterie, bread, pickles, preserves, olives and olive oil. Has a small range of organic products. Also runs a café.

Godminster Vintage

Godminster Farm, Bruton, Somerset BA10 0NE

T: 01749 813 733

E: sales@godminster.com

W: www.godminster.com

Godminster's dairy herd has been certified organic since 1999 and their milk is used in this unusually creamy vintage organic cheddar. The cheese is coated in a distinctive burgundy wax and is available in individual truckles that are round or heart shaped. The range now includes a beetroot and apple chutney, hand-baked cheddar crackers with rosemary or garlic and vodkas flavoured with fruits and roots from the farm. All of these items are available mail order or on the website.

Halzephron Herb Farm

62 Fore Street, St Ives, Cornwall TR26 1HW

T: 01736 791 891

E: orders@halzherb.com

W: www.halzherb.com

Cornish farm growing herbs free from pesticides and artificial growing agents. The herbs are sold dried or processed as marinades, sauces, dips and dressings. Also produces herb honey, a wonderfully aromatic mixture of Cornish honey and rosemary, and a range of herbal remedies. The products are available by mail order but, if you are in the area, the shop is well worth a visit.

Hambleden Herbs

Rushall Organic Farm, Devizes Road, Rushall, Wiltshire SN9 6ET

T: *01980 630 721*

E: *info@hambledenherbs.com*

W: *www.hambledenherbs.com*

Organic dried herb specialists, supplying over 300 culinary and medicinal herbs from an award-winning range of 130 organic herb based products, including delicious herb teas, a selection of herbal tinctures, infusions and over 60 culinary herbs and spices. Guaranteed free from artificial flavours, colours, preservatives or additives of any kind, the herbs are GM free and 100 per cent vegan.

Oil in the Raw

St Dominick, Saltash, Cornwall PL12 6TE

T: *01579 351 178*

E: *olive@oilintheraw.co.uk*

Supplies raw, unrefined, natural, unblended organic extra virgin olive oil from single estates and organic table olives direct from the Greek producer. Also wholesale in bulk or bottled.

Organic Smokehouse, The

Clunbury Hall, Clunbury, Nr Craven Arms, Shropshire SY7 0HG

T: *01588 660 206*

E: *info@organicsmokehouse.com*

W: *www.organicsmokehouse.com*

Soil Association-registered organic smokehouse for salmon, cheese and other foods. Organic Food Awards winner in 2003-4 and 2004-5. Products available from the farm, local farmers markets, fine food retailers and via mail order.

Steenbergs Organic Pepper & Spice

The Spice Factory, Unit 6 & 7 Hallikeld Close, Barker Business Park, Melmerby, Ripon, Yorkshire HG4 5GZ

T: *01765 640 088*

E: *enquiries@steenbergs.co.uk*

W: *www.steenbergs.co.uk*

Supplies organic spices, herbs, blends and peppers including organic saffron and vanilla. Many products are sourced direct for freshness and provenance. Has over 60 organic blends including curries, rubs and a range of organic and fair trade, flavoured sugars. Is a Fairtrade licencee for spices

with the UK's first spice range to carry the Fairtrade Mark. There are stockists around the UK and the products are also available online and via mail order. Bulk orders also accepted. Email newsletter and information available on website. Sister company Steenbergs Organic Tea (www.steenbergs-tea.com) supplies organic and fair trade loose leaf tea – sourced direct from tea estates in Sri Lanka and India. Chinese organic green and white teas also available. The products are certified by the Organic Food Federation.

Cakes

Cakes by Ann

6 Carron Court, Hamilton, Lanarkshire ML3 8TD

T: *01698 336 448*

E: *Info@cakesbyann.co.uk*

W: *www.cakesbyann.co.uk*

Wedding cakes and celebration cakes created using only the finest ingredients.

The Organic Chocolate Cake Company

The Lodge, Oxford Street, Kingsdown, Bristol BS2 8HH

T: *0117 9273 954*

E: *mail@toccc.co.uk*

W: *www.toccc.co.uk*

Founded in Bristol in 1985, the Organic chocolate Cake Company is the longest established organic cake maker in great Britain. Their secret recipe ensures a cake that is moist to the very edge, which is soaked in vintage character port, then layered with plum jam and buttercream. The premises are 100 per cent nut free, with ample off road parking. Viewings and tastings by appointment only.

Village Bakery Melmerby Ltd, The

Melmerby, Penrith, Cumbria CA10 1HE

T: *01768 898 437*

E: *info@village-bakery.com*

W: *www.village-bakery.com*

Natural good taste is the secret of The Village Bakery's organic success and it has made its reputation by swimming against the tide of the use of additives and preservatives in mass produced snack bars, breads and cakes. Instead it uses natural processes, artisan methods and interesting ingredients to make its award-winning ranges. Also offers a special dietary range which is gluten, wheat and dairy free and is suitable for vegetarians. Some lines are also suitable for vegans.

Aspall

The Cyder House, Aspall Hall, Debenham,
Debenham, Suffolk IP14 6PD

T: *01728 860 510*

E: *info@aspall.co.uk*

W: *www.aspall.co.uk*

Established in 1728. Since 1946, Aspall's orchards have been grown and managed to organic standards. Certified by the Soil Association, they produce organic apple juice, cyder vinegar, balsamic vinegar, white and red wine vinegar. All products are made using the juice of the whole fruit to ensure that maximum flavour and aroma can be found in the bottle. To maintain this quality their products are free from concentrates and artificial flavourings. Eight generations of the family have been making cyder for 280 years without compromising quality for price. Available in local health food stores and supermarkets.

Avalon Vineyard

The Drove, East Pennard, Shepton Mallet,
Somerset BA4 6UA

T: *01749 860 393*

E: *pennardorganicwines@mail.com*

W: *www.pennardorganicwines.co.uk*

Family run organic vineyard and fruit farm. Organic wines, traditional cider, organic mead, organic apple juice and organic fruit wines. Soil Association registered. Mail order available. Free tasting available in vineyard shop for people in the area.

Black Isle Brewery

Old Allangrange, Munlochy, Ross-shire IV8 8NZ

T: *01463 811 871*

E: *greatbeers@blackislebrewery.com*

W: *www.blackislebrewery.com*

Soil Association-registered independent brewery producing organic beers. Also approved by the Vegetarian Society. Available to buy online and also via mail order.

Cairn O' Mohr Fruit Wines

Cairn O' Mohr, East Inchmichael, Errol,
Perthshire PH2 7SP

T: *01821 642 781*

E: *cairnomohr@btconnect.com*

W: *www.cairnomohr.co.uk*

Mail order suppliers of fruit wines fermented from fresh Pershire berries, including strawberry, raspberry, bramble, elderberry and the intriguing Spring Oak Leaf and Autumn Oak Leaf wines. Also non-alcoholic elderflower 'champagne'. Stockists in

Edinburgh include Royal Mile whiskeys and Peter Green. Call for a pricelist or visit the website for an order form.

Ethical Fine Wines

Cambrian House, 51 Broad Street, Chipping
Sodbury, Bristol BS37 6AD

T: *01454 313 300*

E: *info@ethicalwine.com*

W: *www.ethicalwine.com*

Specialises in selling sustainable, organic, biodynamic and fairly traded wines, many from small producers. The list is available online for fast, efficient delivery within the UK. The wines are selected by Susan McCraith, Master of Wine, who founded the company in 2007. Hampers and gifts are also available. There is a wealth of useful, down-to-earth information on the website as well as full tasting notes and background information on each wine. Prices range from as little as £3.99 to £50 per bottle and wines come from all over the world.

Luscombe Organic Drinks

Luscombe Farm, Colston Road, Buckfastleigh,
Devon TQ11 0LP

T: *01364 643 036*

E: *info@luscombe.co.uk*

W: *www.luscombe.co.uk*

Producers of a range of organic juices and soft drinks, using fresh ingredients and none of the 'short cuts' associated with standard drinks production so there are no salty after-tastes of additives or preservatives. The range includes pear & apple juice, apricot & apple, ginger beers brewed-in-the-bottle, Sicilian lemonade and Elderflower Bubbly.

Organic Champagne

Upper Floor, 5 Regent Street, Cheltenham,
Gloucestershire GL50 3UE

T: *01242 244 620*

E: *sales@organic-champagne.co.uk*

W: *www.organic-champagne.co.uk*

Organic Champagne is a specialist online organic retailer, providing organic drinks for retail customers through their website. The wines, beers and soft drinks are sourced from the best suppliers around the world, giving you fine quality organic drinks all in one place. All you have to do is choose!

Organic Spirits Company Ltd, The

London & Scottish International Ltd,
Meadow View House, Tannery Lane,
Bramley, Surrey GU5 0AB

T: *01483 894 650*

E: *office@londonandscottish.co.uk*

W: *www.junipergreen.org*

Supplies organic gin, rums, vodka and Scotch whisky. Juniper Green is the world's first Organic London Dry Gin, distilled and bottled in the heart of London. All the ingredients are 100 per cent organic. In 2004 it won the International Gold Medal in the Wine & Spirits Competition. In total 12 medals have been won in 8 years. For more information, visit the web site www.junipergreen.org. UK5 Organic Vodka is smooth and clean with a hint of fruit esters. It was awarded a Gold Medal in the International Wine & Spirit Competition, reflecting the judges' opinion that it is a very fine quality organic vodka. For more information, visit the web site at www.uk5.org. Papagayo Organic Spiced Rum and Papagayo Organic White Rum are made with organic rum from Paraguay. Highland Harvest Organic Scotch Whisky is a blend of three organic malt whiskies and organic grain and has a smooth, full-flavour finish.

Pitfield Brewery & Beer Shop

Unit 1 The Nursery, London Road, Great Horkesley, Essex CO6 4AJ

T: *0845 833 1492*
E: *sales@pitfieldbeershop.co.uk*
W: *www.pitfieldbeershop.co.uk*

Currently produces 14 organic beers as well as organic country wines. The Beer Shop is now online and is also appears at Farmers Markets in the South east. Certified by the Soil Association.

Sedlescombe Organic Vineyard

Hawkshurst Road, Cripp's Corner, Robertsbridge, East Sussex TN32 5SA

T: *01580 830 715; Freephone 0800 980 2884*
E: *enquiries@englishorganicwine.co.uk*
W: *www.englishorganicwine.co.uk*

England's leading organic vineyard, established in 1979 and located in East Sussex, producing a range of award-winning white, red and sparkling wines, as well as fruit wines, fresh fruit juices, liqueurs and cider. All all organic and vegan-registered. Open to the public for daily tours of the vineyard, woods and winery plus tastings. If you want to get involved and spend some time in the vineyard check out www.wwoof.org or visit their Rent-a-vine Club – an ideal gift for wine-lovers at www.rentavine.co.uk.

Sussex Wine Company, The

47 South Street, Eastbourne, East Sussex BN21 4UT

T: *01323 431 143*
E: *sales@thesussexwinecompany.co.uk*
W: *www.thesussexwinecompany.co.uk*

Supplies a range of organic and biodynamic wines from around the world. Offers UK delivery service and case discounts.

Vinceremos Organic Wines

Munro House, Dukes Street, Leeds LS9 8AG

T: *0800 107 3086*
E: *info@vinceremos.co.uk*
W: *www.vinceremos.co.uk*

The UK's longest established organic drink specialists with the largest selection of organic wines – delivered to your door. The catalogue features a huge range of organic (and biodynamic) wines from around the world, including many award winners, as well as organic beers, ciders, spirits, liqueurs and fruit juices. There's even an organic single malt whisky! The vast majority of their products are suitable for vegetarians and vegans. Trade and export customers are also supplied. Write or call for a free catalogue or visit the website.

Vintage Roots Ltd

Farley Farms, Bridge Farm, Reading Road, Arborfield, Berkshire RG2 9HT

T: *0800 980 4992*
E: *info@vintageroots.co.uk*
W: *www.vintageroots.co.uk*

Offers the most comprehensive range of organic drinks available in the UK with wines, beers, ciders, spirits, liqueurs, juices, cordials – and even olive oils and chocolates. Deals only with officially recognised and certified organic and biodynamic suppliers. 'Organic' is not a sideline of the company: it's been their only business since they started in 1986. With over 350 products, there is something to suit all tastes and pockets, from gold medal-winning vintage champagne to everyday great value vin de pays wines from Southern France. All are available by mail order, you can mix your own case or get them chosen for you. Call for a free wine list. Trade enquiries welcome.

Westons Cider

The Bounds, Much Marcle, Ledbury, Herefordshire HR8 2NQ

T: *01531 660 233*
E: *tradition@westons-cider.co.uk*
W: *www.westons-cider.co.uk*

Westons award-winning premium organic cider is traditionally-produced and made from the finest organic cider apples which meet Organic Certification UK5. Matured in old oak vats, it has a ripe apple aroma and well-balanced taste. Westons Cider Visitor Centre is open all year round. Visitors can take a tour around the mill and see how cider is made and then go to the shop where they can sample free all the perry and ciders available. Or they can walk through the award-winning Henry Weston Garden into the bottle museum which is

GreenPhotographic
▬▬▬▬ Wedding Photography

Specialising in high quality, eco-friendly photography
throughout the South West.

www.greenphotographic.com
info@greenphotographic.com   07966613086

---

located in a converted cow shed and houses over
1000 different bottles. Meals are also served in the
Scrumpy House Restuarant.

THE DREAMY DETAILS

Stationery

CherryGorgeous

*Parke Lane House, Park Lane, Leeds, West
Yorkshire LS5 1AA*

T: *0113 308 2027*

E: *dee@cherrygorgeous.co.uk*

W: *www.cherrygorgeous.co.uk*

A small, innovative business, which prides itself on
providing beautiful wedding stationery that reflects
a customer's lifestyle. The emphasis is on style,
individuality and creating a bit of character that will
blow away the old clichéd concepts of what a
wedding should be. Environmental issues are taken
seriously, and an intrinsic part of the business; all
the card is recycled, the company is carbon neutral
and they offset all the carbon used in delivering
wedding stationery. So you can be sure that not
only does your wedding stationery look fabulous
but it's as environmentally sound as possible.

Exotic Paper Company Ltd, The

*Poo Corner, Old Down Business Park,
Emborough, Somerset BA3 4SA*

T: *01761 233 818*

E: *exoticpaper@elliepoopaper.co.uk*

W: *http://elliepoopaper.co.uk*

Manufacturers and distributors of 100 per cent
recycled papers with natural inclusions such as
straw, grass, coffee, hair, marshland, etc.They stock
a complete range of Ellie Poo stationery and gift
items (100 per cent recycled paper from elephant
dung). A bespoke handmade and machine-made
papermaking service is offered. Approved by NAPM
(National Association of Paper Merchants) and
BAFTS (British Association of Fair Trade Shops).

Green Elephant

*11 Caroline Close, Kingskerswell, Newton
Abbot, Devon TQ12 5JL*

T: *01803 872 703*

E: *sales@greenelephant.org.uk*

W: *www.greenelephant.org.uk*

Gifts and stationery made from 100 per cent
elephant dung paper. All the products are imported
from Thailand where they are made by local people
living near the Thai Elephant Conservation Centre.
Each item sold helps to save Asian elephants by
providing a safe future for them and also an income
for the people living alongside them. Give a gift
that is both thoughtful and memorable and which
will not only be a topic of conversation but also for
conservation. Choose from notebooks and journals,
photo albums and address books, writing sets and
pencil boxes or why not invest in some elephant art
– paintings by elephants on dung paper!

Seed Prints

*32 Felcott Road, Walton on Thames,
Surrey KT12 5NS*

T: *07929 027 534*

E: *tara@seedprints.co.uk*

W: *www.seedprints.co.uk*

Produces screen-printed wedding stationery and
greetings cards, using recycled card and paper. All
items are printed by hand, using traditional silk
screens. Envelopes are hand-printed to match and
hand-folded. The range, which includes photo
albums, notebooks, ribbon-tied packs of cards and
wall art, can be viewed on the website or you can
request a bespoke design.

Vinatis Paper

*Studio One, 7 Chalcot Road, Utopia Village,
London NW1 8LH*

T: *020 7193 3993*

E: *info@vinatispaper.com*

W: *www.vinatispaper.com*

A socially conscious enterprise, promoting recycled
and handmade paper based bespoke wedding
stationery.

British Wild Flower Plants

31 Main Road, North Burlingham,
Norwich NR13 4TA

T: *01603 716 615*
E: *office@wildflowers.co.uk*
W: *www.wildflowers.co.uk*

Growers of 400 species of native wildflower plants, in plugs, 7cm, 9cm and litre pots. Also offers seed sourcing and collecting, wildlife garden planning and a consultancy service for management plans. Recent projects include the saltmarsh planting around the Millenium Dome, show gardens at Tatton Park and Hampton Court, sea defences at the Channel Tunnel entrances and over 3,000 wildlife gardens nationwide. A specific sales area and information centre is on-site for visitors, including access and facilities for the disabled.

Catkin Flowers

3 North End Cottages, North End,
Fulbeck, Grantham,
Lincolnshire NG32 3JR

T: *01400 272 344*
E: *catkinflowers@tiscali.co.uk*
W: *www.catkinflowers.co.uk*

Passionate about natural, seasonal flowers and about producing flowers in a sustainable way. The majority of the flowers are grown in their own cutting garden at Belton Garden Centre, near Grantham, or bought from other UK growers, which considerably reduces the air miles involved in their range. Also runs a series of exclusive flower or garden-related courses throughout the year, involving practical, hands-on tuition in a relaxed atmosphere at their Belton studio.

Eco Bouquet

Heathcote Way, West Drayton,
Middlesex UB7 7RE

T: *020 3239 8640*
E: *info@valueflowers.net*
W: *www.valueflowers.net*

An ethically-inspired online florist delivering bouquets with a personal message card anywhere within the UK by courier. The floral gifts are sourced from a network of local florists that are committed to social, ethical and environmental standards. The aim is to improve the quality of flower farm working conditions, minimise damage to ecosystems, conserve biodiversity, and enhance environmental quality for future generations.

Flowers & Plants Association

266-270 Flower Market, New Covent Garden
Market, London SW8 5NB

T: *020 7738 8044*
E: *info@flowers.org.uk*
W: *www.flowers.org.uk*

As the UK's not for profit organisation promoting cut flowers and indoor plants, the Flowers & Plants Association has a list of members who supply ethically-sourced products as well as great ideas on how to arrange and get the most from your blooms on their website. Whether you're planning a green wedding or simply want to find out more, there's over a thousand pages of really useful information answering every query.

Imogen Stone

T: *0844 818 4480*
E: *customer.service@imogenstone.com*
W: *www.imogenstone.com*

Imogen Stone's florists have been creating floral designs for many years, with an extensive portfolio of weddings. They create beautiful floral designs using the finest fresh flowers combined with scented herbs and interesting foliages. Imogen Stone is also a Fairtrade licencee, using fair trade flowers wherever available.

Sweet Loving Flowers

3 Vane Hall Place, Machynlleth,
Powys SY20 8DQ

T: *01654 700 112*
E: *orders@sweetlovingflowers.co.uk*
W: *www.sweetlovingflowers.co.uk*

Grows beautiful, seasonal cut flowers without artificial chemicals or fertilisers. If ordered in time they can even grow flowers specifically for you. They can supply flowers to arrange yourself, make up simple arrangements or work together with a florist of your choice. Their flowers don't travel huge distances and are not grown in heated polytunnels so use far less fuel than most flowers available.

The Organic Flower Company

Jubilee House, Oswestry, Shropshire SY10 8DF

T: *01691 683 866*
E: *felicity@tofc.co.uk*
W: *www.tofc.co.uk*

The very best ethically grown flowers, beautifully presented, by people who really care. Organic, UK-grown and fair trade flowers available to order online for next day delivery. Each bouquet is made to order using fresh, seasonal flowers which have been grown with care, arranged with pride and sent out to your loved ones to say 'hello', 'well done'.

Hapi Bean Soy Candles

36 Octavia Court, St Pauls Way, Watford,
Hertfordshire WD24 4UW

T: *07947 464 186*
E: *info@hapibean.co.uk*
W: *www.hapibean.co.uk*

Sells only 100 per cent pure and natural soy wax candles made from GM free, pesticide free and herbicide free soybeans. Soy wax is a sustainable resource and contains no chemicals which means very little or no soot release. Each candle is handpoured in Hertfordshire. Currently sells tea lights in different size boxes and bags, and soon selling pillar candles and other varieties. Everything business-related is sourced from eco friendly companies and local suppliers.

Petal Pot, The

Arcania, Llandyfaelog, Kidwelly,
Carmarthenshire SA17 5PE

T: *01267 267 899*
E: *enquiries@petalpot.co.uk*
W: *www.petalpot.co.uk*

Supplies real flower petals for use as confetti or table decoration at weddings and many other celebrations, such as naming ceremonies and festivals. The original blend of real flower petals, mixed by hand, is a vibrant celebration of nature's colours. Also offers different combinations of flower petals to suit particular colour schemes. All blends are totally natural, 100 per cent biodegradeable and available unscented or fragranced with oils of rose and jasmine.

Green Photographic

7 Richard's Terrace, Millbrook,
Cornwall PL10 1RT

T: *07966 613086*
E: *info@sarahamysmith.com*
W: *www.greenphotographic.com*

Offers a high quality, low impact wedding photography service throughout the South West of England, striving to provide a service that is as respectful to the environment as possible. All stationery used is printed on recycled paper, all electricity and fuel used in conjunction with photographic commissions is offset with an annual donation to carbonfootprint.com. Photographer

Sarah Smith specialises in reportage wedding photography meaning that from beginning to end, your wedding day will be documented in a classic style using a combination of colour and black and white photography. She and her assistants pride themselves on being unobtrusive photographers – allowing your wedding day to run just the way you want without the photographers stealing the show.

MyWeddingStory.co.uk

14 Richmond Gardens, Canterbury,
Kent CT2 8ES

T: *0800 916 9369*
E: *info@myweddingstory.co.uk*
W: *www.myweddingstory.co.uk*

Beautiful, relaxed photography in a modern story telling style. But MyWeddingStory is so much more. They're carbon neutral, use recycled local products wherever possible, and cut down on their impact on the environment any way they can. They are also one of the few UK companies to supply vegan albums. Check out the website or make an appointment to visit them in their beautiful gallery built for them by local carpenters from FSC managed timber (it has also cut the daily commute down to 20 metres!).

Olivia Brabbs Photography

20 Vicarage View, Leeds,
West Yorkshire LS5 3HF

T: *0113 275 2560*
E: *info@oliviabrabbs.co.uk*
W: *www.oliviabrabbs.co.uk*

Olivia's style of photography is known as wedding photojournalism or documentary which means rather than direct and choreograph your wedding, she will be there to quietly observe and record the atmosphere, the spontaneous moments, the friendships and the little details. The resulting images are stylish, modern and most importantly natural. Your wedding day is all about you and your unique style and for that reason Olivia offers a bespoke pricing structure which can provide coverage to suit all plans from the most intimate civil partnership through to the most epic of events! From green business practices such as online proofing through to options for UK-produced coffee table books, Olivia takes environmental issues seriously and is always delighted to work with clients to help them achieve their goal of a green wedding. She also takes on a range of private commissions including lifestyle portraits, corporate imaging and documentary projects. She is based in Leeds, West Yorkshire and offers coverage across Yorkshire and beyond.

Ethical Party Bags

3 Freer Close, Houghton on the Hill,
Leicester, Leicestershire LE7 9HU

T: *07948 343 653*
E: *sales@ethicalpartybags.com*
W: *www.ethicalpartybags.com*

Provides an alternative to the traditional party bag as the bags and contents are either fairly traded, recycled, organic or from a sustainable source. Take a look and see the amazing bags made from recycled juice cartons or the high quality fair trade mini footballs. They also stock the eco friendly range of Sheep Poo cards – perfect for a birthday, invitation or thank you card.

Little Cherry

2, Duke Street, Windsor, Berkshire SL4 1SA

T: *01784 470 570*
E: *info@littlecherry.co.uk*
W: *www.littlecherry.co.uk*

The first complete solution for environmentally friendly children's parties, with a range of products including recycled, organic and biodegradable tableware, eco friendly party decorations, sustainable wooden toys, recycled stationery, ethically sourced natural cotton party bags and an extensive range of eco friendly partybag fillers.Incorporating a 'Quick Shop' option for busy Mum's and 'Go Totally Green' option for adult parties.

Wooden Wonders

Farley Farm House, Chiddingley,
East Sussex BN8 6HW

T: *01825 872 856*
E: *woodenwonders1@btopenworld.com*

Established in 1994, this is one of a group of family-owned companies sharing a common vision for conservation, the environment, sustainable farming and forestry. It is the first craft manufacturer trading in giftware to be awarded the Forest Stewardship Council's accredited wood mark for some of their pebbles, guaranteeing that wooden products come from sound forestry practise and have not contributed to the destruction of woodlands anywhere. Their famous wooden pebble is the basis for most of the products and is formed by a special crafting process that imitates the way fragments of rock are turned into smooth pebbles on the seashore. Like seashore pebbles, each of the pebbles is a unique shape, which combined with the beauty of the wood grain brings out the wonder of wood. The original pebble has grown into a full range of practical and ornamental wooden gifts for both individuals and corporate promotions alike. Using in-house laser engraving facilities these gifts can be personalised to clients individual requirements.

Zigzag Bunting

Harewood House, Longparish, Andover, Hampshire SP11 7AH

T: 01264 720 806
E: info@zigzagbunting.com
W: www.zigzagbunting.co.uk

Beautiful and stylish eco-friendly cotton bunting made from gorgeous fabrics and handmade at a family business in rural Hampshire. Perfect for decorating wedding venues, gardens or children's parties, and equally at home indoors or outside. The bunting can be used time after time. Bespoke bunting for wedding decorations is a speciality: have your own bunting made and you can use it for all your family parties.

THE GIFT LIST

Biggreensmile.com

87 St Leonards Road, Chesham Bois, Amersham, Buckinghamshire HP6 6DR

T: 0845 230 2365
E: customerservices@biggreensmile.com
W: www.biggreensmile.com

Sells an extensive range of green, ethical, recycled and eco-friendly gifts and gadgets that will help you to help the environment, with lots of ways to save water and energy and reduce your carbon footprint. Works closely with suppliers to ensure that their products are the most environmentally friendly of their type on the market.

Centre for Alternative Technology Mail Order

Centre for Alternative Technology, Machynlleth, Powys SY20 9AZ

T: 01654 705 959
E: mail.order@cat.org.uk
W: www.cat.org.uk

An extremely popular mail order catalogue, Buy Green By Mail supplies environmental books and products around the world. It contains over 700 items including all CAT's publications, plus a large selection from the shop. Aims to offer a speedy service wherever you are. All profits go to the educational work of the Centre. Call for a copy or visit the online shop.

Complete Wasters Greengifts

The Green Place, 6 Cossington Road, Sileby, Loughborough, Leicestershire LE12 7RS

T: 01509 815 181
E: info@completewasters.co.uk
W: www.completewasters.co.uk

The Green Place is a mini eco centre, wildlife garden and shop with a range of eye catching gifts and products, all with an environmental, sustainable and fair trade theme. Mail order is also available from the website.

EcoCentric

14 Bacon Street, London E1 6LF

T: 0207 739 3888
E: info@ecocentric.co.uk
W: www.ecocentric.co.uk

An eco homewares and gifts store – full of ethical and sustainable designs and energy saving ideas. Co-founded by TV designer Oliver Heath, the site offers a wide range of stylish eco-home and lifestyle goods, from recycled glass, energy saving gadgets, low energy lighting, home accessories, bamboo towels, organic bedding and soft furnishings to ethical toys, stationery and eco friendly and fair trade gifts. All of the products and homewares use low levels of energy, are crafted from sustainable or recycled materials, are recyclable or are ethically produced. Perfect for your wedding gift list, too.

Ecomundi

Unit 4, St Martin's Court, Route des Camps, St Martin, Guernsey GY4 6AA

T: 01481 235 580
E: sales@ecomundi.co.uk
W: www.ecomundi.co.uk

Sells the latest eco, ethical and fair trade products designed to promote a more sustainable lifestyle. The extensive range includes eco gadgets such as solar powered radios, biodegradable catering supplies, recycled stationery, fair trade jewellery and toys, natural organic healthcare products, fair trade food and drink and energy saving devices. Ecomundi is part of The Mundi Group which includes the mondomundi chain of fair trade shops.

Ethical Home Boutique

10 Aisthorpe Road, Sheffield, South Yorkshire S8 8SZ

T: 07896 753 463
E: info@ethicalhomeboutique.com
W: www.ethicalhomeboutique.com

An innovative and fresh online store which offers a gift list service ideal for weddings and other celebrations. Believes that buying products that adhere to high ethical standards does not mean that you should have to compromise on choice, quality or beauty. As a result they have built – and are continuing to extend – a site that offers an excellent range of beautiful homeware products. The site has a professional list service providing a friendly and stress free way of compiling a gift list. So if you want your celebration to extend far beyond the guests by encouraging the purchase of fair trade and green products then this site is the place to visit. All the products have been carefully chosen because they are fair trade and eco-friendly – so enjoy your celebration and help to make the world a better place in the process.

Ethical Superstore

16 Princes Park, Team Valley Trading Estate, Gateshead, Tyne & Wear NE11 0NF
T: *0845 0099 016*
E: *shop@ethicalsuperstore.com*
W: *www.ethicalsuperstore.com*

Delivers the widest range of eco-friendly and fair trade products including the best selling brands and the very latest products sourced locally and globally. Check out the ethical hampers, gift sets and wrapping service, fair trade greetings cards and activist books, CDs and DVDs, and fortnightly new products review. Top selling eco products include the award-winning Eco-kettle, Eco Balls, Dryer Balls and the energy saving Electrisave. The first UK mail order company to offer a carbon offset delivery service in association with Climate Care. Be prepared to be inspired by the huge product range!

ethicalonestopshop.com

Suite 3, 125-129 Witton Street, Northwich, Cheshire CU99 5DY
T: *0845 130 9474*
E: *info@ethicalonestopshop.com*
W: *www.ethicalonestopshop.com*

ethicalonestopshop.com was launched in August 2005 by Emma Smith, as a result of ethical concerns regarding trade and consumerism and an increasing awareness of humanity's impact on the planet and its inhabitants. The aim was to make it as easy as possible for people to shop ethically. The first site was a retail site from which Emma sold ethically-sourced products directly to customers. Two years later, and now in partnership with fellow director Collette Bentley, she has taken a giant leap forward in order to be what it says on the tin... an ethical one-stop shop! They have re-launched the site as an online ethical shopping centre featuring a large number of retailers and covering a wide range of departments and products.

Fairgift Ltd

Long Rock Industrial Estate, Penzance, Cornwall TR93 0FG
T: *0870 803 3226*
E: *info@fairgift.co.uk*
W: *www.fairgift.co.uk*

An online store stocking a collection of stylish and high quality household items to treasure. The products are predominantly handmade in small quantities, so it is the perfect source of original gifts or to set up a wedding list with a difference. Everything is fair trade, so every item is a gift that gives twice. It provides a beautiful and practical item for your home and for the producer groups in Africa, Asia and Latin America, it helps build a positive future for their families and wider community. Free UK delivery on orders over £30 and a 14 day money-back guarantee on all purchases.

Ganesha

3-4 Gabriel's Wharf, 56 Upper Ground, London SE1 9PP
T: *020 7928 3444*
E: *shop@ganesha.co.uk*
W: *www.ganesha.co.uk*

Ganesha is for fabulous furnishings and eclectic home style – all fairly traded from India. Products include stylish kauna-phok pads for low-level lounging, indoors and out and organic bed linen and accessories made from reused/recycled post-consumer waste, alongside quality handmade furnishings from the simple to the extravagant. Members of the British Association for Fair Trade Shops (BAFTS) and most products are sourced through IFAT (International Fair Trade Association). Extending markets for marginal producers and supplying the UK with life-enhancing goods, Ganesha is supporting an alternative vision of trade.

Get Ethical Trading Ltd

Unit 4. St Martins Court, 436 Essex Road, St Martin, Guernsey GY4 6AA
E: *info@getethical.com*
W: *www.getethical.com*

An online ethical shopping site from a joint venture of fair trade companies including Mondomundi and Earth & Wear, with a product range including fair trade Mexican jewellery, hemp clothing, re-chargeable batteries, garden tools and ethical trainers. In the online consumer magazine Ethical Matters you can find out about ethical issues such as consumer boycotts, eco-tourism and ethical finance. Read bad company investigations, browse ethical consumer surveys and plan green days out. Subscribe to their newsletter for monthly updates on products and information.

Green & Easy

Unit 12 Court Farm Business Park, Bishops
Frome, Worcester, Worcestershire WR6 5AY
T: *0845 257 0550*
E: *info@greenandeasy.co.uk*
W: *www.greenandeasy.co.uk*

Promotes and sells environmentally friendly products and services for the home and garden. The aim is to provide both clear and regularly updated information on a wide range of green issues, and a range of products and services to satisfy the desire to be more eco-friendly. The site has been designed for people of all ages who want to take whatever simple steps they can towards being more environmentally friendly, and who appreciate a one-stop-shop for information and guidance to suit their busy, modern lifestyles. Awareness of an individual's contribution to greenhouse gas emissions, or 'carbon footprint', is growing enormously. It's not practical for most of us to make radical changes in our lives to reduce our footprints, but the site offers easy options to do whatever you can.

Green Apple, The

Rose Cottage, 1 Chapel Lane, Ryton-on-
Dunsmore, Warwickshire CV8 3EU
T: *07732 435 393*
E: *enquiries@the-green-apple.co.uk*
W: *www.the-green-apple.co.uk*

For ethical shopping with style, the Green Apple stocks a wide and varied range of eco and ethical products, from bamboo fibre clothing to chicken doorstops made from recycled fabrics. They have a great gift section, full of unusual items that are hard to find elsewhere. They carbon-neutralise the journeys of any products that have travelled a long way to get to them and they also give 1 per cent of their yearly profits to charity.

Green Eyed Frog

Ashdeyne House, Wetheringsett Road,
Mickfield, Stowmarket, Suffolk IP14 5LH
T: *0141 416 1448*
E: *sales@greeneyedfrog.co.uk*
W: *www.greeneyedfrog.co.uk*

Ethical online gift store for the individualist with a green conscience. Organic, fair trade, recycled and eco gifts for all the family that don't cost the earth. Specialises in gifts for children and babies including blankets, wooden toys, solar and brick construction sets. For adults browse the homeware, garden, gadgets, jewellery and organic toiletry departments to find that special wedding gift. For the personal touch a bespoke gift wrap service is available.

More Than Gifts

PO Box 8164, Nottingham NG11 8WF
T: *0115 974 6229*
E: *enquiries@morethangifts.co.uk*
W: *www.morethangifts.co.uk*

A online shopping store specialising in authentic, handmade quality gifts from around the world and providing gift solutions for all occasions. Many of the items are sourced from fair trade suppliers and small village communities, which ensures that the producers of the goods are working in safe conditions and receiving fair wages.

Natural Collection Catalogue

Department 7306, Sunderland SR9 9XZ
T: *0845 367 7001*
E: *orders@naturalcollection.com*
W: *www.naturalcollection.com*

Since 1999, Natural Collection has been at the forefront of ethical retail, promoting fair trade and environmentally considered products. The award-winning range includes organic cotton and fair trade clothing and accessories, items for your home and garden, energy saving gadgets, organic cosmetics, eco cleaning products like Ecover and much more. Each item is carefully researched and selected to promote ecological and sustainable manufacturing practices. To order visit the website, call or email.

Natural Store, The

2 Rochester Gardens, Hove,
East Sussex BN3 3AW
T: *01273 746 781*
E: *info@thenaturalstore.co.uk*
W: *www.thenaturalstore.co.uk*

An online store for new brands and ideas, natural luxury and organic living, with a stylish mix of over 3,500 products ranging from fashion to interiors, beauty to food, children's wear to garden products. Ring or look at the website for more information.

Nigel's Eco Store

55 Coleridge Street, Hove, East Sussex BN3 5AB
T: *0800 288 8970*
E: *helpme@nigelsecostore.com*
W: *www.nigelsecostore.com*

An online retailer of environmentally friendly products you'll love. Inspired by stylish, innovative and functional eco design, Nigel has handpicked a variety of products and gifts that help you save money, reduce your carbon footprint and live a more planet-friendly life. The range features something for everyone including home furnishings, kitchenware, gadgets, office products, kids toys and energy saving devices. All products sold are environmentally sound and made of organic, recycled and energy efficient materials, they will not only look great in your home, but will help to reduce your contribution to global warming.

Only Fair

High House Farm, Downham Market, Norfolk PE38 0HJ

T: *01366 386 974*
E: *sales@onlyfair.co.uk*
W: *www.onlyfair.co.uk*

A web based gift shop specialising in fair trade gifts, with a range including ceramics from Peru, jewellery from India and stationery from the Philippines. Aims to stock a wide range of affordable gifts to appeal to everyone's taste and also runs a fair trade party scheme in the West Norfolk area.

Sell for Good Ltd

2 Mount Place, Lewes, East Sussex BN7 1YH

T: *01273 486 015*
E: *holly@ourgreenweddinglist.com*
W: *www.ourgreenweddinglist.com*

An online wedding gift registry, enabling couples to select from a wide range of ethical, environmentally friendly, recycled, environmentally beneficial and energy efficient goods, which are also good quality and aesthetically pleasing.

So Organic

Eagle House, 7 Turnpin Lane, Greenwich, London SE10 9JA

T: *0800 169 2579*
E: *enquiries@soorganic.com*
W: *www.soorganic.com*

An online, one-stop shop for all of the non-food products needed to support an organic lifestyle. Offering everything from organic cotton washable nappies to organic candles and everything in between, So Organic makes organic lifestyle shopping easy. Delivery is fast to all over the UK and Europe, sometimes even next day, and the huge range means there's no need to visit several stores to find what you need. So Organic is the first online multi-brand retailer to be certified by the Soil Association. A mail order catalogue is also available.

Starfish Fairtrade

Unit 10, Kempleton Mill Twynholm, Twynholm, Kirkcudbright, Dumfries & Galloway DG6 4NJ

T: *01557 860 000*
E: *sales@starfishfairtrade.co.uk*
W: *www.starfishfairtrade.co.uk*

Fairtrade products and ethical gifts ranging from bedspreads to Buddhas, including handmade

ceramics for herbal teas, speciality incense and re-usable shopping bags. All fair trade, all handmade, and all with a low carbon footprint for earth friendly living.

BuyOnceGiveTwice

Benwell House, Convent Lane, South Woodchester, Gloucestershire GL5 5HR

T: *01453 832 440*
E: *lisa@buyoncegivetwice.co.uk*
W: *www.buyoncegivetwice.co.uk*

www.buyoncegivetwice.co.uk is a unique online auction site that helps charities by simply recycling luxury auction lot 'waste' at no cost. Generally when a charity holds an auction, its supporters pay thousands of pounds for a luxurious and often unique prize. However, frequently the supporter is busy and does not have time to redeem their lot so it simply doesn't get used. Now through BuyOnceGiveTwice it is recycled making more money for charity. Lots can be donated by charities or buyers. Also individuals are able to donate lots for their favourite charity such as, for example, a week's holiday in a donor's house in the South of France. The founders of BuyOnceGiveTwice, Mia Woodford and Emma Leschallas have a vision of an online charity auction portal that is designed to maximise life events by selling items that are not suitable for charity shops. They plan to change the way that people shop, and the site has been developed to respond to the changing attitudes.

Good Gifts Catalogue, The

Radius Works, Back Lane, Hampstead, London NW3 1HL

T: *020 7794 8000*
E: *orders@goodgifts.org*
W: *www.goodgifts.org*

The Good Gifts Catalogue offers you the chance to get people something they really want for Christmas. Instead of the usual pair of socks, you could get your loved ones an African Farmyard. Don't worry that they won't have space for it because in fact it will be given in their name to a family in Africa, for whom it will be a life-changing experience. There are hundreds of different gifts from £3-£3,000, all guaranteed to make a big difference. You could plant chilli hedges to protect villagers' crops from marauding elephants, provide the National Library for the Blind with a new Braille book, clear 25 square metres of minefield or protect an acre of rainforest. Unlike other similar catalogues, all the money received will not be put into general funds or spent on related projects. What you choose is exactly what is given.

Living Generously

PO Box 1121, Bristol BS48 2XZ

T: *0870 626 0982*

E: *info@livinggenerously.com*

W: *www.livinggenerously.com*

Gifts that change lives with the world's largest choice of charity gifts and direct-giving opportunities. Know exactly who, what and where is benefiting from your gifts. Beautiful gift packs available with all gifts, ranging from child sponsorship to fresh waterwells. Social investment opportunities are available for individuals and corporate giving.

Oxfam Unwrapped

Oxfam House, John Smith Drive, Oxford, Oxfordshire OX4 2JY

T: *0870 410 5030*

W: *www.oxfamunwrapped.com*

Launched in 2004, Oxfam Unwrapped is still a novel solution to finding original presents – and beating poverty and suffering at the same time. It's the perfect way to buy for friends and relatives – fanatical DIY dads, aunts with green fingers or fussy friends who seem to have everything. Customers can choose from over fifty gift ideas including the ever-popular goat, safe water, toilets, teacher training and mango plantations. Prices range from £5 for school text books to £1,700 to create a classroom. Kids can join in too with 20kg of fertiliser for £6,100 school dinners for just £6 or planting 50 trees for £8. Or if you leave your present-buying a bit late, you can now choose e-cards.

Save the Children

1 St John's Lane, London EC1M 4AR

T: *0207 012 6928*

E: *j.engelking@savethechildren.org.uk*

W: *www.savethechildren.org.uk/wishlist*

Runs a virtual gift range called Wish List, with a range of 24 gifts, such as Sneezing Elephant. This is a chilli plant elephant kit, costing £68. Crops often get trampled by elephants, but elephants don't like chilli so if chilli is wrapped around the fence it protects the crops from getting squashed. Something Plumpy is a month's supply of Plumpy'nut for a severely malnourished child and costs £20. Plumpy'nut is a special high-protein, high-energy peanut butter that can be sent out to emergency situations around the world for severely malnourished children. The complete gift range is available for review online. The gift chosen is actually sent out by Save the Children (rather

than the money going into a general fund) and every gift has been identified by their country teams to meet the specific needs of the children and communities they aid. The gifts are given in the name of the recipient who receives a card.

Send a Cow

The Old Estate Yard, Newton St Loe, Bath BA2 9BR

T: *01225 874 222*

E: *info@sendacow.org.uk*

W: *www.sendacow.org.uk*

Send a Cow is a Christian charity that enables poor farmers in Africa to become self-reliant by providing them with livestock, training and advice. It works with some of the most vulnerable groups in Africa, including children orphaned by war, families affected by AIDS, and disabled people. The Send a Cow Special Occasions Gift Catalogue is available online. The catalogue offers the chance to give livestock and other assistance such as cows, goats, pigs, or bees – in the names of your loved ones. In return you can choose to receive attractive gift cards in the post, or send e-cards to your friends and family.

Trees for Cities

Prince Consort Lodge, Kennington Park, London SE11 4AS

T: *020 7587 1320*

E: *info@treesforcities.org*

W: *www.treesforcities.org*

An independent charity working to improve the environment in London and other cities by involving local people in tree planting and landscaping projects. The work is targeted on the poorest parts of the capital with projects in schools, housing estates, streets and other public spaces. Call for further information.

Trees for Life

The Park, Findhorn Bay, Forres, Moray IV36 3TZ

T: *0845 458 3505*

E: *trees@findhorn.org*

W: *www.treesforlife.org.uk*

An award-winning, internationally known conservation charity based in Scotland whose vision is the regeneration and restoration of the Caledonian Forest and the reintroduction of all the missing wildlife species. Trees for Life also supports within its vision statement a strategy and programme for the restoration of the Earth's ecosystems. Provides a newsletter, volunteer work weeks, tree planting and educational services.

THE HONEYMOON

French Letter Condoms

E: info@frenchlettercondoms.co.uk
W: www.frenchlettercondoms.co.uk

Designers and manufacturers of condoms using fairly traded rubber. A royalty from each pack goes to ensure a fair payment to workers on the rubber plantations, and assists with healthcare and pension provisions.

Yes Intimate Lubricants

3L Trading, PO Box 214, Alton,
Hampshire GU34 3WY

T: 08456 448 813
E: isis@yesyesyes.org
W: www.yesyesyes.org

Intimate lubricants made by the leading manufacturer of premium, pure and natural intimacy products. Yes is the only range of Soil Association-certified organic personal lubricants in the world and is also Vegetarian Society-approved. The range includes a water based dual action vaginal moisturiser and lubricant and a long lasting oil based product, available in 25ml, 75ml and 125ml packs. Yes is hypoallergenic and free from parabens, glycerin, grapefruit seed extract and hormones. The elegant and tasteful packaging ensures discretion and also makes Yes ideal for a unique and sensual present. Buy online or use the 24-hour orderline for discreet delivery.

Argyll Hotel

Isle of Iona, Argyll PA76 6SJ

T: 01681 700 334
E: reception@argyllhoteliona.co.uk
W: www.argyllhoteliona.co.uk

Relaxed, friendly hotel on the seashore in the village of Iona. Cosy lounges with open fires and books, a plant filled sun lounge and spacious dining room, all overlooking the Sound of Iona. 'Cottagey' bedrooms with kettles, period furniture, and en-suite facilities. Provides freshly-prepared, home cooking using local produce and seasonal homegrown vegetables from their own organic garden and caters especially for vegetarians using wholefoods. Has a residents' and table licence. Green Tourism Scheme Gold Award and Soil Association-certified.

Bloomfield House

146 Bloomfield Road, Bath, Somerset BA2 2AS

T: 01225 420 105
E: info@ecobloomfield.com
W: www.ecobloomfield.com

This elegant, beautifully restored Georgian Bed and Breakfast (B&B) was recently taken over as Bath's first eco-hotel and conference centre. The grade II listed building has elements of a truly sustainable hotel. All food served is organic, local and fair trade. Rooms are from £100 per night, including breakfast. Prices for fully-catered conference facilities quoted individually. House-trained children and, by arrangement, pets are welcome. Guests who travel to the hotel by long distance public transport or bicycle get 10 per cent off the standard bed and breakfast rate.

Bruach Mhor

Fionnphort, Isle of Mull, Argyll PA66 6BL

T: 01681 700 276
E: heather@bruachmhor.ndo.co.uk

B&B in a comfortable, modernised crofthouse in Fionnphort, half a mile from the ferry to Iona, the beautiful isle where St Columba landed in the sixth century. Lovely beaches, coastal and mountain walks and wildlife. Vegetarian, vegan and traditional breakfasts made using organic, home-grown vegetables wherever possible. Also serves local fish and meat.

Buttervilla

Buttervilla Farm, Polbathic, St Germans,
Torpoint, Cornwall PL11 3EY

T: 01503 230 315
E: info@buttervilla.com
W: www.buttervilla.com

Buttervilla is a Soil Association-certified organic farm set in 15 acres of exceptionally beautiful countryside, which is perfect to roam and relax in. The owners care for their land in a sustainable, natural and eco-friendly way and have an abundance of wildlife. They have never used chemical sprays so the environment is clean, pure and influenced by the Atlantic breezes – the south Cornish coast just two miles away. Local and seasonal produce is used for breakfasts and evening meals, including the freshest day-caught fish, with everything sourced from organic suppliers whenever possible. In-season fresh vegetables are from an extensive kitchen garden. Comfortable large double en-suite rooms with all the modern conveniences and eco-friendly solar heated power showers. With a wealth of glorious beaches, beautiful woodlands and historic towns and villages on the doorstep Buttervilla is the perfect place for couples looking to chill out and eat well.

Cumbria House

1 Derwentwater Place, Keswick,
Cumbria CA12 4DR

T: *01768773171*

E: *green@cumbriahouse.co.uk*

W: *www.cumbriahouse.co.uk*

Accommodation provider and holder of the Cumbria Tourist Board Responsible Tourism Standard. The owners' aim is that your stay in their guest house in the Lake District should be socially responsible and have as small an environmental impact as possible. Your breakfast will be freshly-cooked and come mainly from local sources, your coffees and teas are amongst the 30 plus fair trade items that are used, and they will give you a discount if you don't arrive by car. They do, however, expect you to make a donation to their conservation fund for the Lake District Tourism and Conservation Partnership. Although the majority of guests are hill walkers, they welcome all, including families, groups and solo travellers – and well behaved dogs are also accepted. Those who share their environmental aspirations are especially welcome.

Dartington Hall & Dartington Hall Trust

The Elmhirst Centre, Dartington Hall, Totnes,
Devon TQ9 6EL

T: *01803 847 100*

E: *bookings@dartingtonhall.com*

W: *www.dartingtonhall.com*

Offers a wide range of facilities for day meetings, residential conferences and special functions. Facilities in the mediaeval courtyard include 12 meeting rooms (the largest of which is the Great Hall), the Barn Theatre, 51 bedrooms and a range of function rooms. Bed and breakfast may be booked on an individual basis. Organic and free range produce is used when possible. Meals and drinks are available in the White Hart bar and dining room.

Deepdale Backpackers and Camping

Deepdale Farm, Burnham Deepdale,
Norfolk PE31 8DD

T: *01485 210 158*

E: *info@deepdalefarm.co.uk*

W: *www.deepdalefarm.co.uk*

This award-winning eco-friendly hostel accommodation and campsite on the beautiful north Norfolk coast is set in an Area of Outstanding Natural Beauty (AONB). You can choose from a range of accommodation, including private ensuite rooms, tipis, camping, group hostel and dorm beds. The campsite offers tipis and camping pitches for tents and small campervans.

Facilities include a cafe, information centre, supermarket, shops, walking and hiking, cycling, watersports and kiting, with a bus service running to and from the front door, so you don't need to drive during your visit. The hostel is in converted 17th-century barns, incorporating eco-friendly technologies and traditional building methods. A fully equipped kitchen and sitting room are available. The campsite spreads across five grass paddocks and has modern toilet and shower facilities. All visitors are asked to consider the environment: there are recycling facilities around the site and a large amount of information about non-car transport including buses, walking and cycling – bike hire is available. Trees are planted around the farm and site each year and wind turbines are planned for the future.

East Lochhead House, Cottages and Gardens

Largs Road, East Lochhead,
Lochwinnoch, Renfrewshire PA12 4DX

T: *01505 842 610*

E: *admin@eastlochhead.co.uk*

W: *www.eastlochhead.co.uk*

Four self-catering cottages ranging from a studio to three bedrooms set on two acres of gardens 25 minutes from Glasgow. Four stars (STB), AA Five Red Diamonds and in the Michelin Guide. Awarded Gold in the Green Business Tourism Scheme and is a member of international Slow Food organisation. Winner of VisitScotland Thistle Award for sustainable Tourism in 2006.

Eco-Lodge

Station Road, Old Leake, Boston,
Lincolnshire PE22 9RF

T: *01205 871 396*

E: *gclarke@internationalbusinessschool.net*

W: *www.internationalbusinessschool.net*

The Eco-Lodge opened in 2003 and was built from wood grown and harvested in Lincolnshire. It was part-funded by a European Union, Lincwoods project grant. The energy sources are wind power and a large wood-burning range. It is open all year round. Drinking water is supplied from the mains; filtered rainwater is supplied for washing. The eco-lodge provides comfortable living accommodation including a kitchen, two bedrooms, a shower room and a veranda. Sleeps four.

Farm & Cottage Holidays

Victoria House, 12 Fore Street, Northam
Bideford, Devon EX39 1AW

T: *01237 479 146*

E: *enquiries@holidaycottages.co.uk*

W: *www.holidaycottages.co.uk*

Enjoy the freedom and the beauty of South West England with over 850 holiday cottages, hand-picked, throughout Cornwall, Devon, Somerset and Dorset. All situated in coastal and rural locations, they range in size and character from farms, barn conversions and log cabins to waterfront apartments, country mansions and quaint fisherman's cottages.

Feather Down Farms

Manor Farm, Westworldham, Alton, Hampshire GU34 3BD

T: *01420 80804*
E: *info@featherdown.co.uk*
W: *www.featherdown.co.uk*

Feather Down Farm Days holidays provide one of the most unique holiday experiences in Britain. Located in beautiful farmland and nature reserves, the farms create a unique experience – in harmony with the gentle rhythm of rural life. A Feather Down Farms holiday is made for people searching for something small scale and genuine – far from today's mass-produced, plastic holiday packages.

Fforest Camp

Bridge Warehouse, Teifi Wharf, Cardigan, Ceredigion SA33 3AA

T: *01239 623 633*
E: *info@coldatnight.co.uk*
W: *www.coldatnight.co.uk*

A green, luxury campsite based on the River Teifi in Pembrokeshire, West Wales. Stay in a Nomad, tipi or luxury dome with breakfast included and full self-catering kitchen outside your tent, including all equipment. Weekend, midweek and full weeks available. A wide range of outdoor activities are also available through their sister company, Fforest Outdoor. Choose from canoeing down rapids in the Teifi Gorge, sea kayaking with seals and dolphins on Cardigan Bay or coasteering at the Witches Cauldron. Low impact breaks run from March to October – call for details.

Glenloy Lodge and Wildlife Holidays

Glenly Lodge Banavie, Fort William PH33 7PD

T: *01397 712 700*
E: *info@glenloylodge.co.uk*
W: *www.glenloylodge.co.uk*

Jon and Angela offer a warm welcome at Glenloy Lodge, a former hunting lodge at the entrance to secluded Glen Loy, with stunning views over the Nevis Range. They have eight comfortable ensuite rooms, with a sun lounge and TV lounge with multifuel stove, exclusively for the use of guests. Close to the Caledonian Canal and only seven miles from Fort William, it is ideally suited for walking,

cycling, bird watching and fishing. They are a STB 3-star Guest House, members of the Walkers and Cyclists Welcome schemes and the Green Tourism Business scheme. Breakfast includes fresh fruit salad and porridge along with a traditional Scottish grill. Evening meals are available with vegetarian options a speciality. Children are welcome. Prices from £30-£35 B&B, with child discounts and rates for longer stays.

Graianfryn Vegetarian Guest House

Penisarwaun, Caernarfon, Gwynedd LL55 3NH

T: *01286 871 007*
E: *info@fastasleep.me.uk*
W: *www.fastasleep.me.uk*

Set in spectacular countryside on the edge of Snowdonia and close to Anglesey's sandy beaches, this is an ideal centre for touring North Wales or for a walking, climbing or beach holiday, situated just three miles from Llanberis at the foot of Snowdon. Graianfryn, an early Victorian ex-farmhouse, is beautifully furnished and offers luxurious accomodation. The delicious meals are imaginative, created on the premises and exclusively vegetarian, wholefood and organic where possible.

Hazelwood House

Loddiswell, Kingsbridge, Devon TQ7 4EB

T: *01548 821 232*
E: *info@hazelwoodhouse.com*
W: *www.hazelwoodhouse.com*

Hazelwood House, set in lush South Devon countryside, reflects this beautiful setting in the food it serves. Every attempt is made to use the fresh, locally grown, organic produce for which Devon is so well known. The accommodation is gracious and comfortable with 14 bedrooms (most of which are ensuite). Surrounded by 67 acres of untouched woodland, meadows and river valley it is the perfect place to relax, reflect and refuel. A variety of events are run throughout the year including concerts, theatre, art courses and talks. Hazelwood is a popular location for civil weddings, whether the occasion is a satin-slippered affair in the old chapel or a wellies and umbrella celebration by the boat house, there is a unique opportunity for any creative idea for a ceremony.

Heartspring

Hill House, Llansteffan, Carmarthen SA33 5JG

T: *01267 241 999*
E: *info@heartspring.co.uk*
W: *www.heartspring.co.uk*

Heartspring is superbly sited, overlooking a stunning coastal conservation area with magnificent sea views in West Wales. The house has been lovingly restored with an emphasis on the use of toxic free, environmentally friendly materials and the rooms are all decorated with natural paints and varnishes. There is pure spring water from every tap, and solar heating panels for hot water. All meals are fully organic and vegetarian. Individual retreats, mini-breaks and self-catering holidays can also be tailor-made with the optional addition of complementary therapy and teaching sessions such as massage, healing, profound relaxation and many others, from local practitioners.

Highdown Organic Farm
Highdown Farm, Bradninch, Exeter,
Devon EX5 4LJ

T: *01392 881 028*

E: *svallis@highdownfarm.co.uk*

W: *www.highdownfarm.co.uk*

Highdown is peacefully situated in the heart of the beautiful Devon countryside with stunning views of the surrounding area. Coasts and moors are a short drive away and Exeter is only 10 miles. There are two self-catering cottages, sleeping seven and four plus a romantic hideaway for two. All are fully equipped and decorated to a high standard with their own gardens. Offers a local organic delivery service and home produced organic eggs. Short breaks available. Open all year.

Home Place Farmhouse Spa
Home Place, Challacombe, Barnstaple,
Devon EX31 4TS

T: *01598 763 283*

E: *markandsarah@holidayexmoor.co.uk*

W: *www.farmhousespa.com*

Nestling amidst the atmospheric moorland of Exmoor in a tranquil river valley is Home Place with its five acres of lake and meadowland to relax in. Accomodation is self-catering in an adjoining holiday cottage. Treatments available include stone massage, aromatherapy, slim gel body wrap, massage and Indian head massage and Elemis Spa treatments. Also has a swim-spa, floatation tank, steam room and rasul. Two night B&B packages from £110pp.

Lancrigg Vegetarian Country House Hotel
Easedale, Grasmere, Cumbria LA22 9QN

T: *01539 435 317*

E: *info@lancrigg.co.uk*

W: *www.lancrigg.co.uk*

In its Lakeland mountain setting, Lancrigg is situated in 30 acres of private grounds and woodland, just half a mile from Grasmere village. The hotel offers individually-styled rooms, some with four-posters and whirlpool baths, and international vegetarian

cuisine. There is an extensive organic wine list. Cost is between £65 and £110 per person per night for dinner, bed and breakfast, depending on room. Special diets are catered for.

Landmark Trust, The
Shottesbrooke, Maidenhead, Berkshire SL6 3SW

T: *01628 825 920*

E: *info@landmarktrust.org.uk*

W: *www.landmarktrust.org.uk*

Independent preservation charity that rescues and restores architecturally interesting and historic buildings at risk, giving them a future and renewed life by letting them for self-catering holidays. Once a building becomes a Landmark its holiday rental income pays for its upkeep but money to save other buildings at risk has to be found elsewhere. Full details of all the more than 180 Landmark Trust buildings are available in the Landmark Handbook, price £11.50 inc p&p. The Trust also manages Lundy, an island 11 miles off the North Devon coast famous for its wildlife and natural beauty (see www.lundyisland.co.uk).

Low Craiglemine Farm Holidays
Low Craiglemine, Whithorn, Newton Stewart,
Wigtownshire DG8 8NE

T: *01988 500 730*

E: *enquiries@lowcraiglemine-farm-*
holidays.co.uk

W: *www.lowcraiglemine-farm-holidays.co.uk*

Two lovely self-catering cottages on an organic, Demeter-certified farm with beautiful beaches, amazing skies and friendly animals and people. Low Craiglemine Organic Farm is set near the southerly tip of the Machars peninsula in Dumfries & Galloway. The accommodation has been tastefully refurbished to provide a comfortable place to relax and unwind. Go and enjoy the wildlife, flora, bird-watching, archaeological interests, spectacular cliffs and sandy beaches.

Moss Grove Organic Hotel
Grasmere, Cumbria LA22 9SW

T: *01539 435 251*

E: *enquiries@mossgrove.com*

W: *www.mossgrove.com*

Following 10 months of renovations, detailed research and innovative thought the Moss Grove Organic Hotel boasts a host of eco-friendly features blended with uncompromising quality. From the organic clay paints to the filtered water throughout the property, the ethos of reducing environmental and carbon impact is applied. The eleven individual rooms with spacious bathrooms are individually decorated to high standards. The wallpapers were chosen from Cole and Son, London, who produce screen printed wallpapers with natural inks, the carpets are woven by Goodacre Carpets of nearby Kendal, the organic natural clay paints were supplied by Earthborn in Cheshire and the beds are handmade from reclaimed timbers or from sustainable sources and made by Derbyshire company Indigo. To reduce the use of manmade chemicals in the fire retardants, wherever possible natural alternatives have been used instead. So throughout the property wooden blinds are used instead of curtains and leather chairs and settees rather than fabrics. All the water is filtered directly from the mains feed into the property to remove the chlorine and pesticides, aerated taps are fitted to reduce water wastage, and 3 litre/6litre dual flush toilets go without saying. Each bathroom boasts underfloor heating, spa bath and shower, and organic toiletries.

Natural Retreats
Aislabeck Units 1-3, Hurgill Road, Richmond, Yorkshire DL 10 4SG
T: *0161 242 2970*
E: *info@naturalretreats.com*
W: *www.naturalretreats.com*
Set in the heart of some of the most beautiful and secluded countryside in the UK, Natural Retreats offers residences of unparalleled luxury. The concept is simple, yet unique: to combine the highest levels of luxury and sensitive development with the most dramatic locations the UK has to offer within the boundaries of its National Parks.

Old Post Office Vegetarian Guest House
Llanigon, Hay-on-Wye, Herefordshire HR3 5QA
T: *01497 820 008*
W: *www.oldpost-office.co.uk*
A very special find at the foot of the Black Mountains in the hamlet of Llanigon, this guesthouse is a 17th century Grade II-listed building with oak floorboards, beams and luxury king-size beds in en-suite rooms, with a comfortable guests' sitting-room and a relaxed atmosphere. Offers a superb vegetarian/vegan breakfast. Nearby there are lovely walks in the outstandingly beautiful Brecon Beacons National Park. Other activities close by include pony trekking, canoeing, paragliding and mountain biking. Prices from £30pppn-£35pppn.

Organic Holidays
Tranfield House, 4 Tranfield Gardens, Guiseley, Leeds LS20 8PZ
T: *01943 871 468*
E: *lindamoss@organicholidays.com*
W: *www.organicholidays.co.uk*

Accommodation on organic farms and organic smallholdings (includes self-catering and catered) and bed and breakfasts, guest houses and small hotels where organic produce is used according to availability in the UK, Ireland, Europe and the rest of the world.

Paskins Town House Hotel
18/19 Charlotte Street, Brighton, East Sussex BN2 1AG
T: *01273 601 203*
E: *welcome@paskins.co.uk*
W: *www.paskins.co.uk*
Paskins has resolutely cast aside ordinariness in favour of its own values. It is stylish and genuinely 'green' in outlook and just yards from the beach and close to the centre of things. Its nineteen attractive rooms, with the odd four-poster, all are impeccably clean and snug. Breakfast, taken in a memorable art deco room includes a varied menu of organic traditional and inspired vegetarian food.

Poachers Hideaway
Flintwood Fam, Belchford, Horncastle, Lincolnshire LN9 5 QN
T: *01507 533 555*
E: *info@poachershideaway.com*
W: *www.poachershideaway.com*
Luxury self catering holiday cottages in the heart of the Lincolnshire Wolds. With 170 acres of ancient woodland, wildflower pastures, natural hedgerows and water meadows to explore, Poachers Hideaway is a perfect place to relax in 5-star holiday cottage accommodation. Holistic therapy treatments are also available. Awarded Silver by the Green Tourism Business Scheme.

Primrose Valley Hotel
Primrose Valley, Porthminster Beach, St.Ives, Cornwall TR26 2ED
T: *01736 794 939*
E: *info@primroseonline.co.uk*
W: *www.primroseonline.co.uk*
A nine-bedroom Edwardian villa with a REN Therapy Room, which aims to combine a memorable guest experience with a minimal impact on the environment. Showcasing and supporting their local suppliers and environmental organisations is key to their ethos and they are proud to be corporate supporters of the Cornwall Wildlife Trust, platinum supporters of the Marine Conservation Society and board members of CoaST, the Cornwall Sustainable Tourism Project.

Strattons Hotel

4 Ash Close, Swaffham,
Norfolk PE37 7NH

T: *01760 723 845*

E: *enquiries@strattonshotel.com*

W: *www.strattons-hotel.co.uk*

A small independent, family-run, boutique hotel secluded in the historic market town of Swaffham in Norfolk. It's an award-winning green hotel, with a chic restaurant serving organic and locally sourced produce in an innovative, modern English style. Art, design, luxury and comfort feature strongly throughout the hotel, with individual, eclectic bedrooms. Swaffham is situated in the Brecks, a unique and beautiful landscape stretching across Suffolk and Norfolk, and is ideal to enjoy healthy walking, jogging, cycling and horse riding on the ancient track ways and peaceful forest trails.

The Hall

Milden, Lavenham, Sudbury,
Suffolk CO10 9NY

T: *01787 247 235*

E: *Hawkins@thehall-milden.co.uk*

W: *www.thehall-milden.co.uk*

Offers bed and breakfast in a listed 16th-century Georgianis-style farmhouse or large group self-catering in Tudor barns, with a walled garden, meadows, ponds, period furniture and spacious bedrooms. Explore the farm nature trail and award-winning woodland. There are also longer distance circular walks and a children's activity pack. Gold Award winner for green tourism in Suffolk.

The Hytte

Bingfield, Hexham,
Northumberland NE46 4HR

T: *01434 672 321*

E: *sgregory001@tiscali.co.uk*

W: *www.thehytte.com*

Close to Hexham and Hadrian's Wall, this unique property is fully accessible and provides the ideal country retreat for friends and family get togethers with the added luxury of a sauna and hot-tub spa. The Hytte (pronounced hutta!) sleeps 8 and has been built in the style of a Norwegian timber lodge, along with a turf roof, and has views across open countryside. The open plan living area has vaulted ceilings and a log burner. Members of the Green Tourism Business Scheme and holding a Gold Award for their committtment to the environment. Full environmental information on the website.

The Manor House Stables

The Manor House, Timberland Road, Martin,
Near Lincoln, Lincolnshire LN4 3QS

T: *01526 378 717*

E: *sherryforbes@hotmail.com*

W: *www.manorhousestables.co.uk*

The restoration of this 18th-century, Grade II-listed stable block has been achieved using all natural, earth friendly materials, local builders and traditional methods. There are two units of quality self-catering accommodation which can be rented separately or together. Both units have exposed beams, lime-washed walls and wood-burning stoves. The first floor 'Hayloft' (sleeps four) is relaxing and welcoming with a spacious open plan living/kitchen whilst the ground floor 'Bothy' (sleeps three) is warm and cosy with direct access to a small private garden. Special care has been made to make The Bothy as wheelchair friendly as possible. The stable walls are insulated with cotton, hemp or wood fibre and below the ground floor lies layers of insulating limecrete and recycled glass. Natural and environmentally friendly paints and wood finishes have been used throughout the building and the hot water, underfloor heating and cast iron radiators are fuelled by a wood pellet boiler and solar panels. Natural materials have been used everywhere. Real wood floors are covered with braided wool rugs and recycled cotton mats. Fabrics are soft and natural and colours are warm and earthy. The luxury mattresses are made of organic Welsh wool, the sheets are cotton (mostly organic) and the beds covered in linen bedspreads or cotton quilts.

The Rectory Hotel

Crudwell, Malmesbury, Wiltshire SN16 9EP

T: *01666 577 194*

E: *info@therectoryhotel.com*

W: *www.therectoryhotel.com*

The Rectory hotel is a beautiful 12-bedroomed, elegantly furnished period house set in three acres of Cotswold stone walled garden. Recently renovated, it is an ideal base from which to explore the Cotswolds, Tetbury, Bath and the ancient town of Malmesbury. The wood-panelled restaurant overlooks the garden with its sunken Victorian pool. The chef heads an experienced team which offers food made from only the finest, freshest local ingredients, organic where possible. Their delicatessen, The Rectory Kitchen & Cellar in Cirencester, stocks local, sustainable and seasonal food with a range of carefully selected wines and ciders. They cater for any event from picnics to dinner parties. Their new pub, The Potting Shed, across from the hotel, provides quality seasonal British produce with great beers and wine. The large vegetable garden grows organic, seasonal vegetables and herbs for use in the pub, hotel and deli.

Tremeifion Vegetarian Hotel
Talsarnau, Soar Road, Talsarnau,
Gwynedd LL47 6UH
T: *01766 770 491*
E: *enquire@vegetarian-hotel.com*
W: *www.vegetarian-hotel.com*
Small vegetarian hotel with spectacular views over the river estuary looking towards Portmeiron and close to Harlech beach. Offers a relaxing and friendly environment, with excellent home-cooked vegetarian and vegan cuisine. Organic produce is provided from the garden when possible and there is an organic vegetarian wine list. No smoking throughout.

Wheems Farm
Eastside, South Ronaldsay, Orkney KW17 2TJ
T: *01856 831 537*
E: *christina.sargent@wheems.fsworld.co.uk*
W: *www.hostel-scotland.co.uk*
Organic farm offering self-catering for families and groups in a converted barn a quarter of a mile from sandy bays and overlooking cliffs. Clean bed linen, cooking facilities, shower and fridge, and a camping area. £170 per week, £35 per night for up to 8 people and camping from £3 pppn. Supplies Soil Association-certified organic vegetables and organic eggs.

Bicycle Beano Cycling Holidays
Erwood, Builth Wells, Powys LD2 3PQ
T: *01982 560 471*
W: *www.bicycle-beano.co.uk*
Sociable cycling holidays on the idyllic lanes of Wales and England with delicious vegetarian cuisine, which is mostly organic (lunchtime veggie and meat options available). Lively friendly groups, running over two to seven days, from April to September. Tours in Snowdonia, Pembrokeshire, the Wye Valley in Wales, and Shropshire, the South Downs, and the Vale of the White Horse in England.

Cotswold Walking Holidays
5 Tebbitt Mews, Winchcombe Street,
Cheltenham, Gloucestershire GL52 2NF
T: *01242 518 888*
E: *cotswoldwalks@star.co.uk*
W: *www.cotswoldwalks.com*
Long-established walking holiday company located in

and specialising in the Cotswolds. Unique routes for self-guided holidays featuring some of the most beautiful villages in Europe. Accommodation, luggage transfer, route notes and maps are all included. The Cotswold Way is a speciality and private groups are welcome. Guides are also available.

ecoescape
E: *info@ecoescape.org*
W: *www.ecoescape.org*
ecoescape® is a green travel guide and online directory of environmentally friendly places to stay and visit. It is a meeting place for green travellers to raise awareness of sustainable travel in the UK and promote responsible escapism globally.

Green Gateway Farm Accomodation
c/o Devon Wildlife Trust, Cricklepit Mill,
Commercial Road, Exeter, Devon EX2 4AB
T: *01392 279 244*
E: *contactus@devonwildlifetrust.org*
W: *www.devonwildlifetrust.org/wildlifetourism*
Helps farmers to look after wildlife habitats on their land and offers a free training course to help diversification projects on wildlife rich farms. Choose from a list of Green Gateway farms offering bed and breakfast or self-catering accomodation. One of the greatest pleasures of staying on a farm is discovering the secret wildlife havens that are hidden from general view. Imagine the chance to enjoy these places right on the doorstep of your accomodation, dusk or dawn, undiscovered by anyone other than the farmers and their guests.

Greenways Holidays Ltd
The Old School, Station Road, Narbeth,
Pembrokeshire SA67 7DU
T: *01834 860 965*
E: *enquiries@greenwaysholidays.com*
W: *www.greenwaysholidays.com*
Provides a selection of packaged and tailor-made walking, cycling and explorer holildays in the unique and beautiful Pembrokeshire countryside. Routes include the Pembrokeshire Coast Path, South of the Landsker and the Celtic Trail Cycle Route – all of which are available 'car free'. Takes care of every detail – from luggage transfer to cycle hire, leaving you free to enjoy the countryside you have come to enjoy.

Hiddenglen Holidays
Laikenbuie, Grantown Road, Nairn,
Highland IV12 5QN
T: *01667 454 630*
E: *muskus@bigfoot.com*
W: *www.hiddenglen.co.uk*

Watch deer and woodpeckers amongst the abundant wildlife on a tranquil croft. Acommodation includes spacious lodges, a chalet and a caravan, all well equipped and clean, and with a beautiful view over the loch and native woods. Visitors can collect eggs and feed pet lambs (if any). The site is safe for children with play area, bikes and a boat. Near mountains, sandy beaches and Moray Firth dolphins. Offers tipi or camping in return for help. Voluntary work through WWOOF. Photos on website. No smoking.

Ramblers Countrywide Holidays

Lemsford Mill, Lemsford Village, Welwyn Garden City, Hertfordshire AL8 7TR

T: *01707 386 800*

E: *info@ramblerscountrywide.co.uk*

W: *www.ramblerscountrywide.co.uk*

Ramblers Countrywide Holidays are synonymous with some of the finest walking holidays throughout the UK. Escape the pressures of modern life and join a group of new friends to share the experience of discovering the country's magnificent and diverse landscapes, centres of history and traditional villages. Designed to be fun and hassle free, the small group walks into the hills and sightseeing on foot will keep you away from the crowds and ensure that you see the best sights. The day hikes are a great way to have an active holiday and to make your spirits soar. The holidays are based on flexibility, informality and an absence of regimentation.

Scottish Cycling Holidays

87 Perth Street, Blairgowrie, Perthshire PH10 6DT

T: *01250 876 100*

E: *info@scotcycle.co.uk*

W: *www.scotcycle.co.uk*

Self-guided groups and tailor-made tours in Scotland, England, Ireland, Austria, France Holland, Italy, Portugal, Sardinia, Spain, Czech Republic, Hungary, Poland, Sicily and Slovenia. The bicycle is the perfect way to travel and enjoy to the full the scenery, heritage and hospitality of the destinations. Also provides accommodation, bike hire, maps, routes and full back-up.

The National Trust Working Holidays

Sapphire House, Roundtree Way, Norwich, Norfolk NR7 8SQ

T: *0844 800 3099*

E: *working.holidays@nationaltrust.org.uk*

W: *www.nationaltrust.org.uk/volunteering*

The National Trust runs around 400 working holidays every year throughout England, Wales and Northern Ireland, so whether you fancy anything from carrying out a conservation survey and herding goats to painting a lighthouse or planting trees they will have something to suit you. Working holidays range from two to seven days and from £80 a week including food and hostel-type accommodation. No previous experience is necessary, as you will be led by trained volunteer leaders and staff. You just need to be team-spirited, enjoy being outdoors in beautiful locations and not mind getting your hands dirty!

Turus Mara

Penmore Mill, Dervaig, Isle of Mull PA75 6QS

T: *08000 858 786*

E: *info@turusmara.com*

W: *www.turusmara.com*

Runs boat trips for viewing wildlife and sea birds and cruise tours from the west side of Mull.

Walk Awhile Walking Holidays

Applegarth, Boughton-under-Blean, Kent ME13 9PE

T: *01227 752 762*

E: *walk@walkawhile.co.uk*

W: *www.walkawhile.co.uk*

Provides three sustainable walking holidays in Kent with easy access by public transport: walk the Pilgrims Way, discover rural Kent or walk the White Cliffs. These self-led and guided walking holidays are available all year round. Walk Awhile is accredited as a Silver buisness by the Green Tourism Business Scheme (GTBS) and is a member of Responsible Travel. The well-researched walks come with local support and back-up, and your luggage will be transfered each day. Enjoy locally sourced packed lunches and stay in period ensuite accommodation in old inns along the trail. On self-led walks your tracker is also on hand at the end of a phone to help you if you run into difficulties along the way.

Wild Explorer Holidays

Skye Environmental Centre, 7 Black Park, Broadford, Isle of Skye IV49 9DE

T: *01471 822 487*

E: *iosf@otter.org*

Organises residential courses to study the Hebridean wildlife and heritage. Each trip visits one set of islands. Profits from the trips are put back into conservation projects and the local community.

Wild in Scotland

166 High Street, Edinburgh EH1 1QS

T: *0131 478 6500*

W: *www.wildinscotland.com*

Wild in Scotland is an established overland tour

company with 10 years experience in offering informative and active sightseeing tours; primarily focusing on Scotland's Highlands and Islands but also to other UK destinations too. Specialising in three to nine-day tours, the company offers a range of over 12 tours to off-the-beaten-track castles, hostels and thatched blackhouses. Using mini coaches taking up to 16 people the tours aim to provide the feel of going away with a group of friends rather than the crowd and incorporate seeing some of Scotland's most stunning scenery and sights with wilderness, wildlife, history and folklore.

Europe & Further Afield

Baobab Travel

Old Fallings Hall, Old Fallings Lane,
Wolverhampton WV10 8BL

T: *0121 314 6011*

E: *enquiries@baobabtravel.com*

W: *www.baobabtravel.com*

A specialist eco-tour operator, born out of a combination of a love of Africa and travel, and a desire to work actively with and support local communities in the Developing World. The company endeavours to take travellers to places that represent the very essence of Africa and sustain the local economies that are visited.

Bushmans Kloof Wilderess Reserve & Retreat

Over the Pakhuis Pass, Cederberg Mountains,
Near Clanwilliam 7430 South Africa

T: *21 685 2598*

E: *info@bushmanskloof.co.za*

W: *www.bushmanskloof.co.za*

Bushmans Kloof is an oasis of ancient myth and untamed beauty, surrounded by mystical, staggering rock formations, open planes and deep ravines. 270km from Cape Town, this exclusive retreat is a safe haven providing sanctuary for diverse wildlife, including 35 species of mammals and more than 150 bird species, as well as extraordinary botanical richness that encompasses 755 indigenous plant species. With over 130 rock art sites within the 7,500 hectare reserve, this South African Natural Heritage site is proud custodian to the ancient Bushman culture, and has a Heritage Centre displaying rare San artefacts. Majestic views, invigorating outdoor activities, supreme luxury and comfort, award-winning cuisine and soothing spa treatments complete an unforgettable experience amidst the wonders of nature. Winner of the Relais & Châteaux Environment Trophy 2007 and Tatler Travel Guide Top 101 Hotels in the World 2008.

Cortijo Romero

23 Cottage Offices, Latimer Park, Latimer
Road, Chesham, Buckinghamshire HP5 1TU

T: *01494 765 775*

E: *bookings@cortijo-romero.co.uk*

W: *www.cortijo-romero.co.uk*

Offers year-round alternative holidays in the Alpurjarra mountains of southern Spain, a magnificent natural park and UN Biosphere Reserve, with one of the best climates in Europe. It is a stunningly beautiful site and provides comfortable accommodation, full board with vegetarian food and an excellent pool. Other aspects include a day excursion, t'ai chi or yoga, and expressive dance. There is also a wide range of 20-hour personal development courses, led by top facilitators and, for a half-price green holiday, an ambitious Tree Planting Project.

Cycle Rides Ltd

PO Box 2440, Bath, Somerset BA1 6XG

T: *01225 428 452*

E: *jerry@cyclerides.co.uk*

W: *www.cyclerides.co.uk*

Long-established company running bike tours in Italy, France, Spain and Holland, with trips from Vienna to Prague, Prague to Budapest, etc. Travel by ferry or Eurostar. Tours range from laid-back pottering to challenging. Participants cycle independently on carefully researched routes so you choose your own pace. Provides a full back-up service and luggage carriage.

Earthwatch Institute

267 Banbury Road, Oxford,
Oxfordshire OX2 7HT

T: *01865 318 838*

E: *info@earthwatch.org.uk*

W: *www.earthwatch.org/europe*

Earthwatch is an international science and education charity which supports over 130 scientific research projects worldwide through individual supporters, volunteers' financial contributions and corporate funding. Its research concentrates on countering detrimental environmental change by supporting the conservation of the planet's heritage. The Earthwatch volunteer programme provides an opportunity for the general public to work directly in the field with scientists, on projects ranging from Dolphins of the Ionian Sea in Greece to Lions of Tsavo in Kenya. Projects last from two to 21 days. You can become an Earthwatch supporter for as little as £2.50 a month. Supporters receive regular mailings on events, activities and volunteering opportunities.

Equine Adventures

Long Barn South, Sutton Manor Farm,
Bishops Sutton, Hampshire SO24 0AA

T: 01962 737 647

E: sales@equineadventures.co.uk

W: www.equineadventures.co.uk

With over 50 rides in five different continents, Equine Adventures offer a superb range of riding holidays, with rides for experienced riders and holidays for those who want to learn to ride. All the trips, whether in the UK or further afield, encompass magnificent scenery, suberb riding and wonderful food. And in many places they include fabulous wildlfe viewing too.

European Waterways

35 Wharf Road, Wraysbury,
Middlesex TW19 5JQ

T: 01784 482 439

E: sales@gobarging.com

W: www.gobarging.com

Their luxury floating hotel barges cruise the magical inland waterways of seven European countries, along canals, rivers, lakes and lochs. Your floating hotel cruises gently along, whilst you relax, enjoy the fine wines and excellent cuisine, the company of fellow passengers, whether new friends, family, or old acquaintances. There are also guided tours in air-conditioned mini buses around castles, markets, battlefields and ancient monuments, or choose to take a gentle bicycle ride down the tow path. Whatever you do, their dedicated and highly trained professional staff will be there to look after you. English speaking captains ensure a safe and yet exciting passage along your chosen route. The all-inclusive price has no hidden extras, with all meals, wine, an open bar and excursions included. Prices start from £1,650 per person sharing a double cabin. Exclusive charters for up to 12 passengers are available.

Gecko Travel

94 Old Manor Way, Portsmouth,
Hampshire PO6 9NL

T: 023 9225 8859

E: frontdesk@geckotravel.com

W: www.geckotravel.com

Offers culture and adventure, off the beaten track, in small group, organised tours (with a maximum of nine people) in SE Asia, and aiming to maintain a responsible travel ethos. Adventures include elephant riding, jungle night hikes, canoeing, kayaking or just sitting back and watching life go by. Beach stays are included on many of the tours and homestays, liveaboards, spa resorts, cookery courses and shopping can be added to all the current itineraries. Accommodation is normally 3-star and locally or family-owned. Areas covered are Thailand, Malaysia, Sri Lanka, Laos, Cambodia, Yunnan and Vietnam. Gecko Travel takes great care to ensure that their practices in Southeast Asia not only provide exciting and memorable holidays for those who travel with the company, but that they make positive contributions to the region as well. To learn more about how they foster responsible tourism see the company's Statement of Endeavour and Responsible Travel Policy on the website. An online brochure is available.

GSE Ecotours Ltd

75 Scotney Gardens, Maidstone,
Kent ME16 0GR

T: 0870 766 9891

E: admin@gse-ecotours.com

W: www.gse-ecotours.com

A specialist tour operator offering unique Kenyan village homestays to give tourists and travellers the opportunity to experience rural Kenyan culture and contribute to an operation that aids local economies and helps to protect and sustain the region's natural resources. To fully absorb local culture and customs, visitors stay as guests with host families and are invited to assist with everyday tasks such as meal preparation, handicrafts and harvesting grass for livestock. The homestay package includes all accommodation, meals, transfers and ground transportation and guide services. Also included are excursions to local national parks and game reserves, to allow visitors to appreciate Kenya's majestic landscape, wildlife and natural habitats.

Inntravel

Nr Castle Howard, York, Yorkshire YO60 7JU

T: 01653 617 788

E: inntravel@inntravel.co.uk

W: www.inntravel.co.uk

Offering a range of active and relaxed holidays across Europe, Morocco and North America, including walking, cycling, skiing and self-catering, Inntravel promotes responsible tourism by closely following guidelines to benefit local communities, protect the environment and minimise pollution. The self-guided walks and cycles explore rural areas, and luggage is transported ahead. Itineraries are flexible to suit the pace of the traveller and many of the family-run hotels used offer local, organic produce and have an environmental policy to reduce pollution. Travel by rail is used wherever possible and the offset of carbon emissions is encouraged for air travellers.

La Maison Du Vert

Le Bourg, Ticheville, Vimoutiers,
Normandy 61120 France

T: *233 369 584*

E: *mail@maisonduvert.com*

W: *www.maisonduvert.com*

An English-owned vegetarian hotel, B&B and restaurant situated in a stunning Normandy valley with 2.5 acres of beautiful organic landscaped gardens. Offers a wide choice of delicious vegetarian and vegan meals made with home-grown organic vegetables, served with a choice of organic wines, local organic cider and beers. Relax in colourful gardens, walk or cycle in the peaceful countryside full of wildlife or explore the local picturesque towns, bustling markets, seaside resorts, Monet's and other gardens and glorious chateaux. Only one hour from Caen port or three hours form the tunnel and Calais. Also has a self-catering townhouse for up to 12 people at Saint Savinien in the warm and sunny Charente Maritime, in South West France. The gite is beautifully furnished and has 5 double bedrooms each with its own shower-room and can sleep up to 12. Saint Savinien is a lovely old medieval town built around the beautiful Charente river. There is a delightful leisure island with swimming pools, cycle hire and boats that take you along the river to historic Saintes. Only 45 minutes from the golden sandy beaches and famous La Rochelle. Prices start at only £290 per week. More detail available online.

Naturetrek

Cheriton Mill, Cheriton,
Alresford SO24 0NG

T: *01962 733 051*

E: *info@naturetrek.co.uk*

W: *www.naturetrek.co.uk*

Britain's largest specialist wildlife tour operator, offering a wide selection of expert-escorted birdwatching, botanical and natural history holidays all around the world. These range from wildlife cruises (especially in such key regions as the Arctic, Antarctica, Galapagos Islands, etc), whale-watching holidays, birdwatching and botany holidays throughout Europe, safaris in Africa, tiger tours in India, polar bear trips, Himalayan wildlife treks, etc, all expertly guided by leading naturalists. The company is highly regarded and has achieved AITO's top level, 3-star Responsible Tourism accreditation. Its detailed 'responsible tourism policy' may be found on the website. The company pays to carbon-neutralise all travel by its customers and staff, and raises large sums for conservation organisations such as Butterfly Conservation, the Environmental Investigation Agency, the Zoological Society of London, and the World Land Trust, amongst others.

North South Travel (NST)

Moulsham Mill Centre, Parkway,
Chelmsford, Essex CM2 7PX

T: *01245 608 291*

E: *brenda@northsouthtravel.co.uk*

W: *www.northsouthtravel.co.uk*

Travel agency offering discounted fares to destinations worldwide, together with full travel agency backup. Profits are channelled to grassroots projects (especially ones that benefit disadvantaged sectors of the community or that contribute to the promotion of sustainable tourism) in Africa, Asia and Latin America through the NST Development Trust.

Paperbark Camp

571 Woollamia Road, Woollamia,
New South Wales, Australia

T: *2 4441 6066*

E: *info@paperbarkcamp.com.au*

W: *www.paperbarkcamp.com.au*

Located just 2.5 hrs drive from Sydney on the unspoilt NSW south coast, the tented accommodation at Paperbark Camp is ecotourism at its best. Combining a unique Australian bush experience with great food, tranquil surroundings and genuine hospitality, guests can get back to nature in style and comfort whilst exploring the famous white beaches and National Parks of Jervis Bay. Thoughtfully placed amongst the spotted gums and Paperbark trees on the banks of the Currambene, the twelve safari style tents feature solar powered lighting, private en-suite and a wrap around verandah from which to enjoy the peace and ambience of the pristine bush environment.

Reef & Rainforest Tours Ltd

A7 Dart Marine Park, Steamer Quay,
Totnes, Devon TQ9 5AL

T: *01803 866 965*

E: *mail@reefandrainforest.co.uk*

W: *www.reefandrainforest.co.uk*

Offers small scale, natural history tours to Costa Rica, Madagascar, Ecuador, Peru, Indonesia, Honduras. and more. Eco-friendly lodges and local guides are used wherever possible. Activities include riding, canoeing, wildlife spotting, snorkelling, scuba diving and nature walking. Also provides tailor-made itineraries and school educational trips for A-level and university students.

Responsibletravel.com

3rd Floor Pavilion House, 6 Old Steine,
Brighton, East Sussex BN1 1EJ

T: *01273 600 030*

E: *amelia@responsibletravel.com*

W: *www.responsibletravel.com*

An online directory that provides the world's largest selection of responsible and eco-travel holidays and accommodation. Its mission is to change tourism by promoting and campaigning for great travel experiences that also benefit conservation and local people. Offers thousands of pre-screened holidays and accommodations catering for a diverse range of interests. Whether you want to stay at a B&B in Scotland or with a Thai hilltribe, go on safari in Africa or take a beach holiday in Greece, responsibletravel.com can cater for your needs. Visit the website to book your next holiday and register to receive a fortnightly emagazine with offers and articles.

Saddle Skedaddle Biking Holidays

Ouseburn Building, Albion Row, Newcastle
Upon Tyne, Tyne and Wear NE6 1LL

T: *0191 265 1110*

E: *info@skedaddle.co.uk*

W: *www.skedaddle.co.uk*

Cycling and holidays throughout the UK, Europe, Asia, USA, Central and South America and New Zealand. Adventures, with something for everyone, designed to give an insight into local cultures whilst experiencing the thrills of biking – from gentle rides in Norway and Ireland to the best mountain biking in Europe and the Americas. Complementing the overseas programme are their monthly UK weekends which range from Beginners to Expert.

Sunvil Holidays

Sunvil House, Upper Square, Old Isleworth,
Middlesex TW7 7BJ

T: *020 8568 4499*

E: *holidays@sunvil.co.uk*

W: *www.sunvil.co.uk*

Established for 38 years, Sunvil is a fully-bonded independent tour operator specialising in carrying small numbers of clients to areas 'off the beaten track'. In 2004, they were awarded 2-star recognition by the Association of Independent Tour Operators (AITO) responsible tourism scheme and their Africa programme gained the much coveted 3-star level. In 2006, they became one of the first tour operators to ask their clients to offset the carbon emissions caused by their flights through an offset scheme. The money raised through this scheme will be invested into carbon-neutral projects in the areas that the company travels to.

The Tide Has Turned

3 The Square, Beaminster, Dorset DT8 3AS

T: *01308 861 488*

E: *hello@thetidehasturned.co.uk*

W: *www.thetidehasturned.co.uk*

Offers individually designed travel services created for each client. Travellers get their ideal experience, as they specialise not in a predetermined destination but in giving people a unique, personalised holiday at a price they can afford. One of the country's first ethically-certified travel companies, The Tide Has Turned has joined the ranks of a prestigious group of national firms with ethical company status awarded by the Good Shopping Guide. By carefully selecting suppliers and business partners they preferentially support owner-managed local businesses and ethically-run companies all over the UK. Travel is planned for clients in a holistic way which not only reduces carbon emissions, but relies on transport and accommodation providers who also act as ethically as possible – treating their suppliers and employees fairly and using their profits justly, whilst respecting the environment.

Travel Matters

10 Blandfield Road, London SW12 8BG

T: *020 8675 7878*

E: *travelmatters@dial.pipex.com*

W: *www.travelmatters.co.uk*

Small holiday company offering a service of booking holidays to South West France as well as other conservation areas in West Algarve. Guided walking, mountain biking and horseriding can be arranged locally.

Travelroots

52 Avenue Road, London N6 5DR

T: *020 8341 2262*

E: *info@travelroots.com*

W: *www.travelroots.com*

Offers responsible eco-tourism holidays to quality destinations across the world. The key aim is to be sensitive to the local community and environment, offering a low impact means of enjoying foreign cultures. Furthermore, all the holidays contribute positively to the areas in which they work, and do not cost anymore than an ordinary holiday.

Tribes

12 The Business Centre, Earl Soham,
Woodbridge, Suffolk IP13 7SA

T: *01728 685 971*

E: *greenguide@tribes.co.uk*

W: *www.tribes.co.uk*

Tribes, the Fair Trade Travel company, arranges

quality tailor-made holidays and safaris. The company is run on ethical and responsible principles. Tribes offers holidays such as African safaris, Galapagos cruises, Peruvian rainforest trips, treks (including Kilimanjaro), and short breaks (such as Marrakech weekends). Destinations include Botswana, Brazil, Ecuador, India, Jordan, Kenya, Malawi, Morocco, Nepal, Peru, South Africa, Tanzania, Uganda and Zambia. Friendly, knowledgeable consultants help you plan your holiday, and offer advice on how your trip can really make a difference.

Tucan Travel

316 Uxbridge Road, Acton,
London W3 9QP

T: *020 8896 1600*
E: *uksales@tucantravel.com*
W: *www.tucantravel.com*

Tucan Travel is a specialist adventure travel company offering more than 300 exciting and affordable small group tours worldwide. The focus is on offering travellers the adventure of a lifetime, whilst minimising their impact on the earth. Travel is in five distinct travel styles to cater for all comfort levels and budgets, so anyone can take the adventure of a lifetime. Destinations include Europe, Asia and Russia, East and Southern Africa, the Middle East and North Africa, Latin America and Antarctica. Tour leaders and local guides provide all the information you need about responsible travel, including local customs and social etiquette, efficient use of local resources and environmentally friendly practices such as recycling.

Uplands Escape Ltd

42 Eastleach, Cirencester,
Gloucestershire GL7 3NQ

T: *01367 851 111*
E: *reservations@uplandescapes.com*
W: *www.uplandescapes.com*

Walking holidays to make your soul sing! Uplands is a specialist tour operator founded on principles of sustainable tourism and offering flexible, independent walking holidays based in traditional villages in some of Europe's most stunning upland scenery. Walk in beautiful unspoilt national parks and undiscovered regions of central Italy, southern France, the Pyrenees, Slovenia – and for some dramatic Winter walking – Gran Canaria. Choose from a wide range of self-guided walks to suit all ages and fitness levels, and choose to join up to three organised walks per week. Stay in a single centre base, where your presence will provide a valuable contribution to the lives of the villagers and the local economy. Holidays include the provision of

carbon-neutral car hire for maximum independence, a delicious and lavish daily packed lunch, a handbook full of local information and the full support of a knowledgeable locally based manager.

Wilderness Journeys

3a St Vincent Street,
Edinburgh EH3 6SW

T: *0131 625 6635*
E: *info@wildernessjourneys.com*
W: *www.wildernessjourneys.com*

Wilderness Journeys is an award-winning adventure travel and ecotourism company, offering an inspiring range of adventure holidays which travel into the wilderness regions of the most beautiful destinations on earth. They offer a wide range of small group and bespoke adventure holidays throughout the year, including trekking, mountain biking, ski touring, sea kayaking, canoeing, wildlife and walking safaris. The trips visit Africa, South America and Asia, as well as several European destinations. They are driven by a passion for adventure travel and a desire to share with others the magic of the earth's last remaining wild places and are committed to the principles of sustainable tourism. The adventure holidays are designed to minimise their impact, to support wildlife conservation and to provide inspiring travel experiences in wild nature.

WildOceans & WildWings

577-579 Fishponds Road, Bristol BS16 3AF

T: *0117 9658 333*
E: *wildinfo@wildwings.co.uk*
W: *www.wildwings.co.uk*

Whale and dolphin watching holidays all over the world, led by experienced biologists. The company takes care to put the welfare of the animals first, and this is reflected in how the tours are conducted and in the choice of professional and sympathetic boat operators. Also offers a range of birdwatching tours under the name WildWings and the widest range of environmentally responsible wildlife cruises to the Antarctic and Arctic.

Wind, Sand and Stars

PO Box 58214, London N1 2GJ

T: *020 7359 7551*
E: *office@windsandstars.co.uk*
W: *www.windsandstars.co.uk*

Operating in the Southern Sinai region for more than 15 years, the company's strong working relationship with the Bedouin has contributed to its success. It ensures benefits are fed back into the community via its supporting charity work. The company has twice won the Highly Commended

Award in the British Airways annual Tourism for Tomorrow Awards (1996, 2000) for its pioneering environmental projects and its irrigation project for the ancient Bedouin gardens. In addition, it has significantly contributed to an ethical tourism report by Tearfund, the development charity. It operates around 50 trips a year catering for all ages and interests, ranging from camel safaris and pilgrimages to historical religious sites, to mountain treks, charity projects and school journeys. Additional activities include research or field trips in Sinai's desert and mountain regions and special needs journeys.

World Walks

5 Tebbit Mews, Winchcombe Street,
Cheltenham, Gloucestershire GL52 2NF

T: 01242 254 353

E: walking@star.co.uk

W: www.worldwalks.com

A well-established walking holidays company offering self-guided and group holidays in the UK and Europe, as well as North Africa and New Zealand. Flexible itineraries and personal service at very competitive prices.

USEFUL ORGANISATIONS

Association of Independent Tour Operators (AITO)

133a St Margarets Road,
Twickenham, Middlesex TW1 1RG

T: 020 8744 9280

E: info@aito.co.uk

W: www.aito.co.uk

Long recognised as a leader in Responsible Tourism (RT), AITO requires every member to appoint a Responsible Tourism Manager who ensures adoption of guidelines set by the organisation. AITO operates a recognition system for its member companies in the field of RT, attributing between one and three stars to each company. Three stars is the top achievement and indicates that a company has fully integrated Responsible Tourism into all aspects of its business and destination work. A growing number of companies meet these high standards. To ensure that AITO's RT programme is kept fully up to date, a dedicated RT committee of members and advisors reviews progress and maintains AITO at the forefront of thinking. To find out more about the 140 AITO specialist tour operators and their RT initiatives, visit the website.

British Association for Fair Trade Shops (BAFTS)

E: info@bafts.org.uk

W: www.bafts.org.uk

A network of independent fair trade or world shops across the UK, BAFTS was established in 1995 and is an information, support, and campaigning organisation for its members. For a list of BAFTS shops in the UK visit the website.

British Union for the Abolition of Vivisection

16a Crane Grove,
London N7 8NN

T: 020 7700 4888

E: info@buav.org

W: www.buav.org

Founded in 1898, the British Union for the Abolition of Vivisection (BUAV) is the world's leading organisation campaigning to end animal experiments. BUAV campaigns focus on a variety of vivisection issues from cosmetics testing, household products, chemical and toxicity experiments, medical research, freedom of information, reforming the Home Office Inspectorate, genetic engineering and the international trade in wild-caught and captive bred monkeys for research. The BUAV is at the forefront of the international campaign to end vivisection through public campaigns, hard-hitting undercover investigations, lab animal rescue, high profile media activities, political lobbying, legal and scientific expertise and quality educational, information and online resources. The BUAV is committed to using all peaceful means possible to end animal experiments and promote modern, non-animal research techniques.

CarbonNeutral Company, The

Bravington House, 2 Bravington Walk,
Regent Quarter, Kings Cross, London N1 9AF

T: 020 7833 6000

E: enquiries@carbonneutral.com

W: www.carbonneutral.com

The CarbonNeutral Company was established more than ten years ago and is one of the leading carbon offset and climate consulting businesses helping hundreds of businesses and thousands of people reduce their CO_2 emissions and/or offset them. Every individual or business has a carbon footprint and the company assesses their CO_2 emissions and provides expert advice on reducing it. For those who are looking at neutralising their footprint to 'zero' they provide independently audited offsetting projects; for example, replacing carbon intensive kerosene in India for solar power. The website provides online calculators to assess and offset the

CO2 emissions used in driving, when flying or in the home. There is also an online shop offering low carbon, climate-friendly gifts, toys and wedding lists.

Climate Care

112 Magdalen Road, Oxford,
Oxfordshire OX4 1RQ
T: *01865 207 000*
E: *mail@jpmorganclimatecare.com*
W: *www.climatecare.org*

Climate change is one of the greatest problems facing society today and Climate Care offers people a simple and practical way of working out and offsetting their greenhouse gas emissions. For a small contribution, Climate Care will make emission reductions on your behalf through projects in forest restoration and sustainable energy across the world – see the website for the latest projects. These reductions balance your emissions – making your activities climate neutral. Go to the website to calculate the emissions from your activities and then offset them simply online.

Environmental Transport Association

68 High Street, Weybridge, Surrey KT13 8RS
T: *0845 389 1010*
E: *eta@eta.co.uk*
W: *www.eta.co.uk*

The ETA provides roadside rescue and other great services with a real difference. The aim is to raise awareness of the impact of excessive car use and help individuals and organisations to make positive changes in their travel habits. Other services include cycle insurance, cycle rescue, motor insurance, travel insurance and house insurance. The ETA believes in freedom of movement through sensible use of transport. By joining the ETA you are lending your voice to a growing number of people who believe that we should be a seeking a sustainable transport system in Britain. ETA uses its profits to lobby key individuals, companies and transport policy makers and also works jointly with a wide range of organisations to provide educational materials.

Fairtrade Foundation, The

Suite 204, 16 Baldwin's Gardens,
London EC1N 7RJ
T: *020 7405 5942*
E: *mail@fairtrade.org.uk*
W: *www.fairtrade.org.uk*

The Fairtrade Foundation is a certification body which awards an independent consumer label – the Fairtrade Mark – to products which meet international standards. The Fairtrade Mark appears on products as a guarantee that disadvantaged producers are getting a better deal. There are now over 3,000 products carrying the Fairtrade Mark in the retail and catering markets. Fairtrade makes a difference to over 7 million farmers, workers and their families. It ensures: a price that covers producers' costs; a premium which producers

©Bedruthan

decide how to invest in their communities on projects such as clean water, healthcare, education and the environment; and long term and more direct trading relations. Products include: tea, coffee, chocolate, cocoa, sugar, fresh fruit, dried fruit, juices, biscuits, cakes, snacks, honey, jam and preserves, chutneys and sauces, rice, quinoa, herbs and spices, nuts, nut oil, wines, spirits, ale, confectionery, muesli, cereal bars, yoghurt, ice cream, baby food, flowers, sports balls, cotton products including clothing, homeware and cotton wool. Fairtrade Fortnight is the annual campaign each February to raise awareness about fair trade and to encourage more consumers to positively change the lives of producers in developing countries by choosing fair trade.

Fishonline.org

Marine Conservation Society, Unit 3 Wolf Business Park, Alton Road, Ross-on-Wye, Herefordshire HR9 5NB

T: *01989 566 017*

E: *info@mcsuk.org*

W: *www.fishonline.org*

If you are concerned about declining fish stocks and the welfare of our seas then this website can help you identify which fish are from well-managed sources and/or caught using methods that minimise damage to marine wildlife and habitats. It has been developed by the Marine Conservation Society and designed by Juniperblue with the support of the Esmée Fairbairn Foundation and Marks and Spencer plc. Information on fish stocks in the North-East Atlantic has been obtained from the most recent scientific reports published by the International Council for the Exploration of the Sea (ICES 2003 – www.ices.dk). Information about World Conservation Union (IUCN) assessments and Red List fish species is available at www.iucn.org. More information on fish biology and distribution is available at www.fishbase.org.

Forest Stewardship Council (FSC)

UK Working Group, R8 11-13 Great Oak Street, Llanidloes, Powys SY18 6BU

T: *01686 413 916*

E: *info@fsc-uk.org*

W: *www.fsc-uk.org*

The FSC trademark is found only on wood and wood products that come from forests independently certified as being managed to an internationally agreed set of social, economic and environmental principles and criteria. There are currently over 10,000 FSC-certified products available in the UK, from garden decking, charcoal and garden furniture to wallpaper and kitchen equipment. These can be found in many high street stores and most major DIY shops, such as B&Q and Homebase, Woolworths, Boots and the Body Shop.

Green Tourism Business Scheme

Green Business UK Ltd, 4 Atholl Place, Perth PH1 5ND

T: *01738 632 162*

E: *gtbs@green-business.co.uk*

W: *www.green-business.co.uk*

A not for profit company established to promote green tourism and to run the Green Tourism Business Scheme. The company promotes sustainable tourism and works closely with government and non-government organisations such as Visit Scotland, the Scottish Executive, Tourism & the Environment Forum, Scottish Natural Heritage, Historic Scotland, Scottish Wildlife Trust and the main utility companies in Scotland. Green Business also administers and co-ordinates the Green Tourism Business Scheme providing membership services to over 1000 tourism businesses throughout the UK.

Low Carbon Travel

10 New Park Court, London SW2 1HS

T: *020 8674 4364*

E: *slowtravel@futerra.co.uk*

W: *www.lowcarbontravel.com*

Provides information about slow, low carbon travel and how to go round the world without flying. In 2007-8 Ed Gillespie and his partner Fiona circumnavigated the globe without getting on a plane. This site offers information on their route, a travelogue of their adventures and lots of tips on how to catch cargo ships and travel overland.

Naturewatch

14 Hewlett Road, Cheltenham, Gloucestershire GL52 6AA

T: *01242 252 871*

E: *info@naturewatch.org*

W: *www.naturewatch.org*

A not for profit animal welfare campaigning organisation, aiming to promote the prevention of cruelty to animals and to conduct and support the publication of information concerning animals in furtherance of their welfare. Works strictly within the democratic system and condemns all illegal activity, believing that an evolutionary approach is better than a revolutionary one. Main campaigning areas are animal experimentation, badger baiting and live transport across Europe. Produces the Compassionate Shopping Guide, a cruelty free toiletries range, and information booklets. Also promotes World Animal Day – see www.worldanimalday.org.uk. Naturewatch Foundation, the charitable arm of Naturewatch, supports the improvement and development of animal welfare standards in Eastern Europe, particularly in Lithuania and Ukraine.

Organic Farmers and Growers Ltd
The Old Estate Yard, Shrewsbury Road, Albrighton, Shrewsbury, Shropshire SY4 3AG
T: *01939 291 800*
E: *info@organicfarmers.org.uk*
W: *www.organicfarmers.org.uk*
One of several national organic sector bodies recognised by Defra and one of the UK's largest organic certifiers (organic certification UK2) offering a practical service for organic food production and processing, as well as cosmetic and body care standards. All staff are experienced in the farming and food processing industries and OF&G offers combined farm assurance inspections alongside organic inspections. A regular newsletter is mailed to all members to keep them informed about the latest developments within the organisation and the organic sector as a whole. All standards, plus classified ads and more, are available on the website.

Slow Food
International Office, Via della Mendicità Istruita, 14, Bra, Cuneo 12042 Italy
T: *0172 419 610; UK 0800 917 1232*
E: *international@slowfood.com*
W: *www.slowfood.com*
Slow Food, founded in 1989, is an international organisation whose aim is to protect the pleasures of the table from the homogenisation of modern fast food and life. Through a variety of initiatives, it promotes gastronomic culture, develops taste education, conserves agricultural biodiversity and protects traditional foods at risk of extinction. It has 80,000 members in 100 countries. Its main offices, situated in Bra (Cuneo), a small town in southern Piedmont, employ about 100 people. They are the hub of a close-knit network of local grassroots offices in Italy and abroad, the so-called convivia, which promote the movement by staging events, debates and other initiatives. Thanks to the hard work and enthusiasm of their managers, collaborators and members, they provide continuous feedback to the central offices in Bra. Slow Food also boasts a publishing company, Slow Food Editore, which specialises in tourism, food and wine. Its catalogue now contains about 40 titles and it also publishes Slow, 'a herald of taste and culture', in five languages: Italian, English, French, German and Spanish. Slow Food promotes

scores of projects and activities and The Ark of Taste is a first step in this direction. The aim of this massive project is to identify and catalogue products, dishes and animals that are in danger of disappearing. The operational offshoots of the project are the so-called Slow Food Presidia, through which the Association provides economic support and a media back-up to groups and individuals pledged to saving an Ark product.

Soil Association
South Plaza, Marlborough Street, Bristol BS1 3NX
T: *0117 314 5000*
W: *www.soilassociation.org; www.whyorganic.org*
The Soil Association is the UK's leading environmental charity campaigning for people and planet-friendly, organic food and farming. Set-up in 1946 by a far-sighted group of farmers, doctors and concerned citizens who saw the direct links between farming practice and plant, animal, human and environmental health, the Soil Association has grown into an internationally respected authority on sustainable agriculture and a recognised champion of healthy food. Concerned about the impact of intensive farming practices on the environment, food quality and health, the Soil Association challenges the dominance of industrial agriculture, connected as it is with degradation of the countryside, increases in diet-related illness, mistreatment of animals and the betrayal of public trust in food. It uniquely represents and offers practical solutions to everyone involved in the food chain – farmers, food processors, retailers and consumers. Also works with the media and government to raise awareness about sustainable, organic agriculture. Through its not for profit subsidiary, Soil Association Certification Limited, it certifies over 70 per cent of the organic food, drink, textiles and and health and beauty products sold in the UK, guaranteeing they have been produced to the highest organic standards.

Tourism Concern
Stapleton House, 277-281 Holloway Road, London N7 8HN
T: *020 7133 3330*
E: *info@tourismconcern.org.uk*
W: *www.tourismconcern.org.uk*
Campaigns on human rights issues connected to travel and for more ethical and fairly traded tourism. Tourism Concern is not against tourism, but just wants it to be as good for the people in Southern (Third World) holiday destinations as it is for Western tourists. It has proven time and time again that our

holidays can often bring unwanted consequences and can accentuate poverty in poorer tourism receiving areas. With its Southern partners it recognises that although tourism can be an industry which improves people's living standards and wellbeing, it is only too often something that works to keep them impoverished. The work for change is crucial as Tourism Concern is the only organisation in the UK campaigning solely on these issues.

Vegan Society

Donald Watson House,
21 Hylton Street, Hockley,
Birmingham, West Midlands BA18 6HJ

T: *0121 523 1730*

E: *info@vegansociety.com*

W: *www.vegansociety.com*

Educational charity promoting ways of living free from animal products for the benefit of people, animals and the environment. Provides information on veganism to schools, health care professionals, the media, food manufacturers and individuals. Publishes a quarterly magazine, The Vegan, a shopping guide, The Animal Free Shopper, and a large selection of information sheets and booklets. Also registers vegan products under its trademark scheme. Has a network of local contacts throughout the UK.

Vegetarian Society, The

Parkdale, Dunham Road,
Altrincham,
Cheshire WA14 4QG

T: *0161 925 2000*

E: *info@vegsoc.org*

W: *www.vegsoc.org*

Registered educational charity and an independent voice whose purpose is to promote knowledge of the vegetarian diet. Owns the Cordon Vert Cookery School which offers a wide range of courses for both professionals and those passionate about food. The Society's activities include raising awareness amongst health professionals, increasing awareness in schools, and holding National Vegetarian Week. For members it offers a free quarterly magazine, a members' discount card, and access to a telephone information hotline service. Call for starter pack.

Listings Index

Acknowledgements

'According to chaos theorists, the flapping of a butterfly's wings can cause an earthquake on the other side of the world. You can be that butterfly.'

I'd like to express great gratitude to all the butterflies around me for their support with this book. From both the personal to the professional there are individuals who never cease to amaze me with inspiration, information and fresh ideas. Thank you to Gavin Markham the publisher who has directed and supported the project from the offset and who is loyally married to the cause (no pun intended). Thank you to Katie Fewings, who is constantly spurring my enthusiasm for glam green weddings to unearthly limits and for sharing a common vision. I'd like to pass on huge appreciation to Patricia Henningsson for her creative design marvel and interminable abundance of patience. To my family: my mum who dutifully declares the book's naissance to every interested bride-to be in the valley; my dad, Andrew, and Zoe who really began my journey on the true significance of a greener wedding; my wonderfully wise Granny; and to my sister Steph, who is a true love.

A mention to other special individuals (both near and afar) who have helped with the Green Guide for Weddings:

Adam Vaughan
Amanda Mellett
Amy Carter
Amy Rucco
Angie Gough
Barbara Basford
Barbara Crowther
Barbara Walmsley
Becca Lush Blum
Bridget Stott
Charlie Burton
Claire Watt-Smith
Clio Turton
Corrina McGowan
Daphne Lambert
David Rhode

Dawn Lewis
Dee Grismond
Freda Palmer
Greg Valerio
James Simpson
Jane Kellas
Jane Parritt
Jayne McDonald
Jenny Irwin
Jill Satin
Jo Mackin
Jo Moulds
Kash Bhattacharya
Katherine Cartlidge
Krissy Pemberton
Laura Burgess

Lesley Stratton-Hughes
Lula Lewis
Mary Louise-Clews
Niki Clarke
Paul Handley
Rachael Matthews
Rachel Petheram
Rikke Bruntse-Dahl
Rosie Ames
Rosie Budhani
Tanis Taylor
Verity Hunt-Shepard
Vicky Kyme
Victoria Watson
Vivien Johnston
Wendy Martin

Green Wedding notes

e: weddings@greenguide.co.uk
w: www.greenguide.co.uk

Green Wedding notes

e: weddings@greenguide.co.uk
w: www.greenguide.co.uk

More Green Guides . . .

Copies of our books and guides can be purchased online at
www.greenguide.co.uk or you can usually find them in bookshops,
independent retailers and organic and wholefood stores. If you need help
finding a local store stocking our books please call us on +44 (0) 1945 461 452
or email the publisher via **publisher@greenguide.co.uk**

Our titles include:
ecoescapes

ecoescape: United Kingdom £8.99
ISBN: 978-1-905731-40-4

ecoescape: Ireland £8.99
ISBN: 978-1-905731-29-9

Green Guide – *the directory for planet-friendly living*
The Green Guide is a series of books and directories focusing on green and
natural products, services and organisations, supported by a comprehensive website and
occasional magazine. Find out more at www.greenguide.co.uk

Green Guide Essentials £6.99
ISBN: 978-1-905731-01-5

The Green Guide for Gifts & Giving £8.99
ISBN: 978-1-905731-52-7

The Green Guide to Fashion & Beauty £8.99
ISBN: 978-1-905731-54-1

The Green Guide for Home & Household £8.99
ISBN: 978-1-905731-50-3

The Green Guide for London £12.99
ISBN: 978-1-905731-31-2

The Green Guide for Scotland £12.99
ISBN: 978-1-905731-32-9

The Green Guide for Wales £12.99
ISBN: 978-1-905731-36-7

You can also find the Pocket Green Guides for England, Scotland
and Wales on the website – each costs £2.99.

For retailers & wholesalers
Our books are distributed by **Vine House Distribution Ltd**
The Old Mill House, Mill Lane, Uckfield, East Sussex TN22 5AA
t: +44 (0) 1825 767 396
e: sales@vinehouseuk.co.uk